THE INSTITUTIONAL DEVELOPMENT OF
BUSINESS SCHOOLS

The Institutional Development of Business Schools

EDITED BY
ANDREW M. PETTIGREW,
ERIC CORNUEL,
AND
ULRICH HOMMEL

OXFORD
UNIVERSITY PRESS

OXFORD

UNIVERSITY PRESS

Great Clarendon Street, Oxford, OX2 6DP,
United Kingdom

Oxford University Press is a department of the University of Oxford.
It furthers the University's objective of excellence in research, scholarship,
and education by publishing worldwide. Oxford is a registered trade mark of
Oxford University Press in the UK and in certain other countries

First Edition published in 2014

Impression: 1

Published in the United States of America by Oxford University Press
198 Madison Avenue, New York, NY 10016, United States of America

British Library Cataloguing in Publication Data
Data available

Library of Congress Control Number: 2014942672

ISBN 978–0–19–871336–4

Printed and bound by
CPI Group (UK) Ltd, Croydon, CR0 4YY

Contents

Part III Challenges for the Future Development of Business Schools

Tables and Figures

TABLES

FIGURES

Notes on Contributors

Emilie Biland is an Assistant Professor of political science at Laval University (Québec City, Canada). She is a member of the Centre Maurice Halbwachs (French National Centre for Scientific Research). She trained as a sociologist at the Ecole Normale Supérieure in Paris. Her fields of interest are in public administration and in law and society studies. Her latest article on legal education is: Emilie Biland and Rachel Vanneuville, (2012), 'Government Lawyers and the Training of Senior Civil Servants: Maintaining Law at the Heart of the French State', *International Journal of the Legal Profession*, 19(1): 29–54.

Steffen Blaschke is Associate Professor in Organizational Communication at the Copenhagen Business School, Denmark. He received his habilitation from the University of Hamburg, Germany, and his doctorate from the University of Marburg, Germany. His current research concerns methods and measures for the structures and dynamics of organizational communication.

Eric Cornuel has been the Director General and CEO of EFMD (European Foundation for Management Development) in Brussels since 2000. He holds a degree from Sciences Po (IEP Paris), an MBA from HEC Graduate School of Management, Paris, and a DEA in strategy and management from Paris Nanterre University, together with a Doctoral Certificate in Strategy from HEC Graduate School of Management, Paris, and a Ph.D. in Management, on international network organizations, from Paris Dauphine University. He has been Director of the HEC Institute for Central and Eastern Europe (Paris), and Dean of KIMEP, at the time the leading business and economics school in Central Asia. From 1996 to the present, Eric Cornuel has been Affiliate Professor at HEC Graduate School of Management, Paris. He has taught for fifteen years at various management schools in Europe and Asia, including the Catholic University of Louvain.

Graeme Currie is Professor of Public Management and Associate Dean at Warwick Business School, University of Warwick. He works closely with the senior levels of a number of public service (NHS, police, and local authority), third sector, and private sector organizations. Graeme has completed a succession of research studies funded by the National Institute of Health Research (NIHR), most recently examining the knowledge-brokering role of hybrid middle managers in quality improvement in the care of older people. In his current NIHR funded research, Graeme analyses the critical review capacity of commissioning networks to intervene to reduce unplanned admissions of frail older people to acute hospitals.

Julie Davies is Deputy Chief Executive at the Association of Business Schools and directs the ABS/EFMD International Deans' Programme. She completed a Ph.D. at Warwick Business School in strategic management. Julie is a Fellow of the Chartered Institute of Personnel and Development and the Association of University Administrators. She lectures for the Open University and Birkbeck.

Aurélie Delemarle is an Assistant Professor of Management at ESIEE, a school training engineers, based at Marne-la-Vallée, and part of the University Paris Est (UPEC).

Jürgen Enders is Professor of Higher Education at the School of Education, University of Southampton, UK, having previously worked as the Director of the Centre for Higher Education Policy Studies (CHEPS) in the Netherlands. He has written and (co-)edited fourteen books, and published more than a hundred articles on institutional change in the field of universities and their role in society and the economy. He is an elected member of the Academia Europaea and of the German Academe of Science and Engineering, and Honorary Fellow of the Society for Research in Higher Education.

Ewan Ferlie is Professor of Public Services Management in the Department of Management at King's College, London where he was previously Head of Department. Formerly, he was Professor of Public Services Management at Imperial College Management School (1997–2003) where he was also founding director of the Centre for Public Services Organizations and School Director of Research. He was then a Professor of Public Services Management and Head of the School of Management at Royal Holloway, University of London. In 2008, Ewan was elected an Academician of the Learned Societies in the Social Sciences (AcSS). He is chair of the Society for the Study of Organizing in Health Care, a learned society affiliated to AcSS. He has also been appointed to the national commissioning board of the National Institute of Health Research, Health Services and Delivery Research Programme.

Fernando Fragueiro is President of Austral University in Buenos Aires, Argentina. Prior to this, he was Full Professor of General Management at IAE Business School, Universidad Austral. He has a Ph.D. in Industrial and Business Studies from Warwick Business School, University of Warwick, UK. He is Director and Founder of ENOVA Thinking (2007–present), a learning network of more than 60 Regional CEOs of multilatinas and multinational corporations. He is also an advisory board member of several business schools in Latin America and Europe. He is former Dean of IAE Business School, Universidad Austral (1995–2008), and has been visiting scholar at Harvard Business School, Harvard University (2008–2009). He published, with Howard Thomas (2011), *Strategic Leadership in Business Schools: Keeping One Step Ahead* (Cambridge University Press).

Jetta Frost is Full Professor of Organization and Management at the University of Hamburg, Germany. Since 2013 she has been Vice President at the University of Hamburg. From 2011 to 2013, she was Director of the Competence Centre 'University for a Sustainable Future'. From 2007 to 2012 she was Associated Dean of the School of Business, Economics, and Social Sciences. Jetta Frost received her habilitation and doctorate from the University of Zurich, Switzerland. Her current research interests concern organizational and knowledge governance in universities and multi-divisional firms, innovative organization design, as well as organizational and strategic solutions for the management of value creation.

Gaële Goastellec is a sociologist, an Associate Professor (MER), and she heads the Politics and Organizations of Higher Education research unit at the Observatory Science, Policy and Society, University of Lausanne, Switzerland. She works on socio-historical comparative research into higher education systems. She has recently published: (ed. 2010), *Understanding Inequalities In, Through and By Higher Education,* (SensePublishers); (2014) *Egalité et Mérite à l'Université: Une Comparaison Etats-Unis, Indonésie, France* (EUE); and, with M. Benninghoff, F. Fassa, and J-P Leresche (eds 2012), *Inégalités Sociales et Enseignement Supérieur* (DeBoeck).

Armand Hatchuel is Professor, co-head of the Design Theory and Methods for Innovation Chair at Mines ParisTech, where he has also been deputy-director of the Centre for Management Science. His research has been about the foundations and history of management. He has focused on the role of design activities in the formation of the modern corporation and on the study of the management of innovative firms. With Benoit Weil, he proposed a new design theory (known as C-K design theory) and he created and co-chaired the special group on Design Theory of the Design Society. He co-authored (2010) *The Strategic Management of Innovation and Design* (Cambridge University Press). In 2009, he was elected to the French National Academy of Technologies and is a columnist on management issues for the French newspaper, *Le Monde.*

Fabian Hattke is postdoc in Organization and Management at the University of Hamburg, Germany. Since 2011 he is researcher and project manager in several ministry-funded research projects on science studies and university governance. During the spring term of 2014, he was visiting scholar and associate lecturer at the Zeppelin University

Friedrichshafen. He holds a doctoral degree in Management Science from the University of Hamburg, and a master's degree in Economics from the University of Heidelberg, Germany. His main research interests are science studies and the governance of knowledge work.

Ulrich Hommel is Professor and Chair of Corporate Finance and Higher Education Finance at EBS Business School, Germany. He holds a Ph.D. in Economics from the University of Michigan, Ann Arbor, and completed his habilitation in Business Administration at the WHU, Germany. He has held visiting appointments at Stockholm University School of Business, Stephen M. Ross School of Business (University of Michigan), Krannert School of Management of Purdue University and Bordeaux Business School. He has been Dean, Rector and Managing Director at EBS. He is currently also the Director of Research and Surveys at the European Foundation for Management Development (EFMD) in Brussels and one of the Senior Advisors for EFMD Quality Services. His current research focuses mainly on risk management of non-financial firms and higher education institutions, as well as alternative forms of corporate financing.

Christophe Lejeune is Professor of Strategy and Organization at ESTA School of Business and Engineering in Belfort, France. Until 2012, he was Assistant Professor at the EM-Strasbourg Business School, France. He holds degrees in management (Ingénieur de Gestion and Diplôme d'Études Approfondies en Sciences de Gestion) and a degree in education (Agrégation de l'Enseignement Secondaire) from the Université Catholique de Louvain, Belgium. He holds a Ph.D. degree in economics and management from the Louvain School of Management, Belgium. His research interests include organizational identity, change, and knowledge transfer.

Peter McKiernan is currently the Dean of the School of Management and Governance at Murdoch University, Australia and Professor of Management at the University of Strathclyde, Scotland, where he was interim Head of Department. Previously, he was Head of the School of Management at the University of St Andrews in Scotland. He has been Chairman, Vice President and President of the British Academy of Management (2001–2006) and the first Dean of their Fellows College (2006). He was also Vice President and President of the European Academy of Management (2001–2010). He is a Fellow of BAM (1998) and an original Fellow of EURAM (2012). He was elected as an inaugural Companion of the Association of Business Schools (2007), served on their Executive Board and sits on their Scientific Panel for the European Academic Journal Quality List. He was elected as an Academician of the Academy of Social Sciences in 2006. His research interests are in management and strategy, on which he has published numerous books, including the best seller *Sharpbenders*—and in international peer-reviewed journals.

Josefina Michelini studied Political Science at the Universidad Católica Argentina and Research Methodology at the Universidad de Bologna. Her research focuses on the political approach of leadership, strategic leadership processes in professional service firms (business schools in particular), internationalization processes, organizational change, and talent management. She is now focusing on the professionalization processes of SMEs in emerging markets. She is co-author of several book chapters and academic publications in journals, such as the *Journal of Change Management*, the *International Journal of Business and Emerging Markets*, and *HBR América Latina*.

Stéphanie Mignot-Gérard has been an Associate Professor of Management at the University Paris-Est Créteil (UPEC) since 2009. Her background is in organizational sociology. She holds a Ph.D. in sociology from Sciences Po Paris. Her major research interests are: the reforms of the French higher education system and the transformation of universities' governance; the social effects of university rankings; and the professional careers of graduate students in the field of finance. Her latest article on university governance is: (2012), 'The Collective Behavior of a University in Response to the Excellence Initiatives. Between Reactivity and Microresistance', *Politiques et Management Public* 29 (3): 519–39.

Rajani Naidoo is Professor of Higher Education Management and Director of the International Centre for Higher Education Management at the University of Bath. She completed her Ph.D. at the University of Cambridge. Her research analyses the links between shifts in the global political economy, government restructuring of higher education systems, and organizational change. She has been an expert advisor to numerous international bodies and an international reviewer for the Finnish Academy of Science. She is a member of the research and development steering committee of the European Foundation for Management Development. She is on the Executive Editorial Board of the British Journal of Sociology of Education and is co-editor of a book series on global higher education.

Catherine Paradeise is a sociologist and Professor Emeritus, University Paris Est. Her contributions have recently concentrated on organizational issues and public policies in research and higher education institutions. She has published, 'How Much is Enough? Does Indicators-based Management Guarantee Effectiveness?', in (2012), F. Bourguignon, *Evaluation and its Discontents, Proceedings of the 9th AFD-EUDN Conference*; and 'Tools and Implementation for a New Governance of Universities. Understanding Variability Between and Within Countries', in A. Curaj, P. Scott et al. (eds 2012), *European Higher Education at the Crossroads—Between the Bologna Process and National Reforms* (Dortrecht, Springer).

Andrew M. Pettigrew is Professor of Strategy and Organization at the Saïd Business School, University of Oxford and Senior Golding Fellow, Brasenose College. He was Dean of the School of Management, University of Bath, from 2003 to 2008 and has held academic appointments at Yale University, London Business School, Warwick Business School and Harvard Business School where, in 2001, he was a Visiting Professor. He also holds an Adjunct Professorship at BI, The Norwegian Business School. His research has pioneered the use of contextual and temporal analyses of organizational processes of strategy making, decision-making, change and power. He is the author or editor of sixteen books and has published widely in management journals. He has been elected Distinguished Scholar of the Organization and Management Theory and Organization Development and Change Divisions of the Academy of Management. In 2002, he was the first, and is still the only, non-North American to be elected Distinguished Scholar of the Academy of Management. In 2003, he was elected a Fellow of the British Academy. In 2012 he was awarded the Richard Whipp Lifetime Achievement Award by the British Academy of Management.

James Pringle was the programme manager at Ryerson's School of Health Services Management while enrolled as a doctoral student in the Higher Education Management programme at the University of Bath's School of Management. He is currently an instructor at Ryerson's. His dissertation will offer a qualitative multi-case study exploring Faculty Perception of Branding. In addition, from a practical perspective, he has been a consultant for Academica Group Inc., looking at branding activities in Canadian universities. Related work includes a publication in the *Canadian Journal of Higher Education* entitled 'Understanding Universities in Ontario, Canada: An Industry Analysis Using Porter's Five Forces Framework'.

Nora Ramadan is an associate lecturer at the Faculty of Commerce, Cairo University. Nora has recently completed her Ph.D. at the University of Birmingham, focusing on the vertical relationship between UK university-based business schools and their higher university authorities. Her research interests include vertical relationships, headquarters–subsidiary relations, organizational power relationships, cross-border learning and knowledge transfer. She participated in teaching in Cairo University, the American University in Cairo, and the University of Birmingham, and has presented her work in a number of regional and international conferences.

Andreas Rasche is Professor of Business in Society at Copenhagen Business School. He holds a Ph.D. from EBS Business School, Germany and a habilitation from Helmut-Schmidt-University, Hamburg. His research focuses on corporate responsibility standards (particularly the UN Global

Compact), the political role of corporations in transnational governance, and responsible management education. He regularly contributes to international journals in his field of study and has lectured widely on corporate sustainability and responsibility. His latest book, *Building the Responsible Enterprise* (with Sandra Waddock) was published in 2012 by Stanford University Press.

Ken Starkey is Professor of Management and Organizational Learning at Nottingham University Business School, where he is Head of the Management Division. His current research, teaching and consulting interests include: leadership; management education and the role of the business school; sustainable strategic management; and organization and design science. He has published twelve books and articles in leading journals, such as the *Academy of Management Review,* the *Academy of Management Learning & Education, Strategic Management Journal, Organization Science, Business Ethics Quarterly,* the *Journal of Business Ethics, Organization Studies, Human Relations* and the *Journal of Management Studies.* Recent work on management research and education includes (2007) *The Business School and the Bottom Line* (Cambridge University Press, with Nick Tiratsoo) and a contribution to the Harvard Business School *Handbook of Leadership Teaching* by Scott Snook, Nitin Nohria and Rakesh Khurana (eds 2012) (Sage Publications, with Carol Hall).

Jean-Claude Thoenig is a Director of Research (Emeritus) at the French National Centre for Scientific Research. He is a member of Dauphine Recherche en Management (University Paris-Dauphine). He trained as a sociologist at the University of Geneva. He co-founded the European Group for Organizational Studies and the Ecole de Paris du Management. He was a dean and a professor at INSEAD. His fields of interest are in organizational sociology. He currently works on higher education and research institutions. Among his books are (with Charles Waldman) *The Marking Enterprise* (Palgrave), and (with David Courpasson) *When Managers Rebel* (Palgrave).

Howard Thomas has been a business school dean on three continents: University of Illinois, U.S.; Warwick Business School, U.K.; and Singapore Management University, Asia. He is a past Chair of the Board of the Graduate Management Admissions Council (GMAC), the American Association of Collegiate Schools of Business International (AACSB), the Association of Business Schools (ABS) and the Global Foundation of Management Education (GFME). He is currently a board member of State Farm Bank, U.S., and the European Foundation for Management Development, (EFMD), Brussels. He is also a Member of the Financial Research Council (FRC) of the Monetary Authority of Singapore.His teaching and research interests encompass strategic management and management education. He is a Fellow of the Academy of Management, U.S., the British Academy of Management, the Strategic Management Society and the Academy of Social Sciences.

Alain Vas is Professor of Strategy and Change Management at the Louvain School of Management, Universite Catholique de Louvain, Belgium. He is also Dean of the School. He holds the KBL Research Chair in Change Management at the Universite Catholique de Louvain. He has a Ph.D. in Management Sciences at Paris XII University, France. He is a member of the Centre for Research in Entrepreneurial Change and Innovative Strategies. His research interests are in the areas of organizational change, knowledge creation and transfer, organizational innovation and competitive advantage. He has authored several refereed publications in academic journals, books, and international conferences.

David Wilson is currently Dean of Research at the Open University, U.K. Prior to that he was Deputy Dean of Warwick Business School and Head of Department, Sociology, at the University of Warwick, UK. He was elected a Fellow of the British Academy of Management in 1994 and served as Chairman (1994–1997). He was elected an Academician of the Social Sciences in 2009. He is a Board member, and ex-Chair, of the European Group for Organization Studies (EGOS). He has had a long association with the scholarly journal *Organization Studies*, from Editorial Assistant in 1981 to Editor-in-Chief (1999–2003). He is the author of nine books and over eighty articles on strategic decision-making, organizational change, and strategy, his main research interests.

1

Introduction

Andrew M. Pettigrew, Eric Cornuel, and Ulrich Hommel

This book has two overriding purposes. These are to help further establish the study of business schools as an important phenomenon in the fields of social sciences and management and to assist the development of a forward looking, challenging and realizable research agenda for that field.

The book represents the first fruits of an ambitious research initiative facilitated by the European Foundation for Management Development (EFMD) in Brussels. The EFMD is an international membership organization made up of 800 institutions from academia, business and the public services in 81 countries. The EFMD is a forum for information, research, networking, and debate on innovation and best practice in management and in management education. At a time of substantial change in higher education throughout the world, the leaders of many of these 800 member institutions of the EFMD have called for theoretically informed and methodologically sound research to understand the institutional development of business schools in their changing economic, business, social, and institutional contexts.

Although business education in the higher education sector is over a century old in both Europe and North America, the last forty years is often portrayed as an era of beneficial growth and development. Certainly, the business school has risen inexorably as a teaching and research institution in many countries since the 1960s. For example, from a marginal activity undertaken in the 1950s by a few dedicated institutions, the field of Management and Business Studies (MBS) has now become the single largest area of teaching and research in UK higher education. The growth of MBS in the UK since the mid 1960s now means that, in 2010, 13,000 academic staff worked in the MBS cost centre in UK universities. MBS staff make up 7 percent of the sector while teaching 14 percent of the students. In 2010, one in eight undergraduates, one in five postgraduates and one in four international students were studying MBS.

However, with this golden era of growth have come plenty of inner-directed questioning and outer-driven scepticism about the role, purposes, and impact of business schools and their faculties and students. Some of this scepticism is directed at the relative financial success of business schools, some at the perceived deficiencies of the curriculum in the face of a changing world, some at the apparently disengaged and trivial nature of management research, and others at the perceived connection between the 2008 financial collapse and the ideological commitments of some business schools. Notwithstanding even the cursory examination of business school profiles, there is also a view that business schools are converging to a common type or types and this represents both a failure of leadership and a lack of recognition of the quite different market, political, and cultural contexts in which business schools operate.

This book cannot pick up all these themes, but it can and does address some of them. Crucially we address important issues to do with the change and development of business schools, with branding and ranking and the challenges for the future development of business schools. The introductory and final chapters also offer an assessment of current research and a clear statement of research priorities in a field that is still relatively new and developing. The individual chapters are written by a group of scholars who attended the first EFMD R&D Conference held at the Lorange Institute in Switzerland in February 2012. The scholars come from the fields of strategic management, organization theory, marketing, finance, public sector management, and higher education policy and management. They offer important empirical studies and conceptual developments carried out in the UK, France, Germany, Belgium, and the USA.

In Chapter 2 of this volume, Hommel and Thomas offer a characterization of the field of business school research. They note a disjointed set of research themes expressed in work of uneven depth and quality. In this respect, our field parallels the longer established and related field of higher education management. See, for example, the excellent reviews of the study of universities and their management by Shattock in 2006, 2009, and 2010. Hommel and Thomas note some of the strengths of the higher education management field: the concern with governance practices and their effectiveness; the studies of leadership in universities; the work on entrepreneurialism and managerialism; and the more recent concern with faculty management and the changing professional identities of scholars. Thus far, there have been few quality studies of such phenomena in business school settings.

Hommel and Thomas identify the normative and moralizing tone of some research on business schools. Challenged from within and without over the quality and impact of their teaching and research, there is a great preoccupation with the identity, moral basis, image and legitimacy of management education. Hommel and Thomas also correctly identify a preoccupation in the literature with the strategic development of higher-tier business schools and a consequent lack of interest in the pathway of development of the great majority of business schools throughout the world.

The Hommel and Thomas suggestions for a future research agenda are very much more substantively embedded in the trends facing business schools than theoretically or analytically driven. Thus they point to the trends to deregulate and privatize higher education and their ongoing impact on business school development, together with the pervasive influences of internationalization and globalization. The development of on-line education, and the role of technology in delivering education, with new entrants to the market, are all sources of enhanced competitive pressure. All these factors are influencing the skill base of faculties which are in turn challenging conventional notions of professional identity and faculty management and control. Throughout all this, there is the pervasive concern with the efficacy of different models of business school development.

Of course, in this volume we have made our own commitment to develop a limited set of research themes on business school development. The three themes—change and development of business schools; ranking and branding in business schools; and challenges for the future development of business schools—represent some of the strengths and limitations of existing theoretical and empirical work.

In Chapter 3, Fragueiro and Michelini provide a rare insight into the institutional dynamics of three top European schools: London Business School, INSEAD, and IMD. They focus on the strategic leadership process in all three schools over the period 1990 to 2004. The chapter addresses the internationalization processes in the three schools and examines the role of Boards, Deans, and Faculty in the politics of issue and power mobilization in driving forward the international strategies of each school. The rich contextual and processual treatment of leadership over time is an examplar of the future work needed on the institutional dynamics of business schools.

In Chapter 4, Hattke, Blaschke, and Frost extend our interest in leadership and change into the governance challenges of two German universities. This is archival-based work which construes governance logics as the competition between different value-based conversations. In exploring the shift from more collegiate, participative forms of self-governance towards more managerial and business-like forms, the authors signal the importance for future research of embedding governance studies in the changing contexts and dynamics of higher education.

Chapter 5 by Lejeune and Vas picks up one of the pervasive influences on business school development: the shaping influences of accreditation standards and processes. The chapter examines the influence of accreditation failure and reapplication on business schools' organizational identity. Failed accreditation is seen as a trigger for challenging and changing pre-existing strategies and practices. The resultant change processes are portrayed as tensions between different institutional logics. This chapter again draws on comparative case study work. The on-going research agenda signalled by this study is the need to examine the variety of meanings of performance evident in business schools and, crucially, the factors which shape and sustain different level of performance over time. The determinants of organization performance in business schools is a major theme addressed by Pettigrew in the final chapter of this volume.

Chapter 6 also features comparative case study work and, again, with an international sample of business schools based in the USA, France, and Switzerland. Here Paradeise et al. examine the playing out of the duality of scholarly excellence and practical/professional relevance within the four case studies. Notwithstanding the perennial claim that business schools are converging towards uniformity in policies, practices, and identities, this chapter unravels the possibilities of local diversity in the way the four business schools have coped with the relevance and excellence duality. The possibility of diversity in a converging world is a key theme in the future research agenda articulated in Chapter 13 by Pettigrew. Establishing the extent of convergence and divergence in institutional development is probably one of the most important research challenges in this area and will require a scale of international comparative investigation not yet attempted in the study of business schools.

Part 2 of this volume covers ranking and branding in business schools. The stratification of universities and business schools is now a dominating influence on the character and conduct of higher education institutions. Chapters 7 and 8 are written by Enders and Naidoo, two of the key figures in the fields of higher education policy and management. These chapters are instructive not only in raising the issues of ranking and branding in the general university sector, but also the important requirement for a research agenda on business schools to be in conversation with the larger and better developed scholarly fields of higher education policy and management.

A striking feature of Chapters 7, 8, and 9 is their use of institution theory (Greenwood et al., 2008) to interpret and explain the phenomena they address. Variants of institution theory are also evident in Chapters 4, 6, 11, and 12 in this volume. It is not surprising that a body of organizational theory which received its first empirical referents in educational organization (e.g. Meyer and Scott 1983; Meyer et al 1987; Strang 1987) should continue to be the almost default theory in studies of business schools. The very convergence that institution theory often draws attention to may, in turn, be limiting the rise of a more theoretically divergent body of work on business schools. In Chapter 9, Rasche, Hommel, and Cornuel offer a Foucauldian treatment of control and discipline, which provides both theoretical variety and a challenging message. Here is developed the argument that rankings can discipline and control faculty by enhancing the visibility of individuals' performance, by defining 'normal' behaviour, and, more generally, by shaping how people understand themselves and people around them.

Part 3 of this volume pursues the broad theme of 'challenges for the future development of business schools'. In Chapter 10, Ferlie et al. offer an early stage empirical study of the prospects for, and obstacles to, research collaborations with business schools and other university departments. This is a neglected area of empirical inquiry and one demanding future investment. The other two chapters in this theme by McKiernan and Wilson, and Starkey and Hatchuel are viewpoint contributions which discuss the challenges facing business schools in their changing contexts. Both chapters make a plea for large-scale international comparative research on business schools to map the contours of the development of contemporary business school strategies, structures, practices, and processes.

Finally, in Chapter 13, Pettigrew concludes the book by providing a forward-looking research agenda on the institutional development of business schools. In this chapter, Pettigrew offers a set of principles which might inform the development of a research agenda for a still developing field. These principles include theoretical and empirical embeddedness and the need for research on business schools to be fully located in related developments in the social sciences and management, and in so doing to avoid the trap of intellectual and substantive isolation for the study of business schools. Further principles include the need for research to be linked to substantive problems in the research domain and to be aspirational in terms of theory, method, and empiricism. Pettigrew then articulates and develops three important research themes for future work on the institutional development of business schools. These are: comparative international research to map and measure similarity and variation in the development of business schools; comparative studies which map and explain performance differences between business schools in the same, and in different, geographical and market contexts; and finally, more micro-level studies of the processes, practices, identities and performance of business school faculties in different academic fields and in different nations of the world.

REFERENCES

Greenwood, R., Oliver, C., Sahlin, K., and Suddaby, R. (2008), (eds). *Organizational Institutionalism*. Los Angeles: Sage Publications.

Meyer, J. W. and Scott, W. R. (1983). *Organizational Environments*. Beverly Hills, CA: Sage Publications.

Meyer, J. W., Scott, W. R., and Strang, D. (1987). 'Centralization, Fragmentation and School District Complexity', *Administrative Science Quarterly*, 32, 2: 186–201.

Shattock, M. (2006). *Managing Good Governance in Higher Education*. Maidenhead, Berkshire: Open University Press.

Shattock, M. (ed.) (2009). *Entrepreneuralism in Universities and the Knowledge Economy*. Maidenhead, Berkshire: Open University Press.

Shattock, M. (2010). *Managing Successful Universities*. Maidenhead: SRHE and the Open University Press, Second Edition.

Strang, D. (1987). 'The Administrative Transformation of American Education School District Consolidation, 1938–1980', *Administrative Science Quarterly*, 32, 3: 352–366.

2

Research on Business Schools

Themes, Conjectures, and Future Directions

Ulrich Hommel and Howard Thomas

2.1. INTRODUCTION

Despite the rapid and successful growth of management education, there has been a growing debate about, and significant criticism of, the value of business schools in society (see, for example, Fragueiro and Thomas 2011; Thomas et al. 2013c; Thomas et al. 2013b). As Thomas (2007: 9) noted, 'business schools currently face an image and identity crisis and have been subject to a wide range of critical reviews about their societal status as academic and professional schools'. They are seen as being too market-driven (Bennis and O'Toole 2005; Pfeffer and Fong 2002) and producing research with little practical impact (Hambrick 1994; Hodgkinson and Rousseau 2009; Pettigrew 2001). The classic and timeless criticisms of the narrowness and amoral nature of business school teaching offered by Mintzberg (2004) and Ghoshal (2005) are still widely quoted. Some observers have argued that they need to focus more on their value to society (Muff 2012). Shoemaker (2008: 119) stresses that 'the traditional paradigm of business schools with its strong focus on analytic models and reductionism, is not well suited to handle the ambiguity and high rate of change facing many industries today'.

A common judgement of business schools is, therefore, that their promise is unfulfilled and that they have adopted a consumer focus and sold out to the 'tyranny of rankings' (Khurana 2007; Thomas et al. 2013b, 2013a). The focus on these consumer reputation measures may often lead to a pre-occupation with marketing and public relations rather than on developing new models of teaching and learning (see also DeAngelo and DeAngelo 2005). Indeed, Starkey and Tiratsoo (2007: 8) point out that university administrators often view business schools as 'cash cows' and therefore seek to 'extract the maximum commercial benefit from courses such as the MBA, regardless of what it means for pedagogy and learning'.

There is clearly a 'tipping' point in business school models and paradigms which will lead to a period of experimentation and change in business schools. Therefore, the aim of this chapter is to interpret current research and debates about the future of business schools and, hence, identify possible options for the future of business school research and teaching.

The chapter addresses the following important themes in manage-ment education: the evolution of business schools; the transformation and re-invention of business school models; and the assessment of future direc-tions for the business school in higher education. Consequently, the research issues reviewed in the paper include the following: the history and evolution of business schools; the changing contexts—identity, image and legitimacy—of management education; business school performance metrics including rankings; leadership of business schools and change management; business school models and their innovation and sustainability; and, finally, the influ-ence of globalization in management education.

2.2. HISTORICAL EVOLUTION OF BUSINESS SCHOOLS

As business schools have evolved, there have been a number of pathways to reaching the present state of affairs (see Thomas et al. 2012: 1–3). In the initial 'tradeschool' era (from the late nineteenth to the early twentieth cen-tury), the original purpose of management education was to educate man-agers and improve the public perception of the professional manager. The pioneer U.S. business schools, such as the Wharton School (influenced by Joseph Wharton's belief in Taylor's scientific management principles) and Harvard Business School became the catalysts for the widespread emergence of U.S.-style business schools (note, however, that three other countries—France, Germany and the United Kingdom—had created their own schools of commerce in the nineteenth century to enhance the education of manag-ers). Indeed, the founding of the American Association for Collegiate Schools of Business (AACSB) in 1916 reinforced the image of the U.S. business school. However, many of these schools did little or no research and were described by Simon (1967) as 'wastelands of vocationalism'.

Gordon and Howell (1959) and Pierson (1959) (respectively sponsored by the Ford and Carnegie Foundations), were subsequently asked to address common criticisms that business schools lacked meaningful research output, academic credibility and recognition. Their reports argued for a new business school model anchored in social science disciplines and offering greater academic rigour. This educational model focused ondiscipline-led scholarship with a greater analytical and scientific emphasis. This new vision, in turn, became the dominant logic drivingthe modern business school and its flagship general management programme, the MBA.

However, by the late 1970s, management educators and business leaders started to criticize the scientific emphasis of business schools and the seemingly impractical and irrelevant nature of management research. Notable academic critics (particularly from Harvard Business School) included Livingston (1971), Hayes and Abernathy (1980), and Leavitt (1989). At about the same time, a set of very readable management books emerged from authors such as Jim Collins, Gary Hamel, C. K. Prahalad, Tom Peters and Michael Porter. These books used business cases and well-constructed stories to suggest how managers and leaders should address such strategic issues as competition, diversification, and organizational change. They served the purpose of explaining how academic research might be applied to real-world management problems. As a consequence, their approaches were adopted by the growing generation of managers and aspiring leaders.

European management educators offered similar criticisms. Elite European management schools such as HEC, IESE, IMD, INSEAD, and LBS had offered alternative approaches to global management education(see Thomas 2012). Their models (Thomas et al. 2013b: 10–15) were much more reflective of European traditions, including action learning, practice-engaged research, customized executive education, and, most importantly, a focus on international linkages, activities and research (the INSEAD case is e.g. discussed in Barsoux 2000; Fragueiro and Thomas 2011). Recent years have clearly seen the emergence of a European identity and style in management education (Amdam et al. 2003; Canals 2011) and the same can currently be observed also in the Asian-Pacific context (Brailsford 2012).

When considering the overall historical development of the European business school sector (e.g. described in Engwall and Gunnarsson 1994; Engwall and Zamagni 1998), it is impossible not to notice a degree of mimicry and convergence towards the American model. As discussed by Engwall (2004) for the Nordic countries, 'Americanization' has led to a 'stream-lining' but not a complete eradication of national/regional identity, which is deeply rooted in the diversity of national higher education systems (see also Engwall 1998, 2000; Locke 1985, 1988). Convergence is to some degree also a derivative phenomenon shaped by the 'Americanization' of the underlying business sectors. This is particularly visible in European entrepreneurship education given the strong links to U.S.-style venture financing (Locke and Schöne 2004).

The conventional judgement is now that the business school model is at a turning point and definitely in transition (Thomas and Cornuel 2012). There is a clear need to answer the concerns of some of the following criticisms of business schools (see also Thomas et al. 2012: 2):

- Pfeffer and Fong (2002) indicated that business schools are too market driven and that management research has failed to scale the 'twin hurdles' of academic rigour and practical relevance (Pettigrew 1997).
- Mintzberg (2004) has consistently argued that management is an art, and that the emphasis on analytical models in business schools is misplaced. He demonstrates that the traditional MBA curriculum is too narrow and largely ignores such people skills as leadership and management skills.
- The late Sumantra Ghoshal in a heavily cited paper pointed out the moral decline of business and argued that business schools emphasized amoral theories that, in turn, createdunethical management practices (Ghoshal 2005).
- Recently, Locke and Spender (2011) amplified Ghoshal's argument and pointed out how business school theories, based on financial economics, may have led to managerial choices ignoring issues of culture, managerial behaviour, and ethics.

Indeed, business schools have been criticized for not teaching their students how to develop an ethical and moral compass. Quite apart from shouldering some blame for the global financial crisis, the demise of companies such as Enron is seen as an ethical failure by professional managers. Indeed, Khurana (2007) has noted that a manager's role has over time shifted from 'higher aims' as professionals in charge of a firm's resources to that of 'hired hands' operating as agents on the basis of contractual relationships. As Thomas et al. (2013b: 6) note, a key consequence of this demoralization and de-professionalization of managers is that the self-interest of the relevant parties has overcome proper ethical standards and the principle of trust central to the operation of market capitalism has been eroded. Augier and March (2011) see the role of utilitarianism and marketization in modern management education as the main culprits for the weak professional identity of managers. Clearly, the ethical tradition in business life is in danger because of the lack of training in business schools related to ethical and humanistic principles. Grey (2004), among others, has argued that business schools have become 'finishing schools' for elites to prepare themselves for highly paid, prestigious positions in finance and consulting without confronting them with a thorough examination of the ethical and moral challenges of leadership and requiring them to reflect on their broader roles in society.

These criticisms underscore the scope for management educators to engage in a period of thorough review and reflection about the role, value, aims and purposes of management education. There is a need to examine the role of businesses in society and in areas of corporate social responsibility and sustainability. In this context, business schools need to be more proactive in shaping management practice. Or, to put it in more general terms, they must examine clearly who are the business schools' key stakeholders and what is the appropriate role of a broad stakeholder orientation in business school development? The business school community would also benefit from a more targeted discussion on the appropriate breadth of management education, which links to a long-standing debate in higher education on the continued role of a classical liberal education (e.g. Bok 2006; Delbanco 2012; Harney and Thomas 2013). It also requires the important re-examination of a holistic perspectiveof management education embracing traditions of both analysis and synthesis.

New research agencies such as ABIS, GLRI, PRME, the UN Global Compact, and the 50+20 WBSCB group (see Muff 2013) have emerged advocating the need for business schools to define themselves more explicitly 'as human institutions embracing humanistic and societal values and that management is a creative art rather than a deterministic science' (Thomas et al. 2013a: 17). They are proponents of the view that management education must encompass a broad range of stakeholder perspectives (society, business, government, students, employers etc.). While business school curricula sometimes pay 'lip service' to these topics (Hommel et al. 2012), showing more evidence of reality rather than rhetoric in curricula development is the way forward. Cornuel and Hommel (2012) and Hommel (2009a) argue that globalization forces will help to prioritize these issues by enlarging the influence of different cultural traditions as well as the relevance of business schools operating in distinct economic contexts.

2.3. IDENTITY AND LEGITIMACY OF BUSINESS SCHOOLS

The struggle of business schools for their identity and legitimacy has been extensively analysed by Wilson and Thomas (2012) and this section summarizes their main arguments. Eric Cornuel, Director General of EFMD, wrote in 2005 that 'in the future the legitimacy of business schools will no longer be questioned' and further argued that they had become 'legitimised parts of society' and that 'their role was clear' (Cornuel 2005). Thomas and Wilson (2011), drawing on earlier work by Antunes and Thomas (2007) and Fragueiro and Thomas (2011), outline the various sources of this legitimacy. In the first generation of business schools (from the nineteenth to the early twentieth century), legitimacy could be traced to the creation and growth of managerial employment and the enhancement of managerial status. In addition, this generation saw the introduction of Taylorist management systems (such as accounting and control systems). The second more academically rigorous generation, following the Gordon/Howell and Pierson reports, garnered legitimacy from national governments, which supported competitiveness and the value of business schools, and from universities, which recognized their financial and cash generation potential. The third generation (mid-1980s to present) sees the consumerist foci of image and reputation as achieving wider legitimacy: these include research rankings, citations, global performance rankings, and international accreditation bodies.

'Today, these (early) claims of legitimacy are being questioned to a degree where they seem neither robust nor accurate' (Wilson and Thomas 2012: 369). For example, they point out that the *New York Times* printed several letters on 3 March 2009 which argued that by studying the arts, cultural history, literature, philosophy, and religion, individuals develop their powers of critical thinking and moral reasoning. Hence the study of humanities is believed to be essential to the development of liberal management education (Harney and Thomas 2013).

Indeed, Podolny (2009) is one of many authors who argue that business schools fail to develop these powers of critical thinking and moral reasoning. He also claims that many business school academics are not curious about what really goes on inside business organizations. They prefer to develop theoretical models that obscure rather than clarify the way companies work and believe that a theory's alleged relevance is enough to justify teaching it as a solution to organizational problems. 'They divide the alleged failures of business schools into three categories: knowledge creation (*schools research the wrong things*); pedagogical issues (*schools teach the wrong things*); and ideology, purpose, and leadership (*schools focus almost exclusively on free market economics, are unclear about their roles in academia or the world of practice*)' (Wilson and Thomas 2012: 369). Rather than a complete legitimacy gap, the criticisms of business schools signal that there are areas of ambiguity, conflict, and uncertainty around their legitimate form.

Business schools, according to Crainer and Dearlove (2001), are schizophrenic organizations, which must be both strongly academic and highly practical. There are therefore two sources of legitimacy that business schools must confront (Thomas and Wilson 2011: 447): First, there is an academic component where business schools must demonstrate a strong academic profile. Historically, business schools have followed a 'scientific' model oriented towards the production of knowledge about theories of management. It requires the production of scholarly publications and also the generation of new intellectual capacity through appropriate doctoral programmes. Second, 'there is a fundamental question about the purpose of management research; is it for or about managers?' (Thomas and Wilson 2011: 447). The gulf between theoretical rigour and practical relevance in management research creates clear problems for business school deans. Should they try to emulate the practical foci of other professional schools (e.g. law, medicine, engineering in universities)? In a very important article,Bennis and O'Toole (2005) ask why 'business schools have embraced the scientific model of physicists and economists rather than the professional model of doctors and lawyers'. Indeed, 'consumers' of management education have already pushed hard for an increasing focus on practical relevance in research and teaching.

Why is legitimacy important to business schools (Thomas and Wilson 2011: 446)? First, an organization must be seen as legitimate for its long-term survival. The business school, following Gordon and Howell (1959), adopted an intense and rigorous approach to management education to align with the university system. But, as Shoemaker (2008) stresses, this paradigm with 'its strong focus on analytic models and reductionism is not well suited to handling the ambiguity and high rate of change facing many industries today'. Second, evidence is growing that current business school research is increasingly disconnected from both the liberal pursuit of knowledge, a principle on which universities were founded (Willmott 1998), and from addressing the needs of managers as they attempt to solve management problems. Indeed, the extent to which business schools compete for the highest rankings, the best quality students and faculty, the greatest number of citations in the highest-impact journals, and secure the largest possible slice of research funding suggests that schools exist in an era of 'hyper-competition' (Starkey and Tiratsoo 2007). This presents a serious problem of maintaining organizational legitimacy and financial sustainability (Peters and Thomas 2011).

2.4. LEADERSHIP OF BUSINESS SCHOOLS AND MANAGING CHANGE

The increasing complexity of the dean's role is evident in the strong current criticisms of the business school, including the gulf between rigour and relevance and whether business is an academic discipline. In their many roles, deans face a host of leadership challenges. They are 'variously described as "doves of peace" intervening among warring factions, "dragons" holding internal and external threats at bay, and "diplomats" guiding and encouraging people who live and work in the college' (Rosser et al. 2003: 2). More pragmatically, Starkey and Tiratsoo (2007: 55) note that 'forty years ago running a business school was something a senior Professor might well take as a matter of duty before retirement. Nowadays, deans almost constitute a profession in their own-right, a cohort with unique specialist skills. Deans may be likened to sports coaches: hired to improve performance, fired at will, but with one eye always on building their own careers'. This section summarizes Thomas and Thomas' in-depth discussion of the multi-faceted challenges of leading business schools and the different roles of deans in this context (Thomas and Thomas 2011).

In business schools, deans have typically grappled with issues such as the tension between academic and professional practice (Grey 2002), which they have attempted to address by championing both the academic values of the university/academy and the professional values of their external business constituency without being two-faced (Davies and Thomas 2009). This has led some deans to argue that they can be likened to partners in professional service firms in that they are promoted on the basis of expertise, knowledge, and intellectual capital to deanships (Fragueiro and Thomas 2011). Their subsequent accumulation of social and political capital then leads to the generation of economic and reputational capital for the business school.

Indeed, understanding the broad 'context' of their professional domains is regarded as a key core competence for deans as they set their strategies (Goodall 2009). This broad view of dean leadership implies a thorough awareness of both the internal context and external context of the business school. Leadership and strategy formulation are thus strongly linked to organizational context and meaningful time horizons for planning purposes (Fragueiro and Thomas 2011).

Deans, in their decision-making processes serve as a bridge between external stakeholders, school goals and the faculty's own interests and motivations. Bryman's research on effective leadership points out that academics prefer a minimalist leadership style—not overt dictatorship (Bryman 2007). Thus, leadership using critical debate, communication, collegiality, open examination, and persuasion should dominate bureaucratic control if strategic change and execution is to be successful in academia. A dean must address three critical and essential models in effectively developing the business school's values, purposes, and positioning. The *academic model* refers to the nature and form of the school's research and teaching goals, and priorities. The *economic model* is concerned with how the school will generate the appropriate level of financial resources to sustain its research, teaching, and outreach activities. The *strategic agenda* attempts to align academic strategies with the resources provided through the economic and business models. The role of deans, therefore, is to champion their school's leadership processes and manage, build, and execute their school's strategic agenda over time.

Three key actors in business schools are 'influencers', who shape and guide their institution's decisions and actions. The *dean* is generally entrusted with the school's mission and takes the lead in executing the strategic agenda. The *board* is responsible for maintaining the school's long-term governance, sustainability, and reputation. Finally, the *faculty* has a significant influence on long-term academic and institutional decisions affecting the school's performance and reputation (Fragueiro and Thomas 2011). Leadership processes involve two crucial steps: first, securing at least a winning coalition for strategic initiatives from key actors and, second, motivating the right people to seize these initiatives and make them their own by championing theirsuccessful execution across the business school. In other words, key actors, most often faculty, are required to champion strategic initiatives while deans use their influence and persuasion to overcome resistance and to generate critical resources.

2.5. RIGOUR VERSUS RELEVANCE OF BUSINESS SCHOOL RESEARCH

The way business scholars are conducting research lies at the heart of the criticism levelled against business schools. Lorange (2008) for instance argues that narrow axiomatic research, typically conducted in discipline-oriented academic silos, fails to address the multidisciplinary nature of management challenges today (see also Tranfield and Starkey 1998). Following Mokyr (2002), he sees an over-emphasis on 'propositional' relative to 'prescriptive' knowledge production, which leads to a growing detachment of educational content from business realities. Thomas and Wilson (2011) explain this phenomenon with so-called 'physics envy', i.e., the prioritization of theory-driven research as a means of gaining academic legitimacy. It is in line with the observation that the professional advancement of faculty has become increasingly conditioned on scholarly activities, in particular the demonstrated ability to publish in highly-ranked peer-reviewed journals (AACSB International 2008). In contrast, research-based business schools tend to offer few if any incentives or opportunities to engage in practice-oriented activities, implying that business school faculties suffer from a systemic lack of practice-based experience (as also noted by Podolny 2009). The evolution of institutional funding structures, in particular the growing reliance on proprietary revenue streams, however makes this situation increasingly unsustainable.

As business schools are becoming more stakeholder-oriented, they need to show simultaneous concern for scholarly quality and practical relevance of research. Pettigrew (1997) defined these two dimensions as the so-called 'double hurdle of management research'. He argues that mastering the double hurdle requires the co-production of research, i.e., the involvement of (non-academic) partners throughout the research cycle (Pettigrew 2008). Pettigrew (1997) further hypothesizes that the inclusion of partners in the early stages of scoping a research project will raise the probability of impact.

Starkey and Madan (2001) address the rigour–relevancy gap with a complementary argument. They argue that researchers must find a more equal balance between 'what knowledge is produced' with 'how knowledge is produced' or, following Gibbons et al. (1994), that the scholarly focus needs to shiftfrom the production of M1 knowledge to M2 knowledge. A related point is the dissemination of knowledge and the question of whether funding organizations can gain proprietary access to new knowledge. M2 research takes place in an applied context, i.e. it overcomes the division between fundamental and applied research, and is diffused in the process of production with business scholars and practitioners interacting in heterogeneous teams (Starkey 2002). While Hodgkinson and Rousseau (2009) see strong evidence for the collaborative model impacting research practices, others are more sceptical (Bartunek 2011). Kieser and Nicolai (2005) argue existing deficiencies may be due to the inability of managers to convert scholarly research into knowledge that can be acted on (in the context of success factor research), which has led Kieser and Leiner (2009) to claim that the rigour–relevance gap is actually unbridgeable.

Various researchers have addressed the question of how the rebalancing of rigour and relevance may be accomplished. Starkey and Tempest (2009a) see the business school's infatuation with economics as one of the main factors explaining the inability to link academic research to managerial practice and propose a greater emphasis on philosophy and the humanities. In a companion paper, they suggest a combination of more 'narrative imagination' as well as 'dramatic rehearsal' (based on drama and music) to challenge existing orthodoxies and to transform business schools into institutions with greater creativity and innovation (Starkey and Tempest 2009b). Bartunek (2007) complements this view by identifying the inability of scholars to properly communicate with practitioners as the key issue, which, according to Dossabhoy and Berger (2002), involves a lack of mutual understanding of how to define research quality. Augier and March (2007) view relevance myopia as an alternative explanation. Business scholars disconnect teaching and practitioner engagement from research by excessively contextualizing non-research activities along the spatial and time dimension.

The frequently criticized failure of business scholars to master the 'double hurdle' is the result of the complex interaction of market pressures and institutional policies. Most importantly, research rankings (of journals, citations, and researchers) have evolved into broadly accepted performance measures, which define the academic community as the main if not the only addressee of scholarly knowledge generation. While being recognized as imperfect proxy measures of quality (e.g. Adler and Harzing 2009; Frey and Rost 2010), research rankings have nevertheless established themselves as the dominant metric for faculty management and recruitment and for judging school-level performance (Cooper 2011). Rankings are accused of fostering intellectual isomorphism (Rasche et al. 2013) and of intellectually impoverishing business schools by replacing the faculty's 'taste for research' with a 'taste for publications' (Frey and Osterloh 2011). Frey (2003) as well as Frey and Osterloh (2011) have identified the peer review process as the underlying issue, while Baden-Fuller et al. (2000), Mudambi et al. (2008) and others have proposed a more scientific derivation of research rankings. Unlike rankings, international accreditation systems such as the EFMD Quality Improvement System (EQUIS) generally acknowledge the multiple purposes of research (e.g. Shenton 2007) and, hence, only trigger isomorphic tendencies by execution rather than by design. The role of performance metrics will be further discussed in the next section in the context of general business school rankings and accreditations.

The literature at this point offers few insights about whether the focus on scholarly research is actually paying off for business schools and their stakeholders. Theoretical treatments focus on the role of research as a signalling device for students (Besancenot et al. 2009) and how faculty research bonuses may actually reduce top-end research and journal quality (Besancenot and Vranceanu 2008). What is, however, needed is more in-depth empirical analysis of the linkage between research and institutional behaviour as well as performance. The evidence, for instance, on the demand effects of research (Becker et al. 2003), the role of organizational choices for research productivity (Rasmussen 2000), or the linkage between faculty compensation and research performance in all its dimensions (Remler and Pema 2009; Swidler and Goldreyer 1998; Worrell 2009) is spotty at best and at this point mostly embedded in the general higher education literature.

2.6. REPUTATION AND THE ROLE OF ACCREDITATIONS AND RANKINGS

Reputation as a driver of a business school's competitive position is an elusive concept. It is the product of perceptions and interpretations of institutional stakeholders and tends to be strongly influenced by the school's past behaviour (Clark and Montgomery 1998). The mainstream of the management literature adds to the fuzziness by not carefully distinguishing between its conceptual definition and measurement issues. If we, however, adopt an asset-based view, then a business school's reputational capital can be interpreted as the portfolio value of its intangible assets, of which the institutional human capital base responsible for delivering educational services and new knowledge figures most prominently. It also captures the organizational capacity to maintain, nurture, and develop its human capital base in the future as well as the value associated with the school's brand. Individual asset values represent the present discounted value of future economic benefit streams accruing to institutional stakeholders (Vallens 2008). They are constituent elements of a business school's competitive positioning if they shape the economic behaviour of stakeholders via the school. The asset-based approach differs from (Rindova et al. 2010) by rejecting the view that reputation itself represents an intangible asset or that it has, per se, uncertainty-reducing effects from the point of view of external parties (see also Cornelissen and Thorpe 2002; Rindova et al. 2005).

When the management literature argues that reputation is an 'organizational attribute depicted as a broad multi-dimensional construct whose value is determined through interactions and interrelationships of multiple attributes' (Boyd et al. 2010; Vidaver-Cohen 2007), it merely underlines the difficulties of valuing the business school's intellectual property. Business school management and the market systemically lack robust data on the benefit streams created for stakeholders and also struggle to identify an appropriate discount rate. As a result, market actors are resigned to evaluating reputation using the historical time series of quality proxies. The actual task of selecting relevant indicators and aggregating them into a composite measure has been, de facto, delegated to market intermediaries—the ranking providers (Bickerstaffe and Ridgers 2007). These measures suffer from various deficiencies, among them the subjective weighting applied in the aggregation process, the manipulation potential due to the partial reliance on self-reported data (which is increasingly been addressed with 'Web of Science'-based statistics), the backward-looking nature of the data analysed, as well as the implicit lag structure until school decisions affect quality indicators. Market intermediaries may also rationally deliver biased opinions in an effort to tailor their signals around the prior beliefs of customers, which appears to be particularly relevant for the top end of the business school market (Gentzkow and Shapiro 2006).

The cross-border reputation of business schools is nowadays established on the basis of a two-stage filtering system with international accreditations providing access and international rankings defining the relative competitive position. They should in principle play a complementary role in generating trust in the market with accreditors acting as 'promisers' ('certifiers') and ranking organizations as 'trusters' (Klein 1997). While national accreditation systems are designed to enforce minimum standards, international accreditation systems grant membership in peer-based 'clubs of elite business schools' (Hansmann 1996; Hommel 2010; Urgel 2007), which serve increasingly as a precondition for being recognized by or even admitted to international rankings. Rankings provide an ordinal ordering of business schools based on reputational proxy scores (which may differ with respect to the emphasis placed on inputs, processes and outputs). It is, however, a two-way street with ranking improvements nowadays attracting more and better applicants (Baden-Fuller and Ang 2001; Monks and Ehrenberg 1999; Peters 2007; Policano 2007) and drops in rankings doing the reverse by, for instance, increasing dean turnover (Fee et al. 2005). In other words, rankings measure as well as create or destroy reputation (Baden-Fuller et al. 2000).

Accreditation and rankings play a central role in homogenizing the value perceptions of stakeholders and other market participants (Safón 2009).

Growing unanimity leads to less diffuse quality signals to the market, which in turn raises 'customer' willingness to pay. At the same time, it creates a perverse incentive to manage business schools on the basis of accreditation standards and ranking indicators rather than fundamental 'asset values' (Gioia and Corley 2002; Peters 2007). As a consequence, deans also display a tendency to initiate organizational changes if rankings are out of line with their own perception of their school's competitive positioning (Martins 2005). One can therefore argue with Sauder and Fine (2008) that reputation is shaped by the interplay between two types of mediators—reputational arbiters (accreditors, ranking organizations) and reputational entrepreneurs (senior management teams of business schools).

The disciplining effect of rankings and accreditations prevails despite the fact that they represent noisy quality signals with the 'rules of the game' subject to abrupt and erratic changes. This is, for instance, evidenced by the fact that, according to Dichev (1999), there exists little correlation between the contemporaneous changes of different rankings. More concerning is the fact that market-based validation mechanisms encourage isomorphism and global mimicry (Wilson and McKiernan 2011) in the market for management education, which has also impacted business schools as a workplace with the creation of corresponding disciplining devices and incentive schemes (Rasche et al. 2013).

Business schools are nowadays unwilling participants in the so-called 'rankings game' (AACSB International 2005; Bradshaw 2007; Corley and Gioia 2000). Individual rationality dictates an increase in spending on tangible and intangible assets to achieve accreditation labels or to improve the position in ranking. Given that all business schools have an incentive to act in a similar fashion, they find themselves in a prisoners' dilemma situation with the returns from these investments often below expectations. Refusing to play the game would be equally disadvantageous as they are then threatened with falling behind the competition. Empirical evidence shows that the rank position of top schools tends to be quite stable, while the opposite holds true for the bottom end of the spectrum (Devinney et al. 2006). In other words, the disappointment factor of the rankings game increases over time as deans move lower-tier schools forward with ambitious and costly development programmes.

2.7. THE FUTURE OF BUSINESS SCHOOLS AND THE FUTURE OF THE MBA

There exists by now a fairly broad literature discussing the future of business schools in more general terms (e.g. Cornuel and Hommel 2012; Durand and Dameron 2008; Iniguez de Onzono 2011). These contributions tend to touch upon a combination of the issues raised above and then offer reflections on the way forward in line with the discussion provided so far in this chapter. They for instance also raise issues such as the convergence dynamics between the U.S. and Europe (Engwall 2007), the rapid growth of the Asian business school sector (Brailsford 2012), how to create a global perspective in management education (Ghemawat 2008, 2011), or the contributions of business schools to the wider society (Morsing and Rovira 2011). Overall, this literature offers a variety of loose ends to be picked up by future research. A promising avenue would, for instance, be the study of changing business models, which seem to lead to a fraying of institutional boundaries and the rise of a networked-based provision of management education (Lorange 2012; Thomas et al. 2013c).

Recent years have seen the emergence of a derivative reform discussion focused on the future of the MBA (see Jain and Golosinski 2011 for a summary of the criticisms levelled at MBA education). The MBA degree is in a lot of ways still the centre of the business school universe. Market outlook studies typically focus on MBA enrolments, hiring prospects and salary levels; many journalists cover the MBA market rather than the business school sector. It is undoubtedly a reflection of many business schools focusing on variants of the MBA as their flagship products. Datar et al. (2010) deserve the honour of having given this discussion a more structured and research-based format. Their carefully crafted study of MBA programmes offered by leading business schools around the globe provides strong evidence for the isomorphic tendencies in curriculum design but, at the same time, also flags up the commonalities of the issues to be addressed by the business school sector. MBA-related research is still in the process of emerging (Collet and Vives 2013; Davis and Hogarth 2012; Rubin and Dierdorff 2013; Schlegelmilch and Thomas 2011), but promises to offer complementary analyses of the developmental challenges for business schools with a larger degree of practical specificity.

2.8. RESEARCH OUTLOOK

2.8.1. General Assessment

An important driver of research so far has been the apparent role of business schools as 'defendants'. They are accused of not conducting relevant research, of not producing competent managers, of not positioning themselves as responsible organizations, of not providing an appropriate international perspective, etc. The multitude of criticisms levelled at business schools points towards persisting gaps between societal expectations and developmental achievements. The result is a fairly narrow (and also one-sided) literature focused on institutional shortcomings. Most of the research conducted so far has been qualitative with a significant share also falling into the applied category. Future work should aim to produce 'hard' evidence on the basis of sound empirical work. Very little of that can be found in the literature so far.

A related deficiency of the existing literature is its overwhelmingly normative character. A lot has been written on 'how things ought to be' on the basis of a set of beliefs, which are not necessarily based on scientific principles. Admittedly, this chapter falls to some degree into the same trap as well. This tendency to 'moralize' explains the somewhat ideological character of the debate on what business schools have achieved so far and what is the right way forward. Further, the debate suffers from a certain degree of superficiality, which has become most visible in the discussion on the learning points to be derived from the financial crisis. There has been a lot of lamenting about the 'evil nature' of finance and economics as the increasingly dominant pillar of modern management and very little recognition of the research advances generated by scholars in these fields following the crisis (see e.g. Shiller 2012 and the sources cited therein).

What is needed instead is a better understanding of institutional dynamics—strategically and operationally. This may entail the risk of studying business schools with the same 'weapons' that make research into business schools the subject of criticism in the first place, but it also promises to yield pointed analyses of factors driving institutional performance and development. A clear strength of existing research is its multidisciplinary nature, which reflects the consensus view that the study of business schools needs to go beyond developing a purely functional viewpoint.

There is also a tendency in research on business schools to focus on the top end of the market, probably because leading business schools are subjected to greater public scrutiny and therefore publish more research-relevant information (e.g. by participating in international rankings). The result is however an unsustainable bias in the way scholars are analysing the business school sector. Lower-tier schools (representing distinctly more than 95 percent of the total sector) effectively operate in different markets, face different constraints, and, as a consequence, have different development priorities and trajectories.

There is still a lot of uncharted territory to be explored by future research. A closer look at the general higher education literature delivers a number of important pointers for future developments (see also Pettigrew in this volume). The business school sector is however also at the forefront of higher education dynamics so that the study of new developments can also provide direction for general higher education research in the medium to long term. Both dimensions will be further discussed in the remainder of this section.

2.8.2. Relevant Research Themes in the Higher Education Literature

Existing research on business schools is still fairly narrow, reflecting a pre-occupation with their institutional and behavioural shortcomings. Similar themes can also be found in the higher education literature but the ground covered by those scholars is much broader and offers significantly more depth in certain areas. Both sides would undoubtedly benefit from more active cross-fertilization, in particular because higher education scholars typically have functional specializations other than management. Examples of well-researched areas in the higher education literature that would deserve attention in a business school context as well are:

- *Governance Practices and their Effectiveness.* There exists a fairly broad literature studying different aspects of university governance such as the role of presidents, senates and department chairs, the effectiveness of different governance features and the factors triggering changes in university governance (Ehrenberg 2004; Hirsch and Weber 2001; Tierney 2004). In contrast, very little work has been done to analyse the governance of business schools. While, for instance, there exists common agreement that the inclusion of outside stakeholders via advisory boards or the delegation of decision rights within the school organization are key drivers of performance, no studies of note except Fragueiro and Thomas (2011) have looked at these aspects in greater detail in a business school context.

- *Entrepreneurialism and Managerialism.* While the business school community appears to have accepted the rise of entrepreneurial activities and management-led governance as a fact of life, similar developments in the university sphere have triggered considerable debate. Marginson and Considine (2000), Slaughter and Rhoades (2004), Zemsky et al. (2006), Deem et al. (2007), and many others are examining the effects on, for instance, academic values, the prioritization of learning, and the openness of academic research. These issues are very relevant in a business school context as well.

- *Faculty Management.* There exists a fairly broad literature in HRM and labour economics studying hiring, promotion and compensation issues (Barbezat and Donihue 1998; Bland et al. 2006; Bratsberg et al. 2003; Ehrenberg et al. 2006). By contrast, we still lack a good understanding of the distinctive practices found in business schools and their effectiveness beyond practice-based accounts that they exist. Higher education research further indicates that the faculty profession appears to have reached a crossroads (see also Burgan 2006; Huisman et al. 2002; Levin 2006): universities are in the process of eroding faculty tenure (Ehrenberg and Zhang 2005), are increasing the number of professors on temporary contracts (Feldman and Turnley 2003), are subjecting faculty to HR practices common in the business sector (Bridgman 2007), and are dislodging faculty from university governance (Ehrenberg 2004). Similar issues can be found in business schools today, but have not been systematically studied in a scholarly context.

– *Learning.* There exists a fairly broad literature discussing the state of learning in universities (Ackoff and Greenberg 2008). The future role of a liberal education on the undergraduate level figures particularly prominently in this context (Arum and Roksa 2011; Bok 2006; Delbanco 2012; Harney and Thomas 2013). By contrast, insufficient efforts have been undertaken so far to comprehensively study the educational purpose of business schools (Athavale et al. 2008; Teece 2011) or to explain the relevance of teaching to fulfilling the business schools' societal role (Cornuel and Hommel 2012).

– *Innovation.* Universities in general are being criticized for failing to adjust their operational model to modern times (Christensen and Eyring 2011; Weber and Duderstadt 2010; Wildavsky et al. 2011). They are accused, in particular, of withdrawing behind 'ivy-covered' walls, sticking to a dated operational model and, in the process, failing to respond to the changing professional, economic and technological circumstances of stakeholders. The literature certainly includes similar themes for business schools, but with a more constructive stance to address existing shortcomings.

2.8.3. Study of Current Market Trends and Institutional Dynamics

The business school sector is currently undergoing a process of fundamental transformation with a variety of demand- and supply-side factors affecting the way business schools will conduct themselves in the years to come. As evidence for change is starting to emerge, we can expect to see a rising number of applied contributions detailing the effects on business schools and their competitive environment. Sound scholarly research will in our view require formal empirical inquiries either on the basis of institutional data or surveys. Some of the more important developments and exemplary contributions, mostly from the higher education literature, are:

– *Trend towards Deregulation and Privatization.* Business schools embedded in public universities are facing trickle-down effects resulting from fiscally constrained governments deregulating or even privatizing higher education systems. It involves, for instance, the switch from subsidized to tuition-fee-based degree education, the greater prioritization of entrepreneurial initiatives or the removal of tenure and civil servant status for faculty. Examples of contributions to the higher education literature discussing the nature and impact of this trend can be found in Morphew and Eckel (2009), Priest and St. John (2006), as well as Fethke and Policano (2013).

– *Internationalization, International Alliances, M&A Activity, and FDI.* Business schools worldwide are responding to the forces of globalization by merging with national competitors (e.g. SKEMA in France, AALTO in Finland and Reading/Henley in the U.K.), forging strategic partnerships with foreign business schools, or investing in campus locations in foreign countries (AACSB International 2011; Weber and Duderstadt 2008). No serious effort has been undertaken so far to analyse the performance effects of these initiatives or the impact on competition (Baden-Fuller and Ang 2001 is a noteworthy exception). Even the extent and strategic role of traditional international partnering, e.g. for exchange of students and faculty, has so far not been subjected to scholarly study (except e.g. Bevelander 2012).

– *Rise of For-Profit Management Education.* The majority of business schools are established as non-profit organizations. However, recent years have seen the emergence of a vibrant for-profit fringe, so far mainly serving socio-economically disadvantaged and less qualified students (Hentschke 2011). Cost inefficiencies in non-profit higher education and research-related resource commitments of traditional providers are enabling for-profit competitors to evolve into mainstream players. This development is likely to create more polarity in management education with a rising number of institutions specializing in teaching and learning rather than research. Preliminary assessments can be found in Breneman et al. (2007), Ruch (2003), as well as Tierney and Hentschke (2007).

– *Shift towards On-line Education and the Role of Technology:* Recent years have delivered strong evidence that the demand for academic business degrees is shifting from full-time to part-time and especially on-line programmes (Walsh 2011). Even leading business schools have started to develop on-line streams for their flagship MBAs. At the same time, we can observe the emergence of technology platforms for on-line delivery, some of them in open source space (e.g. Coursera, Academic Earth, MIT OpenCourseWare). These developments promise to have a disruptive impact on higher education (DeMillo 2011; Economist Intelligence Unit 2008) and, in particular, business schools (Fleck 2008; Hommel and Lejeune 2013). Learning platforms provision may be shifting from business schools to new market entrants (e.g. publishing houses, database providers). Faculty may ultimately become dislodged from academic institutions by contracting directly with platform providers. The resulting scale economies may put the so far dominant business model of research-based business schools at risk and trigger an industry shakeout.

– *Convergence of For-Degree and Non-Degree Management Education.* Circumstantial evidence is emerging that business schools are in the process of breaking down the boundaries between for-degree and non-degree education, implying that credits for non-degree coursework can be transferred to for-degree programmes (Hommel 2009b). It is reflective of changing consumption patterns and a shift towards modular design structures in management education (see also Christensen and Eyring 2011).

– *Availability of Faculty Resources.* It is already well documented that business schools are systematically under-producing Ph.D. graduates (e.g. AACSB International 2003; Ivory et al. 2007). The result is a shortage of well-qualified junior faculty (e.g. currently especially visible in the field of accounting), rising salary levels and increasing international mobility of researchers. More evidence is needed to understand flows of doctoral students and graduates as well as the resulting impact on hiring practices and general school development, especially in high-growth markets (see e.g. also Ehrenberg et al. 2010).

– *Sustainability of the Business Schools', 'Business Model'.* The dynamic forces discussed so far coupled with existing demographic trends will increasingly put into question the business model of, in particular, Western business schools. Thomas and Peters (2012) call it 'a bit too luxurious' and identify resource commitments in support of faculty research as the key issue for the future. Educational activities must generate sufficient returns to cover investments in research, which leads to more entrepreneurialism and risk-taking behaviour (Hommel and King 2013). These developments will raise demands for the professionalization of the finance and risk management function in business schools, which are two particularly opaque areas of business school management from a practical as well as from a research perspective (Hommel and Pastwa 2013).

2.9. CONCLUSIONS: WHAT KIND OF BUSINESS SCHOOL?

'The obvious challenge, arising out of the all the constraints, situational contexts and isomorphic tendencies (e.g. rankings, accreditation etc.), is to identify what kind of business school might be more appropriate (and robust) for the future' (Wilson and Thomas 2012: 374). Mintzberg (2004) argues that management is an art and that the managerial task involves a set of practical people-skills. He would favour a greater emphasis on managerial skills and capabilities and the examination of critical and synthetic thinking through study of the humanities and social sciences(see also Harney and Thomas 2013). We argue that business schools will have to make substantial changes in what they research and teach. This means broadening the traditional focus of research and teaching in business schools to look more broadly at wider society, to embrace multi-disciplinary perspectives, and to turn its theoretical perspectives and research foci toward 'big' questions. In turn, this means engaging to a greater extent in policy debates—reclaiming broader issues of healthcare, poverty, and social responsibility as well as issues of work, employment, and society.

A first step would be to develop a strong norm of management learning and to move away from the utilitarian-instrumental perspective of management education. Next to maintaining proper coverage of fundamental management disciplines, educational approaches must extend to fields as diverse as sociology, philosophy, psychology, economics, law, and mathematics. A second step would be to place far greater emphasis on addressing the ethical and moral challenges presented by the various forms of modern capitalism (ranging from the more socially-oriented European-style democratic capitalism to Asian-style state capitalism). In addition, a critical examination of the role of businesses and managers in society should focus on corporate social responsibility as a deeper question about the accountability of managers for their actions and decisions. A third step would be to research and teach 'big questions' generally of an inter-disciplinary nature which impact upon organizations and society. These might include topics such as an examination of why there is simultaneously obesity, poverty, and starvation in a world that is technologically able to feed itself, or the impact and risks of exogenous events such as climate change, disasters and terrorist activities. Finally, as managers operate increasingly globally, business schools themselves will have to become less insular and nationally oriented in order to produce flexible, 'go-anywhere' graduates. An understanding of language and greater contextual and cultural intelligence would seem to be essential parts of the teaching and research curriculum of business schools in the near future.

If schools do not undertake these changes, we believe that they are likely to become less relevant, i.e., they will increasingly be perceived as illegitimate players operating on the side-lines of key social, economic and political debates, and policy decisions. Deans need to have the courage to deviate from the mainstream and build curricula which develop so-called T-shaped individuals i.e. those having achieved significant *disciplinary breadth* through a liberal education involving critical, synthetic and analytic thinking and appropriate *depth training* in the important functions and languages of management education. Unfortunately, the similarity in many business school curricula arises from the mimetic and isomorphic tendencies promoted by, inter alia, rankings and accreditation systems present in the current management education area.

ACKNOWLEDGEMENTS

The authors would like to acknowledge helpful comments and suggestions provided by Andrew Pettigrew and participants of the 1st EFMD Higher Education Research Conference held in 2012 in Horgen, Switzerland. The usual disclaimer applies.

REFERENCES

AACSB International (2003). *Sustaining Scholarship in Business Schools: Report of the Doctoral Commission to AACSB International's Board of Directors*. Tampa, FL: AACSB International.

AACSB International (2005). *The Business School Ranking Dilemma*. Tampa, FL: AACSB International.

AACSB International (2008). *Impact of Research*. Tampa, FL: AACSB International.

AACSB International (2011). *Globalization of Management Education: Changing International Structures, Adaptive Strategies, and the Impact on Institutions*. Tampa, FL: AACSB International.

Ackoff, Russell L. and Greenberg, Daniel (2008). *Turning Learning Right Side Up: Putting Education Back on Track*. Upper Saddle River, NJ: Pearson.

Adler, Nancy J. and Harzing, Anne-Wil (2009). 'When Knowledge Wins: Transcending the Sense and Nonsense of Academic Rankings', *Academic of Management Learning & Education*, 8: 72–95.

Amdam, Rolv Petter, Kvålshaugen, Ragnhild, and Larsen, Eirinn (2003). *Inside the Business Schools: The Content of European Education*. Copenhagen: Copenhagen Businesss School Press.

Antunes, Don and Thomas, Howard (2007). 'The Csompetitive (Dis)Advantages of European Business Schools', *Long Range Planning*, 40: 382–404.

Arum, Richard and Roksa, Josipa (2011). *Academically Adrift: Limited Learning on College Campuses*. Chicago, Il: The University of Chicago Press.

Athavale, Manoj, Davis, Rod, and Myring, Mark (2008). 'The Integrated Business Curriculum: An Examination of Perceptions and Practices', *Journal of Education for Business*, May/June: 295.

Augier, Mie and March, James G. (2007), 'The Pursuit of Relevance in Management Education', *California Managment Review*, 49: 129–146.

Augier, Mie and March, James G. (2011). *The Roots, Rituals, and Rhetorics of Change: North American Business Schools After the Second World War*. Stanford, CA: Stanford Business Books.

Baden-Fuller, Charles and Ang, Siah Hwee (2001). 'Building Reputations: The Role of Alliances in the European Business School Scene', *Long Range Planning*, 34: 741–755.

Baden-Fuller, Charles, Ravazzolo, Fabio, and Schweizer, Tanja (2000). 'Making and Measuring Reputations The Research Ranking of European Business Schools', *Long Range Planning*, 33: 621–650.

Barbezat, Debra A. and Donihue, Michael R. (1998). 'Do Faculty Salaries Rise with Job Security', *Economic Letters*, 58: 239–244.

Barsoux, Jean-Louis (2000). *Insead: From Intuition to Institution*. Fountainebleau: Insead.

Bartunek, Jean M. (2007). 'Academic-Practitioner Collaboration Need Not Require Joint or Relevant Research: Toward a Relational Scholarship of Integration', *Academy of Management Journal*, 50: 1323–1333.

Bartunek, Jean M. (2011). 'What Has Happened to Mode 2?', *British Journal of Management*, 22: 555–558.

Becker, Elizabeth, Lindsay, Cotton M., and Grizzle, Gary (2003). 'The Derived Demand for Faculty Research', *Managerial and Decision Economics*, 24: 549–567.

Bennis, Warren G. and O'Toole, James (2005). 'How Business Schools Lost Their Way', *Harvard Business Review*, 83: 96–104.

Besancenot, Damien and Vranceanu, Radu (2008). 'Can Incentives for Research Harm Research? A Business School Tale', *Journal of Socio-Economics*, 37: 1248–1265.

Besancenot, Damien, Faria, Joao Ricardo, and Vranceanu, Radu (2009). 'Why Business Schools Do So Much Research: A Signalling Explanation', *Research Policy*, 38: 1093–1101.

Bevelander, Dianne Lynne (2012). 'Who Is Engaging with Whom? Internationalizing Opportunities for Business Schools in Emerging Economies', *International Journal of Educational Management*, 26: 646–663.

Bickerstaffe, George and Ridgers, Bill (2007). 'Ranking of Business Schools', *Journal of Management Development*, 26: 61–66.

Bland, Carol J., et al. (2006). 'The Impact of Appointment Type on the Productivity and Commitment of Full-Time Faculty in Research and Doctoral Institutions', *Journal of Higher Education*, 77: 89–123.

Bok, Derek (2006). *Our Underachieving Colleges*. Princeton, NJ: Princeton University Press.

Boyd, B. K., Bergh, D. D., and Ketchen, D. J. (2010).'Reconsidering the Reputation-Performance Relationship: A Resource-Based View', *Journal of Management*, 36: 588–609.

Bradshaw, Della (2007). 'Business School Rankings: The Love-Hate Relationship', *Journal of Management Development*, 26: 54–60.

Brailsford, Tim (ed.), (2012). *Business Education in the Asia-Pacific*. St. Lucia, Queensland: AAPBS.

Bratsberg, Bernt, Ragan, James F., and Warren, John T. (2003). 'Negative Returns to Seniority: New Evidence in Academic Markets', *Industrial and Labor Relations Review*, 56: 306–323.

Breneman, David W., Pusser, Brian and Turner, Sarah E. (eds) (2007). *Earnings from Learning: The Rise of For-Profit Universities*. State University of New York Press.

Bridgman, Todd (2007). 'Freedom and Autonomy in the University Enterprise', *Journal of Organizational Change*, 20: 478–490.

Bryman, A. (2007). 'Effective Leadership in Higher Education: A Literature Review', *Studies in Higher Education*, 32: 693–710.

Burgan, Mary (2006). *What Ever Happened to the Faculty? Drift and Decision in Higher Education*. Baltimore, MD: The Johns Hopkins University Press.

Canals, Jordi (2011). 'In Search of a Greater Impact: New Corporate and Societal Challenges for Business Schools', in Jordi Canals (ed.), *The Future of Leadership Development: Corporate Needs and the Role of Business Schools*. Houndmills, UK: Palgrave Macmillan, 3–30.

Christensen, Clayton M. and Eyring, Henry J. (2011). *The Innovative University: Changing the DNA of Higher Education from the Inside Out*. San Francisco, CA: Jossey-Bass.

Clark, Bruce H. and Montgomery, David B. (1998). 'Deterrence, Reputations and Competitive Cognition', *Management Science*, 44: 62–82.

Collet, Francois and Vives, Luis (2013). 'From Preeminence to Prominence: The Fall of U.S. Business Schools and the Rise of European Asian Business Schools in the Financial Times Global MBA Rankings'. *Academy of Management Learning & Education*.

Cooper, Cary L. (2011). 'Management Research in the UK: A Personal View', *British Journal of Management*, 22: 343–346.

Corley, Kevin and Gioia, Dennis (2000). 'The Rankings Game: Managing Business School Reputation', *Corporate Reputation Review*, 3: 319–333.

Cornelissen, Joep and Thorpe, Richard (2002). 'Measuring a Business School's Reputation: Perspectives, Problems and Prospects', *European Management Journal*, 20: 172–178.

Cornuel, Eric (2005). 'The Role of Business Schools in Society', *Journal of Management Development*, 24: 819–829.

Cornuel, Eric and Hommel, Ulrich (2012). 'Business Schools as a Positive Force for Fostering Societal Change', *Business & Professional Ethics Journal*, 31: 289–312.

Crainer, Stuart and Dearlove, Des (2001). *Gravy Training: Inside the Shadowy World of Business Schools*. Oxford: Capstone.

Datar, Srikant M., Garvin, David A., and Cullen, Patrick G. (2010). *Rethinking the MBA: Business Education at a Crossroads*. Cambridge, MA: Harvard University Press.

Davies, Julie and Thomas, Howard (2009). 'What Do Business School Deans Do? Insights from a UK Study', *Management Decision*, 47: 1396–1419.

Davis, Harry L. and Hogarth, Robin M. (2012). 'Rethinking Management Education: A View from Chicago', *Unpublished Working Paper*.

DeAngelo, Harry and DeAngelo, Linda (2005). 'What's Really Wrong with U.S. Business Schools', *Unpublished Working Paper*, July.

Deem, Rosemary, Hillyard, Sam, and Reed, Mike (2007). *Knowledge, Higher Education, and the New Managerialism: The Changing Management of UK Universities*. Oxford: Oxford University Press.

Delbanco, Andrew (2012). *College: What It Was, Is and Should Be*. Princeton, NJ: Princeton University Press.

DeMillo, Richard A. (2011). *Abelard to Apple: The Fate of American Colleges and Universities*. Cambridge, MA: The MIT Press.

Devinney, Timothy M., Dowling, Grahame, and Perm-Ajchariyawong, Nidthida (2006). 'The Financial Times Business School Rankings: What Quality Is This Signal of Quality', *European Management Review*, 5: 195–208.

Dichev, Ilia D. (1999). 'How Good Are Business School Rankings?', *Journal of Business*, 72: 201–213.

Dossabhoy, Nasswan and Berger, Paul D (2002). 'Business School Research: Bridging the Gap between Producers and Consumers', *Omega*, 30: 301–314.

Durand, Thomas and Dameron, Stéphanie (2008). *The Future of Business Schools: Scenarios and Strategies for 2020*. New York: Palgrave-Macmillan.

Economist Intelligence Unit (2008). *The Future of Higher Education: How Technology Will Shape Learning.* London: The Economist.

Ehrenberg, Ronald G. (2004). *Governing Academia: Who Is in Charge at the Modern University?* Cornell, NY: Cornell University Press.

Ehrenberg, Ronald G. and Zhang, Liang (2005). 'Do Tenured and Tenure-Track Faculty Matter?', *Journal of Human Resources*, 40: 647–659.

Ehrenberg, Ronald G., McGraw, Marquise, and Mrdjenovic, Jesenka (2006). 'Why Do Field Differentials in Average Faculty Salaries Vary Across Universities?', *Economics of Education Review*, 25: 241–248.

Ehrenberg, Ronald G., et al. (2010). *Educating Scholars: Doctoral Education in the Humanities.* Princeton, NJ: Princeton University Press.

Engwall, Lars (1998). 'Asterix in Disneyland: Management Scholars from France on the World Stage', *Organization Studies*, 19: 863–881.

Engwall, Lars (2000). 'Foreign Role Models and Standardisation in Nordic Business Education', *Scandinavian Journal of Management*, 16: 1–24.

Engwall, Lars (2004). 'The Americanization of Nordic Management Knowledge', *Journal of Management Inquiry*, 13: 109–117.

Engwall, Lars (2007). 'The Anatomy of Management Education', *Scandinavian Journal of Management*, 23: 4–35.

Engwall, Lars and Gunnarsson, Elving (1994). *Management Studies in Academic Context.* Uppsala: Uppsala University Press.

Engwall, Lars and Zamagni, Vera (eds) (1998). *Management Education in Historical Perspective.* Manchester, UK: Manchester University Press.

Fee, C Edward, Hadlock, Charles J, and Pierce, Joshua R. (2005). 'Business School Rankings and Business School Deans: A Study of Non-Profit Governance', *Financial Management*, 34: 143–166.

Feldman, Daniel C. and Turnley, William H. (2003). 'Contingent Employment in Academic Careers: Relative Deprivation Among Adjunct Faculty', *Journal of Vocational Behavior*, 64: 284–307.

Fethke, Gary C. and Policano, Andrew J. (2013). 'Public No More Universities: Subsidy to Self-Reliance', *Journal of Management Development*, 32: 525–536.

Fleck, James (2008), 'Technology and the Business School World', *Journal of Management Development*, 27: 415–424.

Fragueiro, Fernando and Thomas, Howard (2011). *Strategic Leadership in the Business School: Keeping One Step Ahead.* Cambridge: Cambridge University Press.

Frey, Bruno S. (2003). 'Publishing as Prostitution?—Choosing Between One's Own Ideas and Academic Success', *Public Choice*, 116: 205–223.

Frey, Bruno S. and Rost, Katja (2010). 'Do Rankings Reflect Research Quality?', *Journal of Applied Economics*, 13: 1–38.

Frey, Bruno S. and Osterloh, Margit (2011). *'Ranking Games', Working Paper No. 39.* Zürich: Department of Economics, University of Zürich.

Gentzkow, Matthew and Shapiro, Jesse M. (2006). 'Media Bias and Reputation', *Journal of Political Economy*, 114: 280–316.

Ghemawat, Pankaj (2008). 'The Globalization of Business Education: Through the Lens of Semi-Globalization', *Journal of Management Development*, 27: 391–414.

Ghemawat, Pankaj (2011). 'Bridging the Globalization Gap at Top Business Schools: Curricular Challenges and a Response', in Jordi Canals (ed.), *The Future of Leadership Development: Corporate Needs and the Role of Business Schools.* Houndmills, UK: Palgrave Macmillan, 177–217.

Ghoshal, Sumantra (2005). 'Bad Management Theories Are Destroying Good Management Practices', *Academy of Management Learning and Education*, 4: 75–91.

Gibbons, M., et al. (1994). *The New Production of Knowledge: The Dynamics of Science and Research in Contemporary Societies.* London: Sage.

Gioia, Dennis A. and Corley, Kevin G. (2002). 'Being Good versus Looking Good: Business School Rankings and the Circean Transformation from Substance to Image', *Academic of Management Learning & Education*, 1: 107–120.

Goodall, Amanda H. (2009). *Socrates in the Boardroom: Why Research Universities Should Be Led by Top Scholars.* Princeton University Press.

Gordon, Robert Aaron and Howell, James Edwin (1959). *Higher Education for Business.* New York: Columbia University Press.

Grey, Christopher (2002). 'What Are Business Schools For? On Silence and Voice in Management Education', *Journal of Management Education*, 26: 496–511.

Grey, Christopher (2004). 'Reinventing Business Schools: The Contribution of Critical Management Education', *Academic of Management Learning & Education*, 3: 178–186.

Hambrick, Donald C. (1994). 'What if the Academy Actually Mattered?', *Academy of Management Review*, 19: 11–16.

Hansmann, Henry (1996). *The Ownership of Enterprise.* Cambridge, MA: The Belknap Press of Harvard University Press.

Harney, Stefano and Thomas, Howard (2013). 'Towards a Liberal Management Education', *Journal of Management Development*, 32: 508–524.

Hayes, R. H. and Abernathy, W. J. (1980). 'Managing Our Way to Economic Decline', *Harvard Business Review*, 58: 67–77.

Hentschke, Guilbert C. (2011). 'For-Profit Sector Innovations in Business Models and Organizational Cultures', in Ben Wildavsky, Andrew P. Kelly, and Kevin Carey (eds), *Reinventing Higher Education: The Promise of Innovation.* Cambridge, MA: Harvard Education Press, 159–196.

Hirsch, Werner Z. and Weber, Luc E. (eds) (2001). *Governance in Higher Education: The University in a State of Flux.* London: Economica.

Hodgkinson, Gerard P. and Rousseau, Denise M. (2009). 'Bridging the Rigour–Relevance Gap in Management Research: It's Already Happening!', *Journal of Management Studies*, 46: 534–546.

Hommel, Ulrich (2009a). 'Upheaval in the Global Market for Management Education and Implications for CEE Business Schools', *Society and Economy*, 31: 235–252.

Hommel, Ulrich (2009b). 'Blurring the Edges: On the Mixing of Degree and Non-Degree Education', *Global Focus*, 3(3): 28–31.

Hommel, Ulrich (2010). 'The Role of International Accreditation for Market Positioning', in HRK (ed.), *10 Jahre Herbsttagung zur Qualität in den Hochschulen: Rückschau und neue Entwicklungen* (Beiträge zur Hochschulpolitik, 7). Bonn: Deutsche Hochschulrektorenkonferenz, 131–135.

Hommel, Ulrich and Lejeune, Christophe (2013). 'Major Disruption Ahead!', *Global Focus*, 7(1): 10–13.

Hommel, Ulrich and King, Roger (2013). 'The Emergence of Risk-Based Regulation: Relevance for Entrepreneurial Risk-Taking of Business Schools', *Journal of Management Development*, 32: 537–547.

Hommel, Ulrich and Pastwa, Anna (2013). 'Risk Management Ante Portas', *Global Focus*, 7: 60–63.

Hommel, Ulrich, Painter-Morland, Mollie, and Wang, Jocelyn (2012).'Gradualism Prevails', *Global Focus*, 6(3): 30–33.

Huisman, Jeroen, Weert, Egbert de, and Bartelse, Jeroen (2002). 'Academic Careers from a European Perspective: The Declining Desirability of the Faculty Position', *Journal of Higher Education*, 73: 141–160.

Iniguez de Onzono, Santiago (2011). *The Learning Curve: How Business Schools are Re-Inventing Education*. Houndmills: Palgrave-Macmillan.

Ivory, Chris, et al. (2007). 'The Future of Business School Faculty'. London: Advanced Institute of Management Research.

Jain, Dipak C. and Golosinski, Matt (2011). 'The Enduring Value of the MBA Degree', in Jordi Canals (ed.), *The Future of Leadership Development: Corporate Needs and the Role of Business Schools*. Houndmills, UK: Palgrave Macmillan, 64–96.

Khurana, Rakesh (2007). *From Higher Aims to Hired Hands: The Social Transformation of American Business Schools and the Unfulfilled Promise of Management as a Profession*. Princeton, NJ: Princeton University Press.

Kieser, Alfred and Nicolai, Alexander T. (2005). 'Success Factor Research: Overcoming the Trade-Off Between Rigor and Relevance', *Journal of Management Inquiry*, 14: 275–279.

Kieser, Alfred and Leiner, Lars (2009). 'Why the Rigour-Relevance Gap Is Unbridgable', *Journal of Management Studies*, 46: 516–533.

Klein, Daniel B. (1997). 'Trust for Hire', in Daniel B. Klein (ed.), *Reputation: Studies in the Voluntary Elecitation of Good Conduct*. Ann Arbor, Michigan: The University of Michigan Press, 97–133.

Leavitt, H. J. (1989). 'Educating our MBAs: On Teaching What We Haven't Taught', *California Management Review*, 31: 38–50.

Levin, John S. (2006). 'Faculty Work: Tensions between Educational and Economic Value', *Journal of Higher Education*, 77: 62–88.

Livingston, J. S. (1971). 'The Myth of the Well-Educated Manager', *Harvard Business Review*, 49: 79–89.

Locke, Robert R. (1985). 'Business Education in Germany: Past Systems and Current Practice', *Business History Review*, 59: 232–253.

Locke, Robert R. (1988). 'Educational Traditions and the Development of Business Studies after 1945 (An Anglo-French-German Comparison)', *Business History*, 30: 84–103.

Locke, Robert R. and Schöne, Katja (2004). *The Entrepreneurial Shift: Americanization in European High-Technology Management Education*. Cambridge, UK: Cambridge University Press.

Locke, Robert R. and Spender, J. C. (2011). *Confronting Managerialism: How the Business Elite and Their Schools Threw Our Life Out of Balance*. London and New York: Zed Books.

Lorange, Peter (2008). *Thought Leadership Meets Business: How Business Schools Can Become More Successful*. Cambridge: Cambridge University Press.

Lorange, Peter (2012). 'The Business School of the Future: The Network-Based Business School', *Journal of Management Development*, 31: 424–430.

Marginson, S. and Considine, M. (2000). *The Enterprise University: Power, Governance and Reinvention in Australia*. Cambridge University Press.

Martins, Luis L. (2005). 'A Model of the Effects of Reputational Rankings on Organizational Change', *Organization Science*, 16: 701–720.

Mintzberg, Henry (2004). *Managers not MBAs*. San Francisco, CA: Berret-Koehler Publishers.

Mokyr, Joel (2002). *The Gifts of Athena: Historical Origins of the Knowledge Economy*. Princeton, NJ: Princeton University Press.

Monks, James and Ehrenberg, Ronald G. (1999). 'U.S. News & World Report's College Rankings: Why They Do Matter', *Change*, 31: 42–51.

Morphew, Christopher C. and Eckel, Peter D. (eds) (2009). *Privatizing the Public University: Perspectives from across the Academy*. Baltimore, MD: The Johns Hopkins University Press.

Morsing, Mette and Rovira, Alfons Sauquet (eds) (2011). *Business Schools and their Contribution to Society*. London: Sage.

Mudambi, Ram, Peng, Mike W, and Weng, David H (2008). 'Research Rankings of Asia Pacific Business Schools: Global versus Local Knowledge Strategies', *Asia Pacific Journal of Management*, 25: 171–188.

Muff, Katrin (2012). 'Management Education for the World: The 50+20 Agenda', *Unpublished Working Paper*.

Muff, Katrin (2013). 'Developing Globally Responsible Leaders in Business Schools: A Vision and Transformational Practice for the Journey Ahead', *Journal of Management Development*, 32: 487–508.

Peters, Kai (2007). 'Business School Rankings: Content and Context', *Journal of Management Development*, 26: 49–53.

Peters, Kai and Thomas, Howard (2011). 'A Sustainable Model for Business Schools?', *Global Focus*, 5(2): 24–27.

Pettigrew, Andrew M. (1997). 'The Double Hurdles for Management Research', in T. Clarke (ed.), *Advancement in Organizational Behaviour* (Dartmouth, VM: Dartmouth Press), 277–296.

Pettigrew, Andrew M. (2001). 'Management Research after Modernism', *British Journal of Management*, 12: 56–70.

Pettigrew, Andrew M. (2008). 'Scholarly Impact and the Co-Production Hypothesis', *Global Focus*, 2(2): 8–12.

Pfeffer, Jeffrey and Fong, Christina T. (2002). 'The End of Business Schools? Less Success Than Meets the Eye', *Academy of Management Learning and Education*, 1: 78–95.

Pierson, Frank Cook (1959). *The Education of American Businessmen: A Study of University-College Programs in Business Administration* (The Carnegie Series in American Education). New York, NY: McGraw-Hill.

Podolny, Joel M. (2009). 'The Buck Stops (and Starts) at Business School', *Harvard Business Review*, June: 62–67.

Policano, Andrew J. (2007). 'The Rankings Game: And the Winner Is...', *Journal of Management Development*, 26: 43–48.

Priest, Douglas M. and St. John, Edward P. (eds) (2006). *Privatization and Public Universities*. Bloomington, IN: Indiana University Press.

Rasche, Andreas, Hommel, Ulrich, and Cornuel, Eric (2013). 'Discipline as Institutional Maintenance: The Case of Business School Rankings', in Eric Cornuel, Ulrich Hommel, and Andrew M. Pettigrew (eds), *The Institutional Development of Business Schools*. Oxford: Oxford University Press.

Rasmussen, Jorgen Gulddahl (2000). 'Changes in Organising and Managing Research in Universities: Reconstruction or Rediscovery', *Tertiary Education and Management*, 6: 271–287.

Remler, Dahlia K. and Pema, Elda (2009). 'Why Do Institutions of Higher Education Reward Research While Selling Education?', *NBER Working Paper Series*, No. 14974.

Rindova, Violina P., Williamson, Ian O., and Petkova, Antoaneta P. (2010). 'Reputation as an Intangible Asset: Reflections on Theory and Methods in Two Empirical Studies of Business School Reputations', *Journal of Management*, 36: 610–619.

Rindova, Violina P., et al. (2005). 'Being Good or Being Known: An Empirical Examination of the Dimensions, Antecedents, and Consequences of Organizational Reputation', *Academy of Management Journal*, 48: 1033–1049.

Rosser, Vicki J., Johnsrud, Linda K., and Heck, Ronald H. (2003). 'Academic Deans and Directors: Assessing their Effectiveness from Individual and Institutional Perspectives', *Journal of Higher Education*, 74: 1–25.

Rubin, Robert S. and Dierdorff, Erich C. (2013). 'Building a Better MBA: From a Decade of Critique Toward a Decennium of Creation', *Academic of Management Learning & Education*.

Ruch, Richard S (2003). *Higher Ed, Inc.: The Rise of the For-Profit University*. The Johns Hopkins University Press.

Safón, Vicente (2009). 'Measuring the Reputation of Top US Business Schools: A MIMIC Modeling Approach', *Corporate Reputation Review*, 12: 204–228.

Sauder, Michael and Fine, Gary Alan (2008). 'Arbiters, Entrepreneurs, and the Shaping of Business School Reputations', *Sociological Forum*, 23: 699-723.

Schlegelmilch, Bodo B. and Thomas, Howard (2011). 'The MBA in 2020: Will There Still Be One?', *Journal of Management Development*, 30: 474–482.

Shenton, Gordon (2007). 'The Role of Research in Business Education', *Global Focus*, 1(3): 14–17.

Shiller, Robert J. (2012). *Finance and the Good Society*. Princeton, NJ: Princeton University Press.

Shoemaker, Paul J. H. (2008). 'The Future Challenges of Business: Rethinking Management Education', *California Management Review*, 50: 119–139.

Simon, Herbert A. (1967). 'The Business School: A Problem in Organizational Design', *Journal of Management Studies*, 4: 1–16.

Slaughter, Sheila and Rhoades, Gary (2004). *Academic Capitalism and the New Economy: Markets, State, and Higher Education*. Baltimore: The Johns Hopkins University Press.

Starkey, Ken (2002). 'New Knowledge Spaces?', *Human Relations*, 55: 350–360.

Starkey, Ken and Madan, Paula (2001). 'Bridging the Relevance Gap: Aligning Stakeholders in the Future of Management Research', *British Journal of Management*, 12 (Special Issue): S3–S26.

Starkey, Ken and Tiratsoo, Nick (2007). *The Business School and the Bottom Line*. Cambridge: Cambridge University Press.

Starkey, Ken and Tempest, Sue (2009a). 'From Crisis to Purpose', *Journal of Management Development*, 28: 700–710.

Starkey, Ken and Tempest, Sue (2009b). 'The Winter of Our Discontent: The Design Challenge for Business Schools', *Academy of Management Learning and Education*, 8: 576–586.

Swidler, Steve and Goldreyer, Elizabeth (1998). 'The Value of a Finance Publication', *Journal of Finance*, 53: 351–363.

Teece, David J. (2011), 'Achieving Integration of the Business School Curriculum Using the Dynamic Capabilities Framework'.*Journal of Management Development*, 30: 499–518.

Thomas, Howard (2007). 'Business School Strategy and the Metrics for Success', *Journal of Management Development*, 26: 33–42.

Thomas, Howard (2012). 'What Is the European Management School Model?', *Global Focus*, 6(1): 18–21.

Thomas, Howard and Wilson, Alexander D. (2011). ' "Physics Envy", Cognitive Legitimacy or Practical Relevance: Dilemmas in the Evolution of Management Research in the UK', *British Journal of Management*, 22: 443–456.

Thomas, Howard and Thomas, Lynne (2011). 'Perspectives on Leadership in Business Schools', *Journal of Management Development*, 30: 526–540.

Thomas, Howard and Peters, Kai (2012). 'A Sustainable Model for Business Schools', *Journal of Management Development*, 31: 377–385.

Thomas, Howard and Cornuel, Eric (2012). 'Business Schools in Transition? Issues of Impact, Legitimacy, Capabilities and Re-invention', *Journal of Management Development*, 31: 329–335.

Thomas, Howard, Thomas, Lynne, and Wilson, Alexander D. (2012). 'The Unfulfilled Promise of Management Education?', *Global Focus*, 6 (2), (Special Supplement): 1–19.

Thomas, Howard, Thomas, Lynne, and Wilson, Alexander D. (2013a). 'The Unfulfilled Promise of Management Education: The Role, Value and Purpose of Management Education', *Journal of Management Development*, 32: 460–476.

Thomas, Howard, Thomas, Lynne, and Wilson, Alexander D. (2013b). *Promises Fulfilled and Unfulfilled in Management Education, Vol. 1* (Reflections on the Role, Impact and Future of Management Education: EFMD Perspectives). Bingley: Emerald.

Thomas, Howard, Lorange, Peter, and Sheth, Jagdish (2013c). *The Business School in the Twenty-First Century: Emergent Challenges and New Business Models.* Cambridge, UK: Cambridge University Press.

Tierney, William G. (2004). *Competing Conceptions of Academic Governance: Negotiating the Perfect Storm.* Baltimore, MD: Johns Hopkins University Press.

Tierney, William G. and Hentschke, Guilbert C. (2007). *New Players, Different Game: Understanding the Rise of For-Profit Colleges and Universities.* Baltimore, MD: The Johns Hopkins University Press.

Tranfield, David and Starkey, Ken (1998). 'The Nature, Social Organization and Promotion of Management Research', *British Journal of Management*, 12: 341–353.

Urgel, Julio (2007). 'EQUIS Accreditation: Value and Benefits for International Business Schools', *Journal of Management Development*, 26: 73–83.

Vallens, Ansi (2008). 'The Importance of Reputation', *Risk Management*, 55: 36–43.

Vidaver-Cohen, Deborah (2007). 'Reputation Beyond Rankings: A Conceptual Framework for Business School Research', *Corporate Reputation Review*, 10: 278–304.

Walsh, Taylor (2011). *Unlocking the Gates: How and Why Leading Universities Are Opening Up Access to Their Courses*. Princeton, NJ: Princeton University Press.

Weber, Luc E. and Duderstadt, James J. (eds) (2008). *The Globalization of Higher Education*. London: Economica.

Weber, Luc E. and Duderstadt, James J. (eds) (2010). *University Research for Innovation*. London: Economica.

Wildavsky, Ben, Kelly, Andrew P., and Carey, Kevin (eds) (2011). *Reinventing Higher Education: The Promise of Innovation*. Cambridge, MA: Harvard Education Press.

Willmott, Hugh (1998). 'Commercialising Higher Education in the UK: The State, Industry and Peer Review'. Cambridge, UK: Judge Institute of Management, University of Cambridge.

Wilson, David C. and McKiernan, Peter (2011). 'Global Mimicry: Putting Strategic Choice Back on the Business School Agenda', *British Journal of Management*, 22: 457–469.

Wilson, David C. and Thomas, Howard (2012). 'The Legitimacy of the Business Schools: What's the Future?', *Journal of Management Development*, 31: 368–376.

Worrell, Dan L. (2009). 'Assessing Business Scholarship: The Difficulties in Moving Beyond the Rigor-Relevance Paradigm Trap', *Academy of Management Learning and Education*, 8: 127–130.

Zemsky, Robert, Wegener, Gregory R., and Massy, William F. (2006). *Remaking the American University: Market-Smart and Mission-Centered*. New Brunswick: Rutgers University Press.

Part I

The Change and Development of Business Schools

3

Leading Breakthrough Initiatives in Business Schools

Fernando Fragueiro and Josefina Michelini

3.1. INTRODUCTION

This chapter focuses on the political approach to the process and context of strategic leadership in three top international business schools, IMD, INSEAD, and London Business School. It attempts to contribute to the comprehension of strategic leadership processes (SLP) by focusing on a set of initiatives undertaken by these schools in following their internationalization strategy. The aim is to understand leadership not as the action of an isolated person but as a set of decisions, actions and events of a group of people over a specific period of time and in a particular organizational setting. Thus, this chapter will identify those key people, activities, competences and features that act as *enablers* and those which are *conditionants* for a particular *breakthrough initiative* to be raised to the strategic agenda, become a decision, and then be executed.

The study of leadership is a topic that has attracted the attention of many researchers for most of the twentieth century, and is still an issue of interest to many academics. However, there is no single definition of leadership. It has evolved from an individual leader perspective to a process and relational approach that refers not only to leaders but also to those that follow them (Yukl 2002; Bryman 2002; Northouse 2001; Gibson et al. 2000; Heifetz 1999; Middlehurst 1993; Bass 1990; Birnbaum 1989; Burns 1978; Cribbin 1972).

But the influence of others is not considered as part of the leadership model until the concept of co-leadership (Heenan and Bennis 1999), shared leadership (O'Toole et al. 2002; Pearce and Conger 2003) or distributed leadership (Fitzgerald et al. 2013; Gronn 2011, 2002; Ancona 2007), is introduced. This integrative perspective on leadership refers to leadership enacted by a group of people, a constellation of co-stars (Denis et al. 2001; Heenan and

Bennis 1999). At this stage, leadership is no longer a process that involves just downward influence on subordinates by a superior, but is distributed among a set of individuals (Pearce and Conger 2003). Even though it suggests an even more expanded role for followers in the leadership process (Pearce and Conger, 2003), and thus, a broader perspective, it remains within a sociological approach to the leadership phenomenon.

Thus far, there is little theory concerning organizational variables such as size, organizational environment and type of strategy that require different behaviours from leaders. Leadership studies seem to be context free (Hunt and Dodge 2001; House and Aditya 1997). Moreover, it can be argued that scholars have mostly approached the field in terms of leadership *in* organizations rather than leadership *of* organizations (Bryman 2002, 1992; Hunt 1991). They have focused mainly on the characteristics of leaders, what they do and how they do it, without addressing the role of the organizational context in which leadership is enacted (House and Aditja 1997).

In connecting leadership with organizations, the approach to the study of leadership, focusing on strategic leadership, represents a further step. However, even though this implies moving forward in relating leadership to its organizational setting, most of the studies on strategic leadership centre predominantly on the content (what leaders do) or on the types of policies and strategies that lead to effective organizational performance (House and Aditya 1997). 'Relatively little attention has been paid to the processes by which strategic leaders affect organizations' (House and Aditya 1997: 447). As a result, while leadership is seen as the process through which leaders influence the attitudes, behaviours and values of others, strategic leadership is considered as the leader's ability to anticipate, to envision, to maintain flexibility, and to empower others to create strategic change as necessary (Hagen et al. 1998).

This study focuses on strategic leadership in organizational settings. It intends to shed light on the set of decisions, actions and events produced by key people in building and executing the strategic agenda in order to achieve the organizational mission, over time. These decisions and actions result from different constraints on contextual factors provided by the setting in which strategic leadership is enacted.

A processual perspective on strategic leadership focuses on its own dynamics, interrelations and interconnections between people, history, culture, time and other contextual factors that influence the strategic leadership phenomenon, over time (Pettigrew 1997). It is designed to account for and explain not only the 'what' but also the 'why' and the 'how' of the links between contexts, processes, and outcomes (Pettigrew 1997). Moreover, a political perspective on the study of the strategic leadership process in organizations—business schools in this case—facilitates the observation of how people use and mobilize power to influence decisions. Such a perspective enables the observation of different interests and demands that arise and compete for organizational attention and resources (Ammeter et al. 2002).

Two characteristics make business schools a particularly attractive scenario for this purpose. Firstly, given the distinctive idiosyncrasy ('loosely-coupled' according to Weick 1976) of the setting, where power tends to be shared and diffused (Cohen and March 1974; Denis et al. 2001, 1996) between the Dean and the Faculty (besides other key constituencies), and where collegiality and a consensus basis characterize academic institutions (Ramsden 1998; Chaffee 1983; Hardy 1991), a political approach enables the observation of strategic leadership as a social influence process with a contextual approach.

Secondly, more than ever, business relies on higher education to prepare students for this rapidly changing environment, expecting it to help develop their critical thinking and analytical abilities (Pfeffer and Fong 2004). As higher education institutions, business schools have a key role in the economic and social context (Crainer and Dearlove 1999), based on their ability to influence the different sectors of the economy, spreading ideas through academic research, developing important relevant knowledge, and serving as a source of critical thought and inquiry about organizations and management (Pfeffer and Fong 2004).

In the last decades, they have become a new kind of space, an 'agora' (Nowotny et al., 2001: 203) in action where different stakeholders and different disciplines interact and learn from each other (Starkey et al. 2004). Thus, they will have new strategic choices to make, relating to how they would prefer to serve the new, networked society (Lorange 2005). A SLP will guide them effectively through the twenty-first century (Van Baalen and Moratis 2001; Hitt 1998) enabling them to respond to demands for business relevance and academic rigour within an ever more globalized environment (Prince 1999; Hitt 1998).

The critical importance of strategic leadership in business schools has been highlighted by some authors (Fragueiro and Thomas 2011; Thomas and Thomas 2011; Trieschmann et al. 2000; Morris 2000; Segev et al. 1999; Twomey and Twomey 1998; Gore et al. 1998; Beeby and Jones 1997). However, only few of them (e.g. Fragueiro and Thomas 2011) reveal how the SLP is operationalized and carried out. An understanding of the way the SLP operates in these institutions makes it possible to understand how they are facing up to the current demands of the business industry, and making strategic choices to enable them to make a response.

Thus, this study remedies three inadequacies in the current literature. These are: first, the scarcity of *empirical studies* on strategic leadership from a processual perspective; second, the lack of links between the leadership and strategy fields; third, scholars' call for studies on leadership processes in organizational settings and from a political perspective.

Therefore, in order to give answers to those demands from the academic world on management, this study will focus on three central topics:

1. Who the key actors are in the strategic leadership process, and how do they interplay in influencing the process of shaping and executing the strategic agenda, while mobilizing their own and others' interests?

2. What are the main features of the inner and outer contexts that influence the School's strategic agenda building and executing, over time; and what influence do they have?

3. How do key actors legitimate their initiatives, and mobilize (build and use) power in order to influence strategic agenda building and execution over time, according to their prioritization of their interests?

In order to give answers to these three questions and understand how the strategic leadership process happens, the study focuses on strategic initiatives representing a *breakthrough step forward*, and not just an incremental one. These are initiatives undertaken by each school in trying to reach their internationalization strategy. A multiple paradigm perspective employing triangulation across theories and paradigms enables us to have greater confidence in the reliability of our findings (Bryman 2002). The methodology selected is primarily qualitative, since it tends to describe the unfolding of social processes (Van Maanen 1979). This approach covers an array of interpretive techniques which seek to describe, decode, translate, and come to terms with the meaning of certain more or less naturally occurring phenomena in the social world (Van Maanen 1979). A combination of a longitudinal approach and comparative case studies (Pettigrew 1990; Yin 1984) were employed to depict the course of events in the schools' external and internal contexts. This enabled us to establish patterns and to examine temporal interconnectedness, looking at past, present and future developments. Longitudinal design permits the study of long-term processes in context. Insights into the time order of variables eventually facilitate causal inferences (Bryman 2002). As a result, causation and connectivity can be determined and patterns identified and explained (Pettigrew 1990).

The chapter is presented in three stages: first, the narrative section describes the three case studies. The focus is on the unfolding of decisions and actions undertaken by the schools' key actors in building and executing the strategic agenda during the 1990–2004 period to enhance and consolidate their international positioning. Next, the conceptual section explores the unfolding of events, establishing analytical themes in order to provide answers to the research questions. Finally, the conclusions are presented and a further research agenda is suggested.

3.2. THREE CASE STUDIES: IMD, INSEAD, AND LONDON BUSINESS SCHOOL

3.2.1. IMD: From an Uncertain Merger to the Global Meeting Place

The Institute for Management Development (IMD) was founded in 1990 in Lausanne through the merger of two Swiss business schools (IMI in Geneva and IMEDE in Lausanne). Its parent Foundation Board consists of 50 executives elected from leading client firms from different countries across the world.

In its short history, IMD has become a major player in the international management education market, building a strong reputation for its widely international executive education and full-time MBA. Given the difficulties that the school had to overcome through the merger process, the fact that IMD is the result of the merger of two educational institutions with different cultures (IMI, with its focus on the geopolitical and macro environment and IMEDE, case-teaching-oriented and committed to the provision of management skills to worldwide executives) has enriched IMD's background story, making the study of strategic leadership as a social influence process at IMD, particularly attractive.

3.2.2. Making the IMI and IMEDE Merger Successful (1990–1992)

Several unsuccessful attempts were made to merge IMI and IMEDE after 1957. However, it was not until December 1988 that members of both the IMI and IMEDE Foundation Boards decided that it would be beneficial to create a big international business school large enough to be not only financially and academically sustainable, but also relevant at a world class level—a top international business school. The decision was made to base the resulting school in Lausanne, where IMEDE's campus was located. To compensate IMI for this location choice, Juan Rada, its director general, was to become the new IMD Dean.

In the following years, IMD's strategy focused on responding to client demands and achieving excellence by strengthening its partnership with industry and adding organizational learning to management development. The school's Board and Dean worked together to set up its governance structure, policies, rules and strategies. However, the fact that Faculty members had not been involved in the merger decision brought great discontent to the school, and the impact of the former schools' long-standing rivalry was somewhat underestimated. 'There were two radically different cultures... IMI had been founded by Alcan, a business that focuses on long-term returns on investment and, therefore, is interested in geopolitics and social stability... IMEDE was founded by Nestlé, which is a business of short-term cash flow, with an interest in management functions—and marketing in particular', Juan Rada declared.

Although IMD's financial performance was excellent in its first year, results in 1991 were not as good as budgeted. Thus, strong measures were taken to avoid a loss, and a modest surplus was thought to be possible. Annoyance and discontent kept growing. The continuous debate, and the lack of clear direction, triggered the Faculty's decision to create a Committee called the 'Faculty College', a 'think tank', which, while not being a decision-making instrument, could influence in a positive manner the orientations and decisions. Excluded from its inception process, IMD's Dean was 'invited' to join the committee's monthly meetings but not to chair them.

The differences between the priorities of the Board, which focused primarily on the school's operating budget, and the Dean's agenda, which prioritized IMD's strategies, triggered additional confusion and dissent. Rada's decisions were usually thwarted by the chairman of the Board's actions, and, despite the Dean's persistent efforts to achieve consensus, decision-making and execution processes became slow and difficult. Moreover, the school's financial performance in 1991 confirmed that its increasing costs were not matched by rising profits. Rada's troublesome relationship with the Board compromised his authority, while unwavering Faculty discontent only compounded his challenges. He decided to resign, and outlined several suggestions for changes to IMD's governance structure. Xavier Gilbert, an IMD Faculty member, was asked to step in as interim director general until the search committee could appoint a new Dean. He led the school through a transition period (1992–1993) with the specific aim of restoring its financial situation in the short term.

By 1992, IMD's situation was difficult. There were different perspectives regarding the future direction of the school. Its deteriorating finances called for an urgent turnaround, and its faculty was divided as to what the school ought to be and do. There were the 'farmers', i.e. those professors that had insisted on being around, doing the work, not competing with the school; and the 'hunters', i.e. those professors who were outside working with companies, teaching and organizing their own programmes. This difference hindered the building of the new school's identity.

3.2.3. IMD's Consolidation and Success (1993–2004)

The Search Committee appointed Peter Lorange as IMD President. He had extensive academic and managerial experience. Things were not as good as he had expected them to be at IMD. There was still uncertainty about the future. IMD had had its image damaged in the business and management education environment. Those were times of much anxiety and anguish. In addition, there was a financial problem. Revenues were not coming in as planned, and the costs were too high.

The Faculty was restless and wanted to get the merger process right. However, some of them were still eager for a more collegial participation in managing the School. Due to his past experience, and on Juan Rada's advice, Lorange was guaranteed the Board's support: he had total responsibility for IMD's management. He immediately stressed his agenda: first, to achieve IMD's financial sustainability; second, to set a clear vision; third, to forge a mutually beneficial partnership with business; and fourth, develop a special focus on 'Faculty' and 'administration'. In turn, to muster the Faculty's support, Lorange wrote a personal letter to every professor, and, based on their feedback, he identified three key priorities: to strengthen the Faculty; to clarify the portfolio of programmes; to reinforce marketing.

As IMD president, Lorange's formal authority was robustly established, but he realized that having the Faculty on his side was crucial. He said to everybody that he would do his best in terms of making decisions that were for the benefit of the School. Lorange was also determined to bring different perspectives and experience to the table, so he drew on key Faculty members originally from IMI and IMEDE to create IMD's Coordinating Committee. He worked hard at promoting certain core values and behaviours, based on IMD's ethical standards as well as institutional ownership, teamwork, transparency, responsiveness, world-class teaching and programme delivery, and meritocracy. He established a non-departmental academic structure, with neither tenure nor titles, in order to avoid Faculty hierarchies. He adapted the workload system in order to develop more transparency among IMD's professors. Compensation systems were adapted so as to stimulate a partnership between IMD and its faculty. A 'buy-back' arrangement was designed for the school, to buy professors' time beyond a threshold of programme delivery workload.

The careful alignment of IMD's culture, its structures and systems to its strategic direction, and the Dean's leadership style made the school's success possible. IMD's recognition as a leading business school has been reflected in international management education rankings. Since Lorange's presidency, a consistent pattern of excellence has raised the school's profile and strengthened its brand. As a result, the school's revenue and profit growth have been impressive.

3.2.4. INSEAD: From Top European Teaching School to Top Research-based School Worldwide

INSEAD is a major player in the international management education industry: one of the world's largest top-tier graduate business schools, with two comprehensive and fully-connected campuses in Europe (France) and Asia (Singapore). Founded as a privately funded independent institution by Georges Doriot in Fontainebleau, France, in 1957, INSEAD was meant to be a global business school based in Europe for executives around the world. Thus, internationalization lay at its core from its inception.

INSEAD stands out among top-tier business schools on three counts. First, it is widely recognized as the world's most global business school (the Asia campus was created in Singapore in October 2000, to better serve INSEAD's regional and global partners). Second, it is the only top business school offering an intensive one-year MBA in international business administration. Finally, its multicultural diversity ensures that no single nationality, style or dogma prevails, either within its faculty or among students.

To explore the SLP at INSEAD fully during 1990–2004, it has been divided into three periods: first, the co-Deanship of Claude Rameau and Ludo Van der Heyden (1990–1993), followed by the co-Deanship of Ludo Van der Heyden and Antonio Borges (1993–1995); second, Dean Antonio Borges (1995–1999); third, Gabriel Hawawini's Deanship (1999–2004). For the purposes of this chapter, the focus will only be on those breakthrough initiatives that enabled the school to become a top international player: deepening the school's research strategy and profile; launching a second campus in Singapore, and the intent to launch a third campus in the US.

3.2.5. Deepening the School's Research Strategy and Profile (1990–1995)

During the 1980s, the school began to shift from being a successful educational institution to a more powerful academic research-oriented organization. It was during this decade that the idea of not only insisting on very good teachers and credibility with companies, but also on the ability to generate research and to compete on the research front with the American schools, became a priority.

By the end of the decade, Claude Rameau and Philippe Naert were INSEAD's co-Deans (1986–1990). Rameau was an entrepreneurial businessman who had been part of the school's foundation. He understood the particular phase INSEAD was undergoing: unless its Faculty got serious about research, it would find itself obsolete. Consequently, transforming INSEAD so that it would be recognized as one of the world's top five business schools implied having critical mass: in terms of faculty size, research, and volume of service proposed.

Naert was an academic who believed INSEAD's lingering weaknesses were the inadequacy of research per capita and its weak image in the 'academic community'. Accordingly, he proposed to increase the size of the permanent Faculty body by about 50 percent and to create a doctoral programme. Thus, INSEAD launched the Ph.D. programme to become better as an academic institution.

In 1990, Ludo Van der Heyden, former head of R&D, took over from Philippe Naert as the new co-Dean, alongside Claude Rameau. The co-Deans had to handle INSEAD's three dimensions: academic; managerial and business; and multi-cultural. However, Van der Heyden's appointment was followed by several new internal and external challenges for INSEAD. Internally, the arrival of new, more research-oriented professors led to the development of two distinct groups within the school's Faculty. Externally, a worldwide recession caused by the Gulf War prompted the cancellation of customized programmes as well as a significant drop in applications and admissions for both INSEAD's executive and MBA programmes.

Consequently, revenues plummeted, and the school posted its first losses in over a decade. The situation worsened over the following years. The drop in market demand was accentuated by heightened competition in the management education sector, forcing the market to become tighter. Such a critical scenario affected INSEAD's research budgets and teaching loads.

In addition, Faculty compensation fell once again, and hindered INSEAD from being a particularly attractive proposition for 'top-flight' academics. This situation provided a forceful reminder of the school's lingering financial vulnerability. INSEAD had gone through a period of strong growth and its on-going development called for the raising of funds. Rameau remembers, 'We agreed... that a fast growth of Faculty would be impossible without new type of financing... I convinced the Board that a capital campaign was the only possibility for really having a push for Faculty recruitment'. In March 1992, the Board agreed to launch a feasibility study which, one year, later delivered favourable initial findings. Supporters of the school, interviewed by the consultants, confirmed that they would back a very ambitious campaign provided that INSEAD could present a clear and convincing development project.

In September 1993, the *Wall Street Journal* rankings rated INSEAD's Advanced Management Programme first in its survey of executive education worldwide. In addition, research centres were developed, and their outputs were immediately transferred to the classrooms. Rameau's tenure had come to an end and Antonio Borges, former Associate Dean of the MBA, was appointed co-Dean in his place, alongside Van der Heyden. Even though the two men respected each other and agreed on where the school should be heading, their styles were not complementary. Borges had spent three years away from academia, as deputy governor of the Bank of Portugal. He was forceful and determined, while Van der Heyden who had always been an academic, was more questioning and consensual, and always positioned himself as a 'primus inter pares'.

Borges was able to use INSEAD's financial distress to press for some urgent changes, including staff salary freezes and a headcount reduction, a slowdown on investments, tightened cost control and a block on recruitment. He was expected to do the external work and Van der Heyden, the internal. However, it appeared that the combination of business and academic skills that had been displayed by the former co-Deanship was no longer at work with the current co-Deans. When Van der Heyden's co-Deanship term came to an end, he made it very clear that he would not be re-elected for a second time, whereas at the same time, Borges stated, 'If you want me to continue I want to be single Dean'. It was at this point that some Faculty members agreed it was time to go to a more traditional structure with one person in charge.

3.2.6. Launching a Second Campus in Singapore (1995–2000)

As soon as he became INSEAD's single Dean, Antonio Borges was clear about his strategic vision and priorities: first, to reinforce INSEAD's economic sustainability so that the school's financial situation would be restored; second, to launch the development campaign so that funds could be raised for academic purposes and high research standards would be achieved; and, finally, to succeed in differentiating INSEAD in the international management education market and enable it to excel. Since he was familiar with the inner workings of the school, he clearly understood how it worked and which levers to pull: setting such a strong academic course at INSEAD required the full support of both the Board and the Faculty.

Changing the orientation of the school was a difficult task. So, he appointed a strong team capable of implementing the policies that he had in mind: the Dean of Faculty (Hubert Gatignon) and the Dean of External Development (Gabriel Hawawini). He started out by addressing the academic level of activity. He focused on recruiting, fostering Faculty growth at a steady rate of 13 percent per year during his tenure. To help attract and retain a research-oriented Faculty, a number of systems and incentives were introduced or changed. The Ph.D. programme had grown strongly and the school devoted a lot of resources to it. But there was a part of the Faculty which did not agree with the school's new strategic direction and with the new systems and processes that were being aligned with it.

Given the complexity of the economic situation during the years 1992 and 1993, Borges decided to deepen INSEAD's research orientation. However, in order to carry out the necessary changes in the systems of faculty compensation and promotion, it seemed crucial to launch a development campaign to raise funds for academic purposes. Thus, INSEAD's first development campaign (1993–2000) achieved €120 million in corporate and private sponsorship. The success of such an ambitious campaign substantiated the school's credibility with the business community, generating not only funds and visibility, but also commitment.

Borges understood that not only high-level teachers and outstanding credibility with companies was required but also the ability to generate research and to compete on the research front with the American Schools. He felt that INSEAD needed to clearly differentiate itself from other top business schools in the world. Thus, during a Faculty meeting, he introduced the idea of opening a second facility so that INSEAD would follow market demands by having a real presence in Asia. Some Faculty members recall that it was Borges who led the issue and that he had Janssen's support. They convinced the Board. There were some key Board members who felt that Asia was the future, and thus, INSEAD should try it. But there was also a lot of resistance that had to be overcome. By 1997, a feasibility study explored the possibility of expanding into Asia. By the end of Borges' mandate, the decision had been taken. It would be Gabriel Hawawini's mission, as new Dean of INSEAD, to deliver it.

3.2.7. Launching a Third Campus in the US (2000–2004)

Gabriel Hawawini was an insider who had belonged to INSEAD, delivering expected results for over two decades. After he had been elected by a majority of Faculty members (it seems relevant to note that he received 90 votes out of 96), the Board appointed him Dean of INSEAD.

Borges' bold agenda of shaping the school's profile to a more research-oriented institution and opening a second campus in Singapore stretched the organization, producing both support and opposition. Thus, the choice of Hawawini as the new Dean can be interpreted as a desire on the part of Faculty to look for a more consensus-oriented and participative leadership style. The Dean's main thrust was to ensure the success of the Singapore campus so he mobilized the entire organization around this mission.

Once the Asian campus was working, the idea arose of launching a third campus in the U.S. The Dean made this initiative his priority, underestimating the Faculty's disagreement due to the difficulties of making the Singapore campus work. He counted on Janssen's support but Janssen was soon replaced by a new Chairman, Cees Van Lede, who was Dutch, an INSEAD alumnus, international, and not ready to face such big decisions. Moreover, the

Committee of Deans was not convinced either and, therefore, they could not present the project to the Faculty.

Then, there was the election to renew the Dean's mandate. Even though the Faculty was not convinced yet, he said he would only stay for another mandate 'if the vote in my favour starts with a 7'. This would force the board's support. But instead of being an election for the Dean, it became an election about whether INSEAD was to go to the United States or not. The vote took place and even though the majority was in favour, the amount of votes was not enough.

3.2.8. LBS: From a Leading UK Business School to Top Ten, Worldwide

London Business School was founded in 1964 as the London Institute of Business Management and as a graduate college of the University of London. Since its foundation and during much of its first decades, LBS focused on the education of British managers. However, towards the end of the 1980s, a broader and more international perspective was gradually developed. In this regard, the School's demography showed steady increases not only in the number of non-UK students but also in its Faculty.

Moreover, since 1990, LBS has gone through an internationalization process with a particular focus on the student and Faculty bodies, to raise the quality of its research to international standards, and to deliver programmes capable of attracting students from around the world. Its high academic research standards have enabled the school to be considered among the top global business schools.

This study addresses the main events for the LBS over the period 1990–2004, which illuminate the strategic leadership processes involved. The study has been divided into three periods: first, making LBS a top league international School (1990–1997); second, deepening the strategy of internationalization, Faculty transformation, and enhancing LBS's visibility and revenues (1998–2002); third, enhancing LBS visibility and fundraising activities (2002–2004). However, as has already been said, for the purpose of this chapter, the focus will only be on those breakthrough initiatives that enabled the school to become a top international player, making LBS a top-league international school.

3.2.9. Making LBS a Top-League International School (1990–1997)

In the mid-1980s, the world showed signs of major economic, technologic, and geopolitical changes. Particularly within Europe, barriers fell and new markets emerged. Within the UK, in particular, the Tory government under

Margaret Thatcher took the lead in deregulation, privatization, and the need to reduce state expenses. From this sprang the idea that business schools could stand on their own two feet and, thus, funding for British students was gradually removed.

At that point, before the funding was removed, LBS had to take a certain number of British students in order to receive government grants. These circumstances drove LBS to take overseas students, who were charged higher fees. Concurrently, the internationalization of business appeared as a robust trend worldwide. This was during Peter Moore's (1984–1989) Deanship at LBS. The school was facing the withdrawal of government support, which would eventually leave it in pretty bad financial shape. People remember there was increasing discontent and anxiety.

On the other hand, in 1988, Fortune Magazine published an article about the top business schools in Europe, considering London Business School second only to INSEAD, the number one within Europe. This acted as a catalyst for the emergent crisis the school was facing. George Bain declares, 'The school had assumed from its inception that it was the best business school in Europe and not short of arrogance in academic institutions, of course. And they had worked on this assumption since they were founded'. This came as a huge shock for the LBS community.

As a result, the Faculty rose up and rebelled against the renewal of the tenure of the current Dean. Thus, the Governing Body understood that there was a need to look for a new vision, fresh ideas. It decided to look for a new Dean from outside the school. The Governing Body looked for a distinguished and successful individual with an entrepreneurial outlook to manage and market the school; someone with a background either in business or management education, who combined academic qualifications with leadership and general management ability. The Dean's objective would be to ensure that the school was transformed in order to be recognized worldwide as one of the most respected centres of management education and research.

In November 1988, George Bain, at that time Dean of Warwick Business School, was invited to be Principal of the London Business School. He would take up his duties in August 1989. This 'actually turned out to be a huge advantage', Bain asserts, since he used that period 'to start seeing a few people... all of the Faculty'. He also spent time visiting around a dozen American business schools and tried to become as well informed as he could about what was going on in the management education industry.

Thus, by the time he took over, Bain already knew what had to be done. He understood there was a need to put LBS on the international map, mostly because the school was already the top business school in the UK. Bain presented his agenda for change in a document called 'Bias Towards a Strategy': a set of guiding principles which compiled and articulated what LBS people alleged needed to be done, in a coherent, unified, and focused way.

The Faculty reacted in a positive manner to Bain's document. People agree they felt released. They had been drifting aimlessly over the previous years, but now they knew what the school's direction would be. Bain recognized that even though he could count on the school's Governing Body, he would need the Faculty's support. Thus, the time he had spent listening to people, before taking over as Dean, enabled him to identify those key Faculty members who supported him and build a team around him: the Management Board Steering Group (MBSG). People agree that this group of four or five people really ran the school on a day-to-day basis. These people enabled the implementation of the new LBS direction.

For LBS to become a top-tier business school within the international market, competing with top business schools, the issue that emerged as a big challenge was internationalization, not only in terms of Faculty, but also of students and the content of programmes and research. This entailed an increase in the size of LBS facilities. But every initiative demanded a sound economic and financial situation.

The most critical tasks were related to the transformation of the academic model in terms of developing a world-class faculty with U.S. research standards and teaching disciplinary balance in order to enhance executive education. Thus, systems and policies were shaped. Faculty compensations became a priority. In this regard, the school moved towards paying salaries that were competitive with U.S. salaries. This would facilitate faculty recruitment. However, transforming systems generated substantial opposition since they were oriented towards performance-related pay and set constraints on consulting.

Given that international salaries and performance were the bases, Bain called attention to the need for a more vocational institution with a balanced excellence so that executive education would be developed. But some Faculty members disagreed, since they believed executive education should be kept in its proper place as a minority activity, not as a central activity. Within the opposition there was the Finance group. Again, Bain explains he dealt with opposition, first, by building coalitions and making sure that what was proposed would have a basis of support. Second, since he truly believes in managing by walking around, he used to walk the halls of the school. Finally, he also focused on building sources of power such as success, setting direction, setting guidelines and communicating them, expertise and listening to people. These permitted him to obtain enough support to deal with the opposition.

In developing faculty, students, and programmes, LBS would also have to tackle the issue of space—becoming a top school in research, and in degree and executive degree education would require more infrastructure. Thus, he developed fundraising in a systematic way, setting up a development office and hiring a development director. LBS managed to raise around 2.5 million pounds for the building of a new library.

In sum, Bain turned LBS into an international player with global contacts, by cultivating the academic and by having a vision. He managed to restore the school's economic health, even though its business model was not transformed.

3.3. LEADING BREAKTHROUGH INITIATIVES FOR INTERNATIONALIZATION AT IMD, INSEAD, AND LBS

Thus far, the chapter has revolved around the main events related to SLPs at IMD, INSEAD, and LBS, in leading their internationalization strategy, during the period 1990-2004. The study has identified three key actors as the main stakeholders (the Board, the Dean, and the Faculty) who interplayed in influencing the process of shaping and executing the strategic agenda for internationalization of each school by putting forward their own interests through a combination of negotiation, skills, and power. Establishing priorities and allocating limited resources accordingly depended, first, on their capacity to build and use power, but also on their capacity to legitimate those initiatives by generating consensus among key people.

To better understand the set of different interests representing key stakeholders, we identified three types of interests related to the role of each key actor within the organizational context of business schools: the main generic interests (MGI). No matter who the key actor is, or under what contextual circumstances he or she acts, these generic interests are applicable to an entire class or group that is differentiated from other groups.

The political analysis of SLPs in a specific organizational setting, such as business schools, facilitates the observation of those social influence processes that unfold among constituents in organizations. It entails the identification of interests and demands that arise and compete for organizational attention and resources (Ammeter et al. 2002) and a single agenda to determine how demands are generated and presented, as well as how power is mobilized to overcome conflict by engaging support for different demands, and produce desired outcomes (Fragueiro, 2007).

The Dean's MGI are: first, setting the school's strategic direction and implementing it (strategic agenda building and execution); second, receiving both Faculty and Board support and collaboration over his or her own initiatives and decisions; third, using the school's performance to validate his or her credibility. As for the Board's MGI, it is: first, the sound governance of the school; second, the school's performance and sustainability; third: the school's reputation. For the Faculty, it is: first, the search for transparent and fair workload and compensation systems. Second, a main driver for professional activity, they seek the school's support regarding their academic career success. Third, like any professional service firm characterized by involvement of the peers in key strategic decisions, the Faculty seeks to influence the school's long-term direction.

Thus, each key actor builds and mobilizes power according to the MGI that prevails over time. Content and prioritization of interests vary according to the influence of contextual features. So far as the inner context is concerned, they are environmental conditions like the school's culture, climate, structure, systems, and performance. The outer context involves the school's location, corporate customer demands, donors and benefactors, governance, alumni, accreditation agencies, economic environment, media rankings, and competition. There are also the stakeholder's personal characteristics (i.e. background, leadership style, skills, and values).

This political analysis of the SLP in business schools, over time, involves four key activities: environmental scanning; issue diagnosis; issue legitimization; and power mobilization (see Figure 3.1). These enablers consist of a set strategic initiatives displayed by the school's key actors in raising a strategic issue in the school's agenda, legitimating it, and mobilizing power to get it decided and executed.

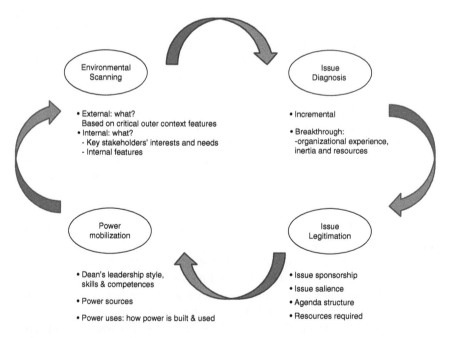

Figure 3.1. A comprehensive and dynamic approach to SLPs
Source: Fragueiro and Thomas (2011)

Figure 3.1 provides a comprehensive and dynamic approach to strategic leadership as a process in context from a political perspective. Environmental scanning enables the observation and understanding of both internal and external scenarios, to identify the key actors and features and how they evolve over time. Issue diagnosis follows direction setting through the generation of strategic initiatives. It facilitates the identification of those initiatives that represent a step forward (incremental) or a radical change (breakthrough) in the school's direction. When these processes are viewed as including a political perspective, with its two intrinsic actions—issue legitimization and power mobilization—firmly supported by leaders' reputations, commitment and integrity, it is possible to use power and influence adequately (Fragueiro and Thomas, 2011). SLPs should encompass both a contextual and a political perspective in order to build a seamless continuum that reinforces leaders' effectiveness and drives organizational advancement.

3.3.1. The Use of Power and its Legitimization

Thus far, the study has identified three key actors (Dean, Board, and Faculty) who exert influence through power mobilization in order to prioritize some issues and to incorporate them in their organizations' strategic agenda. But how do they influence?

Power mobilization and issue legitimization are both crucial parts of the SLP. When focusing on breakthrough initiatives, facts show that they require committed, consistent issue legitimization efforts to sell, articulate and communicate them in a transparent attractive and eloquent way, not only to minimize resistance or opposition but also to motivate all stakeholders by appealing to their aspirations, values and beliefs. These initiatives also call for sponsors to fully exploit the entire range of their power sources—both structural and personal—and power uses so as to ensure successful execution. Figure 3.2 shows how SLPs work from a political perspective.

Figure 3.2 shows power mobilization efforts are characterized by sponsors' leadership styles, deans' skill and competence sets, personal power sources and their utilization of power. Following Fragueiro (2007), the use of power may involve coalition building, information leverage, resource allocation, compensations, ingratiation, goodwill creation, etc. The other mechanism used to garner support for strategic initiatives is issue legitimization, which encompasses leaders' endeavours to sponsor and sell their priority issues to as many people in their organizations as possible by articulating and communicating the value of their initiatives to the successful pursuit of an organization's mission, vision and strategic goals. Issue legitimization also involves three contextual factors: alignment with key actors' MGI prioritization;

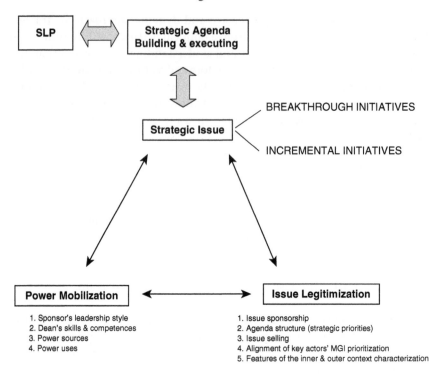

Figure 3.2. A political approach to strategic leadership
Source: Fragueiro (2007)

proper consideration of organizations' salient inner and outer context features; and their size and structure.

Thus, any strategic pursuit varies according the particular interests of each actor and needs to be legitimated by key constituencies, while power is used to overcome resistance and to procure critical resources. These interests prevail over time and their content and their prioritization vary over time according to the key actors' characteristics (their preferences, style and background) and the influence of contextual features from both outer (competition and rankings, corporate customers' demands, economic environment, and donors and benefactors) and inner contexts (performance, culture, climate, systems, and structure). Thus, issue legitimization complements power mobilization throughout SLPs. Legitimization occurs when key constituents to be affected by new initiatives 'buy' them, or at least recognize their value for the organization and for themselves.

Next, the study displays patterns that are found in successful breakthrough initiatives related to issue legitimization:

- Issue sponsorship: Dean as main issue sponsor, who intends to broaden the sponsorship through coalition building.

At IMD, immediately after joining the school as President, Lorange requested input in writing from all members to collect their impressions and overriding concerns. At INSEAD, the Dean expanded and strengthened issue sponsorship through informal communication with key members of Faculty and Board.

- Issue-selling: proactive and intense activity with Faculty, Chairman and members of the Board and key staff, to articulate and communicate the school's vision for these initiatives.

For example, Dean Borges carried out a strong issue-selling process to make both the Board and the Faculty understand and share these initiatives, underlining their relevance in delivering INSEAD's international strategy and success in order to be a top worldwide business school.

- Alignment: Dean's proactive environmental scanning, in considering demands and requirements from the outer context and other key actors in terms of MGI prioritization.

At IMD, Lorange carried out an intensive activity to align key actors' MGI priorities. He focused on identifying those signals that entailed any misalignments such as Faculty compensation systems, which he then shaped. From the very beginning, he argued for the importance of integrating the needs of both the institution and the key actors into the school's vision. Accordingly, he promoted such integration of interests and goals through his consistent behaviour in bringing customers' perspectives to the school. Later, he also redesigned policies, academic systems and structures, and maintained intensive communication with both Faculty and Board.

At INSEAD, the Dean displayed a clear activity of communication in articulating the initiatives he promoted, aligned to the school's strategic initiative, which started under Philippe Naert's Deanship with the creation of the Ph.D. programme, and hiring new Faculty with research competences. He leveraged INSEAD's entrepreneurial and international culture, centring on the school's experience and reputation as a main executive education provider in Asia. Such initiatives were introduced as sequential steps towards the evolution of the School in line with its strategic agenda.

- Agenda structure: the agenda is shaped and modified by breakthrough initiatives that take forward the strategic issue. This requires the above-mentioned strong issue sponsorship, issue selling, and alignment of priorities.

- Corporate customers' demands, competition, and donors and benefactors were critical features in triggering the legitimization of the breakthrough initiatives.

Over recent decades, the more intensive competition and fragmented market in the business school industry raised the importance of the critical role of matching corporate customers' demands and needs. IMD through its main strategy represents a unique example. On the other hand, INSEAD and LBS, while having excellent reputations in this regard, are constantly searching for ways to improve their already excellent standards, and show some degree of concern about IMD's unprecedented success in this matter.

Donors and benefactors denote the external contribution to schools' development, but also recognition from the market and society of the value of the schools' initiatives. A clear example of this could be seen at INSEAD and its capital campaign. People at INSEAD considered the campaign was not only about resources and about capital. In many ways, it was also the ultimate market test for INSEAD. Nobody would support something they didn't believe in.

Rankings represent a relevant message for schools' key actors to introduce breakthrough initiatives to the agenda, when it is needed. A clear example is the legitimization within LBS's recognition of the need to change due to the evidence from Fortune magazine of INSEAD's advantage within the European market. Another example was LBS's and INSEAD's enormous and persistent efforts in shaping their Faculty and profile in order to compete with the top league U.S. schools regarding their research skills and capabilities.

- The pattern of performance in the inner context responds in a similar way to two different phenomena: i) a weak performance triggers the need for change (e.g. Peter Lorange at IMD 1993, George Bain at LBS in 1990); ii) a strong performance supports the risks triggered by new breakthrough initiatives (e.g. Antonio Borges' first and second spells at INSEAD).

In order for the Dean to gain support and exert power, performance and the capacity to deliver results probably represent the most fundamental feature in achieving credibility. This was clearly seen at IMD, with its difficulties during the merger period, where weak performance resulted in the Dean's departure. As for IMD's consolidation and success, focus was mainly exerted not only on superior performance both in terms of economics and financial situation, but also in terms of school's reputation in the international market place.

As for INSEAD, Borges' determination to go forward in shifting the school's profile towards research more oriented to US standards, and, later on, to open a second campus in Singapore, was supported by his ability to strengthen the financial and economic model of INSEAD through a successful capital campaign. Finally, at LBS, Bain's ability to reinforce the School's finances became crucial.

By contrast, weak performance represented an opportunity to introduce dramatic changes. That was the case for IMD's creation, as a result of the IMI and IMEDE merger, and, to some extent, the situation that enabled Bain to introduce breakthrough initiatives in a conservative culture at LBS.

Patterns found in unsuccessful breakthrough initiatives related to issue legitimization

- Little being done towards broadening the sponsorship base.

At INSEAD, in trying to fulfil the initiative of launching a US campus, Hawawini's sponsor was Janssen, the Chairman of the Board, soon replaced by Ces Van Lede.

- Infrequent/weak issue selling.

In the case of INSEAD, there is a misalignment gap between the Dean's priorities and those of the Faculty and Board. Hawawini's sense of urgency, of going forward on the multi-campus or network model business school strategy was not shared by the other key actors. The Faculty, who eventually supported his continuity as Dean, did not agree with such a decision. Rather, they focused on other priorities: consolidation of the Singapore campus and the impact of this campus on the work systems and academic careers. As for the Board, Janssen was replaced by Van Lede, a former INSEAD alumnus with a conservative profile, oriented towards the school's performance, sustainability and reputation and who did not support the Dean's 'risky' initiative.

- Misalignment of key actors' MGI prioritization.

Both the Dean and the Board had a different prioritization for making the merger successful at IMD. While Rada was oriented towards strategic agenda building and executing with impact on the long term, the Board prioritized performance as a short-term demand. To some extent, such misalignment contributed to the Dean's departure.

- Agenda structure: difficulty in competing with other initiatives prioritized by other key actors.

- Outer context features legitimating: corporate customers' demands, donors and benefactors, competition, and economic environment.
- Inner context features de-legitimating: climate, structure, and systems.

Patterns found in successful breakthrough initiatives related to power mobilization were:

- Directive leadership style.
- Skills and competences that enable the deans to understand the context—inner and outer—in which the School was embedded, through constant *environmental scanning*, communicating their ideas, and influencing others through their commitment.
- Power was accrued mostly from personal sources.
- There were specific actions which aimed to articulate their vision, delegating execution and orienting towards achieving results.

All three schools showed a more directive leadership style supported by a comprehensive skill and competence set that enabled them to understand the contexts in which their schools were embedded and to communicate their ideas assertively, influencing others through their own commitment. The deans drew power mostly from personal sources, taking decisive, specific steps to articulate their vision, to delegate execution and to focus their entire organization on reaching the desired outcomes.

Moreover, although position (structural source of power) as Dean or President represents a first step in influencing and shaping the strategic agenda building, however, the field study shows personal sources of power as conditionants for success in both introducing breakthrough initiatives to the agenda and executing them. Among these personal sources of power, delivering results, expertise, resource generation, reputation, and consistency are considered among the most relevant. Finally, uses of power demonstrate a critical role in mobilizing power. Among these, coalition formation, articulation and communication of the vision, rationality, assertiveness, decisiveness, listening and scanning, execution, and delegation are the most relevant.

Examples are: IMD's consolidation and success with the School's unparalleled turnover and positioning in the international market; INSEAD's successful endeavour to reinforce and deepen its research profile and activities, as well as the decision to launch a second campus in Singapore. And, finally, LBS with its initiative to become a top league international school.

Patterns found in unsuccessful breakthrough initiatives related to power mobilization:

- Participative and slightly weak sponsor's leadership style.

- Dean's skills and competences. Likewise, in successful breakthrough initiatives, Deans were shown to be visionary, entrepreneurial, and committed.
- Power sources: position (this pattern is rather weak). Unsuccessful initiatives seem to be related to weak power sources.
- Power use: consensus building.

To make the findings more explicit, the study has organized the foregoing patterns as 'conditionants' and 'enablers'. With regards to conditionants, their importance relies on the fact that the success of the initiatives depends on their presence and how they are enacted —i.e. they are a necessary condition but not a sufficient one. Likewise, enablers are elements that promote or facilitate the success of an initiative.

Conditionants for successful breakthrough initiatives regarding issue legitimization are:

- Intensive and proactive issue selling.
- Critical activity in understanding and aligning priorities of other key actors' MGI.
- Performance. It sometimes appears as a weak feature and, thus, reinforces any trend towards change or otherwise. It appears as a strong feature legitimating the feasibility of initiative (e.g. deepening research strategy regarding the capital campaign).

Conditionants for breakthrough successful initiatives regarding power mobilization:

- Directive leadership style.
- Dean's skills and competence based on his or her capacity to scan the environment both internally and externally, listening in order to enrich his or her own perspective and understanding of the context; political skills to build coalitions, articulating and communicating the vision and its relation to the specific initiative he is promoting to the strategic agenda; the capacity to integrate short-term with long-term interests and individual with institutional interests; the capacity to deliver results mostly through delegation; and the capacity to stand and make the case: to present the initiative and the analysis on which it was based with decisiveness, assertiveness and rationality.
- Power sources, both structural and personal—position, reward, and resource generation and allocation with regard to the structural sources of power and referent, expertise and reputation regarding the personal sources of power.
- Power uses: articulating the vision, building coalitions, rationality, assertiveness, decisiveness, execution, delegation, and environmental scanning.

Enablers for successful breakthrough initiatives regarding issue legitimization are:

- Issue sponsorship—needs a clear sponsor, an organizational key actor. In all cases, the Dean.
- An agenda structure: first, for the issues already in progress within the agenda; second, for the logic and sequencing of those issues in relation to the broad strategic agenda.

With regard to the characterization of features of the outer context that legitimate such initiatives, the study cannot conclude whether corporate customers' demands, donors and benefactors and competition are conditionants or enablers, although they are present in all successful breakthrough initiatives.

Enablers for successful breakthrough initiatives regarding power mobilization are:

- Dean's skills and competences—entrepreneurship and commitment.
- Power sources—position, reputation, and rationality.

3.4. CONCLUSIONS

This chapter presented an empirical study of the political approach of SLPs in three business schools—IMD, INSEAD, and London Business School—in undergoing their internationalization strategy during the period 1990–2004. It is intended to identify those key people, activities, competences, and features that acted as enablers and conditionants for a particular breakthrough initiative to be raised to the school's strategic agenda, become a decision, and then, be implemented.

The analysis has shed light on how the SLP operates in carrying out a particular breakthrough initiative, over time, in terms of who the key actors were and their characterization, how they interplayed, what their main generic interests (MGI) were and how and why they prioritized those interests, over time. Moreover, it has conveyed what the key features of the inner and outer contexts were, and how they influenced the SLP, over time. The research has also analysed, in each case study, how those issues were legitimated by features of both outer and inner contexts, the alignment of key actors' prioritization of MGI, and issue-selling. Finally, the analysis focused on how key actors mobilized power to add some issues to the strategic agenda, according to their prioritization.

However, although the Dean has the primary role in building and executing the strategic agenda, he or she cannot succeed without the explicit support of the most relevant people from both the Faculty and Board. Hence, two leadership activities require particular attention: 1) legitimating the strategic initiative among the other key actors—capacity to articulate and communicate the initiative according to the shared vision and values of the school—as well as being credible due to track-records and results achieved; and 2) mobilizing power—having the necessary resolution for sponsoring and selling the initiative, as well as the capacity to get support from key people, and find the necessary resources to accomplish the initiative. These two activities are particularly relevant when the strategic initiative represents a 'breakthrough' in the strategic direction of the school.

3.5. LIMITATIONS TO THE STUDY

Several circumstances limited our study. First, the conclusions relate solely to the specific case study examples, which involve, in essence, three high status, and high quality private schools during the period 1990–2004: IMD, INSEAD, and LBS. Although the choice of these three schools with their own similarities was deliberate, in order to set boundaries for the study, future research may well include a case study of a high quality European public school to establish a meaningful point of contrast. This would enable an understanding of the SLP to be gained within a more regulated environment, such as that of the public sector, and identify differences between schools which are more dependent on University governance, and embedded within a more bureaucratic context.

Second, as in every study, the perspective chosen enables both researcher and reader to better understand the phenomenon under study. At the same time, by its very nature, it represents limitations. Thus, the political analysis of the SLP in business schools, over time, depends on the particular lens that has been selected: here, one with a political focus. Even though choosing this perspective has facilitated the observation of power and influence, interests and demands, coalitions, goals and objectives, bargaining processes and conflict—among other things—the rational aspect of decisions, actions, and events could not readily be identified.

Third, in looking at the research method chosen for this study, even though the multiple case study method augments external validity and helps guard against observer bias (Yin, 1984), there must be questions as to the extent to which findings are applicable to other contexts, especially those whose organizational characteristics differ from those of business schools.

Fourth, as for the operationalization of the SLP, the selection of categories to identify the SLP may have constrained the analysis. In this regard, strategic agenda building and execution have been chosen, since they suit the political perspective better.

Fifth, if we now consider the particular sets of indicators chosen to analyse issue legitimization and power mobilization, and outer and inner contexts, these may also have limited the research findings. For example, performance issues have been avoided, limiting the issues to positioning and economic outcomes.

Sixth, the period in which the SLP was observed—1990–2004—and the temporal bracketing employed (episodes corresponding to the different Deanships in which each school was divided) constrained the study to some extent. However, given that IMD was founded in 1990, this period was deliberately chosen in order to carry out a better comparison across the three business schools over time.

Finally, a qualitative approach was chosen for the study, since, where processual analysis is carried out, interconnections, dynamics, and interrelations, can be better explained. Quantitative analysis would have enhanced the study. Although this type of analysis was also carried out to augment validity, the study acknowledges that the use of the questionnaires would have improved the data, since semi-structured interviews sometimes present questions which might not fit or that cannot be answered with the depth the research needs for further analysis.

3.6. RESEARCH AGENDA FOR THE FUTURE

The relevance of the leadership phenomenon to management fields is widely acknowledged. The study of leadership has, indeed, been approached with a range of considerations in mind: the person of the leader, and his or her traits and skills; the leader's behaviour; his or her actions in a particular situation; the relationship between leaders and followers; charismatic leadership; different characters of transformational and transactional leadership; shared or joint leadership with a broader and more integrative perspective. Strategic leadership as a process in organizational settings represents an avenue for further exploration in order to deepen the understanding of strategic formulation and implementation.

Finally, the political perspective facilitates a consideration of the interplay among people's interests. In effect, because leadership is understood as a process of social influence, power, and influence represent a central issue in studying leadership.

The field study enables one to recognize that power essentially accrues to personal sources such as the following: the capacity to shape, communicate and articulate a vision; the delivery of results; listening to others; the integration of different people; the location of common ground among them; the integration of goals for the long and short term; the building of confident relationships; consistency; commitment; integrity; political skills in coalition building; resource generation, etc. Particularly, in organizational settings where power tends to be shared, and collegiality and dual authority challenge formal authority, the understanding of leadership and power, with their possibilities and limitations, represent a relevant issue for further research.

The contribution of a contextual approach to the understanding of strategic leadership as a process in business schools is still in its early stages and there is much room for advancing and deepening it. Future research on SLPs in business schools from this perspective can take different avenues. First, SLP for breakthrough strategic initiatives in business schools could be studied in other contexts than Europe, the location of the three schools included in this study. The observation of SLPs in institutions based in the U.S. could be a next step in observing and identifying differences from and similarities with the first study. A market with a more mature culture of postgraduate education in management, strong competition and a tradition of financial contribution from donors to build endowments for long term funding seems to be an interesting scenario to dive into. By contrast, the impact of the external context in totally different environments, like Emerging Markets, where these institutions are flourishing but still relatively new phenomena, calls for research on SLPs in business schools situated in markets like Latin America, Asia, Africa.

Second, SLPs could be studied in university-based business schools. Our study has been focused on three stand-alone institutions. Even though London Business School is part of the University of London, from a governance perspective its autonomy is comparable to independent institutions. In this sense, differences and similarities in the use of power and its legitimization can be identified.

In addition, identifying the key actors seems to be interesting. Dean and Faculty will clearly remain as crucial players, although there could be differences in their relative relevance. A major variance could be the role of the Board. Furthermore, there may be more than just one actor in its place. In the same way, in relation to the key players in university-based business schools, it seems interesting to identify the MGI and their prioritization. The Dean's capacity to define the strategic agenda will probably be lower than in stand-alone institutions.

Another aspect to consider is the role of the other schools within the same university, as relevant features of the context in exerting influence, providing potential synergies or requiring support.

REFERENCES

Ammeter, A. P., Douglas, C., Gardner, W. L., Hochwarter, W. A., and Ferris, Gerald R. (2002). 'Toward a Political Theory of Leadership', *The Leadership Quarterly*, Vol. 13.

Ancona, D. (2007). 'Distributed Leadership in Action', in Ancona, D. and Bresnam, H., '*X-Teams: How to Build Teams that Lead, Innovate and Succeed*', Ch. 9. Harvard Business School Publishing Corporation: Boston, Massachusetts.

Bass, B. M. (1990). *Bass & Stogdill's Handbook of Leadership. Theory, Research, & Management Application*. New York: The Free Press.

Beeby, M. and Jones, W. (1997). 'Business Schools and Corporate Management Development', *Journal of Management Development*, Vol. 16, N° 7.

Birnbaum, R. (1989). 'Presidential Succession and Institutional Functioning in Higher Education', *The Journal of Higher Education*, Vol. 60, N° 2.

Bryman, A. (2002). 'Leadership in Organizations', in Clegg et al. (eds) *The Sage Handbook of Organization Studies*. London: Sage, pp. 276–292.

Bryman, A. (1992). '*Charisma and Leadership in Organizations*. London: Sage.

Burns, J. M. (1978). *Leadership*. New York: Harper & Row.

Chaffee, E. E. (1983). 'The Role of Rationality in University Budgeting', *Research in Higher Education*, Vol. 19.

Cohen, M. and March, J. (1974). '*Leadership and Ambiguity*. The Carnegie Commission on Higher Education.

Crainer, Stuart and Dearlove, Des (1999). '*Gravy Training—Inside the Business of Business Schools*. San Francisco: Jossey-Bass Publishers.

Cribbin, James J. (1972). *Effective Managerial Leadership*. New York: American Management Association Inc.

Denis, J-L, Lamothe, L., and Langley, A. (2001). 'The Dynamics of Collective Leadership and Strategic Change in Pluralistic Organizations', *Academy of Management Journal*, Vol. 44, N° 4.

Denis, J-L, Langley, A., and Cazale, L. (1996). 'Leadership and Strategic Change under Ambiguity', *Organization Studies*, Vol. 17, N° 4.

Fitzgerald, L., Ferlie, E., Mc Givern, G., and Buchanan, D. (2013). 'Distributed Leadership Patterns and Service Improvement. Evidence and Argument from English Healthcare', *The Leadership Quarterly*, Vol. 24.

Fragueiro, F. and Thomas, H. (2011). *Strategic Leadership in the Business School. Keeping One Step Ahead*. New York: Cambridge University Press.

Fragueiro, F. (2007). *Strategic Leadership Process in Business Schools. A Political Perspective.* Thesis submitted in partial fulfilment of the requirements for the degree of Doctor of Philosophy in Management. University of Warwick, Warwick Business School.

Gibson, J. W., Tesone, D. V., and Buchalski, R. M. (2000). 'The Leader as Mentor', *The Journal of Leadership Studies*, Vol. 7, N° 3.

Gore, C., Steven, V., et al. (1998). 'Analysis of the Effect of External Change on the Management of Business Schools within the Higher Education Sector', *Total Quality Management*, Vol. 9, Issue 2/3.

Gronn, P. (2011). 'Hybrid Configurations of Leadership', in Bryman, A., Collinson, D.L., Grint, K., Jackson, B., and Uhl-Bien, M. *The Sage Handbook of Leadership*, London: Sage, Ch. 32.

Gronn, P. (2002). 'Distributed Leadership as a Unit of Analysis', *The Leadership Quarterly*, Vol. 13.

Hagen, A. F., Asan, M. T., and Amin, S. G. (1998). 'Critical Strategic Leadership Components: An Empirical Investigation', *SAM Advanced Management Journal*, Summer.

Hardy, C. (1991). 'Pluralism, Power and Collegiality in Universities', *Financial Accountability & Management*, Vol. 7, N° 3.

Heenan, D. A. and Bennis, W. (1999). *Co-Leaders: The Power of Great Leaderships*. New York, NY: John Wiley & Sons.

Heifetz, R. (1999). *Leadership without Easy Answers*. Cambridge, MA: The Belknap Press of Harvard University Press.

Hitt, M. A. (1998). 'Twenty First Century Organizations: Business Firms, Business Schools, and the Academy', *Academy of Management Review*, Vol. 23, N° 2.

House, R. J. and Aditya, R. N. (1997). 'The Social Scientific Study of Leadership: Quo Vadis?', *Journal of Management*, Vol. 23, N° 3.

Hunt, J. G. and Dodge (2001). 'Leadership Déjà Vu All Over Again', *The Leadership Quarterly*, Vol. 11, N° 4.

Hunt, J. G. (1991). *Leadership. A New Synthesis*. Newbury Park, CA: Sage.

Lorange, P. (2005). 'Strategy Means Choice: Also for Today's Business School!', *The Journal of Management Development*, Vol. 24, N° 9.

Middlehurst, R. (1993). *Leading Academics*. Buckingham: Society for Research into Higher Education and Open University Press.

Morris, H. (2000) 'The Origins, Forms and Effects of Modularization and Semesterization in Ten UK-Based Business Schools', *Higher Education Quarterly*, Vol. 54, N° 3.

Northouse, P. (2001). *Leadership. Theory and Practice*. London: Sage Publications.

Nowotny, H., Scott, P., and Gibbons, M. (2001). *'Rethinking Science. Knowledge and the Public in an Age of Uncertainty*. Cambridge: Polity Press.

O'Toole, J., Galbraith, J., and Lawler, E. E. (2002). 'When Two (or more) Heads are Better than One: The Promise and Pitfalls of Shared Leadership'. *California Management Review*, 44 (4), 65–83.

Pearce, C. L. and Conger, J. A. (2003). *Shared Leadership. Reframing the Hows and Whys of Leadership*. Thousand Oaks, CA: Sage Publications.

Pettigrew, A. M. (1997). 'What is Processual Analysis?', *Scandinavian Journal Management*, Vol. 13, N° 4.

Pettigrew, A. M. (1990). 'Longitudinal Field Research on Change: Theory and Practice', *Organization Science*, Vol. 1, N° 3.

Pfeffer, J. and Fong, C. (2004). 'The end of Business School?' *Academy of Management Learning and Education*, Vol. 1, N° 1.

Prince, C. (1999). 'Transforming the University Business School for the 21st Century.' *Strategic Change*, Vol. 8, N° 8.

Ramsden, Paul (1998). *Learning to Lead in Higher Education*. New York: Routledge.

Segev, E., Raveh, A. and Farjoun, M. (1999). 'Conceptual Maps of the Leading MBA Programs in the US', *Strategic Management Journal*, Vol. 20, N° 6.

Starkey, K., Hatchuel, A., and Tempest, S. (2004). 'Rethinking the Business School', *Journal of Management Studies*, Vol. 41, N° 8.

Thomas, H. and Thomas, L. (2011). 'Perspectives on Leadership in Business Schools.' *Journal of Management Development*, Vol. 30, N° 5.

Trieschmann, J. S., Dennis, A. R., Northcraft, G. B., and Nieme Jr., A. W. (2000). 'Serving Constituencies in Business Schools: MBA Program Versus Research Performance', *Academy of Management Journal*, Vol. 46, N° 6.

Twomey, D. F. and Twomey, R. F. (1998). 'UK Business Schools and Business: Activities and Interactions', *Journal of Management Development*, Vol. 17, N° 3.

Van Baalen, P. J. and Moratis, L. T. (2001). *Management Education in the Network Economy. Its Context, Content, and Organization.* Boston: Kluwer Academic Publishers.

Van Maanen, J. (1979). 'The Fact of Fiction in Organizational Ethnography', *Administrative Science Quarterly*, Vol. 24.

Weick, Karl E. (1976). 'Educational Organisations as Loosely Coupled Systems', *Administrative Science Quarterly*, Vol. 21, N° 1.

Yin, R. K. (1984). *Case Study Research: Design and Methods.* London: Sage.

Yukl, G. (2002). *Leadership in Organizations.* New Jersey: Prentice Hall.

4

Governance Logics in Universities

Organizational Change as Oscillating Conversations

Fabian Hattke, Steffen Blaschke, and Jetta Frost

4.1. INTRODUCTION

Over the past 30 years, universities have been facing intense institutional pressure to change (Eckel and Kezar 2003; Paul 2005; Slaughter and Rhoades 2004). In Germany, for example, a severe legitimacy crisis in the early 1990s forced decision makers to find new ways of organizing higher education (Mayer and Ziegele 2009). Universities have been responding to these institutional pressures with the introduction of New Public Management (NPM) (Bleiklie and Lange 2010; Schimank 2005). This application of corporate management practices to public sector institutions has been deemed successful in many cases (Pollitt 2011). At the same time, the more or less subtle replacement of academic self-governance with managerial hierarchies still poses trouble for many universities (Mora 2001).

The introduction of NPM brings about an escalating number of performance measures, accountability standards, and intensified stakeholder participation. Smaller departments are consolidated into larger schools with proprietary administrative and decision-making structures in order to boost the efficiency of university governance. Scientists are pooled in interdisciplinary research centres with professional fund raising and institutionalized university–industry collaborations. Centralized study-path programmes harmonize teaching formats that used to be structured autonomously by departments and chairs. Libraries, computing centres, and technical support services are concentrated in shared services to cater to larger groups of internal 'customers'. The associated shift of power among governing bodies is a rather rocky endeavour for many universities (Krücken 2003; Salancik and Pfeffer 1974). How these changes in universities are governed remains a central research question in higher education studies. Current research largely takes a macro-level perspective by assuming that university governance is isomorphic with the overall institutional logics or legal frameworks (Birnbaum 2004; de Boer et al. 2007; Shattock 1999). Only a few studies focus on communication, coordinated interactions, and the dynamics of actual governing behaviour (Bryman 2007; McLaughlin 2004; Middlehurst 2004). Thus, there is little explanation of how universities govern organizational change on the micro level.

Our chapter aims to remedy this shortcoming by focusing on interactions among governing bodies that facilitate organizational change. Based on the approach that communication constitutes organization (Cooren et al. 2011; Taylor and Van Every 2000), we conceptualize organizational interactions as conversations among governing bodies. In German public universities, typical governing bodies consist of the university and several department or school executive boards (rector's and dean's offices), various academic and administrative committees, a supervisory board and the state secretary of education (in a liaison role between government and university), as well as department or school councils. Relying on the notion of universities as loosely coupled systems (Weick 1976), we expect any governing body to be potentially coupled to any other governing body through either sporadic or repeated communication. Thus, every governing body may somehow be engaged in setting, debating, deciding, and enforcing the university's issues, all of which naturally happens in conversations.

Conversations among governing bodies constitute organizational change or, as Ford (1999: 488) puts it, 'in a network of conversations where realities are ongoingly being constructed, producing and managing change becomes a matter of shifting conversations'. We develop a framework of governance logics in universities based on these shifting conversations of change. We then analyse two empirical cases of comprehensive reorganizations in German universities due to institutional pressures to change. Our empirical elaboration of the framework shows conversations of change oscillating through the organization. They start with a limited participation in conversations, then diffuse throughout the organization, and come full circle with a medium level of diversity. Although neither stage of change accounts for an exclusive governance logic, our framework shows different governance logics in combinations of vertical and horizontal couplings among governing bodies, which allows for an analysis of how comprehensive reorganizations are governed.

Our contributions are twofold. First, we provide conceptual clarity for a communicative approach to questions of university governance. Our generic framework then allows for the analysis of the micro-level dynamics of university governance, which have received too little study so far. Second, we apply the framework to empirical data in order to show how universities cope with external pressures to change. In particular, we derive dominant governing logics that constitute four stages of change. In addition to these contributions, we sketch out two subsequent fields of research that may benefit from this study, namely, the relation between intentional and emergent change, as well as the interplay between micro and macro levels of analysis.

The chapter is organized as follows. First, we extend two widespread communication models of organizational change by specifying the actors involved in conversations of change. This part of our study develops the theoretical framework for the later analysis of conversations of change. After a brief introduction to the data, we present our cases of comprehensive reorganizations at two German universities based on six years of longitudinal data on meetings of the universities' senates. We then apply the framework to explain governance logics during different stages of change and provide related literature for our qualitative reasoning. Finally, we conclude with a discussion of the findings and implications for further research.

4.2. A TYPOLOGY OF CONVERSATIONS OF ORGANIZATIONAL CHANGE: GOVERNANCE LOGICS IN UNIVERSITIES

Following the idea that change in universities is communicatively constructed (e.g., Gioia et al. 1994; Simsek 1997), we view organizational change as shifting conversations among organizational members (Ford 1999). Generally speaking, change describes differences in form, quality, or state over times (Van de Ven and Poole 1995), which are usually perceived as shifts in organizational goals or values (Porras and Silvers 1991). Only when these differences are compared by juxtaposing forms, qualities, or states, a change can be noticed (Ford and Ford 1995). If organizational change modifies organizational structures, for example, we witness the change in shifting conversations that initiate, argue, perform, and establish the modification of structures.

4.2.2. Types of Conversation and Stages of Change

Relying on the approach of Ford and Ford (1995: 560) who argue that 'change is based in and driven by particular types of communication', we adopt their four types to identify conversations of (1) initiation, (2) understanding, (3) performance, and (4) closure.

Initiation. During this first stage of organizational change, organizations make problems visible, redefine their goals, and recognize opportunities.

Although there is no singular starting point to change (Weick 1979), conversations of initiation feature claims or declarations on what could or should be done (Ford and Ford 1995). Governing bodies and other organizational units try to channel attention to such claims. These conversations are either a reaction to external pressures for change—such as governmental regulations, public politics, or fiscal budgets—or they are proactively initiated internally in order to develop some new conceptualizations of the organization. In either case, they adhere to organizational contexts, such as current strategies, organizational hierarchies, and decision-making cultures (Dutton 1986; Gioia and Thomas 1996).

Understanding. The second stage of organizational change follows with challenges, debates, and discussions of the previously raised topics. Ambiguities, contradictions, and inconsistencies are exposed and resolved. This stage is characterized by the construction and reconstruction of meaning, which takes place in iterative, sequential, and to some extent reciprocal fashion (Gioia and Chittipeddi 1991). This sensemaking (Weick et al. 2005) influences the way organizational change is perceived and, ultimately, how decisions are enacted with respect to external and internal demands (Smirchich and Stubbart 1985). Similar to conversations of initiation, understanding is bound by environmental conditions and organizational contexts. While such conditions (e.g. governmental regulations) already reflect the strategic issues that made conversations in the first place, respective contexts (e.g., organizational hierarchies) take full force only in understanding (Gioia and Chittipeddi 1991; Gioia and Thomas 1996).

Performance. The third stage of organizational change is characterized by conversations of performance in order to produce results that are relevant for the intended organizational change. We argue that these conversations practically translate into devising designs, plans, or strategies, including setting deadlines, showing evidence of completion, and insisting on accountability for fulfilling the underlying conditions. Performance agreements are discussed and negotiated as well as what knowledge, ideas, and initiatives are needed, what they are needed for, and how they are evaluated. Organizations are talked into existence nowhere more than in conversations of performance (Taylor and Van Every 2000; Weick et al. 2005).

Closure. The fourth and final stage of organizational change implies the possibility of harmonious completion. Hence, the primary function of conversations of closure is feedback. Summaries and justifications are made in order to compare differences over time. Organizations figure out what no longer works, consider how the future can or may be different from the past, and how to continue with new possibilities. Some kind of closure is necessary to invoke further organizational change (Ford and Ford 1995). In closure, organizations disengage from former routines and start to find orientation in new settings (Albert 1983). Closure takes organizational change full cycle—a necessary requirement to analyse organizational change in different stages to begin with (Huy 2001; Weick and Quinn 1999). The closure stage should not be reduced to a clearly defined, disruptive endpoint of organizational change. It rather takes the form of a milestone in order to institutionalize responses to organizational change.

Taken together, these four types of conversation and stages of organizational change foster the capability to continuously adapt to changing contingencies. Change is not reduced to something that occurs 'out there' but is produced through shifting conversations (Ford and Ford 1995). It is enacted in and governed by communication. Still, how to apply this staged model to university governance remains an open question. In particular, we do not know which governing bodies participate in the conversations: for example, who initiates change and who is responsible for closing open topics. Without specifying who is involved in conversations of initiation, understanding, performance, and closure, the stages remain metaphorical constructs (Stubbart and Smalley 1999). To elaborate our understanding of how organizational change is governed through the four types of conversation, we suggest that each type involves different combinations of organization members and governing bodies and thus rely on different governance logics. Ford and Ford's (1995) four conversations of organizational change provide a coherent typology for all organizations, including universities.

4.2.3. Participation of Governing Bodies: Vertical and Horizontal Couplings

Universities are broadly conceptualized as loosely coupled systems (Lutz 1982; Rubin 1979; Weick 1976). Their organizational structures are reflected in couplings of governing bodies by communication. On a dyadic level, loose coupling describes communication between governing bodies that is infrequent, random, slow to respond, or weak in nature (Orton and Weick 1990). In contrast, tight coupling between governing bodies describes communication that is frequent or planned, fast to respond, or generally strong of sorts. On a systemic level, loose coupling is a dialectical concept of organizations comprising of both loose and tight couplings (Orton and Weick 1990). For example, two governing bodies may be tightly coupled by decisions on inter-disciplinary study paths, de-coupled in case of decisions on disciplinary research profiles, and loosely coupled regarding decisions on their composition (when one scientific discipline is under-represented in one body, it may be over-represented in another body).

Gioia and Chittipetti (1991) already establish top-down couplings (sensegiving) and bottom-up couplings (sensemaking) as viable perspectives on the way governing bodies participate in conversations of change. Centralized,

managerial governing bodies such as the university executive board establish conversations of change with task forces such as committees and department or school councils. In turn, these decentralized, collegial governing
bodies engage in further conversations, just the other way around. We argue
that sensegiving and sensemaking (Gioia and Chittipetti 1991) feature conversations of change on two independent dimensions, not just top-down or
bottom-up. For example, sensegiving may target decentralized department
executive boards without incorporating the larger collegial participation
of department councils. In the following, we take note from both Ford and
Ford (1995) and Gioia and Chittipetti (1991) in the presentation of our own
typology of governance logics in universities, which anchors conversations of
change in vertical and horizontal couplings among governing bodies.

Vertical couplings. Similar to the distinction between corporate parents
and their divisions or subsidiaries (e.g., Goold and Campbell 2002; Goold
et al. 1994), we distinguish between centralized and decentralized governing
bodies in universities. The degree of (de)centralization depends upon the
extent to which decision authority is centred at the top of an organization
or is delegated down the chain of command to the bottom of the organization. The multi-divisional form is widely acknowledged as one of the most
common organizational forms representing a trade-off between centralization and decentralization, where the corporate parent governs the combined
activities and resources of rather autonomous subsidiaries (e.g., Chandler
1991). In our framework, parental or centralized governing bodies in universities are the state secretary of education (in a liaison role between government and university), the university supervisory board, the university
executive board including the president, vice presidents, and chancellor,
as well as various standing committees to assist these bodies. Accordingly,
subsidiary or decentralized governing bodies are the school and department executive boards, including deans, vice deans, and directors, as well as
school and department councils.

Based on the distinction between centralized and decentralized governing bodies, we distinguish between four types of vertical couplings. Table 4.1
displays these couplings from one governing body to others. (1) *Centralized*

Table 4.1. Vertical couplings among governing bodies (GB)

		To	
		Central GB	Decentral GB
From	Central GB	*1 Centralized Conversations*	*2 Top-Down Conversations*
	Decentral GB	*3 Bottom-Up Conversations*	*4 Decentralized Conversations*

conversation occurs if a parental governing body communicates with another parental governing body; for example, if the university supervisory board informs the university executive board about upcoming changes to legislation. (2) If a parental governing body communicates with a subsidiary governing body we label it *top-down* conservation. (3) If a conversation is initiated by a subsidiary governing body and addresses a parental governing body we term it *bottom-up* conservation. (4) A *decentralized* conservation takes place between subsidiary governing bodies, that is, only among department or school executive boards.

Horizontal couplings. Taking the well-known dichotomy between managerial and collegial decision making (e.g., Birnbaum 2004; Bleiklie and Kogan 2007; Mora 2001), we furthermore distinguish between managerial and collegial governing bodies in universities. Whether governing bodies are considered managerial or collegial depends on the extent to which they invite a narrow or broad participation of status groups in conversations of change. On the one hand, managerial governing bodies are characterized by professionalism, hierarchy, and the primary task of enforcing strategic goals, allocating resources, and satisfying the interests of major stakeholders. They include the state secretary of education, the university supervisory board, the university executive board, as well as department and school executive boards. On the other hand, collegial governing bodies are characterized by academic self-governance, democratic participation, and the primary task of making the voices of all status groups in universities heard. They are comprised of students, tenured and non-tenured faculty, as well as administrative and technical staff, all of whom are represented in bodies such as department and school councils or standing committees.

Similar to the four types of vertical couplings, we distinguish between four types of horizontal couplings. Table 4.2 displays these couplings between governing bodies, too: (1) *Focused* conversations occur if managerial governing bodies communicate with each other, for example, if the university supervisory board informs the university executive board about upcoming changes to legislation. (2) If a conversation is initiated by a managerial governing body and addresses collegial governing bodies, we call it an

Table 4.2. Horizontal couplings among governing bodies (GB)

		To	
		Managerial GB	Collegial GB
From	Managerial GB	*1 Focused Conversations*	*2 Inside-Out Conversations*
	Collegial GB	*3 Outside-In Conversations*	*4 Shared Conversations*

inside-out-conversation. (3) Conversely, if a conversation is initiated by collegial governing bodies and addresses managerial governing bodies we label it *outside-in* conversation. (4) A *shared* conversation among only department or school councils and committees represents a horizontal coupling between collegial governing bodies.

4.2.4. A Framework of Governance Logics

The combination of vertical and horizontal couplings between and among governing bodies yields a framework of governance logics in conversations of organizational change. The term 'governance' refers to the coordination of the plurality and complexity of universities. It involves the enactment of policies and procedures for communication and interaction. Figure 4.1 summarizes the framework with a concentration on four dominant governance logics that derive from all possible combinations of a centralized, top-down, bottom-up, or decentralized coupling and another focused, inside-out, outside-in, or shared coupling. Each governance logic is represented by one quadrant: (A) top-heavy professional; (B) top-heavy

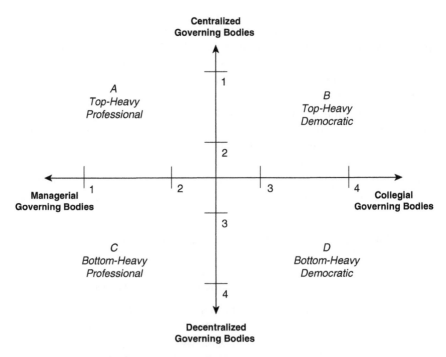

Figure 4.1. Framework of governance logics

democratic; (C) bottom-heavy professional; and (D) bottom-heavy democratic. The term 'professional' refers to the bodies' mainly full-time administrative staff holding a strong formal status with extensive decision autonomy that requires at least some formal educational qualification (Gornitzka and Larsen 2004; Whitchurch 2004). In contrast, part-time members of 'democratic' bodies represent different status groups with a variety of educational levels (students, academics, administrators) and reach decisions only by collective vote.

Top-heavy professional. Centralized, managerial governing bodies address either fellow bodies, other managerial but decentralized, other centralized but collegial, or altogether decentralized, collegial bodies. Consider the following four examples that make up the top-heavy professional governance logic: (1) the state secretary informs the university executive board about budget cuts in state spending on higher education; (2) the university executive board discusses the consequences of the budget cuts with department executive boards; (3) it assigns a committee to draw up a plan of action to counter the budget cuts, and (4); it informs school and department councils of the budget cuts and the plan to counter them.

Top-heavy democratic. Centralized, collegial governing bodies address either fellow bodies, other collegial but decentralized, other centralized but managerial, or altogether decentralized, managerial bodies. Committees that present their plans of action to other governing bodies are a good example of the top-heavy democratic governance logic. They equally represent all status groups in universities (i.e., tenured and non-tenured faculty, administrative and technical staff, and students), which pre-approve any plan of action with a certain commitment from the respective status groups.

Bottom-heavy professional. Decentralized, managerial governing bodies address either fellow bodies, other managerial but centralized, other decentralized but collegial, or altogether centralized, collegial bodies. For example, department or school executive boards are likely to voice their opinion when it comes to dealing with the consequences of budget cuts, whether in their bargaining with the university executive board or in meetings with various councils.

Bottom-heavy democratic. Decentralized, collegial governing bodies address either fellow bodies, other collegial but centralized, other decentralized but managerial, or altogether centralized, managerial bodies. A prominent example of the bottom-heavy democratic governance logic is department or school councils fighting for the rights of the status groups they are made up of. Hence, they frequently call the university supervisory board or the university executive board into question, not least when it comes to bearing the consequences of budget cuts.

We expect neither one of the four governance logics to be exclusive to just one conversation of change. Nonetheless, we argue that there may be patterns or sequences of dominant logics apparent in cases of comprehensive reorganization. In order to trace these patterns, we turn to two in-depth case studies.

4.3. ORGANIZATIONAL CHANGE AT GERMAN UNIVERSITIES: TWO COMPREHENSIVE REORGANIZATIONS

In the following, we introduce our case-based approach to elaborate the framework of governance logics (Eisenhardt 1989; Vaughan 1992; Yin 2009). We contrast two theoretically sampled longitudinal cases of comprehensive reorganizations in two German universities. The first case shows the integration of eighteen departments into six schools at a large, diversified university. This case is later referred to as DU University. The second case illustrates the integration of ten departments into three schools at a small, specialized university. This case is later referred to as SU University. While the change itself is very similar, the chosen universities represent polar types in terms of size and subject diversity: DU University is among the biggest and most diversified; SU University is among the smallest and most specialized state-owned universities in Germany. Table 4.3 highlights some key facts about the two cases. Analysing such theoretically sampled polar type configurations allows for a 'broader exploration of research questions and theoretical elaboration' (Eisenhardt and Graebner 2007: 27) than is possible within a single case. In addition, this approach is especially well suited for longitudinal analysis (Pettigrew 1990). By following this method, we expect to identify governance logics that are specific to reorganizations in small universities, governance logics specific to reorganizations in large universities, and generic governance logics beyond this dichotomy.

Table 4.3. Facts and figures describing the two case universities

	DU University	SU University
Professors	*670*	*145*
Academic Employees	*4090*	*610*
Non-Academic Employees	*6640*	*420*
Students	*40.000*	*6.300*
Study Paths (Majors)	*170*	*25*
Budget per Year	*305 Mio EURO*	*107 Mio EURO*
Duration of Reorganization	*35 Months*	*42 Months*

4.3.1. Method and Data

We substantiate our framework with longitudinal data taken from the senate meetings of the two case universities. University senates are councils in which university members participate on a regular basis in debates of various organizational issues (Birnbaum 1989; Bradshaw and Fredette 2009; Minor 2003). The two case senates consist of professors, academic associates, students, non-academic employees, the president, several consultative members, and guests. Every status group has the right to raise questions, voice its opinion, and propose issues for discussion, either in advance of the meetings or via ad hoc inquiries. Thus, the senate's meeting minutes are an immediate reflection of debates among all internal status groups as well as external stakeholders. We rely on 30 protocols from DU University and 31 documents from SU University.

Our approach to elaborating the framework and to enhancing our understanding of how organizational change in universities is governed has some restrictions that must be considered. Our observation of the couplings is clearly tied to the data source. Of course, conversations may happen outside these senate meetings or behind closed doors. For example, core issues of teaching and research remain largely unaddressed in both cases. In addition, the protocols represent a negotiated reality, meaning that the content of the meeting minutes has to be approved by the senate's members before they are published. This may lead to ex-post rationalization of otherwise ambiguous interpretations and conflicting conversations. To avoid a biased view on the two reorganizations at large, we conducted a document analysis of additional official statements and internal memos. The results are incorporated in the case descriptions in the section 'Sampling the Cases: Context and Content of Meeting Minutes'. The debates in the university senates correspond with the milestones derived from this document analysis. Our narrative examples illustrate how the important issues, such as the organization design or the composition of bodies and their competencies, are extensively discussed in the senate. Last, an application of the framework to this type of data implies that governing bodies noticeably address each other in the four types of conversations. Especially during conversations of understanding, coding this directed form of communication proves to be challenging. Sometimes issues are interpreted by both sides simultaneously, which requires a clarification along the vertical and horizontal dimensions or, in other words, of who is addressing whom. Still, this supports our interpretation of understanding as a polyphonic conversation, as we later show.

4.3.2. Sampling the Cases: Context and Content of
Meeting Minutes

Thirty meeting minutes detail the case of organizational change between the years 2003 and 2006 during which DU University reorganized its 18 departments into six schools. The government first discussed this consolidation in 2002 and released an official report in early 2003. The report asserts that the university's small departments are inefficient due to redundancies in administrative processes. In April 2003, the governing bodies start an initial discussion of the governmental report. The government passes a document for the future development of the university in June 2003, aiming to realize expected synergies by consolidating related departments. In May 2004, the university rejects the government's plan, because the extensive school autonomy is suspected to have negative effects on multidisciplinary teaching and research formats. A revised plan is issued by the government in June 2004, accepted, and formalized by means of an interim statutory document in October 2004. Finally, by April 2005, a new state law establishes six schools. But it is not until February 2006 that the internal restructuring is formalized in a new statutory document and the change comes to a (temporary) end.

The reorganization of ten departments into three schools at SU University is reflected in 31 meeting minutes between the years 2003 and 2006. The merger of the departments is first discussed in 2003, when the government announces large funding cuts that threaten the future of the university. After tedious discussions about ways to ensure the survival of the institution, the ministry develops a financial model for the merged departments in early 2004. This is a critical point for the change since the merger would have stopped without a sustainable budgeting plan. A precondition for the budget approval by the government was a more distinctive research and teaching profile for SU University after the reorganization. In 2005, the state passes a new law that establishes the new organization structures in three schools. The faculty's call for five schools is simultaneously rejected in favour of further specialization in teaching and research. Minor disciplines without an immediate fit to one of the three schools are closed in the process. In 2006, the governance bodies of the new institutions are appointed and the university begins its operations in the new structure.

Turning to the senate's meeting minutes, we find 52 communication episodes concerning the reorganization at DU University and 76 episodes at SU University. The coded data is summarized in Table 4.4. Conversations of performance represent the majority of communication at both universities. The engagement of governing bodies is almost equally distributed at DU, whereas the university executive board at SU is involved in over eighty percent of all conversations. Both universities primarily rely on centralized, top-down, and focused couplings when governing organizational change.

Table 4.4. Summary of codings

	DU University	SU University
Types of Conversations		
Initiation	*9*	*7*
Understanding	*9*	*8*
Performance	*25*	*44*
Closure	*9*	*17*
Governing Bodies		
State Secretary and Supervisory Board	*24*	*25*
University Executive Board	*29*	*63*
School and Department Executive Boards	*28*	*24*
School and Department Councils	*29*	*21*
Committees	*15*	*36*
Vertical Couplings		
Centralized	*20*	*40*
Top-Down	*20*	*26*
Bottom-Up	*5*	*10*
Decentralized	*6*	*0*
Horizontal Couplings		
Focused	*21*	*28*
Inside-Out	*13*	*16*
Outside-In	*9*	*27*
Shared	*8*	*5*

4.4. DISCUSSION: OSCILLATING CONVERSATIONS OF ORGANIZATIONAL CHANGE

Our analysis suggests that conversations of change do not follow a unidirectional sequence but oscillate back and forth. Neither are conversations of initiation necessarily followed by understanding, nor are conversations of performance succeeded by closure, and so on. This finding is in keeping with Ford and Ford (1995) who argue that change does not move in linear fashion from start to finish. However, our analysis also shows dominant governance logics for each one of the four stages of change. Although conversations of change frequently shift from one type to the other, dominant governance logics indicate a systematic participation of governing bodies in times of organizational change. We find that conversations of initiation address a broadening audience, conversations of understanding reassure about matters of change, conversations of performance call for actions among all governing bodies, and conversations of closure display power plays in the final words about organizational change.

4.4.1. Broadening the Audience: Dissemination in Conversations of Initiation

In both our empirical cases, financial considerations and a perceived lack of efficiency trigger changes to the organizational structure. In addition, the supposed absence of a clear profile enforces pressure to change at SU University. Neither case displays a 'grassroots' approach to the comprehensive reorganization. Institutional pressures to change originate with the government's enforcement of new budget constraints to improve input–output relations (Gumport 2000). Our analysis shows how these external pressures to change enter the organizational discourse through conversations of initiation in a top-heavy professional logic (see Figure 4.2).

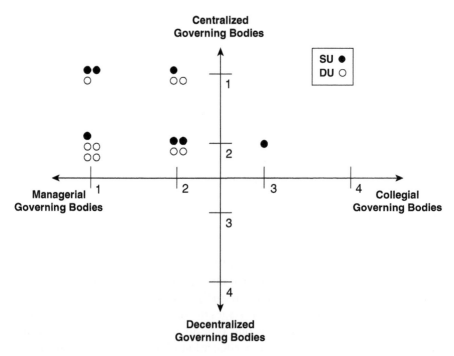

Figure 4.2. Governance logics of initiation

Conversations of initiation put institutional pressures to change on the agenda, but it is nevertheless astonishing how rarely initiatives are brought up by decentralized and collegial bodies. The periphery of power is not able or willing to initiate conversations in such a manner that they appear as important issues in the university senates (Dutton 1986; Dutton and Ashford 1993). In either case, issues are simply put on the agenda by managerial governing bodies through top-down and inside-out couplings, drawing lower organizational levels' and status groups' attention to upcoming actions. Thus, a top-heavy professional logic creates the 'internal sensemaking context' (Gioia and Thomas 1996: 384) that guides the following conversations of understanding, performance, and closure.

There is only one conversation of initiation in our data in which a collegial body initiates conversations of change. In short, the passage from the meeting minutes reads: 'The centralized statutory committee reports on the initial draft for the new organization structure at SU University... So far, the number of schools remains an open and controversial question... The department executive boards are asked to build their opinion about this draft of the statutory document and the designated number of schools'. (SU protocol 2004-07-21, topic 10-D). We clearly see the statutory committee initiating change by setting the agenda for department executive boards. However, when the statutory committee later reports back to the university executive board that 'five schools are the preferred future organization model' (SU protocol 2004–12–01, topic 3), the Deans' opinion is not explicitly mentioned. Officially, there is no involvement of department executive boards even though they are addressed beforehand. Thus, the initiated conversation is either resolved behind closed doors or symbolic in nature. Since the university executive board submits the 'foundation of three schools for the committees' attention' in 2005 (SU protocol 2005–08–29, topic 5) and thereby overrules the committee's recommendation, too, a symbolic involvement seems to be the case.

4.4.2. Reassuring the Matter: Polyphony in Conversations of Understanding

Conversations of understanding do not follow a dominant governance logic. Figure 4.3 shows many 'in-between' conversations expressed in bottom-up and outside-in couplings. Obviously, there is a strong need for all types of governing body to make sense of the issues at hand and understand implications of the initiated conversations. During understanding, a shared language develops in the polyphony (i.e., the multiple but equal voices that constitute organizations; Kornberger et al. 2006; Shotter 2008) of the governing bodies.

The following narratives exemplify the various needs for clarification throughout the organization: 'The president reports on the planning

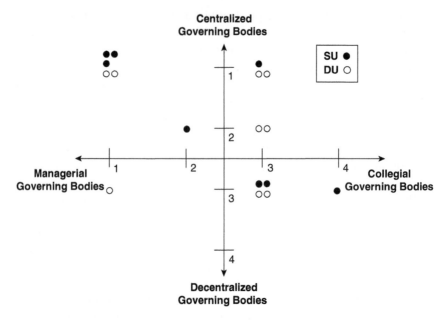

Figure 4.3. Governance logics of understanding

committee's request to clarify which measures... follow from the official governmental report and which planning intervals should be considered. Irrespective of that, upcoming decisions and actions from the state should also be further ascertained' (DU protocol 2003-07-03-604, topic 12). Two months later, this conversation of understanding is followed by a conversation for initiation, as 'the university executive board specifies the structure development plan for the planning and the statutory committee. A further discussion and elaboration of the plan is set on the agenda for the next meetings of the two committees' (DU protocol 2003-09-25-606, topic 12). Clearly, the committees could not enter conversations of performance without further information on the upcoming reorganization and an adjustment of their agenda.

But committees do not simply ask for clarification, they are frequently addressed themselves for a more detailed explanation of their plans. For example, the committee for statutory issues is challenged by the department councils at SU University. 'The department councils raise concerns about the division of research and teaching and especially about the introduction of schools. In the following discussion, the committee's proposal for the transition to schools is further explained and elaborated' (SU protocol 2004-09-28, topic 7-C). Besides, in 2003, the university executive board at SU University asks for more information from decentralized collegial bodies and states that 'the communication with department councils must be enforced, especially in regard to core issues of teaching and research... The university executive board and the department councils [then] arrange a regular meeting to figure out further implications of the reorganization for the core issues' (SU protocol 2003-11-13, topic 8). Thus, department councils are asking committees, committees question the university executive board, and the executive board is asking department councils for additional sensemaking on the initiated conversations. Although related to different issues, every organizational level seeks a common understanding of the issues at hand. This behaviour is essential since polyphonic interpretation of issues may lead to problems when acting on these issues later on (Sullivan and McCarthy 2008).

Centralized and focused communication takes place during understanding at both universities, as well. These couplings of sensemaking are constituted by the university executive board asking the government for clarification of the initiated conversations. In this regard, the two case universities strongly resemble each other: At SU University, 'the president welcomes the state secretary. The secretary then comments on various measures of the concept for university optimization... The president thanks the secretary for his explanations and poses questions on several issues' (SU protocol 2003-12-11, topic 5). At DU University, 'the president welcomes the state's senator for science. The president then repeats core implications of the concept for university development and points out some critical open issues' (DU protocol 2003-05-22-602, only topic). In what follows, the president and the senator seek clarification on these issues. These centralized, focused conversations of understanding take place in early periods of change, in 2003 and 2004. Accordingly, there is a huge effort from centralized bodies to align their voices, at first.

4.4.3. Calling for Action: Top-Heavy Governance in Conversations of Performance

Conversations of performance constitute by far the majority of couplings in both reorganizations. As Gioia and Chittipeddi (1991) point out, these conversations are strongly associated with top-down sensegiving of centralized governing bodies. Accordingly, we see top-heavy governance logic favoured in this stage of change. Conversations of performance are dominated by centralized governing bodies, both professional and democratic (see Figure 4.4). These conversations are performative in that they change a situation, bring forth a structure, or otherwise alter a logic. It is their propositional content that already envisions changes to come (Taylor and Cooren 1997). Therefore, any commitment to a comprehensive reorganization, such as the ones in our cases, necessarily takes place in conversations of performance.

The following examples show how organizational change is talked into existence (Robichaud et al. 2004; Weick et al. 2005). In particular, we

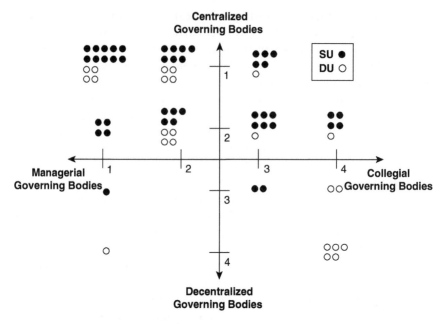

Figure 4.4.   Governance logics of performance

see organizational structures emerge in discussion and then are put into action by assigning personnel to the as yet 'empty boxes' in the organization chart. Consider the case of SU University where 'the university executive board calls upon department executive boards to implement the new internal school structures' (SU protocol 2005-08-29, topic 5). Immediately, 'the university supervisory board... urges the president to take all steps necessary to implement operational school structures, as soon as possible' (SU protocol 2005-09-21, topic 4). In October 2005, the three schools are formally implemented by a new statutory document. But it takes until August 2006 when the president reports that 'the university executive board and the department executive boards have reached consensus on how to assign deans for school executive boards' and immediately 'devises department executive boards to implement the staffing commissions' (SU protocol 2006-08-02, topic 3). Similarly, at DU University, the selection of deans takes place two months after the six schools are legally established by an interim statutory document (DU protocol 2005-01-20-624, topic 4). Thus, and in both cases, conversations of performance include top-down patterns for the allocation of human resources long after organizational structures are formally redefined. By staffing the bodies, conversations of performance literally put organizational structures into action.

Next to the dominant top-heavy governance logics, DU University also relies on democratic bottom-heavy governance logic to bring about change. For the most part, these are conversations where department councils formulate guidelines for diversity, legislative periods, and disciplinary composition of prospective school councils (e.g., DU protocol 2004-11-25-622, topic 16). This difference in governance logics may have several possible reasons. First, DU University could have further democratic procedural rules or a more collegial discussion culture than SU University. However, our data does not support such a systematical difference in governance logics for all types of conversations. Second, the reorganization's scope at DU University could have forced centralized bodies to delegate more action to decentralized bodies. At DU, one single school has the size of the entire SU University. Thus, effectiveness might be enhanced by the higher awareness of critical issues during conversations of performance at the decentralized bodies. Even though this explanation seems rational, we find no such explicit reasoning in the conversations. Third, the lack of department closure may enable decentralized performance conversations at DU University, while department closures cause resistance among decentralized bodies at SU University. The closing of scientific disciplines indeed evokes such strong conflict at SU that the president feels urged to 'recall professors that they are tenured public officials and resistance would lead to official sanctioning... The president recommends to the one's opposing the reorganization either to mentally resign or to directly call for a relocation' (SU protocol 2004-05-26, topic 4). With such resistance, decentralized performance conversations are most likely to fail to correspond to external pressures for change (Ford et al. 2008). Thus, centralized bodies are somehow forced to take the lead through top-heavy governance logics at SU University.

4.4.4. Oscillating Back: The Question of Power in Conversations of Closure

First and foremost, closure is achieved by either managerial or outside-in couplings (see Figure 4.5). Conversations of closure bring organizational change full circle back to the governing bodies that put issues on the agenda in the first place. This finding is in line with the theoretical argument that it takes powerful actors to coordinate and control discourse (Hardy and Philips 2004; Philips et al. 2004). At DU University, we primarily find centralized managerial bodies engaged in conversations of closure. In other words, a small group of organizational members tells the periphery that 'change is complete'. For example, the university executive board closes the discussion on the size of school executive boards by 'keeping the interim statutory document unmodified' (DU protocol 2006-02-09-637, topic 9). This form of power is primarily

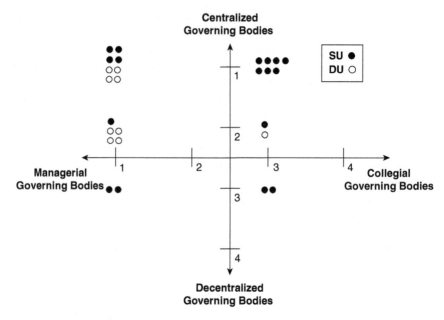

Figure 4.5. Governance logics of closure

grounded in formal competencies and hierarchy structures (Finkelstein 1992). Conversely, in 2004 'the university executive board rejects the government's plans, because the extensive autonomy of schools is expected to be disadvantageous for the university as a whole' (DU protocol 2004-05-27-614, topic 4). Clearly, this control of the discourse is not rooted in hierarchy, because the government has higher authority than the university executive board. It could be explained by the status of the president (Finkelstein 1992) as a spokesman for the university at large. Still, in both examples, further discussion of the issue is (temporarily) ended by the president 'putting his foot down'.

Conversations of closure at SU University are more diverse. Next to the top heavy professional governance logic, we see much participation by collegial governing bodies in final reports on the completion of the reorganization. However, as exemplified in the dissent on the number of schools, conversations of closure from committees have little or no impact if centralized managerial bodies are last to close an issue and not bound to collegial assessments. Formally, this is the case for all committee closures since their competency is restricted to decision preparation and support. Nonetheless, they still have considerable power in that they provide alternative scenarios to choose from. This influence is best illustrated when the university executive board asks the statutory committee to 'evaluate the assignment of decision authority and the division of work among the three schools' (in SU protocol 2005-08-29, topic 5). Four months later, one out of two proposals 'is applied for the future election process of school executive boards' (in SU protocol 2005-12-07, topic 7). As discursive knowledge and power are inseparable (Alveson and Kärreman 2000; Foucault 1980), committees exercise their power by formulating alternatives that are grounded in more detailed expert knowledge on certain issues than the bodies possess who formally have decision authority.

Decentralized governing bodies only bring change to an end in bottom-up couplings in some instances at SU University. For example, the school councils give an account of their constitutive meetings to the university executive board (SU protocol 2006-08-02, topic 3); or, the school executive boards define their final nomenclature after the schools are legally established (SU protocol 2005-10-26, topic 3). In both examples, closure from decentralized bodies is primarily related to issues of comparatively minor significance. Hence, the power of decentralized bodies to initiate and to close important conversations is limited. This finding suggests that the structural power of hierarchy is dominant in both comprehensive reorganizations. In the end, conversations oscillate back to central bodies that initiated them in the first place.

4.5. CONCLUSION

Research on higher education institutions conceptualizes change as a reaction to the pressures of NPM (e.g., Mayer and Ziegele 2009; Schimank 2005), thus addressing the misalignment of organizational structures and perceived environmental demands. Unfortunately, this perspective leaves open the question of how organizations actually govern change. We have presented a framework that remedies the shortcoming of previous research. Based on the notion of universities as loosely coupled systems of governing bodies, we have analysed conversations of change at two universities. Finally, we were able to show that these conversations oscillate through the organization as managerial and collegial governing bodies participate in communication.

Organizational change starts with a limited participation in conversations of initiation, displays diverse engagement in understanding, boosts the broadest integration of governing bodies in performance, and comes full circle with a medium diversity in conversations of closure. Although neither one of these conversations of change accounts for an exclusive governance logic, we see logics with a specific purpose dominate each stage of organizational change: top-heavy professional dissemination of issues in conversations of initiation; polyphony for developing a common understanding; top-heavy governance when calling for action; and the relevance of power in conversations of closure. Conversations of change are pervaded by a number of other logics, too, which highlights once more why universities are frequently conceptualized as organized anarchies (Cohen et al. 1972). Our framework nonetheless shows great heuristic value for the interpretation of the reorganization of two universities. Its application provides both generic and idiosyncratic findings.

Finally, we would like to point out two open issues that were not at the centre of this chapter. The first one is about the interplay between intended and emergent change and the second is concerned with the effects between different levels of analysis. In both regards, we see that our study may provide orientation for further research.

First, we have conceptually combined two communication models of organizational change and extended their classification of governing bodies involved in conversations of change. By doing so, we provided conceptual clarity for the application of the models in a university setting. Still, more research is needed to examine the relationship between intended episodic organizational change represented by the four stages of Ford and Ford (1995) and emergent continuous change as proposed by Weick and Quinn (1999). While episodic change results from external pressures, continuous change originates internally and is driven by organizational instability. Let us briefly illustrate this for the SU University. Four years after the constitution of the three schools, a fourth school was founded. It is devoted to teaching and research in the field of sustainability and originates in an interdisciplinary initiative of the university itself. Studying such emergent developments in universities could complement the derived characteristics of governing logics, as it probably results in other patterns with different characteristics. It might also be fruitful for a deeper understanding of the relation between intentional and emergent change—a central issue in management research on organizational change in general (Pettigrew et al. 2001).

Second, our chapter focuses on relations between governing bodies instead of only using attributional data: it emphasizes communication instead of legal competencies. We offer a framework that allows for an observation of dynamics in university governance, which have received too little study so far. However, while providing clarity for the micro level of university governance, we did not examine how these patterns of communication relate to the discourse on university governance at the macro level of analysis. The mutual interplay between these two levels is especially interesting, not least because most developed countries have currently made a shift away from collegial, participative self-governance towards managerial, business-like forms of governance (de Boer et al. 2007). How micro-level phenomena correspond to macro-level shifts is a central issue on the research agenda of sociological institutionalism (Powell and Colyvas 2008). We think that higher education is a very suitable setting for the analysis of such micro-macro relations and hope that our approach can inform future research in this regard.

ACKNOWLEDGEMENTS

This research is supported by a grant from the German Federal Ministry of Education and Research (Grant No. 01PW11018)

REFERENCES

Albert, S. (1983). 'The Sense of Closure', in K. Gergen, and M. Gergen (eds) *Historical SocialPsychology*. Hillsdale: Erlbaum, 159–172.

Alvesson, M. and Kärreman, D. (2000). 'Taking the Linguistic Turn in Organizational Research: Challenges, Responses, Consequences', *The Journal of Applied Behavioral Science*, 36(2): 136–158.

Birnbaum, R. (1989). 'The Latent Organizational Functions of the Academic Senate: Why Senates do not Work but Will not Go Away', *The Journal of Higher Education*, 60(4): 423–443.

Birnbaum, R. (2004). 'The End of Shared Governance: Looking Ahead or Looking Back', *New Directions for Higher Education*, (127): 5–22.

Bleiklie, I. and Kogan, M. (2007). 'Organization and Governance of Universities', *Higher Education Policy*, 20(4): 477–493.

Bleiklie, I. and Lange, S. (2010). 'Competition and Leadership as Drivers in German and Norwegian University Reforms', *Higher Education Policy*, 23(2): 173–193.

Bradshaw, P. and Fredette, C. (2009). 'Academic Governance of Universities: Reflections of a Senate Chair on Moving from Theory to Practice and Back', *Journal of Management Inquiry*, 18(2): 123–133.

Bryman, A. (2007). 'Effective Leadership in Higher Education: A Literature Review', *Studies in Higher Education*, 32(6): 693–710.

Chandler, A. D. (1991). 'The Functions of the HQ Unit in the Multibusiness Firm', *Strategic Management Journal*, 12(S2): 31–50.

Cohen, M. D., March, J. G., and Olsen, J. P. (1972). 'A Garbage Can Model of Organizational Choice', *Administrative Science Quarterly*, 17(1): 1–25.

Cooren, F., Kuhn, T. R., Cornelissen, J. P., and Clark, T. (2011). 'Communication, Organizing and Organization: An Overview and Introduction to the Special Issue', *Organization Studies*, 32(9): 1–22.

de Boer, H., Enders, J., and Schimank, U. (2007). 'On the Way towards New Public Management? The Governance of University Systems in England, the Netherlands, Austria, and Germany', in D. Jansen (eds.), *New Forms of Governance in Research Organizations*. Dordrecht: Springer Netherlands, 137–152.

Dutton, J. E. (1986). 'Understanding Strategic Agenda Building and its Implications for Managing Change', *Scandinavian Journal of Management Studies*, 3(1): 3–24.

Dutton, J. E. and Ashford, S. J. (1993). 'Selling Issues to Top Management', *Academy of Management Review*, 18(3): 397–428.

Eckel, P. D. and Kezar, A. J. (2003). *Taking the Reins: Institutional Transformation in Higher Education*. Westport: Praeger.

Eisenhardt, K. M. (1989). 'Building Theories from Case Study Research', *Academy of Management Review*, 14(4): 532–550.

Eisenhardt, K. and Graebner, M. (2007). 'Theory Building from Cases: Opportunities and Challenges', *Academy of Management Journal*, 50(1): 25.

Finkelstein, S. (1992). 'Power in Top Management Teams: Dimensions, Measurement, and Validation', *Academy of Management Journal*, 35(3): 505–538.

Ford, J. D. (1999). 'Organizational Change as Shifting Conversations', *Journal of Organizational Change Management*, 12(6): 480–500.

Ford, J. D., and Ford, L. W. (1995). 'The Role of Conversations in Producing Intentional Change in Organizations', *Academy of Management Review*, 20(3): 541–570.

Ford, J. D., Ford, L. W., and D'Amelio, A. (2008). 'Resistance to Change: The Rest of the Story', *Academy of Management Review*, 33(2): 362–377.

Foucault, M. (1980). *Power/Knowledge: Selected Interviews and Other Writings, 1972–1977*, ed. C. Gordon, 3rd ed. New York: Harvester Press.

Gioia, D. A., and Chittipeddi, K. (1991). 'Sensemaking and Sensegiving in Strategic Change Initiation', *Strategic Management Journal*, 12(6): 433–448.

Gioia, D. A. and Thomas, J. B. (1996). 'Identity, Image, and Issue Interpretation: Sensemaking during Strategic Change in Academia', *Administrative Science Quarterly*, 41(3): 370–403.

Gioia, D. A., Thomas, J. B., Clark, S. M., and Chittipeddi, K. (1994). 'Symbolism and Strategic Change in Academia: The Dynamics of Sensemaking and Influence', *Organization Science*, 5(3): 363–383.

Goold, M. and Campbell, A. (2002). 'Parenting in Complex Structures', *Long Range Planning*, 35(3): 219–243.

Goold, M., Campbell, A., and Alexander, M. (1994). *Corporate Level Strategy: Creating Value in the Multibusiness Company*. New York: Wiley.

Gornitzka, A. S. E. and Larsen, I. M. (2004). 'Towards Professionalisation? Restructuring of Administrative Work Force in Universities', *Higher Education*, 47(4): 455–471.

Gumport, P. J. (2000). 'Academic Restructuring: Organizational Change and Institutional Imperatives', *Higher Education*, 39(1): 67–91.

Hardy, C. and Phillips, N. (2004). 'Discourse and Power', in D. Grant, C. Hardy, C. Oswick, and L. L. Putnam (eds), *The Sage Handbook of Organizational Discourse*. London, UK: Sage, 299–316.

Huy, Q. N. (2001). 'Time, Temporal Capability, and Planned Change', *Academy of Management Review*, 26(4): 601–623.

Kornberger, M., Clegg, S. R., and Carter, C. (2006). 'Rethinking the Polyphonic Organization: Managing as Discursive Practice', *Scandinavian Journal of Management*, 22(1): 3–30.

Krücken, G. (2003). 'Learning the 'New, New Thing': On the Role of Path Dependency in University Structures', *Higher Education*, 46(3): 315–339.

Lutz, F. W. (1982). 'Tightening up Loose Coupling in Organizations of Higher Education', *Administrative Science Quarterly*, 27(4): 653–669.

Mayer, P. and Ziegele, F. (2009). 'Competition, Autonomy and New Thinking: Transformation of Higher Education in Federal Germany', *Higher Education Management and Policy*, 21(2): 1–20.

McLaughlin, J. B. (2004). 'Leadership, Management, and Governance', *New Directions for Higher Education*, (128): 5–13.

Meyer, A. D., Goes, J. B., and Brooks, G. R. (1993). 'Organizations Reacting to Hyperturbulence', in G. P. Huber and W. H. Glick (eds.) *Organization Change and Redesign*. New York: Oxford University Press, 66–111.

Middlehurst, R. (2004). 'Changing Internal Governance: A Discussion of Leadership Roles and Management Structures in UK Universities', *Higher Education Quarterly*, 58(4): 258–279.

Minor, J. T. (2003). 'Assessing the Senate: Critical Issues Considered', *American Behavioral Scientist*, 46(7): 960–977.

Mora, J.-G. (2001). 'International Seminar on University Governance and Management: An Overview', *Tertiary Education and Management*, 7(4): 91–93.

Orton, J. D. and Weick, K. E. (1990). 'Loosely Coupled Systems: A Reconceptualization', *Academy of Management Review*, 15(2): 203–223.

Paul, D. A. (2005). 'Higher Education in Competitive Markets: Literature on Organizational Decline and Turnaround', *The Journal of General Education*, 54(2): 106–138.

Pettigrew, A. (1990). 'Longitudinal Field Research on Change: Theory and Practice', *Organization Science*, 1(3): 267–292.

Pettigrew, A., Woodman, R., and Cameron, K. (2001). 'Studying Organizational Change and Development: Challenges for Future Research', *Academy of Management Journal*, 44(4): 697–713.

Philips, N., Lawrence, T. B., and Hardy, C. (2004). 'Discourse and Institutions', *Academy of Management Review*, 29(4): 635–652.

Pollitt, C. and Bouckaert, G. (2011). *Public Management Reform: A Comparative Analysis—New Public Management, Governance, and the Neo-Weberian State*. New York: Oxford University Press.

Porras, J. and Silvers, R. (1991). 'Organization Development and Transformation', *Annual Review of Psychology*. 42(1): 51–78.

Powell, W. W. and Colyvas, J. A. (2008). 'Microfoundations of Institutional Theory', in R. Greenwood, C. Oliver, K. Sahlin, and R. Suddaby (eds.) *The Sage Handbook of Organizational Institutionalism*. London: Sage Publications, 276–298.

Robichaud, D., Giroux, H., and Taylor, J. R. (2004). 'The Metaconversation: The Recursive Property of Language as a Key to Organizing', *Academy of Management Review*, 29(4): 617–634.

Rubin, I. S. (1979). 'Retrenchment, Loose Structure and Adaptibility in the University', *Sociology of Education*, 52(4): 211–222.

Salancik, G. R. and Pfeffer, J. (1974). 'The Bases and Use of Power in Organizational Decision Making: The Case of a University', *Administrative Science Quarterly*, 19(4): 453–473.

Schimank, U. (2005). '"New Public Management" and the Academic Profession: Reflections on the German Situation', *Minerva*, 43(4): 361–376.

Shattock, M. (1999). 'Governance and Management in Universities: the Way we Live Now', *Journal of Education Policy*, 14(3): 271–282.

Shotter, J. (2008). 'Dialogism and Polyphony in Organizing Theorizing in Organization Studies: Action Guiding Anticipations and the Continuous Creation of Novelty', *Organization Studies*, 29(4): 501–524.

Simsek, H. (1997). 'Metaphorical Images of an Organization: The Power of Symbolic Constructs in Reading Change in Higher Education Organizations', *Higher Education*, 33(3): 283–307.

Slaughter, S. and Rhoades, G. (2004). *Academic Capitalism and the New Economy: Markets, State, and Higher Education*. Baltimore: The Johns Hopkins University Press.

Smirchich, L. and Stubbart, C. (1985). 'Strategic Management in an Enacted World', *Academy of Management Review*, 10(4): 724–736.

Stubbart, C. I. and Smalley, R. D. (1999). 'The Deceptive Allure of Stage Models of Strategic Processes', *Journal of Management Inquiry*, 8(3): 273–286.

Sullivan, P. and McCarthy, J. (2008). 'Managing the Polyphonic Sounds of Organizational Truths', *Organization Studies*, 29(4): 525–541.

Taylor, J. R. and Cooren, F. (1997). 'What Makes Communication `Organizational'?', *Journal of Pragmatics*, 27(4): 409–438.

Taylor, J. R. and Van Every, E. J. (2000). *The Emergent Organization: Communication as its Site and Surface*. Mahwah, NJ: Erlbaum.

Van de Ven, A. H. and Poole, M. S. (1995). 'Explaining Development and Change in Organizations', *Academy of Management Review*, 20(3): 510–540.

Vaughan, D. (1992). 'Theory Elaboration: the Heuristics of Case Analysis', in C. C. Ragin and H. S. Becker (eds), *What is a Case? Exploring the Foundations of Social Inquiry*. New York: Cambridge University Press, 173–202.

Weick, K. E. (1976). 'Educational Organizations as Loosely Coupled Systems', *Administrative Science Quarterly*, 21(1): 1–19.

Weick, K. E. (1979). *The Social Psychology of Organizing*, 2nd ed. Reading, MA: Addison-Wesley.

Weick, K. E., and Quinn, R. E. (1999). 'Organizational Change and Development', *Annual Review of Psychology*, 50: 361–386.

Weick, K. E., Sutcliffe, K. M., and Obstfeld, D. (2005). 'Organizing and the Process of Sensemaking', *Organization Science*, 16(4): 409–421.

Whitchurch, C. (2004). 'Administrative Managers—A Critical Link', *Higher Education Quarterly*, 58(4): 280–298.

Yin, R. K. (2009). *Case Study Research*, 4th ed. Los Angeles et al.: Sage.

5

Institutional Pressure as a Trigger for Organizational Identity Change

The Case of Accreditation Failure within Seven European Business Schools

Christophe Lejeune and Alain Vas

5.1. INTRODUCTION

Since the late 1990s, business schools have been confronted by the growing institutional influence of accreditation standards, among which the most famous internationally are AACSB, EQUIS, and AMBA. As of December 2011, there were 643 AACSB accredited schools in 43 countries, 135 EQUIS accredited schools in 38 countries, and 189 AMBA accredited programmes in 81 countries. However, we know very little about the organizational consequences of accreditation standards for business schools. In a provocative essay, Julian and Ofori-Dankwa (2006) have suggested that AACSB accreditation processes may hinder business schools' abilities to adapt to changing environments. In reaction, some authors have responded by showing the benefits and value of AACSB (Romero 2008; Zammuto 2008) and EQUIS (Urgel 2007). In addition, a few comparative studies of existing accreditation schemes have been conducted to highlight their similarities and differences (Roller, Andrews and Bovee 2003; Stensaker and Harvey 2006). Progressively, accreditation standards have led to building an organizational field that confers both legitimacy and social identity on the accredited schools. On the one hand, legitimacy appears to be fundamental for business schools (Durand and McGuire 2005) as well as other organizations (Deephouse 1999). Indeed, accredited organizations ensure that they are congruent with social expectations and professional norms. Nevertheless, accreditation may represent a threat to diversity of business schools in higher education (Proitz, Stensaker and Harvey 2004). Indeed, accreditation standards have a strong influence on business schools and are suspected of pushing them towards mimetic strategies and isomorphism, with limited possibilities for voluntary innovative strategies (Julian and Ofori-Dankwa 2006). On the other hand, accreditation development leads to the creation of two strategic groups of business schools: the accredited schools and non-accredited schools. In line with Peteraf and Shanley's (1997) idea that managers cognitively partition their industry environment, any accreditation creates a group, in which merely belonging—visible through a label—is sufficient for accredited schools to gain a new social identity by being in the same group as 'top quality schools'. Based on these conjectures, schools that have failed to become accredited deserve special attention since they have been faced with both a legitimacy threat and identity discrepancy. To our knowledge, very few studies have been conducted on the consequences of accreditation failure. This research thus aims to fill this gap and it focuses on business schools that once failed to get accredited and decided to re-apply to be accredited later. More precisely, we focus on three questions. (1) Why do business schools not leave the accreditation exercise after a first failure? (2) What dimension of their identity changes during these schools' reapplication period? (3) How do these schools' identities change during the accreditation process? In doing so, we hope to partially answer Julian and Ofori-Dankwa's (2006) call for more research on accreditation stakes.

This paper presents a comparison of multiple case studies of identity changes within seven European business schools that first failed to get EQUIS accreditation until a new application succeeded. The access we were granted to these schools' confidential reports and key actors represents a unique opportunity to better understand the influence of accreditation and subsequent organizational adaptations. In the following section, we present a theoretical framework for accreditation influences on organizational identity. Then, we present our method, and introduce the case studies. Finally, the results are presented and discussed.

5.2. THEORETICAL FRAMEWORK

In recent literature, organizational identity has been increasingly debated (Fiol 2001; Fiol 2002; Hatch and Schultz 2002; Puusa 2006; Ravasi and Schultz 2006; Whetten 2006). Answering the question, 'Who are we as an organization?', the concept of organizational identity has first been defined as the central and enduring attributes of an organization that differentiate it from other organizations

(Albert and Whetten 1985). Many scholars have built on this definition of organizational identity (Dutton and Dukerich 1991; Elsbach and Kramer 1996; Gioia and Thomas 1996). In their study of a university, Albert and Whetten (1985:270) note how central and potentially conflictual elements—utilitarian and ideological—coexist in a university and consequently hybridize its identity by co-locating 'two or more types that would not normally be expected to go together'. Interestingly, these two types of identity have been measured for universities (Gioia and Thomas 1996; Labianca et al. 2001) and seem close to the notion of conflicting institutional logics. More recently, some research has suggested that organizational identity has two components, which are identity claims and identity understandings (Corley and Gioia 2004; Ravasi and Schultz 2006; Whetten and Mackey 2002). Identity claims are defined as affirmations by leaders about who members are as an organization, while identity understandings are defined as beliefs shared by members about who they are as an organization. Nag, Corley and Gioia (2007:843) also make a clear distinction between the labels and the meanings of identity when they affirm that 'identity transformation must go beyond actions taken by leaders and also engage those whose daily practices will be most affected by a new identity'. In a dynamic view of identity (Hatch and Schultz 2002; Gioia, Schultz and Corley 2000), past research suggests that feedbacks from external audiences have a direct influence on organizational identity. In that regard, any failure by business schools to get accredited represents an identity discrepancy that can act as a trigger for identity change (Ravasi and Schultz 2006). Corley and Gioia (2004) suggest three antecedents to identity change: a change in social referents; temporal identity discrepancies; and construed external image discrepancies. For business schools, it seems that the rising development of accreditation standards well represents a change in social referents: the group of accredited schools is a new comparison group to which directors and deans cognitively self-categorize their school, progressively building a new strategic group identity (Peteraf and Shanley 1997). Further, business schools that fail to get accredited are even more interesting cases for studying an identity change. First, such schools experience a construed image discrepancy when school members realize that accreditation auditors and external peers have a poor view of their school. Second, these schools may also go through a temporal identity discrepancy when their members are told and realize that they are not as good ('do not meet the standards') as they thought to be in the past. Therefore, business schools that at first failed and then reapply to get accredited will most likely be confronted with an identity change. However, it is not clear what type of identity components are influenced and how organizational identity change occurs.

Acting as a strong institutional pressure, accreditation standards are likely to influence business schools' organizational identity. Indeed, standards embed institutional logics that are likely to trigger an identity formation process within business schools (Stensaker and Norgard 2001). As professional associations, accreditation bodies act through a theorization process (Greenwood, Suddaby and Hinings 2002) to put into standards what business schools 'do' and what it takes to 'be' a business school, therefore impacting their legitimate identities. Accreditation has been defined as a 'process whereby an organization or agency recognizes an education institution or programme as having met certain predetermined qualifications or standards, outlined by the accrediting organization. Inherent in accreditation activities is the process of self-study and evaluation, guided by standards that are written and endorsed by academic peers' (Hedmo 2002:259). Since accreditation is built upon standards, it thus incorporates professional norms that exert a strong institutional influence on organizations—namely business schools—that are part of a same organizational field. Sherer and Lee (2002) define a standard as 'an accepted way of doing things with an arguable technical rationale'. Standards have also been characterized as 'decentralized institutions', for instance the ISO management standards that firms use to reduce problems that might arise with exchange partners who lack information or fear opportunism (King, Lenox and Terlaak 2005). In that regard, institutional theory appears especially interesting in understanding the influences of accreditation on business schools. Institutional theory (Di Maggio and Powel 1983; Oliver 1991) states that organizations in the same organizational field are underdoing isomorphic—coercive, mimetic or normative—pressures to increase their legitimacy. According to this theory, being similar to others is important in order to be socially accepted and remain credible (Deephouse 1999). For instance, Glynn and Abzug (2002) have added the idea of symbolic isomorphism in a study of conformity in organizational names—which they call organizational identities—and have shown how it supports legitimacy. Behind those institutional pressures, there are actually some 'institutional logics' that are 'the basis of taken-for-granted rules guiding behaviour of field-level actors... the belief systems and related practices that predominate in an organizational field' (Reay and Hinings 2009:629). While many authors have suggested that institutional logics may involve organizational adaptation and identity change (Fox-Wolfgramm, Boal and Hunt 1998; Rao, Monin and Durand 2003; Stensaker and Norgard 2001), recent studies have highlighted multiple—possibly conflicting—institutional logics, as reflective of the rising pluralism and diversity in our societies (Glynn, Barr and Dacin 2000; Pache and Santos 2010; Purdy and Gray 2009; Townley 2002). For instance, Thornton (2002) studied higher education publishing from 1958 to 1990 and distinguished between the editorial (professional) logic and the market logic. In research on quality initiatives in U.S. hospitals, Kennedy and Fiss (2009) have shown that social logics aimed at legitimacy and economic logics aimed at performance improvement coexist although they may be conflicting. Greenwood et al. (2010) have emphasized the coexistence of market logic, regional logic and family logic in Spanish firms and show how certain logics are stronger in certain contexts. In these examples, the number of institutional logics and the degree of their incompatibility contribute to an institutional complexity, against which organizational responses may vary (Greenwood et al. 2011). In this research, we focus on the EQUIS accreditation standards that themselves include multiple logics, the influences of which are not obvious to organizations. In particular, the EQUIS accreditation aims at granting a high quality level (selective logic), but at the same time to help schools improve (formative logic) as EQUIS stands for 'EFMD Quality Improvement System'. EQUIS standards are focused on the needs of the corporate world (professional logic) but also on knowledge creation (academic logic), which are two extremes between which the business schools' pendulum has swung during the twentieth century (Zell 2001). Although these logics are not necessarily exclusive, they may generate some tensions within business schools. To our knowledge, the responses of business schools faced with failure in getting accredited and then deciding to re-apply have not yet been much studied. We aim to fill this gap and explore the institutional influence of accreditation standards on organizational identity, by studying the reactions of seven business schools that once failed before reapplying for EQUIS accreditation. The next section elaborates further on our methodology.

5.3. METHODOLOGY

This research is based upon multiple case studies (Eisenhardt 1989; Eisenhardt and Graebner 2007; Leonard-Barton 1990; Yin 2003). In general, multiple cases are preferred over single-case designs so as to improve the external validity (Dul and Hak 2008). Case studies are the preferred research strategy (1) for 'how' and 'why' questions, (2) when there is little control over events, and (3) when there is a focus on a contemporary phenomenon within some real-life context (Yin 2003). In particular, we focus on European business schools that first failed to get accredited, decided to re-apply and succeeded afterwards in getting the EQUIS accreditation. This choice appears interesting in many respects. First, European business schools seem to have received less attention than their American counterparts (Antunes and Thomas 2007). Second, focusing on schools that first failed an accreditation makes sense in a study of identity change. Indeed, such an accreditation failure may be viewed as an identity discrepancy acting as a trigger for change. Third, focusing on schools that failed and got accredited afterwards helps to maintain the focus on a similar limited timeframe between a failure and a success.

Among the worldwide EQUIS-accredited schools, 41 schools agreed to grant us confidential access to their internal and accreditation reports. Among these, seven European business schools had failed to obtain their first accreditation. For Eisenhardt (1989), a number between four and ten case studies is preferred. Therefore, we chose to make an analysis of these seven European business schools. Due to sensitivities about risks to reputation, the participating schools have been assured of strict confidentiality and anonymity. The failure criterion for their selection was not formally emphasized in the presentation of the research project. Rather, the research was introduced as focusing on 'organizational change during the accreditation process'.

In each school, we spent at least one week on site in 2008. After a first contact with the accreditation manager, we asked to meet about ten people for an interview. The criteria for being an interviewee were that they should: (1) cover the functions or positions of research, teaching and programmes, school management, international relations, corporate affairs, or student services; (2) be a member of faculty or administrative staff; (3) where possible, to have been working in the school for at least 10 years. For the seven schools, we conducted 76 interviews of an hour, on average. These interviews were transcribed and coded. In line with the theoretical framework, a first coding grid was built to classify interview quotes in three categories: (1) EQUIS accreditation (context, content, process); (2) organizational change (resources and activities); and (3) organizational identity (understandings and claims).

Through the coding process, the grid has been improved in an emergent and iterative way. For instance, the category for identity understandings has been progressively divided into three main subcategories (international–local, academic–corporate, formal–informal). For each case study, facts have been positioned on a time line, allowing us to build comparative temporal matrixes (Miles and Huberman 1994) and find underlying mechanisms (Pettigrew 2012). Further, schools' public information (website, brochures, etc.) as well as confidential documents related to the EQUIS process (data sheets, self-assessment reports) were also used. In order to increase the reliability of the data, a triangulation was made between these sources, and with peer review reports, awarding body letters and discussion with experts from the EQUIS team. In particular, our triangulation method consisted in checking the coherence of data gathered through interviews with other sources, either interviews or documents written by EFMD (audit reports, awarding body decision letters) or schools (data sheets, self-assessment reports, progress reports). Together, these data have captured the main features of each case and improved our understanding of them.

5.4. CASE STUDIES

As the seven schools have to remain anonymous, they have first been classified from the oldest first failure to the most recent one. The seven schools that have been studied are located in four different European countries. Each school has been attributed a fictional name going from ES01 to ES07. Table 5.1 summarizes the first application to EQUIS for the seven schools. Among them, four schools were initially neither university-based nor focused on research, but were, rather, focused on teaching with a strong corporate orientation. We present these as four professional schools ('Prof.'): ES01, ES02, ES03 and ES06.

The three other schools are university-based and had been used to conduct research activities before they started the EQUIS procedure. Table 5.1 also includes the recommendations from the peer review committee (PRC) explaining the first failure to EQUIS accreditation. Some of the schools received a letter with a notice of formal failure (ES01, ES02, ES03, and ES05), while others were advised not to formally apply for the awarding body's final decision (ES04, ES06, and ES07), which we assimilated to a first failure, as confirmed by our interviews.

Among the seven schools, some went through a 'guided development' after the initial failure. It consisted in support offered by EFMD to help schools improve on the dimensions mentioned in a previous assessment. In particular, the guided development encompasses visits and reports of an EFMD-based consultant, advising what types of change to support and which priorities to establish. In our set of schools, three schools—ES03, ES05, and ES06—went through such a 'guided development' over periods from one to three years. In addition, ES04 went through EQUIP in 2000. In contrast to EQUIS, EQUIP (European Quality Improvement Programme) consists in an analysis with self-assessment and peer review visits but only to find ways of improvement, without any accreditation at the end (EQUIP has now closed). As ES04 actually applied for EQUIP in 2000, the fact that they were not yet ready for EQUIS accreditation was not that surprising. As the accreditation manager at ES04 claims, 'they [the reviewers] advised that some areas needed to be improved in order to meet the standards. And we just started working on that basically'. However, considering the nature and extent of advice given by EQUIP at this time, it seemed interesting to keep ES04 in our set of case studies. We thus took the feedback from EQUIP as a negative quality assessment for ES04 that involved an identity discrepancy.

We present the original story of our seven business schools below. Although it is difficult to summarize the empirical richness of several cases in a few paragraphs, we hope to help the reader understand the main features of the case studies. For each school, a title suggests the main changes that were implemented between the first failure and the first EQUIS accreditation.

Table 5.1. Overall description of the first application to EQUIS within the seven schools

School	School type	First failure	PRC recommendations	Event type	EFMD support	First EQUIS
ES01	Prof.	1998	Management committee MBA strategy Intellectual capital	Formal failure	/	2000
ES02	Prof.	1999	Faculty size and profile Research Internationalization	Formal failure	/	2000
ES03	Prof.	1999	Research and development Faculty role, involvement and composition Organization and management	Formal failure	Guided Dvlpmt 1999	2000
ES04	Univ.	2000	Mission, vision and strategic plans Governance, alumni Formal programme monitoring Evaluation and review Learning and personal development Time spent on research Faculty management	Advice to develop certain areas	EQUIP program 2000	2006
ES05	Univ.	2001	Clarification of governance structure and decision making Faculty quality and quantity Internationalization Executive education consistent with strategy and resources	Formal failure	Guided Dvlpmt 02–05	2006

| ES06 | Prof. | 2001 | Research
Faculty quality and management
Internationalization
Programmes' coherence, monitoring | Advice not to apply | Guided Dvlpmt 02–04 | 2006 |
| ES07 | Univ. | 2003 | Internationalization of the faculty
Marketing and communication
Courses in English
International content for courses
New pedagogical approach undertaken by faculty at large
Corporate involvement in the school and decision-making
Links with alumni association
A clearly redefined mission statement | Advice not to apply | / | 2006 |

(*) Source: Peer Review Committee's (PRC) reports.

5.4.1. ES01: Creating a Management Structure and Strengthening Research

As a pioneer for EQUIS, ES01 started the accreditation process in 1998 when it had 43 full-time faculty and approximately 2200 students. Its director had prepared for the accreditation process well with the creation of two work groups involving 46 persons during 8 months. Against all expectations, ES01 failed to obtain the EQUIS label. The reasons given by the auditors were three. First, a management committee was needed to cover several programmes that were more or less autonomous. Second, the MBA strategy had to be rebuilt in a more coherent way, avoiding its dispersion across several programmes that had been created as opportunities arose. Finally, auditors also required that ES01 invests more in its intellectual capital and research activities. This was a real challenge for ES01 as its origin was based precisely in its opposition to the university model. In less than a year, the direction of ES01 launched important changes to respond to these recommendations: three management committees were created; the MBA was strengthening and separated from executive education; and several policies aimed at promoting research were introduced (seven new professors were recruited, 25 per cent of time was allocated to research, and a three year research plan was required for faculty, etc.). These deep and rapid changes impressed the auditors greatly in 2000, and allowed ES01 to get the EQUIS label.

5.4.2. ES02: Developing a Sense of Mission and Building Research Capability

As a department of a Chamber of Commerce and Industry (CCI), ES02 had always been anchored in the local context of SMEs. In 1998, the school had 38 full-time faculty and approximately 1700 students. During the 1990s, ES02 had several programmes that were not well positioned at the European level. As a professor told us, 'at this time, the school was like a bunch of flowers' as programme directors had a lot of freedom to seed and let blossom new programmes. The director of ES02 then saw the EQUIS accreditation as a way of creating changes within the school. He created two work groups that involved 74 employees over three months, and nominated the associate director as the EQUIS project leader. The failure, in 1999, to get accreditation with EQUIS revealed three weaknesses: the small size and poor quality of faculty; poor research; and weak internationalization. Following this feedback, the CCI director came to the school and made a threatening speech to the school's members about the consequences if ES02 did not get EQUIS next time. From that moment, the director of ES02 spent a lot of time reassuring staff and explaining the importance of accreditation. He also had to manage a latent tension with CCI since EQUIS could be perceived by CCI as a means for the school to escape its control. In less than a year, ES02 launched big changes to obtain EQUIS: it recruited nine new professors; core faculty saw their time for research increased to 50 per cent; created incentives for research; created an international committee for research; and new strategic partnerships, among which one was for an MBA programme. During their second visit, the auditors observed a deep commitment to improvement within the school. The EQUIS accreditation was then granted to ES02 for a period of three years.

5.4.3. ES03: Sharing Management Responsibilities and Rocketing Research

Created during the 1980s, ES03 is a young management school that had 43 full-time faculty and approximately 1900 students in 2000. Its innovative character and internal dynamism had contributed to its 'success story', reaching the top of the European rankings. In 1999, in order to maintain its competitive advantage, the direction of ES03 decided to engage in the EQUIS accreditation. Confronted with a first formal refusal, the school learned of three of its areas of weakness from the auditors: the level of research; the role, composition and involvement of Faculty; and the organization and management of the school. ES03 then engaged in a 'guided development' process, with the help of EFMD representatives. Over a year, ES03 went through major change to answer the EQUIS auditors' requirements. First, an ambitious five year programme for research was launched, which included: a mandatory doctorate for Faculty and a minimum level of research time; the recruitment of 14 new professors and doctoral students; the creation of a research steering committee, the creation of a DBA programme with a foreign university; the launch of a series of working papers; the foundation of three research chairs, etc. Second, the role and involvement of core faculty in the school management were strengthened, not only through their improved qualifications, but also by the creation of research committees and five positions for associate directors. At the end of this important transformation, a professor acknowledged that 'after this, we could compare ourselves to others... we were not pirates anymore'. During their second visit, the auditors were impressed by these rapid changes and supported a first EQUIS accreditation for ES03.

5.4.4. ES04: Involving Administrative Staff at the Core of Quality Processes

As a leader institution in its country, ES04 had 150 full time faculty and approximately 20 000 students in the year 2000. Being a faculty within a big university, research has always been part of ES04's mission. Since the 1990s, the school had started an internationalization process and EQUIS appeared as a natural step in 1998. At the time, an expert from EFMD advised the school to start the EQUIP process, which was similar to EQUIS but without granting any label at the end. In 2000, the EQUIP auditors advised the school not to apply to EQUIS as the school appeared not to be ready yet. The auditors identified nine areas where improvements were required. In 2001, a new dean with an entrepreneurial approach was elected. Between 2001 and 2006, several changes happened in the school: a Vice-dean for International Relations was created; a pedagogic centre was founded, an 'Executive MBA' was launched; alumni associations were merged; the first IT manager was recruited; there was massive recruitment of administrative staff, mainly among graduate students; an IT-based monitoring and quality assurance system was developed; research institutes were created, etc. This period was perceived as a time of collective enthusiasm around a strong and dynamic administrative core, with the motivation to improve quality at the school. It also increased greatly the expenses of the school. In 2006, EQUIS auditors observed the implemented changes and ES04 was accredited. This was viewed as a crown for the school and a real European and international recognition.

5.4.5. ES05: Redefining the School's Scope and Structure

Being part of a university, ES05 has been created in the 1980s. In 2001, it had some 98 full time faculty and approximately 4500 students. Historically, ES05 was born out of the collaboration between five departments from the faculty of social sciences. Each department could act independently of the school on issues unrelated to management programmes. In 2001, a new dean was elected and decided to launch the school into EQUIS accreditation. The Dean prepared all the documents with a close collaborator. However, ES05 failed to get certification from EQUIS. The auditors had five main concerns and required five areas be improved in the school. From that moment, the Dean decided to enter into a 'guided development' process with the support of EFMD. At the same time, ES05 launched five master programmes, fully in English so as to promote internationalization. This decision implied that the school lost some students who were attached to programmes in their national language. In 2004, an advisory board was created, as well as a cell for public relationships. A first bachelor programme completely in English was initiated, and a first 'Executive MBA' was launched. In 2005, the scope of the school was redefined. From that moment, the school would be the only management department, while the four other departments were excluded from the school and became strategic partners. This had lasting effects in the school and on people's minds. The school grew also in size with the recruitment of 12 new professors, and improved its quality assurance information gathering. In 2006, ES05 reapplied for EQUIS accreditation and it was granted for the first time.

5.4.6. ES06: Strengthening the School with EQUIS Following a Merger

Following a merger, ES06 had some 50 full-time faculty and approximately 1900 students in the year 2000. Although the merger had just been implemented and had led to 14 professors leaving the school, the director of ES06 decided to participate in EQUIP, with the help of an external consultant, to improve the school's image. During 2001, the school had recruited a lot of people, in particular to replace voluntary leavers. Shortly before the auditors' visit, the director switched from EQUIP to EQUIS. After the auditors visited the school, they mentioned some gaps between the school's situation and its vision, as well as in the field of academic research with regard to EQUIS standards. Other weaknesses concerned the school's internationalization, quality and management of faculty, programmes monitoring and management. The auditors noted that 'the new internal governance structure with several committees and a matrix organization is rather complex and not yet established'. In 2002, the director left the school, and a new director was designated to restore trust within ES06. From 2002 till 2004, the school went into a 'guided development' process with the support of EFMD. During his first presentation to the school, the new director explained that the school was approaching bankruptcy, both on financial and academic levels. Then, he proposed to rebuild the school on the basis of common values, which appeared in brochures, the website, and as posters in the school. Several staff meetings were organized to promote participation, and a delegate for accreditation was designated. Former partnerships that were of low quality were ended, and several programmes that did not fit the school strategy were closed. An MBA programme was created in collaboration with an international partner. A new research policy was activated, and the qualifications of Faculty were improved, mainly through Ph.D. achievements. In 2006, ES06 reapplied to EQUIS accreditation, and was accredited the same year.

5.4.7. ES07: Creating an Organizational Project and Restructuring Research Activities

As a major national player, ES07 belongs to a university with a strong international reputation. In 2000, the school had some 35 full time faculty and approximately 1200 students. Under pressure from the university rector, the

Dean of ES07 announced the future application to EQUIS in 2001. Thanks to a small team who prepared the documents, the school sent its formal letter in 2003. Later on, the EQUIS auditors advised ES07 not to apply yet. Although the comments and critics formulated by the auditors (see Table 5.1) were acknowledged and accepted, the lack of internationalization created a shock at the school. Indeed, ES07 had strongly believed itself to be international enough, but came to realize that its levels of internationalization were not sufficient anymore given the standards at that time.

The Dean then created two workgroups to consider the strategy of the school. Several 'green days' were also organized so as to promote a collective spirit. From 2004 till 2006, the workgroups developed a proposal to restructure research activities around three centres of excellence. In parallel, the Dean proposed a new mission statement for ES07. The tasks of administrative staff were reorganized, and a new employee was recruited to manage corporate relations. An international chair was founded to promote exchanges of professors and to welcome visiting faculty. An advisory board was also created, as well as the position of dean for international relations, a marketing plan and a new name in English. In the school, the change project for the preparation of EQUIS had allowed, at least temporarily, professors' individual objectives to converge with the organizational objective of accreditation. In 2006, ES07 sent its application and was accredited the same year for a three-year period.

5.5. RESULTS

The case studies of EQUIS accreditation in seven European business schools are interesting as they represent specific contexts, hence different evolutions of organizational identity and changes. We present here below the answers to our research questions: (1) Why do business schools not leave the accreditation exercise after a first failure? (2) What dimensions of identity change during the reapplication period for these schools? (3) How do these schools' identities change during the accreditation process? The next section summarizes the research results and provides some illustrative quotes.

First, the reasons why the schools being studied have not left the accreditation process appeared to be linked to particular institutional logics. Through our interviews, we have identified two institutional logics that help understand why the studied schools have re-applied after their first failure: (1) a 'national competition' logic with a strong awareness of national market and rankings where accreditation plays a major role as a differentiating asset; and (2) a 'regional recognition' logic with a strong emphasis on European development and the Bologna reform, where accreditation is viewed as a vehicle for geographical attractiveness.

Table 5.2. Relative strength of institutional logics supporting the EQUIS accreditation

Institutional logic	ES01	ES02	ES03	ES04	ES05	ES06	ES07
National competition	Strong	Strong	Strong	Moderate	Moderate	Strong	Strong
Regional recognition	Weak	Weak	Weak	Strong	Moderate	Weak	Weak

To some extent, these logics are close to the market logic and regional logic suggested by Greenwood et al. (2010). Table 5.2 summarizes the relative perceived importance—based on coding the frequency of quotes—of institutional logics within each studied school.

ES01, ES02, ES03, ES06 and ES07 have a strong 'national competition logic' where the EQUIS accreditation was mainly a means to keep a good position, if not to climb, in national rankings or to keep competitive advantages. The following quotes illustrate that logic:

> But for us, our competitors are [list of four national schools], I mean this is impossible. And you can see that in national rankings, it is all about accreditations. If you do not have it, you lose points in the rankings. (ES01, Programme Director)
>
> That was for a positioning issue on the national market. In my opinion, if there were two dimensions that have been promoted so far with EQUIS, this is the contribution to international quality and positioning on the national market. We need EQUIS to exist on the national market, to keep our status. So far, this is it. (ES02, Head of International Relations)
>
> You know, there is this competition logic among business schools, let's call it in that way. And the fact to be accredited puts you almost mechanically to another level. (ES06, Director of Executive Education)
>
> I think that the underlying logic is clearly market oriented. There is a market. So as to attract the right customers, one needs to sell something that is differentiated... And I think that another argument that has played a role was to keep a membership in international networks, especially for exchange programs, one needed to have the label. (ES07, Professor)

Except for ES06 and ES07, a strong 'national competition' logic seems to explain why the period of change between the first failure and first accreditation was short (between one and two years) for those schools under strong competitive pressures. Although undergoing a strong market competition as well, ES06 was in a particular organizational process of strengthening the school following a recent merger. This may explain why the period before the first failure and accreditation took some five years for ES06. As for ES07, the school felt a pressure to get the EQUIS accreditation so as to remain part of an international network where most members were already EQUIS accredited. For ES07, remaining a member of this network was also a source of competitive advantage on its national market, hence the importance of the accreditation.

ES04 and ES05 have a strong or moderate 'regional recognition' logic where the EQUIS accreditation appears as a way to become more attractive in Europe and at the international level, mainly because of a remote geographical or socio-economic distance from central Europe. This institutional logic is illustrated by the following quotes:

> So, we didn't have a lot of competition practically. No real competition. But what we were really afraid of was that when... the doors for our best students would be opened in the schools in [central] Europe, so that we might be losing those students that actually are the key of quality of programmes. If you have no quality students, you cannot offer quality programmes. So our idea was in order to look at competition actually for the top students, for the top universities in the European Union, this is why we wanted actually to upgrade our quality with processes, with internationalization, working with companies to a level of schools that could be our competitors within European Union. (ES04, Professor)
>
> Because when you come to [this country]... which has a low recognition, people will not recognize [our school] immediately as being a good school. So you have to build your own reputation. (ES04, Associate Professor)
>
> I mean my general goal was to really put [our school's city] on the map. And one way is to go for EQUIS, AACSB, AMBA... you could choose any of these accreditations. (ES05, Head of Marketing Section)
>
> We wanted to be an international business school. We had a strong position in the region, and quite a strong position nationally. But we were unknown internationally. (ES05, Professor)

To some extent, the logics of 'national competition' and 'regional recognition' seem to relate to EQUIS's selective and formative logics. While most schools that were studied have decided to re-apply with a 'national competition' logic, these seem to have followed the selective logic of EQUIS to remain (or become) part of the best national schools. As for schools ES04 and ES05 that reapplied with a 'regional recognition' logic, those appear closer to the formative logic of EQUIS to improve their internal quality. As a matter of fact, ES04 started the improvement process with EQUIP with a clear objective of improving quality first. Do these 'national competition' and 'regional recognition' logics affect the schools' identity change in different ways? We now have to carefully look at the changes in identity claims and understandings to answer this question.

Second, the observed changes in organizational identity are presented separately for identity claims and identity understandings. Concerning identity claims, we observe that the seven schools have not all changed identity statements during the re-application phase. Indeed, ES01, ES02, and ES03 made changes in their identity claims only after having received the EQUIS label. In particular, each of them changed their name after the first accreditation. As for ES04, ES05, ES06, and ES07, they clarified their mission and vision before getting their first EQUIS accreditation. Although a 'national competition' logic could have caused us to assume that identity claims would be more rapidly changed, our case studies seem to confirm that identity claims need more time to change than identity understandings (Gioia, Schultz and Corley 2000). Except for ES06, which was consolidating a recent merger, all these schools with a 'national competition' logic changed their name during the re-application phase (ES07) or after their first accreditation (ES01, ES02, and ES03). The schools with a 'regional recognition' logic took five (ES05) or six (ES04) years to revise some identity statements but did not change their name, either during the re-application or immediately after their first accreditation. Table 5.3 summarizes the changes in identity claims, which means the mission, vision, policy, or school's name.

Concerning identity understandings, the schools being studied appear to have changed in different ways. More precisely, our coding method emphasizes three main dimensions, as the result of an aggregation of our codes through an iterative process. These dimensions of changes in identity understandings thus emerged progressively from our data, based on observed regularities. We have called them the local-international, academic-corporate, and informal-formal dimensions. Among the studied cases, the university-based schools (ES04, ES05, and ES07) were traditionally more international and academic, while the other schools (ES01, ES02, ES03, and ES06) were more local and corporate oriented. Interestingly, our study suggests that the only dimension of identity understanding that offers different results within the schools under study is the academic–corporate dimension, which is related to the EQUIS academic and professional logics. The two other dimensions suggest similar changes, which are 'more formal' and 'more international' perceived identities for these schools. While the increased formalism may be attributed to the accreditation process that requires formal reporting and accountability, the increased international identity mainly relies on organizational changes in resources and activities that will be described further. Hereafter, we present each dimension of modified identity understanding with some illustrative quotes.

The 'local–international' dimension is strictly linked with the criteria of internationalization emphasized by EQUIS, and our results suggest that a shift was perceived in all studied schools towards an 'international mind', notably through benchmarking activities. Although many of interviewees recognized that EQUIS was probably not the only cause of the internationalization, they acknowledged its accelerating effect. The following quotes illustrate this shift:

Table 5.3. Changes in identity claims

Phases	ES01	ES02	ES03	ES04	ES05	ES06	ES07
After failure	None	None	None	New mission, vision, strategy	Revised research policy	Reduced mission ambition	Revised mission, strategy, new school's name
After 1st EQUIS	New school name	New school name	New school name	Revised mission statement	...	...	...

Source: Peer Review Committees' (PRC) reports, Progress Reports (PR), Self-Assessment Reports (SAR).

What is the biggest weakness for a school like [our school]? These are schools that are nationally very strong, and that act as, not a monopoly but almost small oligopolies with two or three actors. But no one denies the position of [our school] on the [national] market. As a drawback, it implies that [our school] has never had a reflection on its position at the international level, with ever no deliberate strategy on this international arena. (ES07, Professor)

'[As examples of changes], I would say the focus on programmes offerings in English, the admission of much larger amount of international students, the decision to only offer master programmes in English and not in [national language], which obviously made us lose some [national] students. That was a strategic decision. (ES05, International Coordinator)

When you are teaching in your classroom, you are alone in your classroom and you are not so much aware that you are part of the worldwide business of teaching business and economics. And maybe, one of the most important factors of EQUIS, it is that, as a teacher, we have got the impression that we are part of the international teaching process... We are now much more international, in teaching, not in research because research is international per definition. But not teaching... It's not a paradox. EQUIS changed this part of the school, which is the most resistant to changes. (ES04, Full Professor)

The academic-corporate continuum emerges also from our analysis. As the EQUIS accreditation emphasizes these two logics at the same time, some shifts in identity understandings have occurred in the schools under study, but not in the same direction. In particular, a major shift in identity understandings towards a 'research-based school' has been noticed in the four professional schools studied along with the development of research activities.

I believe that we are going to go from a centre of knowledge transmission to a centre for knowledge creation. And this is due to accreditation. (ES06, Accreditation Delegate)

We went from a school managed by professionals within each discipline to a school managed by professors. Before, they could be professors but they needed to have a corporate experience. They needed to have another experience than the teacher's one. And the true criteria before, today it does still exist, was knowledge about companies... Today, if this criteria still exists, it has a bit decreased because of the research capabilities of recently recruited persons. (ES01, Financial Director)

As for the university-based schools, the shift seems to have mainly increased towards the corporate side through the development of MBA programmes, advisory boards, guest lecturers from companies, etc. Nevertheless, EQUIS seems also to have stimulated research activities within ES05 and ES07, to make them also 'more research oriented'.

We think of it as a positive thing when it comes to business connections and community services or in general, that we more deeply engage business organizations in our programmes or in the education that we give. (ES05, Director of Undergraduate Studies)

And from being very heavy on teaching—and also developing these three new programmes, we put effort into that—I think another contribution I did was really to turn the school around from being education oriented to be more research oriented. (ES05, Head of Marketing Section)

Nowadays, the corporate relationships are much more developed than in the past. Not that it was bad, but it was a set of relationships in a 'good family mother' style. Now, it has become a more strategic element with official corporate partnerships. For instance, there are the business projects for students that allow strong corporate relations. There is a professionalization of corporate relationships. (ES07, Professor)

I think that we were happy to say that 30 per cent of our workload was dedicated to research, no matter what people were really doing. Now, we realize that conducting research is more than simply talking about it. (ES07, Programmes Director)

The formal-informal dimension refers to the formalization degree of processes, goals and structures. Indeed, a formalization movement appeared to be required by accreditation standards, so as to reach accountability by showing achieved results and improvement. Such formalization can also be related to an expected minimal size for organizations, so that they can be international players. Along with an increased size, the atmospheres within several schools were perceived as having changed. Globally, this dimension is linked to the way things are being done, hence the answer to the question of 'who we believe we are as an organization'. More precisely, such changes in identity understandings are linked to the development of formal processes.

Well it has changed a little bit our thinking, and made us more proud of ourselves. But of course, the looseness and informality of that kind of... I mean when I started in '87, there were 30 employees, and now it's like almost 100. So, when an organization grows like that, it has to standardise and become less informal. So, I think that EQUIS has pushed in that direction, pushed us quicker into that kind of formalization process. (ES05, Associate Dean for Research)

Before at the school, there was a joyful climate, a bit childish. Today, this climate has disappeared because everything has to go into processes. So, there is not much places for fun. First, it's professionalism in all sectors. And instead of having big teams that do a lot of things together, we have created different sectors today, it has been extremely divided into sectors. It loses a bit the deep soul of the school. We enter into schemes. This is for sure a point that I consider as being negative. So, it's the same everywhere. Professionalism imposes rigour, and rigour doesn't please to everyone. (ES03, Director for Students Integration)

We were in an oral culture too. And the accreditation system has brought us to formalize more, to structure more... so to go to a written culture. And the fact that it lies on a self-assessment report brings us to structure more than in the past. (ES06, Accreditation Delegate)

Especially, the first time EQUIS forced us to compare ourselves to other schools. And it forced us to formalize and make explicit many things that were informal and implicit, like all values, our culture, our strategy, our objectives, etc. (ES07, Accreditation Manager)

For the professional schools (ES01, ES02, ES03, and ES06), the transformation toward a more 'international', 'academic' and 'formal' organization may have created a perceived risk to their historical identity. Indeed, as these professional schools were typically national, corporate-oriented, and informal, such an evolution promoted a strong change in identity understandings. As for the university-based schools (ES04, ES05, and ES07), the 'international' characteristic was generally perceived as being in the continuity of research activities, while the more 'corporate' and 'formal' identity promoted more rigour in the schools' management. For ES05 and ES07 though, a more 'academic' identity was also perceived, which could fill a likely gap between what these schools claimed to do in research and what they were actually doing. How did these changes in identity understandings take place? We provide an answer to this question here below.

Third, understanding how business schools' identities changed during accreditation requires the description of (1) how the accreditation process was prepared in the schools under study and (2) the nature of organizational changes during that period. These two elements are in fact constitutive of the schools' particular contexts and allow a better understanding of identity evolutions. Concerning the accreditation approach, we have identified three patterns that show the different paths followed by these schools. These paths—A, B and C—have been identified based upon the differences in staff mobilization and representation (view) of accreditation before the first failure, and are described in Table 5.4.

Although there remain several differences between the individual schools, the patterns identified emphasize major characteristics for each path. Concerning Path A (ES01 and ES02), the EQUIS accreditation was prepared during several months as a quality project and had involved a large staff mobilization. The reasons for failure seemed to unveil a misunderstanding of the nature of EQUIS standards and/or the expected degree of development for these. Regarding the EQUIS institutional development, it is worth mentioning that ES01 was the first school ever to have its initial attempt at accreditation rejected. Therefore, one can assume for ES01 and ES02 that the EQUIS standards could easily be misunderstood as very few schools were actually accredited at that time. After the first failure, ES01 and ES02 switched to smaller and more efficient teams for the preparation of accreditation and updated reports. Concerning Path B (ES04 and ES07), the EQUIS accreditation process was triggered by the university rectorship and/or senate, where the EQUIS accreditation was considered as a

Table 5.4. Changing patterns in the accreditation approach

Paths and related case studies	Phase 1: Before first failure	Phase 2: After first failure
Path A: ES01 and ES02	Large staff mobilization Accreditation viewed as a new quality project collectively shared	Smaller efficient project teams for data and reports update
Path B: PES04 and ES07	Selected staff mobilization Accreditation triggered by rectorship as a milestone of a long term evolution	Creation of work groups for discussing and reflecting on strategic issues Less critical self-reporting
Path C: ES03, ES05 and ES06	No staff mobilization (except for data collection) Accreditation viewed as a formality	Larger staff mobilization for project appropriation and/or data collection

Source: Peer Review Committees' (PRC) reports, Self-Assessment Reports (SAR) and internal documents.

milestone on a long term international evolution. ES04 benefited from a larger staff mobilization for EQUIP as a quality project, while ES07 created a small accreditation project team. For the two schools, the data collection required the contribution of every member of the staff (eg. collecting CV). Although not welcome, the accreditation failure was viewed as an opportunity to learn and improve quality. It was especially the case for ES04, while ES07 was a bit more driven by its competitive environment to get accredited. After the failure, both schools created workgroups to share more on strategic issues and reflect on their vision for the future. Concerning Path C (ES03, ES05, and ES06), the EQUIS accreditation was at first viewed as a formality and it was prepared by the schools' directors themselves with only a few selected people around them, as illustrated by the following quotes:

> Before 2001, it was a bad story. We've been shot down. What happened is that we have confused speed with haste. And second fatal error, this no-involvement of the staff. So the project was led on the sly, by a group of 3-4 people among whom a collaborator who was very close to [the former director] and had been hired for that mission. But the project was not shared with the department and program directors. So, it was not a quality system since there were very few people who shared the project. So it could not work. It was destined to be a failure, or it would have been a big makeup to hide a not sustainable success. (ES06, Director of Executive Education)

> The first time, there was a minimal sharing of the project, which was prepared only with some specific people. It was not used as managerial leverage. (ES03, Director General)

And then he [the former Dean] started with the EQUIS process, working with the first Dean of the business school. Because they looked into that and they wrote the SAR almost on their own, with a little small team, and thought... They were really inexperienced, they hadn't the network, they weren't familiar with the process at all. So, they got turned down for EQUIS in 2001... Maybe that was perhaps the first thing he did then. Because it was really after he started. Maybe he started in January, and tried to do it in November. Because he didn't know... absolutely, he hadn't prepared the school, the school wasn't prepared. But he didn't know. So, he was really the one to get it, and the first Dean. They were doing research together. They talked and discussed about that. (ES05, Head of Marketing Section)

After the initial failure, the schools in Path C went through a larger staff mobilization. ES03 switched from a strong 'concentration of powers and decision-making in the hands of a triumvirate' to delegation initiatives. ES05 created a new and narrower school structure and saw its staff more involved and ES06's new director set up a method of 'participatory management, based on empowerment, trust, delegation and control'. For all paths, we observe that staff involvement was necessary at a certain step, much in line with the philosophy of quality improvement and the EQUIS formative logic. Schools in Path A, although under a strong 'national competition' logic, started with a large staff mobilization and became in the end more 'academic'. Schools on Path B increased their staff mobilization during the reapplication process and became more 'corporate'. Schools on Path C started without any staff involvement at all, but had to mobilize it after the failure, and became either more 'corporate' or more 'academic' through the process. Beyond the accreditation approach, it is important to understand the implemented organizational changes that support identity change.

As regards the nature of the organizational changes, we observed that the implemented organizational changes—in resources and activities—created specific organizational contexts where school members could make sense of those changes and progressively see their identity understandings evolve. In that sense, organizational change and identity change are to be differentiated but also enable one another. In short, the nature of organizational changes answers to the question of how organizational identity changes. Table 5.5 offers a synthetic view of the main organizational changes in resources and usual activities that the seven schools went through between their failure and first EQUIS accreditation. In particular, these changes in resources and activities are interesting as they show how the organizational contexts evolved differently within the schools under study and served as support for new identity understandings.

Among the case studies, the difference in time horizons for implementing these changes is striking. For instance, the period between the failure and first EQUIS accreditation for ES02 and ES03 was one year, while it covers five

Table 5.5. Main changes in resources and activities between failure and first accreditation

Changes	ES01	ES02	ES03	ES04	ES05	ES06	ES07
Human resources	7 (5 Ph.D.s) professors being recruited	9 core faculty being recruited (7 foreign)	14 new faculty being recruited (8 Ph.Ds)	First IT manager recruited, increase in admin staff	12 new FTE faculty (from 37 to 49)	Increased **qualification of faculty** (32% Ph.Ds)	More invited international and corporate lecturers
Structural resources	Creation of three committees: management, academic and scientific committees	International research advisory committee	New research steering committee, advisory board, and 5 positions under the director	New Vice-Dean for internationalization, new Public Relations unit, new research institutes, new students' services centre	**Redefined structure** of the school, new business advisory board, career centre, structure for company training, research institute and expertise centres	New advisory board, modernized campuses, end of relations with poor quality partners	Reorganized admin staff and services, corporate cell created, new advisory board, more autonomy in university
Other resources		New international partnerships	Research budget multiplied by 2.6			Budget increase by 15%	Creation of a funding international chair
Research activities	25% of time devoted to research; plan for each professor	50% of time to research for active faculty	No. of days for research multiplied by 2.5		Creation of four research centres of expertise	Creation of research laboratories	Restructure research around 3 centres of excellence
Teaching activities	Clarification of the MBA position ing (director)	More courses in English	Creation of a DBA with a foreign university	New MBA and Executive Education abroad	8 master and 1 bachelor programmes in English, first EMBA	Several closed programmes New MBA with foreign partner, 2 new EMBA	Creation of international EMBA with foreign partners
Other usual activities		2 yearly international research conferences	Launch of a series of working papers	Building of **centralized quality assurance and IT – based monitoring**	Language courses for faculty		

Source: Peer Review Committee's (PRC) reports, Progress Reports (PR), Self-Assessment Reports (SAR).

years for ES05 and ES06 and six years for ES04. Interestingly, there seems also to be a correlation between the time needed to get accredited and the time-consuming aspect of the implemented changes. If we consider ES04, ES05 and ES06, we can see that some changes—emphasized in bold in Table 5.5—required a lot of time to be fully implemented. Indeed, the development and routinization of IT-based quality assurance and monitoring tools needed several years at ES04 before being effective. The redefinition of the scope and structure of ES05, as differentiated from previously associated university departments, also needed time to be implemented and embedded in members' minds. Finally, the qualification of existing faculty at ES06 also needed several years so as to increase the number of existing faculty with a Ph.D. For schools that took one year (ES02 and ES03) or two years (ES01), these changes seem to require less time. For instance, the recruitment of faculty or the creation of research centres, new programmes and research policies were done quite rapidly in these schools. To some extent, ES07 contradicts a bit this argument as similar changes in research structure and programmes were made over three years. A possible explanation may lie in the university setting of ES07, which may require more time to launch organizational changes than a professional school.

5.6. DISCUSSION

This research suggests that accreditation standards represent an important institutional influence on European business schools in an increasingly competitive context, with students' and faculty having enlarged mobility. On the one hand, accreditation labels first appeared as a market signal to differentiate business schools. This differentiation effect progressively decreased while the number of accredited business schools was increasing. On the other hand, accreditation labels also involve sharp legitimacy and identity stakes for business schools that fail to get accredited (or are not yet accredited). Our case studies have suggested that EQUIS accreditation standards influence schools' organizational identities mainly through organizational change in resources and activities. In turn, the renewed identity understandings and claims shape a platform for leading further organizational changes. In short, it means that organizational change and identity change enable one another. This research highlights also the importance of context to understanding organizational change and identity. To some extent, the schools being studied were all successful as they were all finally granted with the EQUIS accreditation. In these cases, an interesting characteristic is the coherence or alignment between the context and pace of change. In cases characterized by a 'national competition' logic and also a professional status (ES01, ES02, and ES03), the changes were usually more rapid and accreditation granted in a short period of time. In cases characterized by a 'regional recognition' logic and a university status (ES04 and ES05), the changes were slower and involved a sensemaking process for most schools' members over a longer period of time. Other cases (ES06 and ES07) are more mixed. With its professional status, ES06 was under a strong 'national competition' logic but took some time to use the EQUIS procedure as a tool to strengthen a recent merger. With its university status, ES07 was under a strong 'national competition' logic and relatively quickly (three years) led to some organizational changes, although starting with a participative process (eg. meetings, workgroups, 'green days') for most schools' members. Finally, the EQUIS accreditation standards themselves incorporate several—sometimes conflicting—institutional logics, which led to different changes in identity understandings among the schools being studied. More specifically, the academic–corporate balance led to 'more academic' identities for professional schools, while it led to 'more corporate oriented' identities for university-based schools. Interestingly, some interviewees in professional schools explained that the new research focus implied by the accreditation standards was actually useful in serving companies better, which was the original objective of professional schools. For a professional school, this means that the 'academic' logic was used as mean to reach the 'corporate' logic as an end, while the contrary ('corporate' logic as a means, and 'academic' logic as an end) could occur in a university-based school. As a matter of fact, the observed dimensions of identity change are strongly linked to the peculiarities of EQUIS standards, which precisely focus on the international dimension, research and corporate connections. In that regard, the observed changes in identity understandings—for the international–local and academic–corporate dimensions—actually correspond to a new 'institutional identity' for the business schools we studied, namely a 'set of claims to institutionally standardized social categories' (Greenwood et al. 2011:346). From this perspective, this research suggests how an 'institutional identity' based on accreditation standards can influence business schools' 'organizational identity'. On the one hand, accreditation standards imply homogeneity in identity claims (quality logo, schools' names, mission statements). On the other hand, members' interpretations and variability in making sense through identity understandings in specific local contexts bring pluralism, hence distinctiveness of organizational identities.

The contributions of this research are three. First, we highlight the role of different institutional logics (national competition and regional recognition) in the adaptation of accreditation standards. If accreditation standards integrate a set of multiple institutional logics on their own (selective–formative, and academic–professional), the accreditation processes were themselves justified in the schools being studied even by some other pre-existing institutional logics (national competition and regional recognition). Second, the concrete organizational adaptations to accreditation standards are of two kinds in these schools: either a change in the acquisition or reconfiguration of resources (human, financial and structural), or the design and implementation of new activities (eg. research seminars, quality monitoring systems). While the first type of adaptation is quicker (development of a 'potential capability'), the second type of change takes more time for its implementation (development of a 'realized capability'). Third, we observe three dimensions of change in identity understandings for EQUIS accredited business schools: international–local; academic–corporate; and informal–formal. Two of these dimensions are strongly related with EQUIS standards (internationalization and academic–corporate balance), while the third dimension is linked to the necessary accountability involved in any reporting activities to support accreditation mechanisms. Nevertheless, this research has also several limits, of which the main ones are as follows. First, a research bias lays in post-rationalizations by interviewees. Thanks to a triangulation of data, this bias has been reduced as much as possible. Second, the guarantee of anonymity for the schools was a heavy constraint on describing the cases, and giving details on the schools' contexts. Third, a comparison with schools that have first failed and then left the process would have been interesting, in order to analyse the identity dynamics, as one could expect no identity change at the end. However, the extreme sensitivity of such cases did not allow us to access these schools. Finally, the EQUIS standards were launched in 1998 and have evolved since that time, which means that the EQUIS recommendations and expectations for the schools we studied may not have been the same with the passing years, especially between ES01 in 1998 and ES07 in 2003.

In this research, we realized that the institutional influence of accreditation standards on organizational identity seems to be closely linked with the notion of business schools' performance, as all the schools improved their quality to get accredited in the end. Therefore, we suggest that future research avenues explore the relationships between institutional logics, organizational identity and performance. Although the links between institutional legitimacy and performance in commercial banks have been studied (Deephouse, 1996 and 1999), much remains to be understood about the role of identity in that relationship. Based on this research, we would suspect that organizational identity has a mediating role in the relationship between institutional logics and performance. The underlying rationality for this conjecture is twofold. On the one hand, it could be that institutional logics push organizations to clarify their identity in 'standardized social categories', which then facilitates somehow an increase in their performance. However, can the notion of performance be considered independently of the institutional logics (eg. accreditation standards)? If the answer is no, there is a tautological risk in such a conjecture. On the other hand, it could be that the 'notion of performance' is not neutral and incorporates certain values that are the basis of ideological or institutional identities. Based on that, the promotion of a certain type of performance strengthens the development of certain institutional identities, which are then constitutive of or feed certain institutional logics. In the two cases, the questions of why and how such a relationship takes form (or not) in certain organizations deserve more research effort.

ACKNOWLEDGEMENTS

We are grateful to the EFMD and the EQUIS team for their support in accessing the accreditation reports, as well as to all participating schools.

REFERENCES

Albert, S. and Whetten, D. A. (1985). 'Organizational Identity', *Research in Organizational Behavior*, 7: 263–295.

Antunes, D. and Thomas, H. (2007). 'The Competitive (Dis)Advantages of European Business Schools', *Long Range Planning*, 40(3): 382–404.

Corley, K. G. and Gioia, D. A. (2004). 'Identity Ambiguity and Change in the Wake of a Corporate Spin-off', *Administrative Science Quarterly*, 49(22): 173–208.

Deephouse D. L. (1996). 'Does Isomorphism Legitimate?', *Academy of Management Journal*, 39(4): 1024–1039.

Deephouse D. L. (1999). 'To be Different or to be the Same? It's a Question (and Theory) of Strategic Balance', *Strategic Management Journal*, 20(2): 147–166.

DiMaggio P. J. and Powell W. W. (1983). 'The Iron Cage Revisited: Institutional Isomorphism and Collective Rationality in Organizational Fields', *American Sociological Review*, 48(2): 147–160.

Dul, J. and Hak, T. (2008). *Case Study Methodology in Business Research*. Oxford: Butterworth-Heinemann (Elsevier).

Durand, R. and McGuire, J. (2005). 'Legitimating Agencies in the Face of Selection: the Case of AACSB', *Organization Studies*, 26(2): 165–196.

Dutton, J. E. and Dukerich, J. M. (1991). 'Keeping an Eye on the Mirror: Image and Identity in Organizational Adaptation', *Academy of Management Journal*, 34(3): 517–554.

Eisenhardt, K. M. and Graebner, M. E. (2007). 'Theory Building from Cases: Opportunities and Challenges', *Academy of Management Journal*, 50(1): 25–32.

Eisenhardt, K. M. (1989). 'Building Theories from Case Study Research', *Academy of Management Review*, 14(4): 532–550.

Elsbach, K. D. and Kramer, R. M. (1996). 'Members' Responses to Organizational Identity Threats: Encountering and Countering the Business Week Ranking', *Administrative Science Quarterly*, 41(3): 442–476.

Fiol, C. M. (2001). 'Revisiting an Identity-Based View of Sustainable Competitive Advantage', *Journal of Management*, 27(6): 691–699.

Fiol, C. M. (2002). 'Capitalizing on Paradox: The Role of Language in Transforming Organizational Identities', *Organization Science*, 13(6): 653–666.

Fox-Wolfgramm S. J., Boal K. B., and Hunt J. G. (1998). 'Organizational Adaptation to Institutional Change: A Comparative Study of First-Order Change in Prospector and Defender Banks', *Administrative Science Quarterly*, 43(1): 87–126.

Gioia, D. A., Schultz, M., and Corley, K. G. (2000). 'Organizational Identity, Image and Adaptive Instability', *Academy of Management Review*, 25(1): 63–81.

Gioia, D. A., Thomas, J. B. (1996). 'Identity, Image and Issue Interpretation: Sensemaking During Strategic Change in Academia', *Administrative Science Quarterly*, 41(3): 370–403.

Glynn, M. A. and Abzug, R. (2002). 'Institutionalizing Identity: Symbolic Isomorphism and Organizational Names', *Academy of Management Journal*, 45(1): 267–280.

Glynn, M. A., Barr, P. S., and Dacin, M. T. (2000). 'Pluralism and the Problem of Variety', *Academy of Management Review*, 25(4): 726–734.

Greenwood, R., Raynard, M., Kodeih, F., Micelotta, E. R., and Lounsbury, M. (2011). 'Institutional Complexity and Organizational Responses', *The Academy of Management Annals*, 5(1): 317–371.

Greenwood, R., Diaz, A. M., Li, S. X., and Lorente, J. C. (2010). 'The Multiplicity of Institutional Logics and the Heterogeneity of Organizational Responses', *Organization Science*, 21(2): 521–539.

Greenwood, R., Suddaby, R., and Hinings, C. R. (2002). 'Theorizing Change: the Role of Professional Associations in the Transformation of Institutionalized Fields', *Academy of Management Journal*, 45(1): 58–80.

Hatch, M. J. and Schultz, M. (2002). 'The Dynamics of Organizational Identity', *Human Relations*, 55(8): 989–1018.

Hedmo T. (2002). 'The Europeanisation of Business Education', in R. P. Amdam, R. Kvalshaugen, E. Larsen (eds), *Inside the Business Schools: The Content of European Business Education*. Copenhagen: Business School Press, 247–266.

Julian S. D. and Ofori-Dankwa J. C. (2006). 'Is Accreditation Good for the Strategic Decision Making of Traditional Business Schools?', *Academy of Management Learning and Education*, 5(2): 225–233.

Kennedy, M. T. and Fiss, P. C. (2009). 'Institutionalizing, Framing, and Diffusion: the Logic of TQM Adoption and Implementation Decisions among US Hospitals', *Academy of Management Journal*, 52(5): 897–918.

King, A. A., Lenox, M. J., and Terlaak, A. (2005). 'The Strategic Use of Decentralized Institutions: Exploring Certification with the ISO 14001 Management Standard', *Academy of Management Journal*, 48(6): 1091–1106.

Labianca, G., Fairbank, J. F., Thomas, J. B., Gioia, D. A., and Umphress, E. E. (2001). 'Emulation in Academia: Balancing Structure and Identity', *Organization Science*, 12(3): 312–330.

Leonard-Barton, D. (1990). 'A Dual Methodology for Case Studies: Synergistic Use of a Longitudinal Single Site with Replicated Multiple Sites', *Organization Science*, 1(3): 248–266.

Miles, M. B. and Huberman, A. M. (1994). *Qualitative Data Analysis*. Thousand Oaks: Sage Publications.

Nag, R., Corley, K. G., and Gioia, D. A. (2007). 'The Intersection of Organizational Identity, Knowledge, and Practice: Attempting Strategic Change via Knowledge Grafting', *Academy of Management Journal*, 50(4): 821–847.

Oliver, C. (1991). 'Strategic Responses to Institutional Processes', *Academy of Management Review*, 16(1): 145–179.

Pache, A.C. and Santos, F. (2010). 'When Worlds Collide: the Internal Dynamics of Organizational Responses to Conflicting Institutional Demands', *Academy of Management Review*, 35(3): 445–476.

Peteraf, M. and Shanley, M. (1997). 'Getting to Know You: A Theory of Strategic Group Identity', *Strategic Management Journal*, 18: 165–186.

Pettigrew, A. M. (2012). 'Context and Action in the Transformation of the Firm: a Reprise', *Journal of Management Studies*, 49(7): 1304–1328.

Puusa, A. (2006). 'Conducting Research on Organizational Identity', *Electronic Journal of Business Ethics and Organization Studies*, 11(2): 24–28.

Proitz T. S., Stensaker B., and Harvey L. (2004). 'Accreditation, Standards and Diversity: an Analysis of EQUIS Accreditation Reports', *Assessment & Evaluation in Higher Education*, 29(6): 735–750.

Purdy, J. M., and Gray, B. (2009). 'Conflicting Logics, Mechanisms of Diffusion, and Multilevel Dynamics in Emerging Institutional Fields', *Academy of Management Journal*, 52(2): 355–380.

Rao, H., Monin, P., and Durand, R. (2003). 'Institutional Change in Toque Ville: Nouvelle Cuisine as an Identity Movement in French Gastronomy', *American Journal of Sociology*, 108(4): 795–843.

Ravasi, D. and Schultz, M. (2006). 'Responding to Organizational Identity Threats: Exploring the Role of Organizational Culture', *Academy of Management Journal*, 49(3): 433–458.

Reay, T. and Hinings, C. R. (2009). 'Managing the Rivalry of Competing Institutional Logics', *Organization Studies*, 30(6): 629–652.

Roller, R. H., Andrews B. K., and Bovee S. L. (2003). 'Specialized Accreditation of Business Schools: a Comparison of Alternative Costs, Benefits, and Motivations', *Journal of Education for Business*, 78(4): 197–204.

Romero, E. J. (2008). 'AACSB Accreditation: Addressing Faculty Concerns', *Academy of Management Learning and Education*, 7(2): 245–255.

Sherer, P. D. and Lee, K. (2002). 'Institutional Change in Large Law Firms: a Resource Dependency and Institutional Perspective', *Academy of Management Journal*, 45(1): 102–119.

Stensaker, B. and Harvey, L. (2006). 'Old Wine in New Bottles? A Comparison of Public and Private Accreditation Schemes in Higher Education', *Higher Education Policy*, 19(1): 65–85.

Stensaker, B. and Norgard, J. D. (2001). 'Innovation and Isomorphism: a Case-Study of University Identity Struggle 1969-1999', *Higher Education*, 43: 473–492.

Townley, B. (2002). 'The Role of Competing Rationalities in Institutional Change', *Academy of Management Journal*, 45(1): 163–179.

Thornton, P. H. (2002). 'The Rise of the Corporation in a Craft Industry: Conflict and Conformity in Institutional Logics', *Academy of Management Journal*, 45(1): 81–101.

Urgel, J. (2007). 'EQUIS Accreditation: Value and Benefits for International Business Schools', *Journal of Management Development*, 26(1): 73–83.

Whetten, D. A. (2006). 'Albert and Whetten Revisited: Strengthening the Concept of Organizational Identity', *Journal of Management Inquiry*, 15(3): 219–234.

Whetten, D. A. and Mackey, A. (2002). 'A Social Actor Conception of Organizational Identity and its Implications for the Study of Organizational Reputation', *Business and Society*, 41(4): 393–414.

Yin, R. K. (2003). *Case Study Research – Design and Methods.* Thousand Oaks: Sage Publications.

Zammuto, R. F. (2008). 'Accreditation and the Globalization of Business', *Academy of Management Learning and Education*, 7(2): 256–268.

Zell, D. (2001). 'The Market-Driven Business School: Has the Pendulum Swung too Far?', *Journal of Management Inquiry*, 10(4): 324–338.

6

Relevance and Excellence in Higher Education Vocational Schools

Business Schools as Institutional Actors

Catherine Paradeise, Jean-Claude Thoenig, Stéphanie Mignot-Gérard, Emilie Biland, Gaële Goastellec, and Aurélie Delemarle

Tensions between practical relevance and academic excellence as defined by quantitative academic outputs occur in most higher education vocational schools. As in other issue-driven fields—law, engineering, agronomy, public health—at the end of the day the worth of knowledge is most closely linked to its capacity to help resolve such practical and professional issues (Rip 2002).

Business schools experience tensions exacerbated by the social and symbolic importance that management education has acquired since the turn of the twentieth century. Many exogenous stakeholders apply pressure to make them more academically excellent, such as private and public funding sources, and the importance given by families and job markets to their quality as defined by ranking metrics. The contradictory demand for professional relevance and academic excellence has become more insistent than ever, due to the growing internationalization of higher education markets.

It was easier to make sense of practical or applied knowledge when the relevance of science was based on know-how. The development of autonomous management sciences that separate the wording of problems from directly operational preoccupations has helped in-depth analysis. Yet, what has been gained by their development is a matter of debate. Disciplinary excellence cannot simply be substituted for practical relevance. Relevance cannot be simply assessed by adding up sources of scientific excellence. Relevance assessment rests upon evaluating the social, moral or technical quality of the solutions proposed in the course of action, which also leans on—among other things—the excellence of the disciplinary knowledge brought into play. If science cannot survive without autonomy, it cannot in the medium term only make reference to its own development, and ignore societal issues and needs, without raising doubts as to its own worth.

A crucial stake is managing the tension between relevance and excellence. Business schools are confronted by the need to prove their legitimacy on two separate scores: academic legitimacy, depending on their peers and based on internally defined academic quality standards, on the one hand; professional legitimacy, established externally by proven relevance on the labour market and in the business world of the diplomas they deliver, on the other hand. This chapter analyses the tensions that arise between those two sources of legitimacy.

Business schools are subjected to exogenous pressures and challenges within their institutional environments. The universities that host them, the agencies that finance them, as well as their own professional associations, keep pushing them to upgrade their quality and to conform to global academic norms and so-called quality practices. Such pressures are not devoid of danger, as the heads of the most prestigious American business schools were already pointing out in the early 1980s (Thoenig 1982).

The hypothesis that will be explored here assumes that despite global standardization frameworks that seem to lock business schools into a kind of iron cage and diffuse homogeneous (when not identical) academic quality criteria and strategic models of success across the world, some relevant (when not major) differences exist in the way each of them constructs solutions to address such exogenous challenges. Sheer imitation is not the name of the game. Local diversity remains rather important. This is clearly the case in the way to handle the relationship between societal relevance and academic excellence. Very diverse organizational approaches are set up and implemented. In other terms, business schools do not function as agents imitating, in a passive manner, a kind of one best way, defined and imposed in a hegemonic manner by an exogenous principal. They are proactive. They behave as institutional actors and entrepreneurs do (Battilana, Leca, and Boxenbaum 2009).

6.1. INSTITUTIONS AS CONSTRUCTED LOCAL ORDERS

Our theoretical and methodological framework revisits the institutional character of business school education and research. It takes issue with an agenda that, in line with a macro-deterministic interpretation inspired by sociological and historical institutionalism schools, is often adopted, for instance, by so-called critical theories, as if global or macro factors at work at societal levels would determine any kind of local organizational evolution (Thoenig 2012). Local orders matter (March and Olsen 1976). Such an actor-centred institutionalism considers institutional factors not as direct causes of practices and norms, but as vectors providing negotiation arenas, power dynamics and interaction resources between various stakeholders, whether inside an organization or external to it (Mayntz and Scharpf 1995; Thoenig 2005). It is up to inquiry to find out how the latter interprets such macro-institutional changes, even when its resource dependence structure gets modified by them, and mobilizes discretionary choices.

Is a business school a local order of its own, whether private or public, whether part of a university or not, whether American or European? The purpose of a field approach is to open the institution, as an organizational black box, and to find out whether, below the surface of formal structures and discourses, its actual functioning may or may not differ quite markedly. It studies what builds its specific identities and it sorts out the collective practices that define their structures and the content of faculty members' roles and tasks. It explores hiring processes, allocation of resources, and remuneration decision making, how research schedules and curricula are built. It identifies which criteria are applied to evaluate the department, the attention paid to rankings in the self-perception of the value of academics and in defining school strategy. It studies the socialization of newcomers.

It focuses on collective action processes and actual outcomes to understand how the qualities and the criteria that ground their reputation and performance are constructed. Even when a business school is more or less loosely integrated into a university (Weick 1976), training and research are produced at the meso-organizational level of schools where resources for action are appropriated and implemented, where academic identities are built, where missions are defined and the internal organization is established. It is also at this level that various stakeholders in higher education assess the school's distinctive qualities.

Our paper presents four case studies of management or business schools carried out in three countries: France; Switzerland; and the USA. They are part of an international research programme covering in-depth analysis of eleven business schools in five countries.[1] They are not representative of all the schools around the world, not even in their respective countries. They were chosen for two reasons. First, each school enjoys a high level of national and international reputation, whether this level of reputation is based on informal and local prestige criteria or on their excellence as measured with reference to explicit criteria and ranking scales.[2] They also illustrate diversity: while they all face the challenge of making excellence and relevance more or less compatible, each addresses the issue in more or less specific ways.

The information analysed is mainly qualitative. It has been collected during field work from the study of archives, analysis of the business schools' websites, shadowing (participation in in-house research seminars, etc.), and semi-directive face to face interviews with professors of various ranks, doctoral students and administrators—on average twenty-five persons per school, each lasting for an average of eighty minutes.[3]

6.2. NATIONAL MODELS AS COMPLEX INSTITUTIONAL CONFIGURATIONS

Although the name 'business school' or 'school of management' has become quite common, university-level training for business remains marked by the institutional milieus and the conditions in which vocational schools of trade and departments of business economics developed.

In the U.S., the worlds of university and business school have long been wedded. Already at the turn of the twentieth century, universities mainly dedicated to the arts and science created the first business schools, but more often than not kept them on their peripheries, as if they suffered from some congenital disease. Their success seemed unlikely in a country where universities were considered the collegially controlled temples of disinterested knowledge in the service of the public interest (Graham and Diamond 1997). To acquire university respectability, business schools had to convince university audiences that they were able to train students in a profession dedicated to the public good and to commercial altruism, capable of mastering the amorality of the markets by skills exceeding operational know-how and practical recipes. The stakes were all the higher at the turn of the twentieth century when the large number of second-rate schools of commerce that had sprouted on the American continent led the promoters of quality training to separate the wheat from the chaff. In 1916, a new association of business schools federating the best universities—the American Assembly of Collegiate Schools of Business, or AACSB—took it upon itself to disseminate good practice and, as early as 1919, to accredit those institutions that observed orthodox university norms. An essential question concerned the teaching staff.

While business schools often hired practitioners as part-time teachers, universities had a core faculty made of professional academics, working full time and with long-term contracts as teachers and researchers. During the 1960s–70s, the idea caught on that the quality of business training had to be tightly linked to the quality of research, that the social sciences had a central role to play as a scientific basis for business research and teaching, and that problems of management were a matter for interdisciplinary approaches. The Ford Foundation generously financed a small number of avant garde university business schools to put those principles into practice. Training for business management became a professional branch in the university on a par with law, medicine or engineering. It became inconceivable that a high-ranking university should not have a good business school, the only exception among the most renowned universities in the United States was (and remains) Princeton. Academic professionalization however came up against an intrinsic limitation: the businessmen and executives educated in business schools serve private interests and therefore might pay little attention to the value of service that could legitimize them as professional schools and fully-fledged components of universities (Khurana 2007).

The French model is quite different: most top-level business schools have developed outside the universities and even today remain outside. The mission of the first schools consisted in training executives for trade. The École Spéciale de Commerce et d'Industrie, created in Paris in 1819 by an enlightened entrepreneur, appeared a major pedagogical innovation at the time and was welcomed by the scientific elites interested in spreading the principles of political economy and the freedom of commerce for the sake of national economic growth. These schools proliferated in the 1870–1890 era. Universities and their academic staffs perceived them with some disdain. The autonomy vis-à-vis the state that such schools had was total as regards financing, curriculum, and internal organization. The fact they were recognized as semi-public institutions was due to their being usually placed under the auspices of the chambers of commerce that furthered their local reputation. The ambition of the best known among them such as Hautes Etudes Commerciales—better known as HEC—was to compete with the state's engineering Grandes Écoles such as the Ecole Polytechnique, the aristocrats of French meritocracy.

In the second half of the twentieth century, the emergence of an executive labour market spurred a new wave of creations of such semi-public schools, but also of private and profit-making schools. The pioneers who created or expanded them, often trained as economists and jurists, found inspiration and funding in the United States, particularly at the Ford Foundation—e.g. HEC and INSEAD. Universities also initiated business training by creating the first Instituts d'Administration des Entreprises as early as 1955.

Yet on the whole, most universities still paid little attention to these initiatives until the turn of the 1970s, when important events took place. In 1968, the French state created a full university called Paris-Dauphine with the privilege of delivering diplomas up to and including doctoral and postgraduate levels. The same year, it set up a specific foundation—the Fondation Nationale pour la Gestion des Entreprises—based on public and private funding, and which massively selected and supported bright French students in getting their doctoral degree in the best American business schools. The *agrégation*, a competitive examination that qualifies people for full professorship in public higher education institutions, was created in management in the early 1980s. Schools, as well as universities, boasted teachers of a new and different kind, timidly welcomed the international scene, and offered management programmes at MBA level and in continuing education. Each of the two worlds remained somewhat aloof. But little by little their relations warmed up. Some schools were allowed to deliver Ph.D. degrees that up till then had been a monopoly controlled by the universities. Universities and schools launched joint training programmes and favoured teacher exchanges. Beginning at the turn of the twenty-first century, the Bologna process sped up the course of affairs by harmonizing grades throughout Europe. In 2007, the French Law called *Liberté et Responsabilités des Universités,* as well as all the schemes set up to face the worldwide higher education market by ensuring universities maintained their autonomy and federating higher education and research institutions, directly challenged the Grandes Écoles. Massive programme-driven public investment supported the renovation of campuses, the diversification of higher education institutions, and the pooling of individual higher education resources into larger consortia offering a complete range of training possibilities, including management, and blurring the radical dualism of the national model.

Little Switzerland presents, paradoxically, a much more diversified landscape. Three sectors coexist on the higher education level alone. The first is more of the vocational type. It includes so-called Écoles Supérieures and Hautes Écoles Spécialisées. Écoles Supérieures either deliver a certificate of training in general management or grant national degrees in sectorial management—hotel and restaurant management, banking, etc. Hautes Écoles Spécialisées offer management courses for students receiving vocational training in a sector other than business. The number of enrolments has increased considerably since they now offer training for all the vocational schools of higher learning.

The second sector combines institutions offering private BA and MBA-type programmes. They are generally more internationally oriented and therefore English-speaking. The American way of teaching management is their benchmark, and they keep away from the traditional academic or university model. Like the Lausanne-based International Institute for Management Development, or IMD—which in many ways resembles its French cousin INSEAD—they take executive continuing education as their priority and do not let MBAs overload their portfolio.

The third sector is made up of university departments devoted to management, called business schools or schools of advanced commercial studies. The University of St. Gallen, created in 1898 as a commercial academy during the golden age of the local lace industry, became a higher school, later a university specialized in public management, commerce, law, and international affairs. Thanks to its business orientation, it ranks today among the major executive training institutions in Europe. The University of Lausanne inaugurated a department of Hautes Etudes Commerciales or HEC as early as 1911. In the 1950s, the University of Geneva too created a new department of HEC. The universities of Zurich and Basle entrust education in management to their department of Economics, Business Administration and Information Technologies, which, in collaboration with its graduate school, delivers diplomas specializing in management. Both Federal Polytechnic Schools in Lausanne and Zurich offer mostly specialized degrees in management of innovation and technology. Broadly speaking, a gradual redefinition of the subjects concerning management can be noted within this third Swiss sector. At the core of the universities, the management sciences are being taken more seriously as departments institutionally distinct from law and economics, developing their own curricula, degrees and resources.

6.3. LOCAL ORDER INSTITUTIONAL DEVELOPMENT PATHS

The differences between national patterns in business education do not cover up the variety of training and research organizations in the management sciences. An obvious observation for Switzerland, this also goes for countries, such as the U.S., that are known for providing a dominant model for business schools. The original vocations of these institutions were diverse, and their response to contextual changes in terms of curricula, teaching methods and research activities differed from one to the other. The dosage between academic excellence and professional relevance is not the same all over, as shown by our analysis of four business schools: City and Strauss in the USA, École in France, Cantonale in Switzerland (see Table 6.1).

At the beginning of the twentieth century, City was set up in an American metropolis as a strictly vocational school. Dedicated exclusively to teaching, it mainly called upon practitioners from the business world to teach on a part-time basis. In 1930, only 46 per cent of them had attended university and 12 per cent held a Ph.D. Its two-year undergraduate curriculum was comprised exclusively of courses in practical accounting, finance, law, and commerce, mainly during night school and aimed at local students, frequently recent immigrants with few qualifications, who for the most part worked during the day. Until the 1950s there were no entrance requirements. City was known as a very efficient channel for climbing up the social ladder: it attracted up to 10000 students in 1942. Yet, though City was somewhat of a cash cow for the university, contributing up to 9 per cent of its total budget after World War II, its purely vocational character was disapproved of. City was close to being shut down by the university president if it did not improve

Table 6.1. The profile of the four business school cases

	City	Strauss	Ecole	Cantonale
Institutional status	School in a private university	School in a public university	Autonomous; linked to a Chamber of Commerce	Department in a public university
Enrollment	5800	2350	2700	2000
Full-time teachers	162	90	120	160
Permanent part-time teachers	#240	#110	# 40	# 40
Rank	Among top 12 in the USA (*US News and World report 2012*)	Among top 12 in the USA (*US News and World report 2012*)	Upper tail of the top 50 in Europe (*Financial Times ranking 2011*)	Lower tail top 50 in Europe (*Financial Times ranking 2011*)

its integration into its university milieu, especially since, as of the early 1960s, enrolment started declining.

From the mid-1950s on, City set up courses that were more generalist and launched research activities. The Ford Foundation strongly recommended it reorganize on a more interdisciplinary basis, admit students following a selection process, recruit teachers according to more stringent criteria—including possessing a Ph.D.—as the only way to survive and prosper in an academic community whose unique criterion should be excellence. In less than twenty years, City underwent a radical transformation. An increasing amount of its funding now comes from outside sources. Self-taught part-timer practitioners have left. The American model of managing university careers is used, paving the way to tenure through peer assessment and applying the 'up or out' principle. Publishing research in top-ranking scientific journals has become a major concern. Performance in class has become less significant in teacher assessment.

City headquarters entrusts the management of its human resources to its faculty, and accommodates their choices without dictating them. Now, City has its own identity as a professional school. Its research output in the field of finance—one of the two departments, together with Management and Organization, which our research focused on during fieldwork—are referred to worldwide. Paying close attention to its young permanent professors who are expected to provide visibility in research, the school increasingly recruits two types of teaching staff. On one hand, a so-called clinical, full-time faculty exclusively dedicated to teaching—and covering 25 per cent of its needs—and a so-called assistant faculty made up of professionals who teach on a part-time basis; on the other hand, teachers who are tenured or on the tenure track, who consider themselves as the only true academics, and whose number dropped from 57 per cent in 2000 to 38 per cent in 2010.

Whereas City had to undergo a hard-hitting revolution in the mid-twentieth century in order to survive inside its private East Coast university, Strauss, settled in a famous West Coast university, has grown and fructified in an institutional context mixing rather than opposing professional and academic references. Over the last decade, it has experienced a gentler evolution dictated by its ambition to attain pure academic excellence.

Strauss is the direct product of an academic initiative that created its mother public university's charter early in the second part of the nineteenth century. Commercial studies were considered right away as a legitimate way for the university to serve local development. To that end, its deans encouraged the recruitment of teachers of disciplines such as law, history, economy, and the social sciences, in the same spirit as liberal arts university colleges do. Practitioners and non-academics generally remained supporting staff. In 1898 Strauss became a business college that offered, like the other colleges on campus, a four-year undergraduate curriculum. Towards 1940, over 1500 students were enrolled. In 1943 the college became a professional school of business administration. It set up a postgraduate programme, and built a research institute, both making noteworthy contributions to marketing, industrial relations, and urban development. The style was clearly interdisciplinary, anchored in the socio-political and economic problems that the university wished to address in applying its academic tools. Thus pioneering contributions mixed political science and law to study relations between public authorities and employer organizations, or sociology, political science, and industrial engineering to study the management of organizations facing industrial risks. Strauss faculty met the teaching and research requirements of a university that ranks among the scientific elite worldwide and collects Nobel Prizes in the most varied domains.

Yet, little by little, the trade-off between excellence and relevance has evolved, with satisfying academic criteria taking precedence over service to local needs in business. Permanent teaching and research staff members are much less multidisciplinary oriented than fifteen years ago. At the outset of the twenty-first century, the Strauss landscape has been considerably modified. The profile of the faculty had changed and, along with it, the contents of courses and research styles. The business school now resembles a traditional college. Vertical authority is weak, whereas autonomy at the base is considerable. It juxtaposes disciplinary silos that—in its eight departments as well as in its research centres—have nothing much to do with each other. The institutional values are carried in the university at large by the dean alone. Each of its departments, and therefore Strauss as a whole, delegates its evaluation to outside assessment sources, the media and other public or private evaluators, that provide rankings of scientific journals, professional and scientific associations, or institutions of higher learning and research. Assessment of teachers' performance is based on their productivity—that is the number of publications they get in A rated journals—regardless of content. Making sense and relevance are considered out of bounds in these evaluations. Some departments advertise their quarterly productivity score on their bulletin boards as if it were a hunting trophy. Conversely, publishing, whether books, essays, or fundamental research, is not considered a valid indicator of academic excellence. In a way, Strauss overdoes signalling its academic quality to ensure its reputation of respectability under the permanent threat of other academics' opinion.

Strauss goes overboard in offering training at all levels: all sorts of MBA programmes, specialized masters, continuing education for executives, including night school. Over 20 per cent of its postgraduate students are recruited abroad. Within the university framework, multiplying sources of funding is an essential vector of its autonomy. While state funding has been cut to less than 12 per cent of the university's overall budget, Strauss has multiplied its resources by receiving donations, setting up specific programmes where it is at liberty to set the enrolment fees, and signing various research contracts. It has thus become a cash cow for the rest of the university, buying off its freedom with respect to campus rules and regulations by being taxed more than the other departments. It can therefore employ talents at their international market price who are out of bounds with regard to the salary grid of its public mother university. In 2008, 18 per cent of the 250 top academic salaries paid by this university were earned by teachers based at Strauss, which boasted only 5 per cent of the university's tenured professors. From then on in, the temptation to claim complete financial and governance autonomy is great, even if both sides hesitate to break the pact whereby the label of 'World Class University' is granted to the school in exchange for large financial contributions.

The case of École, a French leading business school, suggests a mutation of a different sort. Created in the mid-nineteenth century and attached to an influential chamber of commerce and industry, École was supposed to become the French reference for management training, turning business into a respected field of learning. Three major assets allowed it to win its wager: a tough entrance competition between a very large number of excellent and well-prepared candidates—selectivity ensuring elitist reputation; a mandatory training period on the job; and the introduction of teaching methods based on Harvard Business School-type (HBS) cases. Since the 1960s, École has provided solid professional training in fields such as marketing, control, and policy. In addition, meetings and lectures with leading social scientists were meant to build men of culture (female students were not admitted before 1973). However the French public Grandes Écoles of engineers that train the state and industry elites and remain disdainful of business and commerce careers, continued to consider the students of École as being just plain grocers, and not as potential leaders of firms and of national economic development.

Towards the mid-1960s, *École* took a first strategic turn by proposing an American-style MBA on the HBS model. It nevertheless remained unable to reach a level of reputation equivalent to a top of the top Grandes Écoles, and based on a French-style hyper-selective mode of admission. École built up a teaching staff recruited mostly among alumni that the state had funded and sent off to the United States to get a Ph.D. These newcomers, who had a very good academic background—unlike some of the practitioners who were their predecessors—kept in close contact with the business world, to which they were allowed to allocate 20 per cent of their time.

The rising number of new programmes—nearly fifteen masters and specialized masters in 2010, of which 50 per cent are taught in English, and several executive education courses—assembled under the École's brand name, led it to hire a growing number of adjuncts, often recruited among alumni active in business. This was a second turning point. It brought the teaching staff structure into line with international schools such as INSEAD and the London Business School. Financial dependency on chambers of commerce decreased with the multiplication of programmes and the creation of a foundation that also allowed the creation of about twenty endowed chairs.

To break away from its French competitors by basing its policy of excellence on indicators provided by the most eminent international rankings has become a major goal of Ecole. Performance in research, measured by the number of A+ level publications, has thus become crucial in the process of hiring and promoting full-time professors on the Strauss model. The same attention came to be allocated to the localization of Ph.Ds and to the recruitment of more female applicants. The other side of the coin is that teaching, conceiving new programmes and courses, as well as service such as taking part in managing departments and academic affairs, appear to the new professors recruited on tenure-track as an obstacle to publishing and promotion.

Cantonale is one of seven components of a Swiss public university. It is a university business school of a particular sort. Created at the start of the twentieth century to provide professional training in business management for the local environment, its mission was to combine advanced general and technical education. It offered postgraduate training to future merchants, industrialists, bank directors, management teachers, public administrators, and civil servants.

From the very start, it benefited from the international scientific prestige of some of its professors in economics and political science. Thanks to their reputation, and to being well integrated locally in terms of the support of the job market, Cantonale enjoyed full academic status from the 1970s. It then set itself up as a possible rival for the French-speaking upper schools of commerce in France and Canada. A more generous offer in programmes and continuing education for local companies, a masters degree in international management and a one-year masters programme, allowed it to overcome its lack of financial support from the university and of organizational autonomy within it.

Nevertheless Cantonale's institutional environment does not do much to further its ambitions to become a sort of European Wharton School, based on a worldwide standing in finance. Its highly-ranked finance and banking department was successfully raided and taken over by a neighbouring university. The latter is ranked among the best worldwide in technology. It offers more prestige. It also can afford to pay higher salaries. Cantonale has tried to overcome that handicap partly by providing very generous research budgets for its best professors, as well as freeing them from heavy teaching loads and granting them sabbaticals. Cantonale also compensates for its policy of accepting students generously at admission by a high degree of selectivity over the school years—only one student in two is granted a diploma after four years. It thus manages to hold its own in rankings of prestige. Nevertheless, it remains torn between two worlds, thrown off balance between its vocation as a professional trainer for a very lively local milieu, and its ranking in an international competitive environment. This publicly-funded business school remains vulnerable to the policy choices made by its successive deans, and to volatile financial and economic circumstances.

6.4. THE APPEAL OF ACADEMIC EXCELLENCE

Differences between national models and individual institutions cannot conceal the fact that academia has become the main reference point for business schools. Regardless of their respective patterns, all these top institutions now conform to academic norms and practices. It has been the case to a certain extent for at least half a century. Though conforming may mean adopting variable forms and following different paths depending on local contexts, nevertheless the common reference these institutions share and cherish is stronger than the specificities and the origins that distinguish them. The magnet of academic excellence appears more irresistible today than the preoccupation with relevance to professional practice.

Many features make business schools unique in the university academic landscape. For example, they were created relatively late, most only in the nineteenth century, and, except for a few—mainly based in the U.S.—are outside, or on the periphery of, the public universities, properly speaking. Their promoters, who were often also their benefactors, belonged to the modernist employers of the times, whether or not connected to public authorities. Ad hoc and diversified paths of financing were adopted. Teachers were active businessmen who sometimes worked alongside university professors. But teaching careers did not usually begin with the schools. Training programmes were free of certification and harmonization constraints. They were in the main concentrated on practical applications. They ignored the social sciences' disciplinary anchoring and barriers, at a time when disciplines themselves were not yet organized in their own right. The guiding spirit in training for business management was first and foremost the need to find practical solutions for real-life problems, eventually leaning on innovative teaching methods. Finally, many schools limited certification to awarding the title of 'alumnus'.

The four cases under scrutiny belong to two different categories. Strauss and Cantonale were created in public universities, made their reputation as business schools, and developed programmes in coherence with their contexts. City and École were created as professional schools—one outside, the other inside a university—that were dedicated to business executives and middle management training. But, despite those major differences, the four schools experienced the same difficulties in being as acknowledged by the academic world as they would have liked. For, in the eyes of the academic establishment, they bore the double stigma of being professional and geared to financial profit training.

From the 1960s, in their quest for respectability, these schools gradually benefited from the escalating specialization of managerial functions and occupations in the real world. This specialization backed the diversification of training according to domain and level of proficiency. Step by step, all four of them developed MBA curricula and lifelong learning for executives, if not standardized programmes such as executive MBAs. They rode the wave of entrepreneurial fashions—for instance public management in Europe in the 1970s, finance in the 1990s, sustainable development and corporate social responsibility in the years after 2000. The 1980s inaugurated a glorious era for occupations in business. Salaries exploded. Entrepreneurship was highly valued. These trends upgraded the number and quality of applicants for those programmes. Business schools became even more selective at the same time as they improved their placements on the labour market, thus gaining in prestige, whatever their past history.

The expansion and disciplinary diversification of these schools on the lookout for academic respectability brought about the creation of a permanent, full-time teaching staff governed by classical academic criteria, feeding the activities of national learned societies or associations, such as, in the U.S., the AACSB or the American Academy of Management. Two of the institutions observed, anchored in public universities—Strauss and Cantonale— did so very early on. Such was later to be the case for École in the 1960s, an institution linked to a chamber of commerce, and for City, a school attached to a private university. The trend was also prompted by the academic turn taken by the Ford Foundation in the 1960s. It considered business education informed by social sciences as a key resource for better informed and more rigorous business practices. The expectation that social sciences could serve social engineering in business was strengthened by recruiting many social scientists—in fields such as organization studies and psychology—available on the academic labour market (Cochoy 1999). Professionalizing teachers encouraged rationalizing methods of hiring them. This in turn contributed to generalize quality criteria on national and internationalizing labour markets, at least as far as the top of the basket was concerned.

Academization also led teachers in management to adopt academic norms and values that drew them still further away from the business world. It was first the case with the rise of disciplines during the 1970s in American business schools, which led to organizing teaching staffs in departments according to academic or professional criteria rather than managerial standards. Guided by a battery of journals, generating their own celebrities, business schools made a decisive step towards academic excellence by turning their backs on the logics of practical relevance. It paved the way for the next academic turn that led after the 1980s to the spectacular rise of neo-classical economics as a general pattern of thinking for business schools in all disciplines, from finance to marketing and strategy. The collateral consequence was to shut the door on other epistemological traditions such as those stemming from law or from comprehensive social sciences.

Doctoral degrees became the passports to disciplinary identity and the academic labour market. By ricochet, the community of academic peers, backed by professional academic associations, and through their journals and symposia, gained control over quality judgments on academics and schools. The value of a school was calibrated following the outputs of its permanent faculty, measured in particular by the sum of contributions to referee journals. Therefore each school developed a series of specific incentives based on promotions, bonuses, and in-house socialization. As a corollary, the books written for practitioners lost their value when assessing academics' scientific quality.

The professionalization of teaching staffs and its corollaries—the role of publications in standard university journals for quality assessment, the fact that disciplinary departments allocate more importance to research than to teaching, the standardization of degrees—induced a paradoxical consequence. They have turned professional schools into disciplinary-driven rather than issue-driven systems that would usefully serve business community practices.

6.5. TENSIONS BETWEEN EXCELLENCE AND RELEVANCE

During the 1980s, approximately twenty years after the Ford Foundation formally put forth its doctrine on business schools, leaders in American universities wondered about the risk that academization might in fact negatively affect their relevance in terms of training business professionals. The stakes were even higher at the start of the twenty-first century, when business schools started worrying about how rankings might impact their own image and financial resources (Espeland and Sauder 2007).

The Ford Foundation had argued in favour of approaches backed by disciplinary know-how as being the best way to contribute to issue resolution in the field of management, based on interdisciplinary projects or research centres. But over a period of twenty years, something different took place. The steamroller of disciplinary logics crushed considerations of business management, leaving it wide open to a multiplicity of theoretical adventures. That unwanted drift was reinforced by the all-important place given to research assessment according to strictly disciplinary or academic criteria. Little time, and only a narrow space, is now left over for renewing pedagogical approaches to concrete issues and professional business practices. These are no longer at the core of business education, which concentrates rather on disciplinary issues. Business management's contribution is in fact no longer anyone's key item on his or her professional agenda. Specialized journals publish theoretical and methodological articles that have most of the time little to do with entrepreneurial activity. 'Publish or perish' pushes scholars to conform rather than innovate. It also encourages the study of micro problems with little practical added value as long as they fit into predefined theoretical frameworks and they conform to standard research protocols. The ties between disciplinary research on management and the real world are stretched out. The growing gap with the real world is strikingly evident in the preference expressed—whatever the field—for model-building based on secondary analysis of large data banks to the detriment of qualitative research. Such analyses are accused of lacking rigorous methods, and of being too slow to attract academics obsessed by publication records—to the point where it impacts the very epistemological foundations of disciplines such as marketing or strategy.

Far from encouraging them to develop practical applications, the demand for peer evaluation in each discipline motivates the schools to recruit publishing scholars. Hence, they dry up the taste for research based on consultancy in the world of business and field-based observation, which used to be considered all-important for management professors, keeping them in touch with professional practices and highlighting their contributions to knowledge.

Finally, the growing and even irresistible need to demonstrate the school's performance according to the excellence indicators emphasized in rankings—number of publications, selectivity, internationalization, placement and remuneration of graduates, etc.—has led the business schools to base their programmes on uniform standards. With the exception of some customized continuing education for companies, the contents of doctoral and MBA programmes are practically interchangeable, with the major consequence that education has become indifferent to local labour markets, when it has not lost touch with local and sectorial issues. It corresponds rather to serving an international social elite sharing standardized know-how and designed to occupy the top—because the best paid—niches in the hierarchy of the labour market.

6.6. TRADE OFFS BETWEEN RELEVANCE AND EXCELLENCE

Confronted by the irresistible attraction of the reference to academic logics, each of the four schools of management has invented its own way to loosen tensions between the quest for academic excellence and professional relevance.

City responds mainly by implementing an academic vision of quality, while remaining able nevertheless to insist on relevance when necessary. That position harks back to the 1960s. City seeks to compete with the best schools of management in the U.S. This is not an easy proposition for a school that began far down the ladder, did not belong to the elite club of Ivy League schools, and had not gathered enough resources to attract star professors on the academic market. To win its place at the top of rankings and remain there, it adopted two ad hoc but complementary strategies. It tracked down a celebrity prepared to compromise on the salary in exchange for the school's very attractive location, i.e. a Nobel Prize winner who owns and manages a hedge fund. City also counts on its own staff. Faculty members carefully assess and advise their younger colleagues on tenure track, hoping that solidarity and reciprocity among generations will result in loyalty to the school. Departments also reward their 'good citizens'—those who pay their dues to the community (department or school)—by granting them symbolic personal distinctions throughout their entire career.

These strategies have paid off. While the average salary is between 15 and 20 per cent lower than in other business schools, despite the high cost of living in the town where City is established, most of the professors remain loyal. None of them have been bought out by other schools over the last nine years, except for the 50 per cent of the teachers on tenure track who did not get tenure. The teaching staff also accepts it should give time and energy to promoting the image of their school. For instance considerable budgets are allocated to organize high-level seminars with academic stars, as a way to promote research, but also public relations. More informally, doctoral students as well as the most senior faculty members, are encouraged to get on the phone to sing the praises of City to potential students and colleagues. Service is still provided quite spontaneously by academics.

Building a community identity is a way of creating an attractive image of the school and its departments at relatively little cost. Nevertheless City also pays careful attention to its position in national and international rankings. An administrative department is dedicated to collecting data and communicating with the ranking agencies, going so far as helping specialized journalists create indicators. City may never succeed in the future in displacing the Ivy League business schools from the top rankings. But, aside from the unique assets derived from its location in a major financial metropolis, its reputation is also linked to its original educational strategy. Its undergraduate programme includes a period abroad. Its MBA programme proposes many optional courses in the U.S. The organization of its curriculum is open to adaptations. Students are carefully selected according to academic performance but also for their personal talents and for network resources that will later make them excellent ambassadors for the school.

The quest for excellence goes together with the construction of City's originality. As the faculty and the dean see it, impacting the real world is not a priority for enhancing research and training curricula, which observe rather the standards of the accreditation agencies. That is notably the case in the finance department—the academic spearhead for a school established at the heart of world finance. It is true that, in this field, academic excellence and professional relevance today are made for each other! That state of mind is expressed on City's website, which makes its academic quality the main distinctive asset of its MBA programme. That does not mean that relevance is dropped altogether in practice, even if it is not placed in the limelight. A large number of adjuncts who teach in some 300 specialized options are practitioners. They bring to the programme their business experience and spare full-time faculty members the trouble of teaching practical subjects, allowing them to concentrate on the so-called 'main' topics—i.e. those which have an academic objective. Is it a winning strategy in terms of recognition of the quality of its students? As far as placement is concerned, City has been very successful, mainly in finance. 98 per cent of its MBA graduates rapidly get a job, with salaries often higher than those of Ivy League business schools.

City professors acknowledge that their research agendas are mainly of interest to the academic peers inside their discipline. Yet they are aware that, in disciplines such as finance, practitioners read their work and draw inspiration from it. They also care about public opinion, as their response to the crisis of the fall of 2008 demonstrates. Quick to react, City's finance professors published three books at the behest of the school Dean, aimed at a public of practitioners, taking time out of their precious research quota to compile and communicate on previous publications. In an emergency that so endangered the image of finance, they felt the imperative need to act as good citizens of their institution, even at the price of temporarily lowering their academic performance.

Strauss had successfully maintained a fair balance between academic excellence and professional relevance up to the 1980s. The internal landscape has since profoundly changed. The school has in practice been unable to keep its distance from the steamroller of academic excellence.

Strauss claims to offer its students general culture, but the promise is difficult to keep. The MBA students, as well as undergraduates, are unanimously in favour of a rather narrow operational specialization that pays on the labour market and justifies their investment in higher education. At the same time, teachers have withdrawn into their disciplinary identities and interests, which in a few short years diluted their interest in contemporary social and economic challenges. Interdisciplinary hybridization—traditionally high in the school—has fallen to zero, or almost zero, in recent years. Themes such as industrial relations, the management of organizations at risk and social responsibility have disappeared, or at best hung on in the margins. Most of the talented academics involved in such cross-disciplinary topics migrated to other academic spheres or were not replaced upon retiring. The ones remaining have been marginalized. This turn took several forms. For instance the MBA course in strategy now begins with a class on auction economic theories, followed by a glimpse at games theory, and it omits all the contributions of the social sciences of organizations. Strauss thus went through the financial, then the economic, crisis of 2008 without—unlike City—launching the least initiative to make sense of it.

What are really considered as relevant at Strauss are the specifically economic and financial aspects in the life of a company and the utilitarian aspects of individual action. The social dimensions of action in specific cultural, political, organizational contexts are considered secondary. The disciplinary oyster has snapped shut. Neo-classical economics has become hegemonic and taken possession of all fields, from strategy to marketing, finance or psychology, imposing its epistemological credo. Ten of the twelve tenured professors in the strategy department hold Ph.Ds in pure economics. Institutional economics—which had a brilliant and eminent position—has become persona non grata. Hypothetical–deductive theories have become the very symbol of scientific respectability. Such and such a full professor of marketing, political science or cognitive psychology with authoritative, internationally acknowledged works, is more or less rudely pushed aside for not conforming to those epistemological norms.

To sum up, except for a few rare exceptions, Strauss professors—in particular the younger ones—just do not care much about the professional relevance of the knowledge they produce. Academic recognition is self-sufficient, as if what is deemed good for the university is ipso facto good for society.

At *École*, the huge tension that set the old faculty members against the younger generation has calmed down with the triumph of excellence over relevance as old faculty stock has now retired.

In the 1980s, École occupied an eminent position at the national level. The internationalization of higher education inspired its new CEO in the 1990s to enhance its visibility by applying the norms embedded in the international rankings indicators. The strategy to join the club of the best business schools in the world was clearly announced. The CEO has became powerful enough internally to implement that strategy methodically since the start of the Third Millennium, when massive retirement facilitated a new vision of what quality means in terms of recruitment and organization. Modes of managing human and financial resources were specifically geared to recruiting an international teaching staff balanced in terms of gender and with strong publishing potential in the most prestigious academic journals, excused from most institutional tasks by the reinforcement of the managerial line, and from specialized professional teaching, thanks to the increase of the number of adjuncts. All the young professors at École now hold Ph.Ds from the so-called best institutions, of which 95 per cent are American or British. The salaries on offer aim to be on a par with those of other business schools in the world league in which École would like to play, though it does not entirely succeed in doing so.

These recent changes spurred strong ethical and normative tensions between the different generations of professor, the older ones putting forward their institutional contributions—as programme directors, department heads, and so on—and their participation in the business world, and the young ones exhibiting the list of their top-level publications. The gap is also particularly blatant in disciplines whose technical and epistemic framework is closest to national or local professional norms and rules, and thus the least likely to produce international-level publications. There are therefore not many full-time professors in law, management control, or accounting. They have been marginalized and labelled as being non-publishers, or may even be forced to resign. Tensions concerning values are multiplied by income disparities, due to the inversion of the salary pyramid to the benefit of the younger professors, who were bought at their price—the highest possible—on the international market. In that new division of labour, senior members, devoted to the cause of the institution, felt depreciated in symbolic terms, as well as in terms of career gratification, by the younger members who, though less involved in teaching and in supporting the school, were better paid on the basis of their publication index. The evolution called for restructuring the teaching staff around a new division of labour.

On one side, in most business-driven professional fields, such as public accounting or law—from which the school cannot expect many international publications—full time academic faculty members have been massively replaced by an army of adjuncts and part-time teachers whose main activity is business. They are not incentivized to publish and are not considered as part of the faculty. Their value comes from their experience in the business world that allows them to deliver up-to-date instruction in MBA programmes, specialized masters or continued education. They are given good students whom they could possibly hire in their own companies.

On the other side, faculty membership is restricted to those who ensure academic performances as assessed by international criteria. They concentrate mostly on routine academic courses, avoid institutional loads, and devote their time to academic research, which the school encourages by providing bonuses for A ranked publications.

École has thus opted for a radical solution to the dilemma between excellence and relevance. Like City, it farms out relevance to adjuncts and senior tenured professors and entrusts its quest for excellence to the young teachers, based on individual incentives. But unlike City, it has relied on its new faculty's self-interest to reorganize the school as the sum of utilitarian actors, with the risk of losing its *affectio societatis*.

Last but not least, Cantonale has been led to perform a delicate balancing act on two fronts: between research and training; and between economics and the other disciplines.

Like École and Strauss, Cantonale's division of labour is pragmatic. A single discipline—economics—makes it one of the best European business schools for research, while the other disciplines prioritize the professional relevance of instruction aimed at managers and executives in their local surroundings.

On one hand, academic human resources management, as well as the division of labour between faculty members, and the relation between research and teaching, aims to improve research outputs according to internationally recognized norms. Yet, on the other hand, Cantonale remains dependent on specific local needs and on competition with other local training institutions. These two, opposed approaches exist side by side in the school. One is local and stresses relevance by training individuals who will later locally join the ranks of jurists, certified public accountants, etc. The other is cosmopolitan and stresses excellence: it targets top-level executives and international leaders, on the one hand, and top research scholars in economics, on the other.

This situation fuels disagreements and bargaining inside the business school. The obligation to teach undergraduate classes in French, for instance, means a relevant reduction of the recruitment pool of the faculty. It also aggravates tensions between locals and cosmopolitans. On the one hand, only some of the locals aspiring to become tenured professors are excused from the heaviest loads of teaching and administrative duties and receive financial support. On the other hand, given the average salaries that the university can afford, and attracted by very attractive research and working conditions from competing business schools, young celebrities are hunted out on the international market.

6.7. CONCLUSIONS

This chapter has studied relevance and excellence issues as viewed by four business schools through specific institutional development lenses, considering them as local orders constructed by institutional entrepreneurs. In synthesis, the case studies suggest two conclusions.

First, the four schools reacted in a broadly identical manner to some external requirements, such as global standards and rankings. They consider academic excellence as a strategic outcome. For instance, they responded to the requirement of excellence assessed in particular by publications in A rank scientific journals. They also experience issues linked to tensions between relevance and excellence. All of them have recomposed their internal division of labour, the purposes being to try and answer the demands on both fronts. They have segmented their teaching staff, first of all according to the criterion of whether they can publish. On one hand, professors tenured or on tenure track, generally young and cut off from the real business world, are recruited and possibly promoted thanks to their productivity and potential as so-called publishers. They teach mainly undergraduate programmes or graduate seminars. On the other side, teachers active in business, experienced practitioners who have no publishing requirement, are recruited in various capacities. These contingent faculty members deliver their practical know-how to students in professional courses and to practitioners in continuing education. The first make up the faculty whose members have access to specific academic rights and privileges. The second are adjuncts, affiliates, professors of practice, who are external to the faculty, loosely connected to the department, often part-timers and with rather short contracts.

Second, and despite identical evolutions of their macro or global environment, each business school proactively throws together solutions to manage tensions between relevance and excellence that, though playing within the same parameters, ends up with a variety of results. Local diversity remains quite important.

For instance the segmentation between the two worlds, one being academic and the other being operational, induces different sorts of tension in the four schools. North American business schools entered into academic logics earlier than European schools or university departments of commerce, which however may enter the new era of so-called excellence more forcefully. The first were subjected to the constraints of accreditation much earlier than Europe, which was only really hit in the year 2000 (Rostan and Vaira 2011). In the American cases, academic criteria and practices have for a long time now been frequently endorsed by the most senior and highest ranking members of permanent teaching staffs with the objective of producing research whose social relevance is neither a stake nor a mission, leaving the issue of relevance to adjuncts teaching practical courses. In the European cases, excellence and relevance have also more recently come to co-exist in two separate spheres, more or less peacefully, depending on the situation. Two different strategies are used to manage issues linked to research. Each has a different impact on the way the question of relevance is considered.

The first strategy consists in applying a hunter–gatherer sort of economy. It means governing according to the market. Such is the case at Strauss, at École and, partly, at Cantonale. Gatherers attach no importance whatsoever to loyalty. Coexistence within the school only comes from the convergence of individual, opportunistic interests. Market opportunism is considered a turn of mind perfectly compatible with the academic ethos and a legitimate way of regulating inward and outward mobility with the advantage of creating no moral obligations. Gatherers are solely attached to individual output in matters of publication and reduce the institution to the sum of academic individualities governed by a management responsible for incentives and controls.

The second strategy means governing by socialization and integration. It is a farming strategy within a community culture, based on accompanying the new recruits, as is the case at City, where professors share a sentiment of collective responsibility towards their younger colleagues. Socialization or farming creates a sense of obligation and reciprocity in the academic community that helps promote loyalty, and thus restricts the rate of turnover of professors and their sensitivity to comparative salaries on the academic market (Paradeise and Thoenig 2011).

The crisis of 2008 revealed another notable difference between these two models. City, which generates an esprit de corps and solidarity, reacted to the threat that business schools might be undermined by the crisis. Strauss and École, obsessed by proving their academic excellence, remained passive.

Another relevant difference between business schools as local orders is linked to the power relations between their internal components. Whatever the school, the link between relevance and excellence is more or less conflictive, in line with the intrinsic connection between academic disciplines and practice, or between undergraduate programmes, graduate programmes and executive education. In disciplines or departments such as finance, where academia generously feeds into practices in the real economy, two factors count: academic excellence, as a resource for practical action, and the bridges connecting the two worlds (Lépinay 2011). Tension between the two logics is therefore relatively contained, as can be seen at City but also in most of the departments of finance in the other schools. By contrast, tension is at its highest in disciplines such as accounting, where there is a huge gap between publishing in high-ranking international academic journals—mostly driven by economic modelling—and what counts for professional relevance in the real world. Cantonale provides a good example of the degree to which relevance weighs upon the strategic hesitation of deans in a school largely turned towards the local context but also anxious to be considered for its academic excellence.

Current tensions between the two ways of appraising the managerial sciences—practical relevance vs. academic excellence—have led to considerable restructuring of the schools. Business schools in the 2010s have little in common with those of the 1980s or even the 2000s in Europe. But changes leave room for rather important variations among them, bringing one to the conclusion that no single or hegemonic organizational way has emerged to manage the tensions associated with these transformations.

6.8. A FORWARD LOOKING RESEARCH AGENDA

To consider the institutional development of business schools through the lenses of self-constructed social system dynamics opens up a wide range of issues for further research agendas.

Research should test the hypothesis that differences observed between schools are not only induced by chronological variations in the development of the same global pattern that would force them into the iron cage. Europe, for instance, was as usual a late follower of innovations first developed in the U.S. To be exposed to global excellence standardization does not exclude successful diversification across countries and single institutions. Such a possibility deserves further and more detailed observation on a larger population of business schools. This should include countries such as India and China in which several education and research professional schools clearly aim at joining the international upper ranks. Do they, for instance, develop local orders that are able to explore and implement sustainable and alternative strategies and organizational modes of functioning?

In-depth comparative approaches shall help to get a better understanding of potential mid-term evolutions and opportunities. Such an approach would also address a major worry often expressed nowadays. Is the business school sector exposed to the major risk, the bubble of its arrogant development since the 1990s—in terms of production volume, of financial profits, of less attention to third missions (Laredo 2007) and of declining academic quality return—of being less positively assessed by major external stakeholders such as labour markets and steering authorities?

The evolution of the cases of the four institutions during the recent decades suggests that each of them, in its own way, has been able to launch drastic reform options and to change in an endogenous manner. Path dependency is not as important as one may expect. And local diversity may persist.

Knowledge production would also benefit from additional scientific investment to explore new theoretical frameworks and to generate empirical facts to test them. Institutional theory as a theoretical approach, for instance, may still contribute provided one key pre-requirement is accepted: it must give up its earlier macro-environmental determinism and allocate major attention to the role of actors and action. Fruitful approaches have been made, which analyse local orders when heterogeneous or even competing institutional logics coexist under the same institutional roof (Greenwood and Hinings 1996).

Two more specific but relevant questions emerge out of the four cases covered by our paper. Both relate to the capacity of academic institutions to generate sustainable organizational integration between societal relevance and academic quality.

One refers to the inner functioning of a business school, as well as to its single departments and its education and research programmes. Various disciplines coexist to which members belong from very different academic and epistemic professions and scientific communities. How far does the fact that several business schools face growing difficulties—at least as compared with a few years ago—lead them to favour interdisciplinary programmes and cooperation,? This is, for instance, the case for economics approaches influenced by so-called rational theories—including large quantitative, even statistical, models of inquiry—on the one hand, and, on the other hand, social science approaches—sociology or political science—that give academic credence to qualitative and case-based in-depth understanding of actual social configurations. Another cleavage is manifest between experimental and clinical psychologists.

A second facet relates to the status of business schools inside universities. Presidential and senate levels of the campus, as well as science, social science, and humanity, often consider them as not being legitimate, academically speaking, and care more about the financial surpluses they generate.

Less indirect sets of evidence are required to trace interactions between organizational actions and cognitions in use, between power dynamics or resource dependencies, and knowledge references mobilized as coordination when integration vehicles. To make excellence and relevance compatible, to set up sustainable coexistence between different disciplines, implies that business schools have, more than ever, to address challenges to their function as hybrid organizations working in academically hybrid institutional environments. Cognitive systems building shared languages for action provide ways to keep such hybrid systems together. Managing business schools, for instance, also implies some skills in cognitive architecture (Michaud and Thoenig 2003).

ACKNOWLEDGEMENTS

This research has been funded by the French national funding agency (Agence Nationale de la Recherche), Project PrestEnce ANR–09–SOC–011 in the frame of the Programme, 'Sciences, technologies et savoirs en société 2009'.

REFERENCES

Battilana, Julie, Leca, Bernard, and Boxenbaum, Eva (2009). 'How Actors Change Institutions: Towards a Theory of Institutional Entrepreneurship', *The Academy of Management Annals*, 1: 65–107.

Cochoy, Franck (1999). *Une Histoire du Marketing. Discipliner l'Économie de Marché.* Paris, La Découverte.

Espeland, Wendy, N. and Sauder, Michael (2007), 'Rankings and Reactivity: How Public Measures Recreate Social Worlds'. *American Journal of Sociology*, 1: 1–40.

Graham, Hugh D. and Diamond, Nancy. (1997). *The Rise of American Research Universities. Elites and Challengers in the Postwar Era.* Baltimore: the Johns Hopkins University Press.

Greenwood, Royston and Hinings, C. R. (1996). 'Understanding Radical Organizational Change : Bringing Together the Old and the New Institutionalism', *Academy of Management Review*, 4: 1022–1054.

Khurana, Radesh (2007). *From Higher Aims to Hired Hands: The Social Transformation of American Business Schools and the Unfulfilled Promise of Management as a Profession.* Princeton: Princeton University Press.

Laredo, Philippe (2007). 'Revisiting the Third Mission of Universities: Toward a Renewed Categorisation of University Activities', *Higher Education Policy*, 4: 441–456.

Lépinay, Vincent (2011). *Codes of Finance. Deriving Value in a Global Bank.* Princeton: Princeton University Press,

March, James G. and Olsen, Johan P. (1976). *Ambiguity and Choice in Organizations.* Bergen: Universitetsforlaget.

Mayntz, Renate and Scharpf, Fritz W. (1995). 'Der Ansatz des Akteurzentrierten Institutionalismus', in Renate Mayntz and Fritz W. Scharpf (eds), *Gesellschaftliche Selbstregelung and Politische Steuerung.* Frankfurt: Campus, 39–72.

Merton, Robert K. (1973). 'Recognition and Excellence: Instructive Ambiguities', in Robert K. Merton (ed.), *The Sociology of Science. Theoretical and Empirical Investigations.* Chicago: University of Chicago Press, 419–437.

Michaud, Claude and Thoenig, Jean-Claude (2003). *Making Strategy and Organization Compatible.* London: Palgrave Macmillan.

Paradeise, Catherine (1988). 'Les Professions Comme Marchés du Travail Fermés'. *Sociologie et Sociétés*, 2: 9–21.

Paradeise, Catherine and Thoenig, Jean-Claude (2011). 'Réformes et Ordres Universitaires Locaux', in Georges Felouzis and Siegfried Hanhart (eds), *Gouverner l'Éducation par les Nombres? Usages, Débats et Controverses.* Bruxelles, De Boeck: 33–52.

Paradeise, Catherine and Thoenig, Jean-Claude (2013). 'Academic Institutions in Search of Quality. Local Orders and Global Standards', *Organization Studies*, 2: 195–224.

Rip, Arie (2002). 'Science for the 21st Century', in Peter Tindemans, Alexander Verrijn-Stuart, and Rob Visser (eds), *The Future of Science and the Humanities.* Amsterdam: Amsterdam University Press, 99–148.

Rostan, Michele and Vaira, Massimiliano (eds) (2011). *Questioning Excellence in Higher Education. Policies, Experiences and Challenges in National and Comparative Perspective.* Rotterdam: Sense Publishers.

Thoenig, Jean–Claude (1982). 'Research Management and Management Research', *Organization Studies*, 3: 269–275.

Thoenig, Jean–Claude (2005). 'Territorial Administration and Political Control. Decentralization in France', *Public Administration*, 3: 685–708.

Thoenig, Jean–Claude (2012). 'Institutional Theories and Public Institutions: New Agendas and Appropriateness', in B. Guy Peters and Jon Pierre (eds), *The Handbook of Public Administration*. London: Sage, 169–179.

Weick, Karl E. (1976). 'Educational Organizations as Loosely Coupled Systems', *Administrative Science Quarterly*, 21: 1–19.

NOTES

1. It covers a total of 27 departments in three disciplinary fields (history, management, chemistry) in two institutions per country and in five different countries (France, the USA, Italy, Spain, Switzerland). In a sixth country, the People's Republic of China, three influential business schools were studied.

2. A distinction can be made between recognition and excellence as academic evaluation modes (Merton 1973).

3. A detailed presentation of the theoretical and analytic frameworks of this research programme has been provided in a separate article (Paradeise and Thoenig 2013).

Part II

Ranking and Branding of
Business Schools

7

The Academic Arms Race

International Rankings and Global Competition for World-Class Universities

Jürgen Enders

7.1. INTRODUCTION

The pursuit of the label 'world-class' university is spreading across the globe. Internationally, nationally and organizationally, excellence in international higher education has become a matter of policy that affects diverse interests. International rankings form an important input and stimulation in this positional competition for 'world-class' status in times of global educational expansion and the global inter-connectedness of higher education (Enders 2004). This paper analyses the processes by which the field of international higher education has changed due to the influence of rankings, which provide input into the construction of global competition for the 'world-class' university.

In order to explore the functioning of rankings, and their impact on political and organizational responses, the paper draws on institutional field theories (DiMaggio and Powell 1983; Fligstein and McAdam 2012). Field theories depict universities as organizations existing with other organizations—'key suppliers, resource and product consumers, regulatory agencies, and other organizations that produce similar services and products' (DiMaggio and Powell 1983: 65)—within a common institutional framework. The field is held together by regulation, cognitive belief systems, and normative rules, and provides social structures that have attained a certain degree of resilience, providing stability and meaning to social life (Scott 1995; Jepperson 1991). The institutional field perspective also provides a relational approach in understanding organizations within a field as being imbedded in complex relations of power and in hierarchical positions competing for legitimacy and resources (Naidoo 2004).

The early neo-institutional literature tended to depict organizational fields and their members as passive recipients of institutional frameworks and emphasized organizational continuity, but notions of embedded agency (Battilana and D'Aunno 2009) and socially skilled actors (Fligstein 1997) allow the capture of a more dynamic field perspective (see also Sewell 1992). From this perspective, the emergence of international rankings can be seen as the entry of a new actor into the field providing input for field change (Sauder 2008) by constructing globally defined standards for success and failure in international higher education.

By favouring a certain institutional logic established within the heterogeneous field of higher education—research reputation—international rankings subordinate competing field logics, providing new tools for constructing legitimacy and positional advantage within the field. Rankings do institutional work in the globalization of higher education by constructing a sub-field of 'world-class universities' and take part in distributing the symbolic capital (Bourdieu 1988) within the field. If they are powerful enough, rankings contribute to the establishment of belonging and distinction, and set rules and criteria for those who are or want to be members of the club. Value statements of better and worse, and of climbing or falling, provide important signals to the universities and other actors within the field, for example policy makers who want to know where their best universities are and where improvement is needed to compete organizationally and nationally within the international field. Rankings affect the political dynamics within the field and stimulate investments in line with the rules of the ranking game as everyone strives to improve their competitive position. In this very sense, rankings provide rhetorical devices (Wedlin 2011) with potentially important material consequences—some of which get enacted as self-fulfilling prophecies.

In this view, rankings are key elements in (trans)national governance: they provide an arena for contestation between actors about what the appropriate criteria for comparison, success and legitimacy are. They also contribute to determining organizational standards and help to define the legitimate players in the field.

This paper discusses how international rankings are socially constructed, and provide a means for creating social order in the bewildering world of modern international mass higher education, as well as being an arena for contestation about constructing new boundaries, and defining a heartland and a periphery. How these boundaries are constructed is to a large extent dictated by the international reputational hierarchies that already prevail, biased towards research reputation. This framework is further used for investigating a growing number of governmental policies and organizational strategies that buy into the ranking game. Potentially detrimental effects of the ranking explosion are discussed, i.e. financial costs in a zero-sum game, organizational isomorphism, and the reduction of diversity in a higher education dominated by international ranking standards. The conclusion discusses the role of international rankings for field dynamics and provides a sketch of a forward-looking research agenda for the study of rankings in the multi-level and multi-actor dynamics of international higher education.

7.2. SETTING THE STANDARDS: THE CONSTRUCTION OF INTERNATIONAL RANKING AND ITS IMPLICATIONS

Following the example of the US News ranking, a growing number of commercial media and research institutions have begun to release rankings nationally as well as worldwide. In their overview of these rankings, Usher and Medow (2009) reported that at the time of their study, there were a minimum of 26 rankings worldwide. International rankings include the Academic Ranking of World Universities (ARWU) by Shanghai Jiao Tong University, the Times Higher Education World Reputation rankings, the QS World University ranking (the latter two split up from the *Times Higher Education Supplement*–QS World University ranking), the Leiden University ranking, and the Taiwan Higher Education Evaluation and Accreditation Council ranking.

What international rankings do and communicate can be exemplified by the ARWU and the Times Higher Education ranking, currently the two most influential international rankings.

The ARWU ranking was first published in June 2003 by the Centre for World-Class Universities and the Institute of Higher Education of Shanghai Jiao Tong University, China, and then updated on an annual basis. ARWU never intended to provide a holistic ranking of universities around the world but was initiated to benchmark the research performance of Chinese universities and to provide tools for Chinese policy making to boost the country's position in the global competition for research excellence. Initially, the global success story of the ranking came as a surprise to its initiators. ARWU uses six indicators to rank world universities: the number of alumni and staff winning Nobel Prizes and Fields Medals; the number of highly cited researchers selected by Thomson Scientific; the number of articles published in the journals *Nature* and *Science*; the number of articles indexed in the Science Citation Index—Expanded; the number of articles indexed in the Social Sciences Citation Index; and per capita performance with respect to the size of an institution. The university ranking is based on the weighted sum of scores on these indicators in which Nobel Prizes and per capita performance count for 10 per cent each and the other four indicators for 20 per cent each. More than 1000 universities are ranked by ARWU every year and the best

500 are published on the web, aggregating their performance in the different fields of research and providing a ranking position for each university as well its scores. For instance, in 2009, Cambridge ranked as number 4 and MIT as number 5, with 0.7 percentage points difference in their scores, while the difference between the 5th (MIT) and 6th (Caltech) ranked universities was 4.7 per cent. In the ARWU, larger universities, as measured by the number of academics or by a higher academic staff to student ratio, perform better; so do universities in countries with a larger population, more public expenditure on education and research, and English-language countries. Except for the language, these variables are indicators of better resources at either the organizational or the national level. The most recent ARWU ranking of the Top-100 universities is clearly dominated by the U.S. (n=53 universities), followed by the U.K. (n=9), Australia (n= 5), Germany and Japan (n=4), France, Sweden and Switzerland (n=3).

The Times Higher Education ranking aspires to provide a holistic ranking of the world's universities, and advertises itself as 'the world leading formula' for judging world class universities across all of their core missions—teaching, research, knowledge transfer and international outlook. Times Higher Education uses 13 indicators grouped into five areas: research (volume, income and reputation, weighted as 30 per cent of the total score); citations (30 per cent), teaching (the learning environment, 30 per cent), international outlook (staff, students and research, 7.5 per cent), and industry income (2.5 per cent). Like the ARWU, larger universities, universities and countries with better resources, and English-language countries perform better. While the Times Higher Education claims to make a holistic ranking, its indicators and their weighting imply a dominant role for research output (publications, citations) and research reputation (actually measured twice: by a survey of a university's perceived research excellence, and a survey of prestige in both research and teaching, curiously used as a teaching quality indicator). In consequence, the most recent Times Higher Education ranking of the top 100 universities is—like the recent ARWU ranking—clearly dominated by the U.S. (n=46 universities), followed by the U.K. (n=10), Australia, Canada and the Netherlands (= 5), France and Germany (n=4). Differences in methodology do, however, matter since we find eight universities in the Times Higher Education top 100 from Asian countries (China, Hong Kong, Korea, and Singapore) not included in the ARWU top 100.

The current measures and representations of these rankings are the outcome of an on-going and sometimes heated methodological debate (van Raan 2007; Harvey 2008) that concerns a whole range of issues: the validity and reliability of the indicators (e.g. the strong reliance on publication and citation data dominated by the (bio-medical) sciences); the weighting of indicators (being subjective and arbitrary); the use of reputational data from perception surveys (reputation and performance are correlated but by no means identical); the ordering of universities in ranks (that overemphasize small, insignificant differences among universities); or the effect of changes in indicators and formula for ranking positions. Each year, considerable amounts of resources are actually spent and a considerable number of experts are consulted to improve the rankings and to boost their legitimacy. In 2010, the Times Higher Education, for example, undertook a major overhaul of its ranking methodology. The challenge of producing the 'best' and most popular international ranking of universities is indeed a competitive race in its own right.

Such important methodological debate overshadows, however, the fact that it is the simplistic beauty of rankings and the hidden work of constructing world-class universities at a global level that empowers them so that 'they travel widely and are easily inserted into new places and for new uses' (Espeland and Sauder 2007: 36). Rankings do Aristotelian science as Foucault (1971) has analysed it: things get classified, sorted into different categories and vertically ordered. This process makes it easier to access and process information, and simplification often makes information seem more authoritative. Lists are reassuring and simple sound bites of information have their own beauty. March and Simon (1958) have shown how such processes of simplification obscure the discretion, assumptions, and arbitrariness that unavoidably infuse information. Consequently, uncertainty and contingency get absorbed. Paradoxically, information appears more robust and definitive than it would if presented in more complicated forms.

Rankings construct their object of comparison—the university—and make this object comparable by introducing the idea that potentially all universities around the world belong to the same class of objects. The differences in context, conditions, and missions of universities get suppressed, leading to their de-contextualization within the rankings. Rankings turn qualities into quantities within a metric that allows the production of a hierarchy of universities with a simple and clear rank order. Differences between universities thus become a matter of better or worse within a pre-defined space of performance, a value statement that excludes non-hierarchical alternatives. Qualities that cannot be expressed in quantities disappear, are marginalized and become de-valued. What is not countable does not count. Rankings produce what they measure: an imagined world-class university that can be calculated according to standardized norms of excellence.

This process of social construction, inherent in all international rankings but in our case exclusively or dominantly based on research performance, has several implications.

A first critical significance of rankings is the fact that they are produced and communicated by new actors—organizations that emerge external to the field while providing an input into the struggle for competitive advantage within the field (Sauder 2008). Certainly, the scientific field has always been the locus of a competitive struggle for positional advantage, in which the issue at stake is scientific authority and related symbolic (reputational) capital. Peers have observed each other's work and have made judgments about each other's products and performance via more formalized processes (e.g. in peer-review-based decisions about publications or funding) as well as via informal processes (e.g. citations, invitations, informal talk). Such processes traditionally unfolded within largely autonomous and closed scientific fields following a specific professional logic in which 'producers tend to have no possible clients other than their competitors... a particular producer cannot expect recognition of the value of his products... from anyone except other producers' (Bourdieu 1975: 23). The construction of excellence in international rankings builds on judgments that have traditionally been acts within scientific fields based on tacit understandings and informal communication. Ranking organizations use value statements like this, which are provided by scientific communities (e.g. in reputational surveys), and are constructs of scientific authority produced within scientific communities but provided by commercial organizations (e.g. publication and citation data banks), or data provided by universities (e.g. numbers of staff and students). Rankings can rely on this field-specific logic as a resource of legitimacy and power. Resistance against the basic logic of international rankings from within the field is hard to organize since they 'borrow' their authority from a powerful professional logic of the scientific field itself. Critiques of rankings from within the field rather concern issues of methodology, as well as of their political use by other actors and audiences.

They follow, however, their own logic and assumptions in gathering, weighting, aggregating and communicating their calculative representations of universities. In doing so, rankings are challenging the informal field logic by making status hierarchies widely visible publicly, easily understandable, and usable for a variety of actors, last but not least policy makers and organizational management. Rankings introduce new actors to an established field and do powerful institutional work eventually by transforming the relationships and powers among field members as well as by providing audiences external to the field of producers with 'information' that can be used to assess the field and demand field change (Sauder 2008).

Second, and related to the first point, the most influential international rankings are either exclusively or dominantly based on indicators reflecting research-related reputation as a perceptual construct and/or of performance output measures constructed by scientific communities. International rankings select and favour a specific logic—research excellence—within the field over others. The uses of the field of higher education are manifold, resulting from the particular combination of scientific and educational, social and economic, cultural and ideological roles. Higher education contributes to the production and application of scientific knowledge, the social development and educational upgrading of societies, the selection and formation of elites, and the generation and transmission of ideology. This range constitutes the key tasks of higher education, albeit with different emphases depending on the historical period, the national context, and indeed the type of university concerned. Like many other fields, higher education is thus characterized by a constant struggle between different and eventually competing institutional logics. Rankings contribute to this struggle by favouring the logic of cutting edge scientific knowledge production over other logics.

They also favour research in certain disciplines over others and contribute as well to the reputational struggle between different disciplinary and inter-disciplinary communities within the scientific field. Publication and citation cultures and norms vary considerably across academic fields, and rankings rely on bibliometric counts that favour a certain publication culture developed in the hard sciences, over-representing the bio and medical sciences while under-representing publication cultures not dominated by English-language international peer reviewed journal articles. Because of the growing influence of rankings on political and organizational choices, decision makers are likely to weight some disciplines more heavily than others when allocating resources. Pressure will also grow in all fields of research to comply with ranking-relevant standards of publication leading to a colonization of other fields of research by the publication culture of the sciences.

Third, one of the side effects of rankings has been that the university as an organization is becoming an object as well as a subject in the on-going construction of excellence. Universities have to some extent always been concerned with the construction and preservation of reputation. Yet, such reputation-focused activities have traditionally been played out via individual academics and academic units, and the reputation they lend to their organization. Public-sector reforms inspired by New Public Management principles have evolved around the globe that already stressed the strategic actorhood of the university as an organization, changing and increasing managerial spaces within universities, and evaluating and benchmarking universities as a whole (Krücken and Meier 2006; de Boer et al. 2007). The responsibility and accountability of universities has expanded beyond traditional bureaucratic areas of control, and the university as an organization becomes a focus and locus of governance within the field. The rise of international rankings has further accelerated the discourse of universities as corporate and global actors. Once reputation gets calculated and made visible in a simplistic measure of 'university performance', and comparisons with other organizations around the globe can supposedly be easily made, reputation is being shifted from the level of individual scholars to an organizational issue to be dealt with by responsive management (Power et al. 2009).

In consequence of ranking criteria, we can further note how a certain type of world-class university serves as a role model for the ranking criteria and consequently their outcomes. Global comparisons are made most prominently in relation to one model of the university, the comprehensive research-intensive university. This university model, most prominently developed in the leading U.S. American research universities, lends itself to the formation of a single global competition constructed in the rankings that build on established notions of what constitutes a 'world-class university' (Marginson and van der Wende 2007). The success of American universities in these rankings and their current domination in the emerging global field is the consequent outcome of the social construction of 'world-class' in doing rankings. Other models of universities that would, for example, focus on undergraduate teaching, regional development, or certain fields of research only can by definition not successfully compete in the beauty contest organized by the rankings. By prioritizing and favouring a certain university model, rankings set standards for inclusion and exclusion and provide role models of legitimate and successful ways of organizing universities as organizations. They also reinforce a trend in scientific knowledge production that had already developed before international university rankings came into existence: the rising collaboration in high-impact science across university boundaries in which world-class research universities play a leading role. Recent scientometric research documents the way that multi-university authored papers are the fastest growing type of publications, increasingly stratified by university rank, and more likely to become the highest-impact papers when the collaboration includes a top-ranked university. 'Thus, although geographic distance is of decreasing importance, social distance is of increasing importance in research collaborations' (Johns et al. 2008: 1261).

Fourth, rankings implicitly support the idea of organizational vertical stratification as a standard for success in the field of higher education. In some countries, e.g. France, Japan, the U.K., U.S., vertical stratification and related status hierarchies among their universities developed long before national and international rankings entered the field. Such patterns of national stratification could, however, reflect different roles for universities within specific contexts and conditions: universities' scientific role showing the leading research universities at the top; the role of prestigious teaching-oriented organizations reproducing a societal elite; or a mix of both functions. In many countries, vertical stratification played, however, a minor or less visible role, and universities traditionally enjoyed broad parity of status, and of regulatory and financial treatment. Nowadays, vertical stratification has become an issue also in those systems where there is a marked shift to engage with global league tables.

Finally, international rankings do what national rankings do but they do it on a global scale, providing measures that can easily be aggregated to point at success and failure, and the rise and fall of countries in the emerging field-specific global competition. Certainly, comparing countries' success in rankings is problematic in many ways. Rankings ignore national and organizational contexts and conditions, and, most importantly, regulatory regimes and the availability of funding. They ignore the size of a country and of its higher education system, or the dominance of English as the language of science that works in the favour of the few countries that also dominate the landscape of international journals. The simplistic beauty of rankings, and their standardized, de-contextualized, commensurate measures, unfold, however, not only seductive and coercive power within inter-organizational competition but for international competition as well, including a new space for transnational governance.

7.3. PLAYING THE RANKING GAME: POLICY INITIATIVES AND ORGANIZATIONAL RESPONSES

With international rankings, especially the global ranking of research performance, the field of higher education has entered a truly global space for the exertion of transnational governance, of global competition between countries and between universities as global actors in their own right. Higher education systems that were once protected, as closed national preserves, are now 'open' systems exposed to global reputational competition. The rankings quickly achieved great attention in higher education, in international and national politics and public arenas, and influence transnational governance, national and organizational policy behaviour.

Organizations at the transnational or supranational level have been quick to interact with international rankings in various ways. Rankings themselves have become an issue of transnational governance. In 2004, for example, UNESCO and the U.S.-based Institute for Higher Education Policy initiated a process for self-regulation and self-monitoring of rankings. The creation of an international expert group led, as a first step, to a code of conduct and good practice for the ranking business (the Berlin principles) and subsequently to the establishment of an Observatory on Academic Ranking and Excellence that aims to be a system to audit the auditors. This process will, however, only gain credibility if it is used by the majority of the main ranking compilers and if it can show some independence from these. In 2008, the European Commission took its initiative to create a new 'European' ranking that would pay more attention and respect to the diversity of the field of higher education, and is expected to counter-balance rankings being dominated by the Anglo-Saxon and Asian ranking organizations. The resulting U-Multirank project is now being conducted by a consortium of European research centres whose basic approach is to compare only institutions which are similar and comparable in terms of their missions and structures (van Vught and Ziegele

2012). Field-based rankings will focus on a particular type of institution, and develop and test sets of indicators appropriate to these institutions by using a grouping approach rather than a league table approach. The design will compare not only the research performance of institutions but will include teaching and learning as well as other aspects of university performance. This indicates a rather self-reinforcing process of ranking expansion and proliferation where the development and use of rankings and their measures to alter perceptions of the field is likely to spur the need for new and better measures and systems, in search of the most appropriate and authoritative ranking.

Transnational organizations, such as the European Commission, the OECD, UNESCO, or the World Bank have also been buying into the competitive logic of international rankings. In recent years, the field of higher education and research has been rediscovered as a major driver of innovation for national, regional and global economic growth. A new grand narrative of the role of the field of higher education has emerged. As universities are increasingly seen as important parts of innovation systems, they are prioritized as a core institution for the global competitiveness of the knowledge-based economy and therefore a key strategic area for transnational and national policy. This goes together with the emergence of a set of generic higher education and research policies, and a competitive turn in the transnational governance of the field. Transnational and supranational organizations have themselves discovered the potentially powerful and coercive logic of stocktaking, benchmarking and reporting on world regions and countries according to their standards and policy templates (Enders and Westerheijden 2011). Policy scoreboards, record cards and the like provide synthetic, easily-readable, and widely-distributed overviews of what has been achieved and not achieved in countries. Naming, blaming, and shaming of countries can impose enormous pressure on national policy makers even though they are formally speaking participating in an unbinding international political process based on voluntary agreement. This competitive turn in the political management of the transnational governance of higher education co-evolved with the rise of international rankings that have quickly been picked up by international organizations. Policies for building world-class universities or excellence in higher education have indeed been advocated as internationally applicable instruments for better regulation and system design by the EU, the OECD, UNESCO, and the World Bank (European Commission 2005; Godin 2003; Sadlak and Cai 2009; Salmi 2009). Next to the rankings themselves, international organizations provide a further driver for governments to implement policies to maintain or build 'world-class' universities in their national systems (Hazelkorn 2011).

In Europe, targeted evaluation and funding for research in selected universities were first developed in the U.K., while nowadays processes of policy formation and implementation for being 'world class' in the field of higher education are observable in many if not all continental European countries. Vertical stratification has thus become an issue in many national systems where international pressures allow agile institutional entrepreneurs within the system to reconfigure it.

Germany's science and higher education system has, for example, been characterized by sectoral differentiation (universities, vocational higher education, public research organizations), while universities were considered roughly equal in terms of prestige, quality and political 'treatment'. International rankings undermined traditional beliefs about the high international standing of German university-based research as well as beliefs about a more or less equal performance of German universities. In 2005, the German Excellence Initiative was launched by the Federal government and the *Länder* to improve the international standing of German universities and to provide targeted funding on a competitive basis to selected universities to enable them to compete on a global scale. France recently developed its own approach for excellence policies, which introduced major changes to the conception of the field of higher education. As in Germany, some academics, programmes or universities were more renowned than others, but governments of different political hues often declared that their main objective was to secure national equality and fight against imbalances that might occur between regions or universities. Excellence policies mark a break with this long tradition and aim to increase differentiation among universities. Further, these policies aim at developing regional synergies and new forms of common governance among universities, selective Grandes Écoles and research organizations in order to weaken the traditional divide between these sectors within the field. A similar trend has been detected in ex-communist countries including Russia, China, and many Eastern European countries.

More and more Asian countries are also joining this academic arms race of greater investment into national standing in the global field of higher education. For instance, China's 211 and 985 projects, Japan's Centre of Excellence in the Twenty-First Century programme, Taiwan's 'five-year–fifty-billion' programme and South Korea's Brain Korea 21 are political initiatives in these countries to improve the research capacity of selected institutions or research units, thereby facilitating their ability to compete for world-class status. In Latin America, countries like Argentina, Brazil, and Chile are sending their selected universities into the competition; and Arab Gulf states have also announced their aspirations, including the establishment of new research universities, such as in Saudi Arabia.

In sum, we are witnessing a veritable process of international policy diffusion in global higher education. The international pressures allow agile institutional entrepreneurs within the national system to reconfigure it, potentially consolidating their own national positions of advantage and inhibiting challenge. Deliberate stratification of universities by the State can be understood in relation to such strategies of exclusion. And national academic elites are suspected of being quick to welcome the plans for designating research-intensive universities. Social networking among these elites and with political actors might then play as much of a part in the selection of a privileged core as any more objective indicators of academic outputs.

According to neo-institutionalist perspectives, there are well known isomorphic drivers to explain the diffusion of the 'world-class university' narrative over time and across national contexts (Meyer et al. 1997). Changes in beliefs about the appropriate ways of running modern and efficient higher education and research systems lead to isomorphic pressures to engage with policies for 'world-class' universities. Such policies are an example of the social construction of appropriate goals, means, and ends. Policy choice is based on fads, revered exemplars, or abstract templates, and social acceptance of the policy approach might happen in different ways: a) leading countries serve as exemplars; b) international organizations serve as model-builders and norm-setters; c) expert groups theorize the effects of a new policy, and thereby give policy makers rationales for adopting it.

The work of Espeland and Sauder (2009) has shown that universities have little chance to escape from this academic arms race. Buffering universities from rankings is difficult if not impossible—depending on the regulatory environment and the position of the university—while governmental policies add to the pressures presented by the international rankings. International rankings and national policies for 'world-class' universities play out in the very heartland of the academic system—the struggle for reputation as symbolic capital, and related benefits in economic and social capital.

Rankings, reputation management and branding have in fact a mutually reinforcing effect. Rankings provide signals to universities to engage in reputation management and branding (Naidoo and Beverland 2012). In the most general—and frequently unaddressed—sense, rankings make universities think about themselves as an organization. By comparing and ranking universities as a whole they contribute to the idea that the organization matters, that the strategic actorhood of universities as organizations has to be developed, that reputation management and organizational branding are needed.

In a more specific sense, rankings use indicators that invite universities to actively engage in influencing their performance according to the ranking standards as well as their image in the eyes of relevant others. Buying Nobel Prize winners provides, for example, an expensive though fast track to climb in the ARWU rankings—improvements in the ranking position will show up immediately. Merging with other (more) research-intensive universities or public laboratories provides further means to quickly gather success in publication and citations as well as the critical mass needed in the ranking game. Establishing carrots and sticks for academics to publish more in English language, international peer reviewed journals provides another popular route to success that needs, however, years to reach fruition. The same holds for 'picking the winners' and privileging the core of research active academics while creating a divide between them and the teaching active staff. Establishing graduate schools as well as tenure-track systems in the global competition for young academic talent may count twice—in terms of publication and citation production as well as internationalization. In these and other ways, rankings and their indicators, which started their life external to the organization, have the potential to be internalized into the very dynamics of the university, with its self-management reactively aligning internal measures and policies with the indicators informing the rankings.

As regards branding, prestige surveys of rankings offering halo-susceptible opinions are the most obvious examples of where universities can try to manage their perception by others. Marketing and public relations activities, assuring the use of the university's brand in all its public appearances, increasing international alliances and global networks, all provide examples of tools for organizational perception management. More and more universities also use rankings to brand themselves: to market themselves by using the simplistic representation of their success in rankings. Some are even courageous enough to announce their future ambitions to climb the rankings as part of their image projects. The success and failure of university leaders, sometimes also their salaries, may be tied to organizational success measured by ranking positions. Obviously, such practices provide additional legitimacy to the rankings. When universities put their rankings on their websites, brochures, or press releases, they are complicit in producing and disseminating identities that align with rankings, which in turn may shape their internal processes of identification. Positional competition in rankings thus partly plays out in an image game, a process that works at the edges but seems to become more edgy. In a domain of intangibles, the greater the uncertainty and ambiguity of a product, the stronger the potential effect of skilfully managed activities aiming at their perception by relevant others. In consequence, it becomes a real question to what extent branding and the co-production of images in the ranking game reflects or deviates from a university's reality: a 'circean transformation from substance to image' that Gioia and Corley (2002: 107) discussed while looking at the impact of business school rankings.

7.4. THE POTENTIAL COSTS INVOLVED: WASTE, ISOMORPHISM, AND NEGLECT OF DIVERSITY

International competition and vertical stratification in higher education have become visible around the globe, including a growing number of regions and countries where there is now a marked shift to engage with international rankings and related global competition. Governments are privileging a core of universities to represent their country in this race. Universities develop strategic responses to adapt to the performance criteria and standards created by international rankings and the incentives set by their governments to engage in the global competition for to be world class. Investments made in this international arms race are not necessarily wasted but there is a real challenge due to the competitive dynamics that govern such expenditures.

More and more governments are introducing market or quasi-market competition into their higher education systems and universities are invited to participate in an international and national rivalry for 'global talent', students and faculty members, and resources centred on research reputation. International rankings are a most visible symptom of massification and globalization, as well as a driver for the increasing trend toward competition between universities in both national systems and in the international field. This 'arms race' is already costly and is likely to become even more costly in the future when more and more countries and universities engage in this competition. And when everybody invests, very few will gain a competitive advantage, if any. The competition continues at a higher level of performance, which is likely to set incentives for further investment into the academic arms race.

Playing the ranking game may also have perverse effects on national and organizational strategies. Actions might be taken that are not aligned with public policy goals but that have the sole aim of moving up the list(s). Allotted public funds then risk being wasted as well. In discussing research on the effects of rankings in the U.S. and the U.K., Dill (2009: 102) speaks of a 'highly costly, zero-sum game, in which most institutions as well as society will be the losers'. The research suggests that the normative standard of rankings rather distorts the assumed link between information on academic quality and university efforts to improve academic standards. As a consequence, many universities have responded to ranking competition by investing in managing research reputation and an increasingly costly market for research stars, shifting disciplinary priorities towards high impact fields, setting incentives for increasing research output, and by investing into marketing and branding activities that push up their perceived standing within the field, with limited attention to actually improving academic standards. The distorting influence of this arms race unfolds because privileged world-class universities provide a financial standard for all of higher education. They present spending targets for less elite universities that wish to compete. Behind such aspirations lie the spread and intensification of international higher education as a 'winner-take-all market' (Frank and Cook 1995) in which small differences in performance translate eventually into large differences in reward.

In addition, international rankings are likely to fuel organizational isomorphism within the global field of higher education, leading universities to change their focus and mission in response to rankings. International rankings contribute to deliberate stratification by constructing new boundaries and defining a heartland and a periphery. How these boundaries are constructed is to a large extent dictated by the international reputational hierarchies that already prevail, which are centred on research reputation. While policy makers and organizational leaders might emphasize the importance of organizational diversity, universities of different types, missions and conditions are considerably affected by the same set of ranking indicators. The world-class research university thus becomes the ultimate template for success. It becomes the Holy Grail which many universities are striving for, even if only a few of them will be successful. However, competition according to normalized ranking standards will lead to the imitation of the best and thus to a further standardization of research universities internationally. Policy makers and organizational leaders act rationally and strategically when they try to become what is measured while what is measured becomes increasingly accepted and normalized. Paradoxically, rankings may thus contribute to the erosion of differentiation that already exists within the field and potentially threatens to flatten out diversity among organizations.

In this context, concern for the wider purposes of higher education seems to have few effective champions. The public mission of higher education (Calhoun 2006; Enders and Jongbloed 2007) is challenged by these developments. What seems likely to happen is a loss of reputation attached to other purposes of universities than their research function. The privileging of academic research outputs leads to the consequent reduction in the diversity of organizational missions; or, at least, the subordination of those other missions to research. Issues of access and equity, the role of higher education for social mobility, the quality of teaching and learning, the contribution of a university to the community and regional development, to name but a few examples, do not play a significant role in international rankings. This risks reducing the diversity, adaptability and resilience of the higher education system as a whole; something of central concern for public policy and the governance of higher education and research.

7.5. CONCLUSIONS AND FURTHER RESEARCH

This paper has argued that the rise of international rankings in higher education forms a visible symptom of global educational expansion and global inter-connectedness in the field while rankings also provide important input into field dynamics. The entry of international rankings into the field shows how field dynamics can change due to the emergence of new actors within the field that rationalize informal field dynamics and externalize its logic in widely visible quality judgments according to their own systems. International rankings interact with traditional field dynamics by selecting the dominant logic of research excellence as the ultimate standard for inclusion and exclusion at the competitive apex of the field, neglecting other logics within the heteronomous field. They perform an Aristotelian science of classification, hierarchization and de-contextualization, producing 'magical numbers' (March 1996) in the construction of standards for the world-class university that are easily communicable and digestible. The simplistic beauty of ranking systems supports their seductive and coercive power, allows them to travel easily and lends itself to uses in multiple contexts of the international field.

International rankings do institutional work within a multi-level and multi-actor field. They affect the constant struggle for multiple and competing logics of higher education within the organizational field as well as within the political field. In this view, rankings are new key elements in the (trans)national governance of the field. They provide an arena for contestation between actors about what the appropriate criteria for comparison, success and legitimacy are. They stimulate investment according to the rules of the ranking game as universities, as well as countries, strive to improve their competitive positions. By defining universities around the globe as their primary object of comparison, rankings support the conception and construction of the university as a corporate and global actor, as a focus and locus of governance within the field. Reputation and reputational risk are matters that continue to concern the traditional professional logic within the field, but increasingly the emerging organizational logic of the strategic actorhood of the university matters as well. By making national comparisons for competitive standing easy and widely recognized, rankings trigger a process of regulatory competition to be 'world class' in higher education. The promulgation of policies to be 'world class' as universally applicable policy tools, as well as the growing number of countries engaging with excellence policies, seems to suggest processes of international diffusion and convergence. Whether brought by international organizations and epistemic communities or direct competitors, governments have little choice, the thinking goes, but to invest in the international academic arms race. The analysis shows the usefulness of such a multi-level and multi-actor perspective on field change and institutional logics within a heteronomous global field, and in conclusion some implications for future research are outlined.

First, international rankings remind us that the diffusion of global templates for field change needs to be enacted to unfold their seductive and coercive power. 'Globalization' does not just happen to us but needs actors as carriers of new ideas and narratives, as well as the reactivity of other actors within the field to be enacted. The line of argument presented in this paper draws attention to a line of inquiry that goes beyond overt processes of adoption and compliance, and calls for the examination of negotiation on the ground, implementation, and rejection. Some research has been done to investigate universities' reactivity to rankings, showing that it 'takes two to tango'. Moreover, the field is not just populated by ranking organizations and universities. Rankings have also entered the international and national policy arena although little is known about the dynamics of the international spread of rankings themselves or about the political diffusion and uptake in international organizations and national policy making. While we gain some purchase from a neo-institutionalist perspective on 'world polity' and international policy diffusion, this strand of research does not pay a great deal of attention to the processes of their enactment on the ground and assumes rejection to be the 'exception to the rule' of globalization.

To date, no systematic comparative empirical research has sought to explore the factors driving and forming the rise of rankings and related policies for world-class institutions across the world. Such research has the potential to offer original insights into the policy dynamics and the logics of contestation and change in the heteronomous field. In order to understand the policy dynamics, conceptual frameworks addressing agenda change (Baumgartner et al. 2006; Kingdon 1995) provide further conceptual inspiration and empirical tools by simultaneously following ideas and actors. Attention needs to be paid to international and national actors who are influential in framing the problems and suggesting solutions, as well as to actors trying to block the process, denying access to new issues and taking into account conflicting interests, power relations and strategic actorhood. 'Shifts in framing' point to the role of ideational factors for explaining policy making trajectories and policy transformations; that is the influence of causal narratives in the conception of policies. We can assume that in a political sub-field like higher education—which has been deeply rooted in national traditions and normative beliefs—ideational factors provide an important factor for political change. The study of ideational change will also point to deeper 'discursive turns' in the social re-construction of the role the field is expected to fulfil within society and the economy.

Second, variety in the regulatory and normative order of higher education can be expected to mediate the reactivity of universities to rankings and stratification policies, and related field change. The political, social, and cultural contexts in which universities exist affect how they operate and how they can interact with templates for global competition. The traditional degree of vertical stratification within the national field, the autonomy in running a university, the resource dependencies of universities, and their ability to acquire new funds, all vary depending on their legal status and reliance on public budgets. Accounting for contexts and conditions is not just of relevance for understanding strategic organizational behaviour but for our conceptualizations of institutional logics in universities as hybrid organizations and field change. In his influential study of universities' reactivity to rankings, Sauder (2008) argues that field changes cannot be explained by change in institutional logics, since the logics of vertical organizational ordering, and of competition according to the logics of the marketplace, began before the introduction of the rankings. While this holds for a highly stratified and marketized system like the one in the U.S., international rankings diffuse such logics around the globe and into very different parts of the world where such logics have traditionally not prevailed. International rankings penetrate very different national fields: what comes as a rationalization of well-established orders in one context forms a remarkable exogenous shock in a different context. Future research thus also needs to pay systematic attention to variations to organizational responses to rankings and stratification policies: the conditions that influence the mechanism and degree of their unfolding discipline in organizations in different regulatory and normative contexts. As institutional research on organizational hybrids and related field dynamics is still relatively scarce, and understanding of organizational responses to institutional complexity and change is partial, much work remains to be done (Greenwood et al., 2011).

Third, the aggregate outcome of organizational reactivity to rankings and stratification policies lends itself to the further study of competition and stratification within the field, on the global as well as on the national level. Under certain conditions, there is the probability that reputational and material gains generate further gains in an exponential way. Bourdieu's theory of capital accumulation (Bourdieu 1975) as well as Merton's Matthew effect (1968) would predict a growing inequality within the field due to self-reinforcing mechanisms. Under conditions of a zero-sum game (in terms of available material and immaterial resources) the gains of some would lead to the consequential losses of others. Since status competition is characterized by closure, the membership of the elite would remain largely stable over time. Where this pattern changes, it would not be on the side of greater access but of greater closure leading to a more intensive concentration of status at the very top. This could shift to a 'saturation effect', which would lead to a new 'equilibrium' via the institutionalization of status hierarchies, and a situation in which mechanisms for the reproduction of inequality become dominant. Under certain conditions, stratification might, however, 'fail'. The field might be more or less saturated and mobilization of interest and resources might become marginal, confirm the status quo ante, or lead to minor further stratification effects. Stratification might also not appear due to policy design. National and organizational resources might be insufficient, might not be concentrated enough (spreading all over the field), or might not be sustainable (creating a very limited temporary shock within the field). Stratification might also not appear due to 'contesting the game': competition for to be world class in research might be accompanied or followed by actors and actions calling for political intervention to re-balance the field. Such actors can be expected to make use of the multi-functional role of universities and claim a neglect of functions other than elite science.

International rankings contribute to the competitive turn in higher education and affect diverse interests internationally, nationally, and organizationally. As such rankings proliferate and interact with other changes in the (trans) national governance of higher education, further research is needed to more fully understand and theorize the role and impact of these systems in the field of higher education.

REFERENCES

Battilana, Julie and D'Aunno, Thomas (2009). 'Institutional Work and the Paradox of Embedded Agency', in Thomas B. Lawrence, Roy Suddaby, and Bernard Leca (eds) *Institutional Work: Actors and Agency in Institutional Studies of Organizations*. Cambridge, U.K.: Cambridge University Press, 31–58.

Baumgartner, Frank. R., Green-Pedersen, Christopher, and Jones, Brian D. (2006). 'Comparative Studies of Policy Agendas', *Journal of European Public Policy*, 13(7): 959–974.

Bourdieu, Pierre (1975). 'The Specificity of the Scientific Field and the Social Conditions of the Progress of Reason', *Sociology of Science Information*, 14(6): 19–47.

Bourdieu Pierre (1988). *Homo Academicus*. Cambridge: Polity Press.

Calhoun, Craig (2006). 'The University and the Public Good', *Thesis Eleven*, 84(7): 7–43.

De Boer, Harry F., Enders, Jürgen, and Leysite, Liudvika (2007). 'Public Sector Reform in Dutch Higher Education: The Organizational Transformation of the University', *Public Administration*, 85(1): 27–46.

Dill, David D. (2009). 'Convergence and Diversity: The Role and Influence of University Ranking', in Barbara M. Kehm, and Bjørn Stensaker, (eds), *University Rankings, Diversity, and the New Landscape of Higher Education*. Rotterdam: Sense Publishers, 97–116

DiMaggio, Paul J., and Powell, Walter W. (1983). '"The Iron Cage Revisited": Institutional Isomorphism and Collective Rationality in Organizational Fields', *American Sociological Review*, 48(2): 147–60.

Enders, Jürgen (2004). 'Higher Education, Internationalisation, and the Nation-State: Recent Developments and Challenges for Governance Theory', *Higher Education*, 47(3): 361–382.

Enders, Jürgen and Jongbloed, Ben (2007). 'The Public, The Private and the Good in Higher Education and Research', in Jürgen Enders, and Ben Jongbloed (eds), *Public-Private Dynamics in Higher Education. Expectations, Developments, and Outcomes*, Bielefeld: transkript, 9–38.

Enders, Jürgen and Westerheijden, Don F. (2011). 'The Bologna Process: from the National to the Regional to the Global, and Back', in Roger King, Simon Marginson, and Rajani Naidoo (eds) *Handbook on Globalization and Higher Education*. Cheltenham/Northampton, M.A.: Edward Elgar, 469–484.

Espeland, Wendy N. and Sauder, Michael (2007). 'Rankings and Reactivity: How Public Measures Recreate Social Worlds', *American Journal of Sociology*, 113(1): 1–40.

European Commission (2005). *Mobilizing the Brain Power of Europe: Enabling Universities to Make their Full Contribution to the Lisbon Strategy*. SEC (2005) 518.

Fligstein, N. (1997). 'Social Skill and Institutional Theory', *American Behavioral Scientist*, 40: 387–405.

Fligstein, Neil and McAdam, Doug (2012). *A Theory of Fields*. Oxford: Oxford University Press.

Foucault, Michel (1971). *The Order of Things. An Archaeology of the Human Sciences*. New York: Pantheon Books.

Frank, Robert and Cook, Philip J. (1995). *The Winner-Take-All Society: Why the Few at the Top Get So Much More Than the Rest of Us*. New York: Martin Kessler Books.

Gioia, Dennis and Corley, Kevin G. (2002). 'Being Good versus Looking Good: Business School Rankings and the Circean Transformation from Substance to Image', *Academy of Management Learning and Education*, 1: 107–121.

Godin, Benoit (2003). 'The Emergence of S&T Indicators: Why did Governments Supplement Statistics with Indicators?', *Research Policy*, 32(4): 679–691.

Greenwood, Royston, Raynard, Mia, Kodeih, Farah, Micelotta, Evelyn R., and Lounsbury, Michael (2011). 'Institutional Complexity and Organizational Responses', *Academy of Management Annals*, 5: 317–371.

Harvey, Lee (2008). 'Rankings of Higher Education Institutions: A Critical Review', *Quality in Higher Education*, 14(3): 187–208.

Hazelkorn, Ellen (2011). *Rankings and the Reshaping of Higher Education. The Battle for World-Class Excellence*. New York, N.Y.: Palgrave Macmillan.

Jepperson, Ronald L. (1991). 'Institutions, Institutional Effects, and Institutionalism, in Walter W. Powell, and Paul J. DiMaggio (eds) *The New Institutionalism in Organizational Analysis*. Chicago: University of Chicago Press, 143–163.

Johns, Benjamin F., Wuchty, Stefan, and Uzzi, Brian (2008). 'Multi-University Research Teams: Shifting Impact, Geography, and Stratification in Science', *Science*, 322(5905): 1259–1262.

Kingdon, John. W. (1995). *Agendas, Alternatives and Public Policies*, New York: HarperCollins.

Krücken, Georg and Meier, Frank (2006). 'Turning the University into an Organizational Actor', in Gili S. Drori, John W. Meyer, and Hokyu Hwang (eds) *Globalization and Organization: World Society and Organizational Change*. Oxford: Oxford University Press, 241–257.

March, James G. (1996). 'Continuity and Change in Theories of Organizational Action', *Administrative Science Quarterly*, 41(2): 278–287.

March, James G. and Simon, Herbert A. (1958). *Organizations*. New York: Wiley.

Marginson, Simon, and van der Wende, Marijk (2007). 'To Rank or To Be Ranked: The Impact of Global Rankings in Higher Education', *Journal of Studies in International Education*, 11(3/4): 306–329.

Merton, Robert K. (1968). 'The Matthew Effect in Science', *Science*, 159(3810): 56–63.

Meyer, J. W., Boli, J., Thomas, G. M., and Ramirez, F. O. (1997). 'World Society and the Nation-State, *American Journal of Sociology*, 103(1): 144–181.

Naidoo Rajani (2004). 'Fields and Institutional Strategy: Bourdieu on the Relationship between Higher Education, Inequality and Society', *British Journal of Sociology of Education*, 25(4): 457–471.

Naidoo, Rajani and Beverland, Michael (2012). '*Branding Business Schools: Academic Struggles with the Strategic Management of Reputation*'. Paper presented at the

EFMD Higher Education Research Conference, Lorange Institute of Business, Zürich, 14–15 February 2012.

Power, Michael, Scheytt, Tobias, Soin, Kim, and Sahlin, Kerstin (2009). 'Reputational Risk as a Logic of Organizing in Late Modernity', *Organization Studies*, 30(02&03): 301–324.

Sadlak, Jan and Cai, Liu N. (2009). *The World-Class University as Part of a New Higher Education Paradigm*. UNESCO European Centre for Higher Education, Shanghai Jiao Tong University: Cluij University Press.

Salmi, Jamil (2009). *The Challenge of Establishing World-Class Universities*. Washington, D.C.: World Bank.

Sauder, Michael (2008). 'Interlopers and Field Change: The Entry of U.S. News into the Field of Legal Education', *Administrative Science Quarterly*, 53(2): 209–234.

Sauder, Michael and Espeland, Wendy N. (2009). 'The Discipline of Ranking: Tight Coupling and Organizational Change', *American Sociological Review*, 74(1): 63–82.

Scott, Richard W. (1995). *Institutions and Organizations*. Thousand Oaks, CA: Sage.

Sewell, William H. (1992). 'A Theory of Structure: Duality, Agency, and Transformation', *American Journal of Sociology*, 98(1): 1–29.

Usher, Alex and Medow, John (2009). 'A global survey of university rankings and league tables', in Barbara M. Kehm and Bjørn Stensaker (eds), *University Rankings, Diversity, and the New Landscape of Higher Education*. Rotterdam: Sense Publishers, 3–18.

van Raan, Anthony F. J. (2007). 'Challenges in Ranking Universities', in Jan Sadlak, and Liu NianCai. (eds), *The World-Class University and Ranking: Aiming Beyond Status*. Bucharest: UNESCO-DEPES, 87–121.

Van Vught, Frans, and Ziegele, Frank (2012) (eds). *Multidimensional Ranking: The Design and Development of U-Multirank*. Dordrecht: Springer.

Wedlin, Linda (2011). 'Going Global: Rankings as Rhetorical Devices to Construct an International Field of Management Education', *Management Learning*, 42(2): 199–218.

8

Branding Business Schools

Academic Struggles with the Management of Reputation

Rajani Naidoo and James Pringle

8.1. INTRODUCTION

A series of structural and ideological transformations since the 1980s linked to globalization and the ascendance of neo-liberal political frameworks have resulted in the destabilization of traditional mechanisms governing higher education institutions (Parker and Jary 1995). The prising open of higher education to market forces has shifted the idea of the university as an institution governed by an autonomous republic of scholars (Brubacher 1967) towards the idea of the university as a stakeholder institution organized and managed as a business enterprise (Bleiklie and Kogan 2007). In addition, crises of legitimacy facing the higher education sector have been met with pressure for universities to import marketing and management principles from the private sector as symbolic of a modernized, strategic and globally competitive university management. These factors, as well as intense forms of competition for domestic and international students in the face of major reductions in public funding (Currie and Vidovich 2000), have combined to transform universities into organizational actors responsible for the strategic management of reputation. This has, in turn, led to the perception of the university brand as a valuable asset.

Branding as a marketing concept has become increasingly common in higher education over the last decade as universities search for new ways to position themselves in a competitive marketplace (Argenti 2000; Hemsley-Brown and Goonawarddana 2007). However, research into branding in higher education is at an early stage. In their systematic review of the marketing literature, Hemsley-Brown and Oplatka (2006: 333) conclude that branding has barely made its mark in higher education research. A small number of viewpoint studies have been published which analyse branding in higher education in generic terms (Temple 2006), or focus on the problematic relationship between branding as practised in the for-profit corporate sector and its application to public systems of higher education (Jevons 2006; Maringe 2005). As Hemsley-Brown and Goonawarddana (2007) indicate, empirical investigations of branding are few and far between. In general, such studies focus on how various brand attributes are perceived by external stakeholders, particularly students, and how student choice in higher education operates (Ali-Choudhury et al. 2009; Bennett and Ali-Choudhury 2009; Chapleo 2010).

However, as Karreman and Rylander (2008), writing from an organizational studies perspective indicate, branding does not merely target external stakeholders but is also potentially directed at organization members. They illustrate how branding can be viewed as a management and leadership practice which contributes to the processes in which meaning in and about the organization is shaped. The marketing research also reveals that employees' engagement with, and enactment of, the values and vision of the brand becomes a key element in differentiation strategies and thus provides competitive advantage for companies (Hatch and Schultz 2008; Schultz et al. 2000). The relationship between the brand and those working within the university is thus fundamentally important. Academic faculty, in particular, by the very nature of their productive activities in relation to research and teaching may be perceived to be one of the main embodiments of the university brand. It is interesting to note, however, that with the exception of Waeraas and Solbakk (2009) there has been little empirical investigation on how academic faculty respond and contribute to branding activity.

Our paper addresses this gap by drawing on Lury's (2004) conceptualization of the brand as an interface, which enables a set of relations and exchanges. While her focus is on brands and consumers, our focus is on how brands feature as a locus for organizational members' sensemaking around organizational and professional identity. Our paper therefore contributes to scholarship on branding as a historically-shaped mode of practice that operates in different ways in the context of specific historically institutionalized sectors. Our study is also likely to generate insights for higher education institutions on branding as a marketing, management, educational, authentic (Beverland 2009) and ethical process.

We begin by presenting an overview of key insights in the branding literature, which offer important definitions, concepts and insights into corporate branding strategies. Drawing on Bourdieu's theoretical framework, we develop an analysis of the interaction of branding practices with the organizational characteristics and the internal culture of higher education in relation to academic faculty. This is followed by an exploratory empirical study of a business school in the United Kingdom.

8.2. CORPORATE BRANDING

Branding as an economic organizing principle and as a marketing strategy has increased in significance in the context of what has been called the 'image' economy, in which the production and consumption of signs rivals the production and consumption of physical products and services. In a world where a surfeit of images co-exists with a deficit of attention, branding is able to simplify, differentiate and narrate a range of economic and social values (Guillet de Monthoux 2004; Schroeder 2002). Complex global corporate strategies, which sometimes result in 'brand wars', have been accompanied by increasing output and intellectual rivalry between scholars from various disciplines, including Marketing, Organizational Studies, Anthropology and Cultural Theory, over who has made the most significant contribution to the study and practice of branding.

The early marketing literature conceptualized brands as condensing a complex web of messages, which acted in umbrella-like fashion to encompass a diverse set of products or services that offered customers a brand promise, usually relating to quality. Within this research, the consumer was positioned as a passive receptor of brand messages. Later research and corporate practice understood that brand equity was only achieved when consumers became immersed in the brand and acted as co-producers. Cultural theorists such as Celia Lury (2004) have developed the concept further by conceptualizing brands as an interface that enables a set of relations between products and services through time, and a two-way exchange between producers and consumers. Brands work by differentiating themselves from other brands, integrating with cultural signs, and developing associations in the minds of the customer. The marketing literature also indicates that organizations that are competing on the basis of their ability to communicate what they stand for are in many aspects becoming more 'expressive' (Schultz et al. 2000). In other words, brands have moved away from the mere promise of quality towards the expression of emotions and symbolic values. Hearn (2008) has also demonstrated how brands have become the sign of different types of social identity, which summon consumers into a relationship with it. Thus the brand does not just create products but also acts as a specific cultural resource for the construction of social identities, relationships, lifestyles and particular types of community (Arvidsson 2006; Holt 2002). The brand is thus only realized in the complex interactions between producers and consumers and can never be fully managed and controlled. Brand communities, whether virtual or geographically defined, can contribute to the enhancement of the brand. On the other hand, anti-brand campaigns can be launched which subvert logos and straplines to apply pressure on companies to live up to their brand promises. Finally, brands can be defined as a value-generating commercial asset recognized in law and by corporate accounting practices (Hearn 2008).

This outside-in orientation of various brand management approaches has also been complemented by an inside-out orientation, which highlights the important roles that employees play in building brand equity (De Chernatony 2006; Lomax and Mador 2006). Schultz et al. (2000) and Hatch and Schultz (2008) have pointed to the importance of the alignment of internal organizational culture with external image and strategic vision. There is therefore increasing recognition that employees are key to building relationships with stakeholders and are an integral part of the brand itself (Thomson and Hecker 2000). Proponents of the 'inside-out' orientation argue that employees' engagement with, and enactment of, the values and vision of the brand becomes a key element in differentiation strategies and thus provides competitive advantage for the company (Ahmed and Rafiq 2003; Punjaisri 2007). Mahnert and Torres (2007) emphasize three core principles within their conceptualization of the internal branding construct. They argue that committed employees reflect and deliver desired brand values to consumers, that good communication ensures that the brand promise is realized internally and externally, and that all levels of the organization need to be permeated in order to align the behaviour and attitudes of management and staff. The influential concept of 'brand citizenship' has also been widely applied. This refers to individual voluntary behaviours outside of role expectations 'that are not directly or explicitly acknowledged by the formal reward system, and which, in aggregate, enhance the performance of the organization' (Burmann and Zeplin 2005: 282).

For the purposes of our study, we draw on the various disciplinary literatures on branding in higher education to conceptualize branding as a strategic asset which can be positioned to distil and project intended organizational attributes and values at the interface of relationships between producers, consumers and brand-workers for cultural value and competitive advantage. Branding is both outward and inward facing. In other words, branding is conceptualized as constructing relationships with external stakeholders but it is simultaneously a management practice with the potential to shape meanings, values and practices within the organization. For the purposes of this paper our primary focus is on how academic faculty engage with branding.

We turn now to an analysis of the extent to which 'brand logic' has been institutionalized in the context of higher education. Our analysis is in two stages. We draw first on the work of Pierre Bourdieu to develop a conceptual analysis of how the logic of branding is likely to become re-contextualised within higher education as a historically-shaped institutional site with its own internal culture, organizational identity and values. Second, we present the results of an exploratory study of branding in a business school. We focus on how brands are constructed, adopted and resisted intra-organizationally by managers and academic faculty.

8.3. HIGHER EDUCATION AS AN
ORGANIZATIONAL FIELD

Bourdieu's work on higher education as a specific institutional site, particularly his concepts of 'field', 'capital', and 'habitus' make an important contribution to understanding the dynamics of practice within higher-education institutions. The organizational field concept has a lineage dating back to Durkheim and draws heavily on accounts of the social construction of reality (Berger and Luckmann 1966) while remaining within a materialist base. It has received attention in management studies through the work of the new institutionalists, who have developed the concept to depict a group of organizations within a common institutional framework held together by regulation, cognitive belief systems, and normative rules, and which compete for legitimacy and resources (Powell and DiMaggio 1991). However, while much of the new institutionalists' work leans towards isomorphism, Bourdieu's framework emphasizes that the field is not a product of consensus but the dynamic product of a permanent conflict. The institutional field perspective is a useful theoretical frame, as it provides an analytical perspective and a mediating context linking business schools to the external environment. It also provides a relational approach that focuses on the interactive processes between and within schools.

Although Bourdieu's work on higher education has been developed in the context of France, the application of his concepts to other national contexts indicates the significant contribution his work can make to the study of higher education in general (Naidoo 2004; Tomusk 2000). According to Bourdieu, social formations are structured around a complex ensemble of social fields in which various forms of power circulate. The relative autonomy of fields varies from one period to another, from one field to another, and from one national tradition to another (Bourdieu 1988). The field of university education is conceptualized as a field with a high degree of autonomy, in that it generates its own organizational culture consisting of values and behavioural imperatives that are relatively independent from forces emerging from the economic and political fields (See also Prichard and Willmott (1995) for their conception of higher education as a restricted field of production).

The activities in the field revolve around the acquisition and development of different species of capital, which may be defined as particular resources that are invested with value (Bourdieu 1986). The types of 'capital' invested with value in the field of higher education are termed 'academic' and 'scientific capital', and consist in the first instance of intellectual or cultural, rather than economic assets. Bourdieu differentiates between 'scientific capital' which is related to research renown and is the most powerful capital in the field; and 'academic capital', which is linked to managerial power over the instruments of reproduction of the university body. We would add that other forms of capital, including economic capital, have and will become increasingly powerful as higher education loses its relative autonomy. Individuals and institutions are located in various positions of hierarchy dependent on the type and amount of field-specific capital they possess.

Bourdieu (1977) introduces the concept of 'habitus' to indicate how social practice within fields is generated. He defines habitus as a system of lasting and transposable dispositions which, by integrating past experiences, functions at every moment as a matrix of perceptions, appreciations, and actions. This inclines actors to act and react in specific situations in a manner that is not always calculated and that is not a conscious adherence to rules. According to these definitions, the 'dispositions' represented by the habitus are not fixed and unchanging but 'strategy-generating'. In his major empirical studies on higher education, (Bourdieu 1988, 1996) illustrates the operation of an academic habitus, which orientates practices that revolve around a belief in, and struggle for, the acquisition of scientific and academic capital internal to the field of higher education. These practices are based on a systematic suspension, or even inversion, of the fundamental principles of the economy. The operation of a general academic habitus operating across different national contexts has been confirmed by empirical studies in other national contexts and time periods (Henkel 2005; Naidoo 2000).

Bourdieu's concepts are closely linked to various emanations of practice theory that focus on the interactions between the actions and interactions of actors and institutional contexts. Taking the three concepts of field, capital, and habitus together, practice in the field of higher education is therefore shaped by an academic habitus that engenders in individuals a 'disposition', below the level of consciousness, to act or think in certain ways. Practice also depends the network of objective relations between positions that individuals or institutions occupy in the field. We incorporate within Bourdieu's framework the 'institutional work' approach developed by Lawrence et al. (2009) to focus on the everyday practices and routines that enable both the maintenance and the transformation of institutions. Most importantly, their approach enables us to incorporate the conscious intentions of actors, which are largely absent from Bourdieu's work. Individuals and institutions implement strategies in order to improve or defend their positions in the organizational field in a competition that has historically been relatively autonomous from economic forces but which nevertheless consists of deeply ingrained rules, values, and professional protocols. Organizational fields can thus be regarded as structured systems of social positions that have an impact on faculty interactions with branding. The 'incumbents' are those located in powerful positions in the field, who will seek to preserve the type of power that is effective in the field and thus the status quo. The 'challengers', who are located in dominated positions, will attempt to challenge the existing criteria and distribution of orthodox power effective in the field (Battiliana and D'Aunno 2009).

8.4. BRANDING IN HIGHER EDUCATION

In many respects, branding is a continuation of earlier struggles in the field. Reputation struggles were always part of the university. The sociology of intellectual work indicates that institutions and scholars have long engaged in various forms of rivalry that included the symbolic destruction of rival scholarship and wars over reputation. These reputation- enhancing strategies, however, drew on criteria, practices and representations that were based on the academic criteria, mainly scientific capital, invested with value within the institutional field of higher education. Reputation was gained through institutional processes controlled by academic peers. The hierarchical ordering of universities and faculties was thus internally judged and then projected outwards and accepted as legitimate by external stakeholders.

In contemporary times, higher education reform has ushered in new systems of external accountability (Naidoo 2008). In addition, changes in state regulation and funding, pressures for the transformation of universities from institutions for the elite towards institutions that were opened up to larger segments of the population, the requirement for performative excellence, the construction of national and global quasi-markets and the positioning of students as consumers (Naidoo et al. 2011) have combined to propel universities to engage with forms of marketing practices that are more closely aligned to the corporate world. Contemporary branding practices therefore attract the concentration of financial and administrative resources and introduce an outer-directed process of conscious organizational projection, packaged and distributed according to external performance measures and market criteria.

Our theoretical framework therefore fosters an understanding of branding as the embodiment of values and images linked to market and corporate imagery, and to popular culture, which is implemented in an institutional site that was historically protected from the direct impact of market forces and which remains organized around deeply embedded institutional logics linked to the contestation between scientific and academic capital.

8.5. BRANDING BUSINESS SCHOOLS

We turn now to our exploratory case study. Our study is part of a larger study in which multiple cases of business schools from several countries were presented and discussed at a workshop on branding. Our case study is relatively small in size consisting of around 2100 students. It offers a range of programmes including undergraduate, postgraduate (including specialized M.Sc.) and Ph.D. programmes, as well as executive education for individuals and organizations. It also offers a full, part-time and executive MBA programme. The School has a faculty of around ninety teaching and research staff with a support team of around seventy managerial and administrative staff. Research is structured around six issue-based subject groups, which span functional disciplines. These groupings contain cross-functional research centres, which focus and formalize major research initiatives.

We chose a single case study of a business school in order to explore a research area where both theory and empirical study is at an early stage and where the phenomena could be examined directly in a real-world context and could inform professional practice (Eisenhardt and Graebner 2007). The qualitative case-study approach enabled us to capture the micro-level interactions of individuals and their everyday practices in relation to branding and the meanings they ascribed to them (Barley and Kunda, 2001). In-depth semi-structured interviews were conducted with senior managers including the Dean and members of the Executive Committee, with academics ranging from professors to lecturers across subject groups as well as those with management responsibilities for teaching programmes. Interview questions were based on a list of core themes that included an identification of the different components of the brand and the extent to which this resulted in synergies or contradictions. There was also a focus on emotional and cognitive responses to branding and the individual practices related to branding work. In addition, academic leaders were asked how particular manifestations of the brand functioned as a managerial strategy within the organizational setting of the business school and as a positional strategy within the competitive institutional field of UK business schools. Academic faculty were questioned on the extent to which the brand acted as a carrier of values and meanings and were asked to elaborate on their own situated practices related to branding work. In addition, documentary evidence such as strategy documents, programme brochures, web-based material and visual images including crests and logos were analysed to ascertain the institutionalization of the brand. The case study will begin by focusing on the key features of the school's branding initiatives. It will then consider how faculty members respond to these initiatives.

8.6. BRANDING INITIATIVES AND IMPLEMENTATION STRATEGIES

Branding initiatives in the School began with the arrival of a new dean. He appointed the first Director of Corporate Relations, who was responsible for a range of activities including developing a marketing and branding strategy and directing a team of marketing and web design professionals. A consultancy company was employed to develop a branding strategy resulting in a 'Brand Identity and Style Guide' document. This outlines the importance of a strong brand and prescribed various modes of operation including how the School should be named. It communicates the branding messages and values that should be conveyed and the 'tone of voice' to be used in all communications which should be 'intelligent, authoritative and warm'. It also specifies the logo design, including size for all stationery and develops a power-point template for internal and external presentations. Colour palettes are assigned for all promotional material relating to particular academic programmes.

The current Dean values the previous Dean's approach and has built on his branding approach. Wall plaques with the names of corporations that the School works with were highly visible on the Dean's instructions. A large wall with photographs of members of the Faculty and administrative staff has been replaced by photographs of students. In the interview, the Dean positioned the School mainly in relation to London Business School, Said Business School, Lancaster University Management School and at other times to European institutions such as INSEAD. In creating an organizational position and identity within the field of business school education, the Dean located the School in relation to an elite in a national field, with some overlapping into a European field.

While recognizing key differences between these institutions, the Dean was able to outline certain classificatory norms and values that he sees as important in both associating and differentiating the brand. Research excellence was seen as extremely important. He noted the proliferation of research seminars in the School and the academic recognition of the School's faculty worldwide as 'informal branding work'. The School's position in various ranking systems and its accreditation status was also seen as an important part of the brand and he directed a great deal of attention to this aspect. The concept of branding in response to both 'academic' and 'business' values was an important point for discussion. The Dean also distinguished the School from other schools by size and argued that the relatively small size creates a supportive and friendly environment and avoids a factory style approach to education. Ethics and good citizenship were also seen as important components of the brand.

The Dean's interview, as well as interviews with other members of the senior management team, show that, for senior managers, branding functions to articulate and legitimize the School's position within the hierarchy of institutions within the field. Associations and affiliations are an important part of the branding process—both in terms of the kinds of organizations with which the business school works, as well as the academic institutions with which it collaborates. Branding work also signals the academic institutions that the School distances itself from. It represents itself as a member of an elite group involved in cutting-edge work with high impact at national and international levels. Great emphasis is placed on performance in league tables, the National Student Satisfaction Survey, and the Research Assessment Exercise.

An analysis of the website, promotional material, and interviews with senior managers reveals that research excellence forms a fulcrum around which other features of the branding message are located. In addition, strong historical traditions in relation to images and logos and high scientific capital were used to leverage the brand. The Dean's message on the website and various interviews focus on 'research intensity', 'innovation', 'knowledge creation', 'scholarship', and 'excellence'. In the promotional literature, research is said to provide real world application and relevance, and the quality of teaching is enhanced by synergies between research and teaching. Senior managers proclaim with pride that unlike other business schools, all research professors and senior managers, including the Dean and the Deputy Dean, teach. At the same time, the majority of study programmes have a strong focus on career enhancement and employability. Distinction has been created by developing undergraduate programmes that attract high achieving school leavers to programmes that include placement opportunities in blue chip companies. A strap line reflecting this has been developed and is highly visible in all course brochures and other promotional material.

What is striking was that branding work from its very inception reveals a competing hierarchy of attributes. Closer analysis of documentation and interview data indicate that the intended features of the brand include multiple and competing attributes related to rankings, employability, blue skies research, knowledge capitalization, internationality, and the role of the business school in society. Managers grappled with these attributes and did not appear to attempt to resolve multiple branding claims; rather, the competing claims appeared to assist managers in responding to competing internal and external pressures for legitimacy.

8.7. BRANDING INTERPRETATION

While the above section has mainly concentrated on how branding activities attempt to diffuse particular messages, values, and norms throughout the organization, this section will show how branding reception acts as a vehicle for contestations of such messages, values, and norms.

We found a range of responses from academic faculty pointing to a more fluid engagement with the brand than might normally be assumed. An important insight was that in many cases branding interpretation by individuals was not fixed and static but fluid, with faculty positioning and repositioning themselves in different ways throughout the interview. For some faculty, particularly scholars of a certain generation and critical orientation, the concept of branding took on negative connotations, as they perceived it as the intrusion of the market into the academic realm and the inappropriate influence of business ideology. These respondents were more comfortable with the term 'reputation', which they saw as more 'open', 'democratic', 'academic', 'scholarly', 'real', and legitimately gained. Branding on the other hand was perceived by this group of faculty as more instrumental, manufactured or as a marketing ploy. These respondents were also unaware that a branding strategy document was in existence and had not noticed the emergence of the strapline.

The vast majority of faculty, however, felt that the School had a relatively 'soft' branding strategy. They knew and respected the professional staff working on marketing in the School and felt that the marketing professionals in turn respected their identities as academics. Faculty felt comfortable with the branding approach used as they felt that a hard and artificially coherent branding strategy would be counterproductive to the quality of research and teaching. They felt that the high levels of autonomy enjoyed by faculty and the fact that competing research paradigms could 'live and let live' was important to their professional status, identities, and work.

Differential responses to branding appeared to be most closely related to research and managerial status. Branding activities appeared to pose significant identity threats to research productive faculty. They were in general either indifferent to branding activities, stating that 'branding is something that just floats above us', or 'it is detached from what we do', or hostile, expressing doubts whether scarce resources and time could not be better spent. When introduced to the branding strategy document, faculty in this group did not take it seriously and labelled some of the tips for developing branding messages such as 'write hot, edit cold' as 'business speak'. An analysis of interviews indicated that branding was not considered a legitimate practice as it introduced external, non-academic, market criteria that contaminated higher education as a space that was relatively autonomous from the market.

Branding also had the potential to undermine the criteria through which academics with high research reputations obtained positions of dominance in the field. However, even in this group there was some measure of flexibility. For example, one respondent stated that, 'It is a pity that our brand is not recognised. . . when you look at our performance in research we do so much better than some others'. The relational dimension is brought out here: the self-identification of organizational position and status is self-produced but also reproduced and maintained in relation to the perceptions of others. For this group, branding was also conceptualized as an unwelcome managerial strategy to monitor and manage performance, which signalled for them the erosion of academic autonomy. Faculty with less scientific capital and younger faculty engaged much more readily with the branding strategy. They acted as brand citizens often going beyond their expected role to promote the brand.

Faculty that were both research productive and involved in management roles, particularly in the management of teaching, took branding work seriously enough to engage with it. It was in this group that the shift in responses to branding at different stages of the interview could be most clearly seen. When they responded to branding in the context of their research, they excluded or were indifferent to branding activities. They made a conscious choice not to use the School's PowerPoint template in research presentations because it detracted from the 'scholarly' nature and the 'seriousness' of their research. An Associate Dean noted that while he would always use the official PowerPoint template in his management and teaching roles, he would not necessarily do so at research conferences as research presentations were 'more about the substance. . . and I feel the visualisations detract from it'. They listed their school and university affiliation but did very little explicit branding work at research conferences. Closer questioning revealed that in this role, faculty wished to be primarily recognized as scholars who were part of a disciplinary community. The institutional and school affiliation became less important.

However, when discussing their management roles, their self-positioning changed. When asked how such tensions were managed, one senior respondent stated 'I live them and hold them. . . depending on the role I am playing'. He clarified that he felt that he almost automatically took on a different identity with different responses to branding depending on whether he was acting in his role as an academic researcher or as a manager'. When shown the branding strategy document, they felt that some of the advice—for example how photographs for course brochures should be taken, the language that could be used, and various other suggestions—was helpful. Many regularly used a version of the PowerPoint template when they marketed academic programmes and in relation to student recruitment and student induction events. In this role, rather than branding activities being excluded because they undermined academic capital, we found contestations between 'academic' and 'business' capital within branding activities, particularly in relation to the messages that were sent to students. Faculty discussed the extent to which a balance between employability and criticality could be achieved. There was the strong sense from one faculty member that branding should not be merely geared to profit-making corporations for short-term business needs but also to the longer-term needs of the knowledge society. This person felt that being in a school of management rather than a business school was important because it signified that the School's activities could be geared to the benefit of society as a whole. Many faculty members were keen that sustainability should become a key feature of the brand. In this group there were also discussions around the extent to which the ethical dimensions of research and teaching was constituted as a visible component of the brand. Faculty also raised the importance of 'authenticity' (Beverland 2009) and the dangers of image becoming more important and dislocated from practice.

8.8. CONCLUSIONS AND IMPLICATIONS FOR FURTHER RESEARCH

In conclusion, we identify some continuities with, but also a number of differences from, some of the more common insights of the marketing literature. Our research reveals that the strategic development and implementation of branding in our case study school has been loosely implemented in line with the dominant organizational culture. We also found that the nature of the brand and responses to the brand are shaped by individual agency and the organizational structure and culture of the School. From its very inception, we found multiple, ambiguous, and contradictory voices rather than a single dominant voice of branding.

While branding initiatives were to a certain extent aimed at generating distinction as well as 'distance' from non-research intensive business schools, they were also aimed at developing associations with other business schools, including in an aspirational sense. In addition, our study revealed that rather than generating externally generated attributes, branding was internally generated by drawing on the voice of internal stakeholders and attaching key values, emotions and associations that were already deeply embedded in the cultural fabric of the school. While the initiation of branding was led by the Dean and the Executive Committee, branding was also influenced by faculty, who re-contextualized and resisted branding constructions in their professional activities. Branding activities simultaneously opened up new avenues of meaning and values, introduced conflict, and attempted to provide discursive closure. Rather than seeing this as potentially dysfunctional, we suggest that maintaining a dynamic exchange over branding is essential in a university environment. Indeed, all academic faculty interviewed welcomed the heterogeneous branding approach of the school as they felt that this resulted in the protection of academic autonomy and opened up critical spaces for discussions around aims and ethics. We also suggest that within reason, presenting many organizational faces to different audiences may be crucial in gaining widespread legitimacy in the face of the maelstrom of diverse and competing interests facing higher education institutions (Sillince and Brown 2009).

What then are the implications for further research?

The first point to make is that branding offers an important lens to analyse some of the effects of the restructuring of higher education in the United Kingdom. These transformations have been associated with economic and ideological shifts away from a Keynesian welfare state model and the social compact that evolved between higher education, the state and society over the last century. Instead, a new settlement based on quasi-market forces and neo-liberalism has been implemented (Naidoo 2003; Slaughter and Leslie 1997). In essence, as McGettigan (2013) argues, quasi-market competition has been introduced in conjunction with elements of deregulation and partial privatization and the idea that public universities ought to be organized and managed as business enterprises is gaining widespread influence amongst managers in higher education. The practice of branding in higher education is thus interesting to explore, particularly since public higher-education systems have until relatively recently been shielded from the direct pressures of market forces. Indeed, in many ways, public higher-education institutions have traditionally encompassed professional cultures which have been antithetical to market principles and cultures (Halsey and Trow 1971; Henkel 2005). An analytical focus on the interaction of branding with the organizational characteristics and the internal culture of higher education will therefore generate important insights about an important sector in society, which is subject to changing relations between state regulation and market forces and which is undergoing major transformations.

While our study has focused on a particular type of business school, insights from our theoretical framework would lead us to hypothesize that approaches and responses to branding are likely to differ substantially across the system of higher education, particularly between high and low status universities. Meadmore (1998), in the context of Australia has argued that elite universities do not need to vie for 'positional goods', as they are able to capitalize on the 'cachet of the past'. This includes strong track records in research, intergenerational social capital through their alumni, reserves of wealth and oligarchic traditions. In addition, elite universities are compelled to constrain expansion in order to maintain and maximize their positional status (Marginson 2006). In other words, elite universities with high levels of scientific capital, which are in the upper levels, are likely to develop branding practices that draw on academic attributes, such as scientific excellence, and visual images, such as traditional historical crests, which in effect reinforce the boundary between the field of higher education and the external context. Institutions lower in the hierarchy which do not compete on symbolic and status grounds but rather on volume are likely to pursue branding strategies that draw in externally generated images and messages that erode the distinction between the inner sanctum of higher education and the external world. Bourdieu has also conceptualized disciplines as existing in hierarchy and clustered around what he terms the 'autonomous' pole, comprising the sub-field of restricted production where producers produce for other producers, and the 'heterono-mous' pole, comprising the field of large-scale production where producers produce for external consumers. The autonomous sector is based on the accu-mulation of symbolic capital internal to the field, while the heteronomous sector is subordinated to the demands of economic capital and other princi-ples emanating from the field of power (Bourdieu 1993: 46). We would there-fore expect to find differences in how academics located in different faculties and disciplines respond to branding imperatives. There is therefore a clear need for further empirical studies to examine internal branding across dif-ferent types of universities and disciplines as well as across different national contexts.

A further important area to explore is whether and how brand images and messages relate to the actual and substantive nature of the research, teach-ing and other professional activities engaged in by business schools. At one extreme, we might hypothesize, in the words of one of our informants, that 'branding is something that just floats above us'. In other words, branding can be conceptualized as mere image, which has little relationship to substance. Levitt (1981: 97) has stated that, particularly for more complex and intangi-ble products, judgement is influenced by 'how such products are presented, who presents it' and what messages are communicated by 'metaphor, simile, and other surrogates for reality'. Gioia and Corley (2002) have also convinc-ingly demonstrated that in an image-driven marketplace, it becomes easier to project an image of change rather than engage in actual change. Alvesson (1990) has indicated that in a context where images must act as substitutes for experience, we will have the growing occurrence of 'pseudoactions' which are activities designed to influence the perceptions of an audience while dis-guising actual intent, and 'pseudostructures' which are structures that do not affect the organization's work in a real sense, but instead have legitimizing potential by reflecting the correct values.

Arguably though, even if the relationship between branding and actual practice is tenuous, branding activities in higher education institutions nev-ertheless have material effects and consequences, which are worth exploring. At the most basic level, institutions have to decide to what extent they spend valuable resources, including time and money, on image related enhancement rather than on the actual improvement of teaching and research. In addi-tion, as competition intensifies, the temptation for selective projection, or in the worst-case scenario, for falsification, becomes stronger (Gioia and Corley 2002). The effects and consequences of such actions would be important to explore, particularly in a litigious context where students perceive them-selves to be paying customers. An even more difficult, but crucial, scenario to research would be the extent to which the brand, when developed by senior managers in a top-down manner primarily for the purposes of external projection, nevertheless reflects back into the organization so as to change core cultures, values, and the actual content of teaching and research activities.

Finally, we would urge researchers working on these, and the many other unexplored questions related to branding in higher education, to avoid withdrawing into the disciplinary silos characterized as organizational studies and critical marketing. It is important for further research to bring together the diverse range of disciplinary scholarship to encompass the cultural and managerial dimensions of the production and consumption of brands. Branding in higher education can be most fruitfully conceptualized as a strategic asset, which is positioned to distil and project intended organizational attributes and values at the interface of relationships between producers, consumers and brand-workers for cultural value and competitive advantage. In this sense, insights from critical marketing and organizational studies can helpfully be complemented by cultural studies literature in order to focus on the social constructivist nature of branding. However, it is also important to acknowledge that these analyses offer an important but nevertheless partial view. Edensor and Kothari (2006: 332) for example have referred to the problems of the social constructivist turn and the replacing of the 'use and exchange value of goods' by 'sign value' with no reference to the political economy of the production of difference. In other words, the organizational and cultural underpinnings of research into branding need to be complemented by analyses related to political economy (Dholakia and Fuat Firat 1998; Wasko et al. 2011) in order to investigate the factors involved in the financial valorization of the brand. As universities and business schools are increasingly propelled into a quasi-market environment, the analysis of supply and demand, capital accumulation and monopolization will become increasingly important.

ACKNOWLEDGEMENTS

We would like to thank Mats Alvesson who developed and hosted the workshop on branding at the University of Lund and Michael Beverland for important discussions, which enhanced our thinking on how brands operate in higher education.

REFERENCES

Ahmed, P. and Rafiq, M. (2003). 'Internal Marketing Issues and Challenges', *European Journal of Marketing*, 37 (9), 1177–1186.

Ali-Choudhury, Rehnuma, Bennett, Roger, and Savani, Sharmila (2009). 'University Marketing Directors' Views on the Components of a University Brand', *International Review on Public and Nonprofit Marketing*, 6, 11–33.

Alvesson, M. (1990). 'Organization: From Substance to Image?', *Organization Studies*, 11 (3), 373–394.

Argenti, Paul (2000). 'Branding B-Schools: Reputation Management for MBA Programs', *Corporate Reputation Review*, 3, 171–178.

Arvidsson, A. (2006). *Brands: Meaning and Value in Media Culture* (London: Routledge).

Barley S. R. and Kunda G. (2001). 'Bringing Work Back In', *Organization Science* 12 (1): 76–96.

Battiliana, J. and D'Aunno, T. (2009). 'Institutional Work and the Paradox of Embedded Agency', in T. B. Lawrence, R. Suddaby, and B. Leca (eds), *Institutional Work: Actor and Agency in Institutional Studies of Organization* (Cambridge: Cambridge University Press), 31–58.

Bennett, Roger and Ali-Choudhury, Rehnuma (2009). 'Prospective Students' Perceptions of University Brands: An Empirical Study', *Journal of Marketing for Higher Education*, 19 (1), 85–107.

Berger, P. L. and Luckmann, T. (1966). *The Social Construction of Reality: A Treatise in the Sociology of Knowledge* (Garden City NY: Anchor Books).

Beverland, Michael (2009). *Building Brand Authenticity—7 Habits of Iconic Brands* (London, UK: Palgrave Macmillan), 219.

Bleiklie, I. and Kogan, M. (2007). 'Organization and Governance of Universities', *Higher Education Policy*, 20, 477–493.

Bourdieu, P. (1977). *Outline of a Theory of Practice* (Cambridge Studies in Social and Cultural Anthropology (No.1); Paris: Cambridge University Press), 255.

Bourdieu, P. (1986), 'The Forms of Capital', in G.R. Richardson (ed.), *Handbook of Theory and Research for the Sociology of Education* (New York: Greenwood Press), 241–258.

Bourdieu, P. (1988), *Homo Academicus* (Cambridge: Polity Press).

Bourdieu, P. (1993), *The Field of Cultural Production: Essays on Art and Literature* (USA: Columbia University Press).

Bourdieu, P. (1996), *The State Nobility* (Cambridge: Polity Press).

Brubacher, J. S. (1967). 'The Autonomy of the University: How Independent Is the Republic of Scholars', *The Journal of Higher Education*, 38 (5), 237–249.

Burmann, Christoph and Zeplin, Sabrina (2005). 'Building Brand Commitment: A Behavioural Approach to Internal Brand Management', *Journal of Brand Management*, 12 (4), 279–300.

Chapleo, Chris (2010). 'What Defines "Successful" University Brands?', *International Journal of Public Sector Management*, 23 (2), 169–183.

Creswell, John W. (2007). *Qualitative Inquiry and Research Design. Choosing Among Five Approaches* (2nd ed., Thousand Oaks: Sage Publications), 395.

Creswell, John W. (2009), *Research Design. Qualitative, Quantitative and Mixed Methods Approaches* (3rd ed., Thousand Oaks: Sage Publications), 251.

Currie, J. and Vidovich, L. (2000). 'Privatization and Competition Policies for Australian Universities', *International Journal of Educational Development*, 20 (2), 135–151.

De Chernatony, L. (2006). *From Brand Vision to Brand Evaluation: The Strategic Process of Growing and Strengthening Brands* (Sydney: Elsevier—Butterworth-Heinemann).

Dholakia, N. and Fuat Firat, A. (1998*). Consuming People: From Political Economy to Theatres of Consumption* (London: Routledge).

Edensor, T. and Kothari, U. (2006). 'Extending Networks and Mediating Brands: Stallholder Strategies in a Mauritian Market', *Transactions of the Institute of British Geographers*, 31.

Eisenhardt, Kathleen and Graebner, Melissa (2007). 'Theory Building from Cases: Opportunities and Challenges', *Academy of Management Journal*, 50 (1), 25–32.

Gioia, Dennis and Corley, Kevin (2002). 'Being Good vs. Looking Good: Business School Rankings and the Circean Transformation from Substance to Image', *Academy of Management Learning and Education*, 1 (1), 107–120.

Guillet de Monthoux, Pierre (2004). *The Art Firm: Aesthetic Management and Metaphysical Marketing* (California: Stanford Business Books).

Halsey, A. H. and Trow, M. A. (1971). *The British Academics* (Boston: Harvard University Press).

Hatch, Mary Jo and Schultz, Majken (2008). *Taking Brand Initiative—How Companies Can Align Strategy, Culture, and Identity Through Corporate Branding* (San Francisco, CA: Jossey-Bass).

Hearn, C. (2008). 'Meat, Mask, Burden: Probing the Contours of the Branded Self', *Journal of Consumer Culture*, 8, 197–217.

Hemsley-Brown, Jane and Oplatka, Izhar (2006). 'Universities in a Competitive Global Marketplace—A Systematic Review of the Literature on Higher Education Marketing', *International Journal of Public Sector Management*, 19 (4), 316–338.

Hemsley-Brown, Jane and Goonawarddana, Shivonne (2007). 'Brand Harmonization in the International Higher Education Market', *Journal of Business Research*, 60, 942–948.

Henkel, Mary (2005). 'Academic Identity and Autonomy in a Changing Policy Environment', *Higher Education*, 49 (1–2), 155–176.

Holt, Douglas (2002). 'Why do Brands Cause Trouble? A Dialectical Theory of Consumer Culture and Branding', *Journal of Consumer Research*, 29 (1), 70–90.

Jevons, C. (2006). 'Universities: a Prime Example of Branding Gone Wrong', *Journal of Product & Brand Management*, 15 (7), 466–467.

Karreman, Dan and Rylander, Anna (2008). 'Managing Meaning Through Branding—The Case of a Consulting Firm', *Organization Studies*, 29 (1), 103–125.

Lawrence, T. B., Suddaby, R., and Leca, B. (2009). *Institutional Work: Actor and agency in Institutional Studies of Organization* (Cambridge: Cambridge University Press).

Levitt, H. (1981). 'Marketing Intangible Products and Product Intangibles', *Harvard Business Review*, May–June, 94–102.

Lomax, W. and Mador, M. (2006). 'Corporate Re-branding: From Normative Models to Knowledge Management', *Journal of Brand Management*, 14 (12), 82–95.

Lury, C. (2004). *Brands: The Logos of the Global Cultural Economy* (London and New York: Routledge).

Mahnert, K. and Torres, A. (2007). 'The Brand Inside: The Factors of Failure and Success in Internal Branding', *Irish Marketing Review*, 19 (1–2), 54–63.

Marginson, S. (2006). 'Dynamics of National and Global Competition in Higher Education', *Higher Education*, 52, 1–39.

Maringe, Felix (2005). 'Interrogating the Crisis in Higher Education Marketing: The CORD Model', *International Journal of Educational Management*, 19 (7), 564–578.

McGettigan, A. (2013). *The Great University Gamble: Money, Markets and the Future of Higher Education* (Pluto Press).

Meadmore, D. (1998). 'Changing the Culture: the Governance of the Australian Premillennial University', *International Studies in Sociology of Education*, 8 (1), 27–45.

Naidoo, Rajani (2000). 'Admission Policies and the Politics of Access', *unpublished Ph.D. thesis* (University of Cambridge).

Naidoo, Rajani (2003). 'Repositioning Higher Education as a Global Commodity: Opportunities and Challenges for Future Sociology of Education Work', *British Journal of Sociology of Education* 24 (2), 249–259.

Naidoo, Rajani (2004). 'Fields and Institutional Strategy: Bourdieu on the Relationship between Higher Education, Inequality and Society', *British Journal of Sociology of Education*, 25 (4), 457–471.

Naidoo, Rajani (2008). 'Building or Eroding Intellectual Capital? Student Consumerism as a Cultural Force in the Context of Knowledge Economy', in Jussi Valimmaa and Oili-Helena Ylijoki (eds), *Cultural Perspectives on Higher Education* (Netherlands: Springler Netherlands), 43–55.

Naidoo, Rajani, Shankar, Avi, and Veer, Ekant (2011). 'The Consumerist Turn in Higher Education: Policy Aspirations and Outcomes', *Journal of Marketing Management*, 27 (11–12), 1142–1162.

Parker, M. and Jary, D. (1995). 'The McUniversity: Organization, Management and Academic Subjectivity', *Organization*, 2 (2), 319–338.

Powell, W.W. and DiMaggio, P.G. (1991). *The New Institutionalism in Organisational Analysis* (USA: Princeton Press).

Prichard, C. and Willmott, H. (1995). 'Just how Managed is the McUniversity?', *Organizational Studies*, 18 (2), 287–316.

Punjaisri, Khanyapuss (2007). 'The Role of Internal Branding in the Delivery of Employee Brand Promise', *Brand Management*, 15 (1), 57–70.

Schroeder, J. E. (2002). *Visual Consumption* (London and New York: Routledge).

Schultz, Majken, Hatch, Mary Jo, and Larsen, Mogens Holten (2000). *The Expressive Organization* (Oxford: Oxford University Press).

Sillince, J. and Brown, A. (2009). 'Multiple Organizational Identities and Legitimacy: The Rhetoric of Police Websites', *Human Relations*, 62 (12), 1829–1856.

Slaughter, S. and Leslie, L (1997). *Academic Capitalism: Politics, Policies, and the Entrepreneuiral University* (Baltimore, MD: Johns Hopkins University Press).

Temple, Paul (2006). 'Branding Higher Education: Illusion or Reality?', *Perspectives*, 10 (1), 15–19.

Thomson, K. and Hecker, L. (2000). 'Value-adding Communication: Innovation in Employee Communication and Internal Marketing', *Journal of Communication Management*, 5 (1), 48–58.

Tomusk, V. (2000). 'Reproduction of the 'State Nobility' in Eastern Europe: Past Patterns and New Practices', *British Journal of Sociology of Education*, 21 (2), 269–282.

Waeraas, Arild and Solbakk, Marianne (2009). 'Defining the Essence of a University: Lessons from Higher Education Branding', *Higher Education*, 57, 449–462.

Wasko, J., Murdock, G., and Sousa, H. (2011). *The Handbook of Political Economy of Communications: Core Concerns and Issues* (Oxford: Blackwell).

Yin, Robert (2009). *Case Study Research: Design and Methods*, in The Applied Social Research Series, 51 vols, edited by Leonard Bickman and Debra J. Rog. (4th ed., Applied Social Research Methods Series; Thousand Oaks: Sage Publications), Vol V., 219.

9

Discipline as Institutional Maintenance

The Case of Business School Rankings

Andreas Rasche, Ulrich Hommel, and Eric Cornuel

9.1 INTRODUCTION

Rankings have turned into a dominant force in the context of higher education in general (Hazelkorn 2011) and business schools in particular (Wedlin 2006). A variety of rankings influence the field of management education, including assessments of institutional research output (e.g. the U.K.'s Research Excellence Framework), journals (e.g. the *UT Dallas'* journal list), and individuals' research yield (e.g. ISI's highly cited researcher lists). This chapter is concerned with the rankings of business schools, either on the institutional or programme level (e.g. the *Financial Times* Global MBA ranking or *The Economist's* Which MBA? list). These widely disseminated measures of quality have been criticized from a variety of angles. Some scholars have argued that rankings are based on narrow and manipulable metrics (Adler and Harzing 2009; Dichev 1999), while others have emphasized that the ranks of the top schools are stable over time, creating path-dependent effects (Devinney, Dowling and Perm-Ajchariyawong 2008; Morgeson and Nahrgang 2008). Business schools themselves complain about the significant amount of resources necessary to gather the data for the rankings, particularly as different publishers use different criteria (*The Economist* 2002).

Despite these (and other) attempts to challenge the legitimacy of business school rankings, their importance has grown significantly. Few people would disagree that rankings are here to stay. As Wilson and McKiernan (2011: 462) point out: 'Despite their failings, their ambiguity and their imprecision, business school rankings have become reified'. This points to an interesting puzzle: How can rankings maintain their impact on the field of management education despite their contested nature? This paper addresses this question by discussing the conditions under which rankings are rationalized and become stable institutions that are diffused over time and space. Our analysis theorizes rankings as institutions and builds on insights from the literature on organizational institutionalism (DiMaggio and Powell 1983; Meyer and Rowan 1977). In particular, we are addressing the discourse on institutional maintenance, as we are reflecting on those mechanisms that support rankings' continued impact and relevance.

So far, institutional theorists have explained the maintenance of rankings by pointing to the existence of isomorphic effects among business schools. Wedlin (2007), for instance, shows that schools adopt rankings to legitimize themselves and to be recognized as belonging to a group of like-minded organizations. Corley and Gioia (2000) find that schools face strong pressures to 'play the ranking game' whether they like it or not. Underlying these explanations is the idea that schools respond to isomorphic pressures by complying with widely-accepted standards for evaluating the quality of their degree programmes. While this perspective helps us to better understand why rankings persist despite widespread criticism, they reflect field-level analyses which neglect the role of the individual. We argue that rankings also maintain their status as prevalent institutions because they discipline individuals within business schools (see also Sauder and Espeland 2009). We show that rankings' disciplinary control stabilizes their impact and supports their further diffusion within the field of management education.

We theorize the role of discipline by drawing on the work of Michel Foucault. Foucault's notion of disciplinary control is not focused on direct control or even punishment. Rather discipline unfolds in a more subtle way: it is reflected in and through social relations that rationalize and normalize individual and collective behaviour (Foucault 1978, 1980). Disciplinary control rests in human interaction and cannot be reduced to single individuals. Power is a practice of shaping relations among people and influencing the 'way of being' within organizations (Barker and Cheney 1994). Our argumentation follows a Foucauldian perspective for two reasons. First, Foucault's (1978: 191) analysis of discipline emphasizes the role of the individual and its embeddedness in social relations. Conceptualizing institutional stability in this way helps us to move beyond the field-level perspective of existing work. Second, a Foucauldian perspective allows exploration of how discipline acts as a productive force. Discipline defines what counts as 'true' knowledge and 'normal' behaviour, while at the same time this knowledge also generates further disciplinary effects (Foucault 1980: 52). It is this productive interplay of knowledge and disciplinary power that helps us to explain the maintenance of business school rankings.

By drawing on and extending discussions of rankings' disciplinary function (Finney 2001; Sauder and Espeland 2009), this chapter shows that business school rankings discipline (a) by making individuals' performance visible according to a predefined set of metrics, (b) by homogenizing behaviour and defining what is 'normal' and 'abnormal' within a given context, and (c) by shaping how people understand themselves and the world around them. We suggest that these disciplinary mechanisms influence three properties of rankings as institutions—i.e. their durability, reproducibility, and communicability. Our discussion shows that the influence of disciplinary control on these properties stabilizes rankings as institutions and helps to maintain their relevance.

Our discussion contributes to and extends two scholarly discourses. First, we extend the literature on business school rankings (Dichev 1999; Morgeson and Nahrgang 2008; Wedlin 2011). Although scholars have pointed out that rankings are maintained because business schools operate in an uncertain and fragmented organizational environment and hence adopt rankings to increase their legitimacy (Corley and Gioia 2000; Whitley 1984), this perspective neglects the role of individuals in stabilizing and reproducing this institution across the field. Our analysis attempts to connect the well-established debate of macro-level institutions in management education (Meyer and Rowan 2006) with the more recent emphasis on the individual subject (Vidaillet and Vignon 2010). Second, we contribute to research on institutional theory by incorporating a Foucauldian perspective on disciplinary power into discussions of institutional maintenance. Such a perspective emphasizes the socially constructed nature of rationalized practices and complements the view that institutions are maintained through structural isomorphism (DiMaggio and Powell 1983).

The next section sets the stage for our analysis by conceptualizing business school rankings as institutions, which are embedded into the organizational field of management education. The following section introduces Foucault's understanding of power and, based on that, discusses the various ways in which rankings discipline the behaviour of individuals. The next section shows how these disciplinary effects help to maintain rankings as institutions by enhancing their stability within adopting organizations and by supporting their diffusion throughout the field. The last section discusses the implications of our analysis and outlines a research agenda.

9.2. THEORETICAL BACKGROUND: RANKINGS AS INSTITUTIONS

9.2.1. Institutions and Institutional Maintenance

We define institutions as 'enduring elements in social life. . . that have a profound effect on the thoughts, feelings, and behaviour of individual and collective actors' (Lawrence and Suddaby 2006: 216). Institutions are embedded in organizational fields (Wooten and Hoffman 2008). Early institutional theorists have highlighted that such fields consist of the totality of relevant actors in an area of institutional life (DiMaggio and Powell 1983; Scott 1995). Members of an organizational field share a common meaning system and, as a result, interact more frequently with one another (Scott 1994). Other authors have adopted a more issue-based definition emphasizing that the field itself results from dialogue and negotiation among a diversity of actors around a contested issue (Hoffman 1999; Zietsma and Winn 2005). Organizational fields are constituted in and through the exchanges of a variety of actors with disparate interests about the issue in question.

The question of why institutions persist across time and diffuse across space has been addressed by the literature on institutional maintenance (Guler, Guillen, and Macpherson 2002; Kennedy and Fiss 2009; Strang and Meyer 1993). Institutional orders need to be maintained; they need to be recreated and supported on an on-going basis in order to unfold their full effects. Although institutions by definition exercise social control over adopting organizations and hence are self-reproducing, it would be naïve to assume that institutions simply exist without any kind of maintenance (Lawrence and Suddaby 2006). Early institutional theory conceptualized institutional maintenance largely as structural isomorphism—institutions become stable and diffuse because a population of organizations faces coercive, mimetic, or normative pressures (DiMaggio and Powell 1983). This bird's eye view of maintenance was criticized for its neglect of the social and cognitive processes underlying the reproduction and diffusion of institutions (Hasselbladh and Kallinikos 2000: 700).

Linking maintenance to social and cognitive processes requires the adoption of a social constructivist perspective. The social construction of rationalized beliefs can help to explain why some institutions gain a remarkable diffusion and visibility, while others fade away. Zilber (2010), for instance, adopts a discursive perspective and shows how the diffusion of narratives within an organization can help to stabilize institutions. Greenwood, Suddaby, and Hinings (2002) demonstrate how professional associations actively manage the creation of shared understandings in an organizational field, leading to the maintenance of institutions (for a similar analysis see Quinn-Trank and Washington 2009). The work by Angus (1993) focuses on how institutions are reproduced through a process of public recognition of compliance, which shapes the continuous rationalization of beliefs and practices associated with institutions, while Zilber's (2002) study shows that the social construction of institutional maintenance is influenced by routinizing the on-going reproduction of members' shared cognitive schemes.

While this stream of literature has significantly advanced our understanding of how institutions are maintained over time and space, the role of disciplinary control in stabilizing and diffusing institutions remains under-theorized to date. Prior research has shown that institutions can be maintained through monitoring (Fox-Wolfgramm, Boal, and Hunt 1998) and that control can also be exercised through the deliberate creation of barriers to institutional change (Holm 1995). These analyses treat control largely as an explicit and formalized organizational activity, but fail to account for the fact that control can also rest on power relations that are less visible and formalized. One notable exception is the work by Townley (1997), who illustrates how disciplining effects are linked to the production of particular types of knowledge in organizations. While discipline has been recognized as one way to conceptualize institutional maintenance (Lawrence 2008), it remains largely unclear how such control rationalizes practices as well as beliefs and hence embeds them into social contexts. Our analysis puts a particular focus on how disciplinary control creates objectifying and subjectifying effects by which organizational practices and beliefs are rationalized into widely recognized institutions (i.e., business school rankings) and, as a result, help to sustain these institutions over time and space.

9.2.2. Business School Rankings as Institutions

While business school rankings have traditionally shaped the North American higher education context (Elsbach and Kramer 1996), the rapid internationalization of the field of management education has made them equally relevant in other geographic regions (particularly Europe and recently also Asia). Nowadays, few deans would disregard the importance of the highly public rankings issued by the *Financial Times* (launched in 1999), *Business Week* (launched in 1988), the *Wall Street Journal* (launched in 2001), and *The Economist* (launched in 2002). The growing homogenization of programme offerings and the increasing international positioning of these programmes reinforce the importance of rankings as ways to measure and compare their quality (Hazelkorn 2011). It is hard to ignore the way that business school rankings have turned into widely disseminated *institutions* reshaping the context of higher education (Pfeffer and Fong 2004).

Understanding rankings as institutions implies an acknowledgement that they reflect 'patterned higher-order effects on the actions, indeed the constitution, of individuals and organizations without requiring repeated collective mobilization or authoritative intervention to achieve these regularities' (Clemens and Cook 1999: 444–445). Rankings also reflect institutions in the sense that they are supported by a variety of organizational practices controlling action outcomes. Rankings do not just exist in abstract disembodied ways, but they become objectified in administrative routines, documentations, numerical work, and, related to that, actors' everyday behaviour (McKinlay and Starkey 1998; Miller and O'Leary 1987).

Following Scott's (1995) analysis of the elements of institutions, we suggest that rankings reflect an institution in three different ways. First, rankings contain *regulative* institutionalized elements, as they establish rules regarding 'what matters' when evaluating business schools and their programmes (e.g., increase in graduates' salaries). Although rankings do not directly monitor compliance, they specify metrics that business schools need to adhere to. (For an overview see Table 9.1.) Second, rankings contain *normative* institutionalized elements, because they create certain expectations within recipient organizations and thus help to define roles and the social obligations attached to them. Understood in this normative way, rankings determine what constitutes appropriate and therefore legitimate behaviour within business schools. Last but not least, rankings also contain *cultural-cognitive* institutionalized elements, since they shape common frames defining what is taken for granted and culturally supported within business schools. For instance, the belief that rankings play a crucial role in the future success of an organization is a deeply embedded belief (Dahlin-Brown 2005).

We analyse rankings as one institution in the organizational field of management education. Various actors mutually influence each other in the context of this field, including, but not limited to: business schools; accreditation agencies; media outlets; government agencies; graduates; consultants; and potential employers. Many of the underlying issues within this field remain contested and are subject to regular debate. For instance, the usefulness of one of the key degrees in management education, the MBA, has been continuously questioned (Bennis and O'Toole 2005), while the practical relevance of business schools' research output remains debated as well (Rasche and Behnam 2009). Rankings are embedded into this contested field, while at the same time acting as a structuring device. Wedlin's (2011) analysis shows that rankings are used as devices to build schools' positions and legitimacy. Her study illustrates how rankings symbolically represent the structure of the field by ordering competing schools and thereby supporting the discursive construction of their legitimacy.

Rankings face a variety of criticisms. Some scholars argue that rankings support a narrow view of science, in the sense that the reputation of a school is measured by faculty publications in a pre-selected list of, mostly, North American journals (Adler and Harzing 2009). Others have criticized rankings' path-dependency. While the position of early entrants remain almost unchanged over time, the positions of new entrants are very dynamic (Devinney et al. 2008). In a similar vein, Morgeson and Nahrgang (2008) find that schools' positions in the *Business Week* rankings remained almost unchanged over the years. There is also a methodological critique arguing that rankings focus on isolated (and manipulable) aspects of school performance and hence are not a good proxy measure for quality (Dichev 1999). In 1998, the *Financial Times'* first attempt to launch a business school ranking

Table 9.1. Selected criteria used by major international rankings

	Employability	Incoming Class	School/ Program Features	Research
The Economist	salary change (pre-MBA to post-MBA); salary percentage of graduates in new jobs after graduation; percentage of graduates with jobs through career service.	average GMAT score; average length of work experience; percentage of women students.	ratio of registered alumni to current students; student rating of programme content; number of overseas countries with alumni.	percentage of faculty with Ph.Ds.
BusinessWeek (Global Full-Time MBA)	effectiveness of career services; usefulness of skills; usefulness of networks; value for money; contacts with businesses.	'calibre' of class.	teaching quality; teaching material; work load; technological tools.	intellectual capital score (calculated based on publications in a list of 20 journals).
Wall Street Journal	recruitment experience; value for money of recruitment effort; skills and abilities of graduates; likelihood of recruiter return.	student characteristics.	career services office; overall satisfaction with a school; faculty expertise.	
Financial Times (Global Full-Time MBA)	salary change (pre-MBA to post-MBA); post-MBA salary; graduates employed within three months; value for money (incl. fees vs. salary).	gender diversity of incoming students internationaldiversity of students.	gender diversity of faculty; international diversity of faculty; international exposure during the programme.	percentage of papers in 45 journals within three years time; percentage of faculty with Ph.Ds.number of doctoral graduates over three years.

Note: This overview does not reflect a complete list of all ranking criteria. Note that some of the publishers do not publicly display their exact ranking criteria, but only refer to general categories (e.g., 'effectiveness of career services'). The table is based on the criteria reported by the different publishers on their respective websites as well as data reported in Wedlin (2007: 29).

was so fiercely criticized that the ranking was withdrawn and relaunched a year later (Crainer and Dearlove 1998). Some universities have even tried to form a coalition to jointly boycott the *U.S. News and World Report* rankings, however without much success (Lemann 1998).

This sustained critique begs the question why business school rankings remain relevant despite their widespread critique. Of course, one straightforward answer would be that the majority of actors in the field of management education desire rankings. In a world without rankings, business schools would lose an important source of legitimacy and differentiation (Corley and Gioia 2000; Wedlin 2011), while potential students and employers would give up an easily accessible measure of reputation and quality. While this answer stresses institutional theory's traditional focus on securing legitimacy, we approach this question by arguing that rankings enforce disciplinary control within business schools leading to stabilizing effects that reinforce their institutionalized character.

9.3. BUSINESS SCHOOL RANKINGS AS DISCIPLINARY INSTITUTIONS: A FOUCAULDIAN PERSPECTIVE

9.3.1. Foucault and Disciplinary Power

Foucault's work has been the extensively discussed and applied in management studies (McKinlay and Starkey 1998) affecting discourses like organization theory (Burrell 1988), human resource management (HRM) (Townley 1993), and business ethics (Crane, Knights, and Starkey 2008). While Foucault's extensive body of work has given insights into a variety of phenomena ranging from the role of madness in Western history to a discussion of the history of sexuality, it is his conceptualization of power and control that has been most frequently discussed by management scholars. Townley's (1993) analysis, for instance, shows how HRM creates disciplinary practices that 'produce' individuals within organizations. She shows that HRM constitutes and produces knowledge in organizations and that this knowledge unfolds disciplining effects. Sewell and Wilkinson (1992) demonstrate how Just-In-Time production systems discipline workers by making their work processes more visible. Our analysis builds upon these accounts, but also reaches beyond them insofar as we discuss the effect of disciplinary control on the maintenance of institutions.

Foucault's analyses are based on a particular understanding of power. Power is not simply introduced from the 'outside' and is also not a property that can be possessed (Foucault 1978: 176–177). Rather, power unfolds through day-to-day interactions among people; it functions as a 'network of relations'. As Foucault remarks, 'in thinking of the mechanisms of power, I am thinking rather of its capillary forms of existence, the point where power reaches into the very grain of individuals, touches their bodies, and inserts itself into their actions and attitudes, their discourses, learning processes and everyday lives' (Foucault 1980: 39). The *individual body* is both the 'object and target of power' (Foucault 1978: 136). The body is understood to be 'analysable' and 'manipulable' in the sense that it can be trained and shaped through disciplinary practices. That is why Foucault talks about 'docile bodies'—bodies that are shaped through discipline. Discipline in this sense reflects one particular form of exercising power. It is not about controlling the entire body or even punishing it through enslavement, but abut limiting the body in terms of deeds, motions, and attitudes (Downing 2008). This controlling of the body is not necessarily repressive. Foucault understands disciplinary power as a productive force, making the body more useful in an economic sense (Foucault 1978: 182–183).

9.3.2. Rankings as Disciplinary Institutions

In his seminal work *Discipline and Punish,* Foucault (1978: 170–192) distinguishes three disciplinary techniques for creating docile bodies. We use these techniques as a yardstick to organize our analysis of how rankings produce disciplinary control over individuals in business schools (for a related analysis in the context of U.S. law schools, see Sauder and Espeland 2009).

Hierarchical Observation through Rankings. The first technique, *hierarchical observation,* aims at organizing individuals so that they are constantly under surveillance, thus making them more visible (Foucault 1978: 170–177). Visibility (i.e. the knowledge of being watched) creates discipline. The point of hierarchical observation is not that there is constant direct surveillance of individuals but that, since people do not know whether they are observed, they behave *as if* they are being watched (Downing 2008). Observation in a Foucauldian sense is more about self-policing than about rigorous external monitoring. Hierarchical observation is not limited to physical observation, but also, and maybe most of all, includes observation through collecting and analysing data about individual behaviour (Giddens 1985: 184; Miller and O'Leary 1987: 239). Of course, rankings require business schools to do exactly that: they produce a significant amount of statistics about various aspects of performance (Wedlin 2006). For instance, the *Financial Times* Global MBA Ranking requires schools to generate information on different subject areas ranging from faculty research to the employment of graduates (Bradshaw 2007). As most schools participate in different rankings simultaneously, producing such data on a regular basis becomes an important part of organizational life, affecting almost all members of the organization.

The availability and continuous production of data enables surveillance of individuals in two interrelated ways. First, as Sauder and Espeland (2009) remark, it makes schools' reputation visible and gives the impression that their performance can be judged easily (even by non-expert audiences). Rankings are released on an annual or at least biannual basis and are swiftly disseminated via print media and the Internet. This high visibility creates disciplining effects. Individuals need to constantly work on improving their performance vis-à-vis a small set of indicators. Any drop in a ranking is easy to identify and usually paired with negative economic consequences, which are likely to feed back to employees (e.g. decreased job security). As Foucault (1978: 175) remarks, this makes surveillance a 'decisive economic operator' and a way of generating higher performance and productivity through discipline. The disciplining effects associated with rankings' visibility are hidden, as they rest on judgments by a network of constituents (e.g., potential students, employers, alumni). Because it is unclear what exactly rankings measure— with opinions ranging from school performance (Dichev 1999) and quality (Sauder and Espeland 2006) to reputation (Corley and Gioia 2000) and customer satisfaction (Zemsky 2008)—the visibility of a school's rank contains a lot of interpretative flexibility. By converting a complex set of (qualitative and quantitative) indicators into an ordinal composite measure, rankings become an attractive reference point to a wide audience of lay judges.

Second, rankings also increase the visibility of individuals' performance within business schools. The systematic documentation and collection of data creates visibility around the performance of individuals (for a related discussion in the context of human resource management, see Townley 1997). For instance, *The Economist* requires data on applicants' GMAT scores, which enhances transparency around the performance of programme managers as well as schools' marketing and admission units. *Business Week* measures the effectiveness of a school's alumni network, making the performance of alumni officers' very accessible. Such indicators objectify the performance of individuals and turn their attention to formerly neglected parts of everyday work life (Sauder and Espeland 2009). Because the individual as a subject becomes socially constructed as an object of knowledge, its intra-organizational visibility increases significantly. How someone contributes to a school's position in a ranking becomes visible. As Foucault (1978) argues, this visibility does not imply direct supervision. Rather it produces self-monitoring behaviour, since actors know that their performance is visible vis-à-vis the indicators specified by rankings. Such self-monitoring objectifies the individual, because it makes people internalize an observer's perspective as a primary view of their selves. In effect, the focus for the constitution of professional identities shifts from substance to external perception.

Normalizing Judgment through Rankings. Foucault's second disciplinary technique, *normalizing judgment*, disciplines behaviour by defining what is commonly perceived to be 'normal'. As Foucault (1978: 182) remarks, 'it refers individual actions to a whole that is at once a field of comparison, a space of differentiation and the principle of a rule to be followed'. Normalizing judgment homogenizes behaviour (because it demands conformity), but it also defines the 'abnormal' and hence uncovers differences between peoples' performance (because it allows gaps to be assessed). Rankings normalize individual behaviour by creating dichotomies through which we classify the 'normal' and exclude what is 'abnormal'. The different ranking criteria act as a guide in this context. For instance, it becomes normal to employ faculty with PhDs (one of the measures for faculty quality by *The Economist*), to focus on directly applicable knowledge (one of the items included by the *Wall Street Journal*), and to consider average industry salaries when placing students (as alumni salaries are measured by the *Financial Times*). This is not to say that schools would neglect these (and other) issues if rankings were non-existent. Rather it suggests that rankings help to create an 'artificial order' (Foucault 1978: 179) within business schools, which defines categories of knowledge that become self-justifying (Barker and Cheney 1994).

The normalization process underlying rankings has a corrective function. It allows the identification of gaps, since it fixes reference points for individual and collective sensemaking. These reference points are perceived as constraints and allow for judging non-observance; they form the basis for comparing, differentiating, and hierarchizing individuals. As Foucault (1978: 180) remarks:

> We have a distribution between a positive pole and a negative pole; all behaviour falls in the field between good and bad marks, good and bad points. Moreover, it is possible to *quantify* this field and work out an arithmetical economy based on it (our emphasis).

The quantification of relevant information supports normalizing judgment, as it enables people to distinguish much more quickly between the normal and the abnormal. Information on business schools' performance is not by definition quantitative. Rankings *convert* qualitative into quantitative information, a practice that is referred to as 'commensuration'. Commensuration simplifies by decontextualizing and depersonalizing knowledge as well as neglecting significant amounts of information (Espeland and Sauder 2007; Espeland and Stevens 1998). However, commensuration also increases the perceived authority of information because it absorbs some of the ambiguity that is attached to qualitative data (March and Olsen 1976). This mixture of simplified, yet authoritative, information supports the corrective function of normalizing judgment: (a) it directs attention to a few selected issues, making the comparison of performance and the identification of gaps much easier (because other facets of performance are deemed irrelevant); and (b) it facilitates longitudinal assessments of normalized behaviour (as long as measures are stable and comparable). The reduction of semantic richness through quantification reinforces rankings' disciplinary control by making people fearful of the humiliating and easily identifiable effects of non-observant behaviour. The laymen's delusion of the cardinality of the ranking measures further strengthens their effectiveness.

Examination through Rankings. Examination combines the two previous techniques and reflects the regular observation of normalization. Examination is a ritualized technique ensuring that individuals are frequently audited and graded. Foucault (1978: 184–185) argues that examinations help to establish knowledge and consequently a 'truth' about individuals. They objectify individuals by imposing power and knowledge relations upon them and by situating them in a network of documentation and writing (Foucault 1978: 189). Rankings do not examine in the sense of physically auditing individual behaviour, but they force schools to regularly produce documents (e.g. about research performance, faculty quality, incoming class features), which fix and capture the subject. The creation of such documents makes it possible 'to classify, to form categories, to determine averages, to fix norms' (Foucault 1978: 190) and hence turn individual subjects into analysable and comparable objects.

To examine via documentation makes each individual a 'case'; it exposes the particularities of individuals and shows the need for further training, correction, and normalization (Schwan and Shapiro 2011). Thinking of rankings as examinations shows Foucault's understanding of the interplay of knowledge and power: rankings establish knowledge about subjects and by doing so also control their behaviour. For Foucault (1978: 188–189) examinations are deeply woven into the organization. Subjects do not directly feel or see the exam; they only feel and reflect on its effects (which may, however, have the character of formal but derivative exams such as tenure decision processes). Examinations constitute the individual as an object, but also, at the same time, affect how individuals constitute themselves. Discipline does not make individuals passive objects but influences their self-understanding and identity construction (Heller 1996; Rabinow 1991)—a process 'by which we assert who we are' (Barker and Cheney 1994: 28). Foucault calls this process subjectification, emphasizing that it is concerned with how people define themselves as 'normal' vis-à-vis their environment.

While some authors have claimed that rankings act as templates for shaping the *organizational* identity of business schools (Elsbach and Kramer 1996; Wedlin 2006), a Foucauldian analysis shows that rankings also shape how *individuals* understand themselves and their work. Individuals experience the effects of the documentation produced by rankings (e.g., in terms of rewards or punishments). These effects steer processes of self-reflection, establishing identities like 'top researcher', 'valued teacher', and 'successful

Table 9.2. Disciplinary effects of business school rankings

	General Description	Rankings Discipline by...	Objectifying Effects on...
Hierarchical Observation	Surveillance of individuals' performance	Visibility	Individual (through self-monitoring and separation)
Normalizing Judgment	Definition of behavioural expectations	Commensuration	Individual (through creating classifications)
Examination	Observation of normalized judgment	Subjectification	Individual (through altered self-understanding)

programme manager'. Although the subject in a Foucauldian sense is embedded in a network of power relations, it is still active in the processes of self-formation. Subjectivity is formed as a product of actors' exposure to and engagement in multiple normalized practices that make the individual observable (Zembylas 2003).

Taken together, the three disciplinary mechanisms show how rankings establish disciplinary control over individuals. All mechanisms discipline by *objectifying the individual*—subjects are turned into objects appearing to be analysable independent of their agency. Hierarchical observation objectifies the individual by enhancing her or his visibility within the organization. This acculturates people to adopt an observer's perspective on their own behaviour, separating them from others. Normalizing judgment objectifies the individual by creating categories into which people can be classified. Examination objectifies the individual by transcribing peoples' features into documentation. The resulting depersonalization makes the individual an analysable object and influences processes of self-formation. The analysis up to this point is summarized in Table 9.2.

9.4. DISCIPLINARY CONTROL AS INSTITUTIONAL MAINTENANCE

We now argue that the disciplinary control exercised by rankings affects their diffusion across time and space. We suggest that disciplinary control has an impact on rankings' durability, reproducibility, and communicability—three properties of institutions which shape the stability and diffusion of rationalized beliefs and practices (Hasselbladh and Kallinikos 2000).

9.4.1 Durability: Maintaining Rankings through Self-Fulfilling Prophecies

Durability is about the enduring nature of an institution: its ability to survive over time despite being challenged (Clemens and Cook 1999). Our analysis frames rankings' durability as resting on self-fulfilling prophecies shaped by disciplinary control.

Rankings' influence on subjectification processes aligns the self-understanding of actors with ranking criteria. This altered self-understanding shapes the cognitive schemes of individuals helping them to suppress alternative interpretations of these criteria. Gill (2009), for instance, shows how researchers change their points of reference for sensemaking when confronted with pressures to respond to narrowly defined research and teaching expectations. If actors alter the way they understand themselves and their work, they reproduce the assumptions embedded in rankings and, as a result, make rankings more durable. Here, the durability of rankings rests on a self-fulfilling prophecy: rankings are durable because what rankings measure influences peoples' self-understanding (and hence the behavioural norms they respond to), which in turn justifies the measures (see also the discussion by Espeland and Sauder 2007). This constitution of actors stabilizes rankings within business schools and creates barriers to change. For instance, if student employability is understood in terms of 'value for money' (e.g. measured by salary increases), then this particular conception of employability is regarded as relevant and justified. The durability of such self-fulfilling prophecies is hard to challenge, as people conceive of themselves as *re*acting to the measures, whereas in fact they are *en*acting them (Weick 1979).

Rankings' durability is also enhanced by the disciplining nature of the visibility they create. Since rankings introduce metrics into business schools that make people comparable, it is easier to distinguish between high and low performers. One possible consequence is that management will raise its expectations regarding high performers, while low performers are seen to have little potential. Framing expectations in this way can create a self-fulfilling prophecy (Eden 1984): raising expectations regarding high performers often enhances their performance. This model of self-fulfilling prophecy has been described as the Pygmalion effect (Livingston 2003) and rests on internalized changes in self-expectancy (e.g. influencing motivation) and supervisor expectations (e.g., influencing leadership style). The Pygmalion effect strengthens the durable nature of rankings, as those employees who are aligned with ranking criteria are more likely to be promoted and/or rewarded, while underperforming employees are likely to leave the organization. The Pygmalion effect reflects a self-selection mechanism that stabilizes the role of rankings within business schools.

The disciplining effects of commensuration also enhance rankings' durability. The metrics produced by commensurative practices create barriers to alternative interpretations of ranking criteria. Codified metrics often act as a source for redesigning existing organizational practices (e.g., reward systems and promotion processes). Redesigning these practices can create another self-fulfilling prophecy: the more such practices are aligned with the metrics propagated by rankings, the more people will enact these metrics over time (Ferraro, Pfeffer, and Sutton 2005). For instance, aligning reward systems with ranking criteria by focusing on specific metrics justifies these metrics and inscribes rankings into organizational practices. This increases the durability of rankings' effects, since challenging the ranking would imply a challenge to fundamental organizational processes underlying the operation of business schools.

9.4.2. Reproducibility: Maintaining Rankings through Enacted Codifications

While durability explains rankings' stability *within* business schools, reproducibility and communicability help to understand institutional maintenance at the field level. Reproducibility refers to 'the capacity to reproduce a rationalized pattern or package in quasi-identical form and enact the relationships it implicates' (Hasselbladh and Kallinikos 2000: 709). The reproducibility of an institution largely depends on how clearly its underlying rules are specified. Rankings rest on highly specified rules, as they discipline through commensurative practices producing aggregated numbers. This formal codification decontextualizes rankings and makes them easily reproducible (as metrics can be enacted quickly in different contexts). For instance, it is easier to reproduce the metric 'average GMAT score' than to reflect on applicants' quality through a narrative account.

It is important to understand that it is not the mere existence of metrics that enables rankings' reproducibility across time and space. Rather it is the *enactment* of these metrics and the social relationships that belong to them that diffuses rankings as institutions. Simply reproducing the metric in a different context is not sufficient, as rankings need to be sufficiently embedded into new organizational settings in order for them to be reproduced. It is the disciplining character attached to commensuration that enables the enactment of rankings within business schools and their successful reproduction throughout the field of management education. Commensuration directs peoples' attention to what is considered to be 'normal', helping them to enact their own organizational reality (Weick 1995). Rankings reproduce because the disciplinary control attached to their commensurative mechanisms helps to embed them quickly in different organizational contexts (see also Giddens 1985 on disembedding mechanisms).

9.4.3. Communicability: Maintaining Rankings through Discourse

We understand communicability as reflecting 'how easily a rationalized package can cross an organizational field, be understood and conveyed to others than those involved in its conception, construction, and initial use' (Hasselbladh and Kallinikos 2000: 710). Communicability is about expressing the key features of rankings in a way that new adopters can easily connect to their basic pillars. We argue that rankings' disciplinary features shape the discourse on management education at the field level and thus enhance the communicability of this institution. In particular, commensuration and subjectification homogenize what language people from *ranked* schools use. Faced with a set of homogenized metrics, people start to use comparable terminology to discuss similar issues. Wedlin (2011), for instance, shows that the stakeholder orientation embedded in rankings helped to construct a 'customer perspective' throughout ranked schools on both sides of the Atlantic. Of course, changes in field-level discourses are also influenced by how people understand themselves and their work. For example, if scholars see themselves as 'high performing researchers' based on the criteria defined by rankings, this particular way of self-understanding is likely to diffuse throughout the community of schools (for a discussion of how language shapes the diffusion of institutions, see Fiss and Hirsch 2005).

As management education reflects a field with a high density, because people from ranked and non-ranked schools are connected and communicate in a variety of ways (Sahlin-Andersson and Engwell 2002), the homogenized discourse created among ranked schools is likely to spill over into the wider discourse on management education. Rankings significantly influence the language actors from ranked and *non-ranked* schools use to describe, compare or benchmark the main features of their field. As a result, organizations interested in 'playing the ranking game' can relate much better to the 'rules of the game' (Corley and Gioia 2000), as the latter are expressed in rather mundane terms resting on established significations and meaning structures. This enhanced communicability makes it easier to frame the adoption of rankings as an opportunity (rather than a threat) influencing the diffusion of the institution within the organizational field. The proliferation of rankings and similar benchmarking mechanisms creates a hierarchical structure infringing on the space of non-ranked schools.

9.5. IMPLICATIONS, CONCLUSIONS, AND
FUTURE RESEARCH

This paper has argued that rankings are able to maintain their status as a widely acknowledged institution because of the disciplinary effects they unfold within business schools. These disciplinary effects make the impact of rankings on schools more durable, while also enhancing their reproducibility and communicability. Taken together, our arguments show the significance of acknowledging the impact of micro-organizational behaviour on institutional maintenance. Of course, rankings also maintain their status as institutions because business schools engage in mimetic isomorphism, adopting rankings to increase their legitimacy vis-à-vis competitors. By contrast, explaining institutional maintenance through disciplinary control emphasizes the role of the 'governed individual' in stabilizing and diffusing institutions. Our analysis shows the usefulness of such a micro perspective on institutional maintenance.

We conclude by outlining a future research agenda for studying the maintenance of business school rankings as institutions. First, there is need to better understand the *socially constructed nature of rankings' maintenance*. Rankings cannot be viewed in separation from the organizational realities they try to portray. Their effects are shaped by the very reality they are attempting to represent. Discipline is a powerful force to structure this reality because it influences the enactment of behavioural norms within schools. Understanding rankings in terms of discipline makes us aware that individuals create many of the opportunities and constraints they subsequently experience as 'given'. Rankings may appear as hard facts representing business schools' organizational reality, whereas, in fact, a school's position within a ranking is influenced by how, and in which ways, disciplinary control unfolds.

As schools are likely to show differences in terms of hierarchical observation, normalizing judgment and examination, our framework can help to explain variation among adopters in responding to rankings (see also the discussion by Corley and Gioia 2000; Espeland and Sauder 2007). Analytically, distinguishing disciplinary mechanisms from their effects is important, since discipline does not necessarily result in unquestioned obedience. For instance, it is possible that discipline results in avoidance or manipulation, particularly when the self-perception of an organization does not match with its position in a ranking (Elsbach and Kramer 1996). Future research needs to identify variations in responses to rankings by differentiating the conditions that influence how discipline unfolds in different organizations, for instance by referring to Oliver's (1991) framework of responses to institutional pressures. As variations in responses are largely invisible to those using rankings, there is a significant degree of uncertainty attached to schools' ranks.

A second area of future research regards the *role of the subject*. As discussed, the disciplinary control exercised by rankings helps to objectify the subject within business schools. Rankings turn the individual into an analysable object that can be compared or benchmarked or managed. Such objectifications bring about a transition of emphasis from the individual subject (with its unique experiences, capabilities, and idiosyncratic character) to the decontextualized role. Organizational duties become decoupled from the individuality of persons and are transformed into predefined roles that can be assigned to different members of a collectivity, as long as people can fulfil the criteria associated with the role (Hasselbladh and Kallinikos 2000). For instance, rankings have helped to decontextualize the role of the researcher by defining good scholarship largely through where and how often scholars publish (rather than what they publish). This makes researchers easier to replace as role specifications depend on a selection of widely diffused criteria rather than assessments of an individual's fit with the organization. In this sense, rankings' communicability enhances the diffusion of role definitions throughout the field. Unfortunately, current research has detached the discussion of rankings from the role of individuals working in business schools. Future research needs to study how rankings help to transform the individuality of persons into predefined roles. This requires bridging the macro-micro divide by investigating how the diffusion of rankings helps to define a 'template' for developing role definitions.

A third research area concerns the *moral dimension of rankings,* which, unfortunately, has remained largely neglected to date. A Foucauldian (1979) perspective emphasizes that disciplinary control is productive—'discipline emerges as an effect of knowledge (while also influencing the latter). As Foucault (1978: 194) writes in *Discipline and Punish*: 'power produces; it produces reality; it produces domains of objects and rituals of truth'. The discipline exercised by rankings produces organizational roles and tasks, performance measures (and their associated documentations), and influences individuals' self-understanding. All of this creates a variety of, often unintended, yet enduring effects, including changes to resource allocation and peoples' status within organizational hierarchies. By standardizing, comparing, and observing behaviour, rankings create winners and losers, both on an organizational as well as an individual level. While research has shown that rankings help to define an 'elite' among business schools (Wedlin 2007), the intra-organizational effects on the individual are less clear. For instance, Gill's (2009) analysis shows that rankings can create fear, anxiety, shame, and feelings of out-of-placeness and may ultimately lead to faculty incivility (Twale and De Luca 2008). On the one hand, such reactions internalize rankings into everyday work routines fostering organizational change. On the other hand, such responses raise a variety of ethical challenges and research questions. Do rankings create unjustified inequality, both among business schools and their staff? Do rankings call for moral compromises (e.g. between 'playing the game' and remaining true to oneself)? Answering questions like these would improve our knowledge about business school rankings in significant ways.

A fourth research area relates to the intermediating role of business schools, which has also not drawn much attention in the literature. Rankings unfold their influence by defining a diversified set of indicators linking the organizational activity portfolio with the individual's task profile and performance. But what prevents individual researchers from altering the weighting scheme applied for performance evaluation by bypassing the intermediator? For instance, the German *Handelsblatt* is publishing research rankings of business scholars employed in German higher education since 2009, which appears to significantly impact professorial hiring decisions. It poses the question of how those rankings, which directly measure the performance of individuals, impact the behaviour of research and teaching staff in a given organization. One key question is whether and how a school's culture affects the uptake of the rankings of individual scholars? Do scholars from institutions in which rankings are seen more critically refrain from such individual performance appraisal?

Understanding and theorizing rankings' continued relevance to the field of management education as resting on disciplinary control implies a shift in emphasis. Rankings not only 'matter' because they provide business schools with an important and highly visible source of legitimacy (Dahlin-Brown 2005), but also because they shape individuals' dispositions toward work and themselves.

REFERENCES

Adler, Nancy J. and Harzing, Anne-Wil (2009). 'When Knowledge Wins: Transcending the Sense and Nonsense of Academic Rankings', *Academy of Management Learning and Education*, 8: 72–95.

Angus, Lawrence B. (1993). 'Masculinity and Women Teachers at Christian Brothers College', *Organization Studies* 14: 235–260.

Barker, James R. and Cheney, George (1994). 'The Concept and the Practices of Discipline in Contemporary Organizational Life', *Communication Monographs*, 61: 19–43.

Bennis, Warren G. and O'Toole, James (2005). 'How Business Schools Lost Their Way', *Harvard Business Review*, 83: 96–104.

Bradshaw, Della (2007). 'Business School Rankings: The Love-Hate Relationship', *Journal of Management Development*, 26: 54–60.

Burrell, Gibson (1988). 'Modernism, Post Modernism and Organizational Analysis 2: The Contribution of Michel Foucault', *Organization Studies* 9: 221–235.

Clemens, Elisabeth S. and Cook, James M. (1999). 'Politics and Institutionalism: Explaining Durability and Change', *Annual Review of Sociology*, 25: 441–466.

Corley, K. and Gioia, D. (2000). 'The Rankings Game: Managing Business School Reputation', *Corporate Reputation Review*, 3: 319–333.

Crainer, Stuart and Dearlove, Des (1998). *Gravy Training*. San Francisco: Jossey-Bass.

Crane, Andrew, Knights, David, and Starkey, Ken (2008). 'The Conditions of Our Freedom: Foucault, Organization, and Ethics', *Business Ethics Quarterly*, 18: 299–320.

Dahlin-Brown, Nissa (2005). 'The Perceptual Impact of U.S. News and World Report Rankings on Eight Public MBA Programs', *Journal of Marketing for Higher Education*, 15: 155–179.

Devinney, Timothy, Dowling, Grahame R., and Perm-Ajchariyawong, Nidthida (2008). 'The Financial Times Business Schools Ranking: What Quality Is This Signal of Quality?', *European Management Review*, 5: 195–208.

Dichev, Ilia D. (1999). 'How Good Are Business School Rankings?', *Journal of Business*, 72: 201–213.

DiMaggio, Paul J. and Powell, Walter W. (1983). 'The Iron Cage Revisited: Institutional Isomorphism and Collective Rationality in Organizational Fields', *American Sociological Review*, 48: 147–160.

Downing, Lisa (2008). *Michel Foucault*. Cambridge: Cambridge University Press.

Eden, Dov (1984). 'Self-Fulfilling Prophecy as a Management Tool: Harnessing Pygmalion', *Academy of Management Review*, 9: 64–73.

Elsbach, Kimberly D. and Kramer, Roderick M. (1996). 'Members' Responses to Organizational Identity Threats: Encountering and Countering the Business Week Rankings', *Administrative Science Quarterly*, 41: 442–476.

Espeland, Wendy N. and Sauder, Michael (2007). 'Rankings and Reactivity: How Public Measures Recreate Social Worlds', *American Journal of Sociology*, 113: 1–40.

Espeland, Wendy N. and Stevens, Mitchell L. (1998). 'Commensuration as a Social Process', *Annual Review of Sociology*, 24: 313–343.

Ferraro, Fabrizio, Pfeffer, Jeffrey, and Sutton, Robert I. (2005). 'Economics Language and Assumptions: How Theories Can Become Self-Fulfilling', *Academy of Management Review*, 30: 8–24.

Fiss, Peer C. and Hirsch, Paul M. (2005). 'The Discourse of Globalization: Framing and Sensemaking of an Emerging Concept', *American Sociological Review*, 70: 29–52.

Foucault, Michel (1978). *Discipline and Punish: The Birth of the Prison*. New York: Vintage.

Foucault, Michel (1979). *The History of Sexuality, Volume 1*. Harmondsworth: Penguin.

Foucault, Michel (1980). *Power/Knowledge: Selected Interviews and Other Writings 1972-1977*. New York: Pentheon.

Fox-Wolfgramm, Susan J., Boal, Kimberly B., and Hunt, James G. (1998). 'Organizational Adaptation to Institutional Change: A Comparative Study of First-Order Change in Prospector and Defender Banks', *Administrative Science Quarterly*, 43: 87–126.

Giddens, Anthony (1985). *The Nation-State and Violence*. Cambridge: Polity.

Gill, Rosalind (2009). 'Breaking the Silence: The Hidden Injuries of the Neo-Liberal University', in Roisin Ryan-Flood, and Rosalind Gill (eds), *Secrecy and Silence in the Research Process: Feminist Reflections*. London: Routledge, 228–244.

Greenwood, Royston, Hinings, C. R., and Suddaby, Roy (2002). 'Theorizing Change: The Role of Professional Associations in the Transformation of Institutionalized Fields ', *Academy of Management Journal*, 45: 58–80.

Guler, Isin, Guillen, Mauro F., and Macpherson, John Muir (2002). 'Global Competition, Institutions, and the Diffusion of Organizational Practices: The International Spread of ISO 9000 Quality Certificates', *Administrative Science Quarterly*, 47: 207–232.

Hasselbladh, Hans, and Kallinikos, Jannis (2000). 'The Project of Rationalization: A Critique and Reappraisal of Neo-Institutionalism in Organization Studies', *Organization Studies* 21: 697–720.

Hazelkorn, Ellen (2011). *Rankings and the Reshaping of Higher Education: The Battle for World-Class Excellence*. Basingstoke: Palgrave Macmillan

Heller, Kevin Jon (1996). 'Power, Subjectification and Resistance in Foucault', *SubStance*, 25: 78–110.

Hoffman, Andrew J. (1999). 'Institutional Evolution and Change: Environmentalism and the U.S. Chemical Industry', *Academy of Management Journal*, 42: 351–371.

Holm, Petter (1995). 'The Dynamics of Institutionalization: Transformation Processes in Norwegian Fisheries', *Administrative Science Quarterly*, 40: 398–422.

Kennedy, Mark Thomas, and Fiss, Peer Christian (2009). 'Institutionalization, Framing, and Diffusion: The Logic of TQM Adoption and Implementation Decisions among U.S. Hospitals ', *Academy of Management Journal*, 52: 897–918.

Lawrence, Thomas B. (2008). 'Power, Institutions and Organizations', in Royston Greenwood, Christine Oliver, Roy Suddaby, and Kerstin Sahlin-Andersson (eds), *Sage Handbook of Organizational Institutionalism*. London: Sage, 170–197.

Lawrence, Thomas and Suddaby, Roy (2006). 'Institutions and Institutional Work', in Stewart R. Clegg, Cynthia Hardy, Thomas B. Lawrence, and Walter R. Nord (eds), *The Sage Handbook of Organization Studies (2nd Edition)*. London: Sage, 215–254.

Lemann, Nicholas (1998). 'Universities Use Rankings, Too', *U.S. News and World Report*, 125: 81.

Livingston, J. Sterling (2003). 'Pygmalion in Management', *Harvard Business Review*, 81: 97–106.

March, James G. and Olsen, J. P. (1976). *Ambiguity and Choice in Organizations*. Bergen: Universitetsforlaget.

McKinlay, Alan and Starkey, Ken (eds). (1998). *Foucault, Management and Organization Theory: From Panopticum to Technologies of Self*. London: Sage.

Meyer, Hans Dieter and Rowan, Brian (eds). (2006). *The New Institutionalism in Education*. Albany: State University of New York Press.

Meyer, J. W. and Rowan, Brian (1977). 'Institutionalized Organizations: Formal Structure as Myth and Ceremony', *American Journal of Sociology*, 83: 340–363.

Miller, Peter and O'Leary, Ted (1987). 'Accounting, and the Construction of the Governable Person ', *Accounting, Organizations and Society*, 12: 235–265.

Morgeson, Frederick P. and Nahrgang, Jennifer D. (2008). 'Same as It Ever Was: Recognizing Stability in the Business Week Rankings', *Academy of Management Learning and Education*, 7: 26–41.

Oliver, Christine (1991). 'Strategic Responses to Institutional Processes', *Academy of Management Review*, 16: 145–179.

Pfeffer, Jeffrey and Fong, Christina T. (2004). 'The Business School "Business": Some Lessons from the US Experience', *Journal of Management Studies*, 41: 1501–1520.

Quinn-Trank, Christine and Washington, Marvin (2009). 'Maintaining an Institution in a Contested Organizational Field: The Work of the AACSB and Its Constituents', in Thomas B. Lawrence, Roy Suddaby, and Bernard Leca (eds), *Institutional Work: Actors and Agency in Institutional Studies of Organizations*. Cambridge/New York: Cambridge University Press, 236–261.

Rabinow, Paul (ed.) (1991). *The Foucault Reader*. London: Penguin.

'Ranking Business Schools: The Numbers Game' (2002), *The Economist*, 14 October, 65.

Rasche, Andreas and Behnam, Michael (2009). 'As If It Were Relevant: A Social Systems Perspective on the Relation between Theory and Practice', *Journal of Management Inquiry*, 18: 243–255.

Sahlin-Andersson, Kerstin and Engwell, Lars (2002). 'The Dynamics of Management Knowledge Expansion', in Kerstin Sahlin-Andersson, and Lars Engwell (eds), *The Expansion of Management Knowledge: Carriers, Flows and Sources*. Palo Alto, CA: Stanford University Press, 277–298.

Sauder, Michael and Espeland, Wendy N. (2006). 'Strength in Numbers? The Advantages of Multiple Rankings', *Indiana Law Journal*, 81: 205–227.

Sauder, Michael and Espeland, Wendy N. (2009). 'The Discipline of Rankings: Tight Coupling and Organizational Change', *American Sociological Review*, 74: 63–82.

Schwan, Anne and Shapiro, Stephen (2011). *Foucault's Discipline and Punish*. London: Pluto.

Scott, Richard W. (1994). 'Conceptualizing Organizational Fields'. in Hans-Ulrich Derlien, Uta Gerhardt, and Fritz W. Scharpf (eds), *Systems Rationality and Partial Interests*. Baden: Nomos, 203–221.

Scott, Richard W. (1995). *Institutions and Organizations*. London: Sage.

Sewell, Graham, and Wilkinson, Barry (1992). ' "Someone to Watch over Me": Surveillance, Discipline and the Just-in-Time Labour Process', *Sociology*, 26: 271–289.

Strang, David and Meyer, John W. (1993). 'Institutional Conditions for Diffusion', *Theory and Society*, 22: 487–511.

Twale, Darla and DeLuca, Barbara (2008). *Faculty Incivility: The Rise of the Academic Bully Culture and What to Do About It*. San Francisco: Jossey Bass.

Townley, Barbara (1993). 'Foucault, Power/Knowledge, and Its Relevance for Human Resource Management', *Academy of Management Review*, 18: 518–545.

Townley, Barbara (1997). 'The Institutional Logic of Performance Appraisal', *Organization Studies*, 18: 261–285.

Vidaillet, Benedicte and Vignon, Christophe (2010). 'Bringing Back the Subject into Management Education', *Management Learning*, 41: 221–241.

Wedlin, Linda (2006). *Ranking Business Schools: Forming Fields, Identities and Boundaries*. Cheltenham: Edward Elgar.

Wedlin, Linda (2007). 'The Role of Rankings in Codifying a Business School Template: Classifications, Diffusion and Mediated Isomorphism in Organizational Fields', *European Management Review*, 4: 24–39.

Wedlin, Linda (2011). 'Going Global: Rankings as Rhetorical Devices to Construct an International Field of Management Education', *Management Learning*, 42: 199–218.

Weick, Karl E. (1979). *The Social Psychology of Organizing*. New York: McGraw-Hill.

Weick, Karl E. (1995). *Sensemaking in Organizations*. Thousand Oaks et al.: Sage.

Whitley, Richard (1984). 'The Fragmented State of Management Studies: Reasons and Consequences', *Journal of Management Studies*, 21: 331–348.

Wilson, David and McKiernan, Peter (2011). 'Global Mimicry: Putting Strategic Choice Back on the Business School Agenda', *British Journal of Management*, 22: 457–469.

Wooten, Melissa and Hoffman, Andrew J. (2008). 'Organizational Fields: Past, Present and Future' in Royston Greenwood, Christine Oliver, Kerstin Sahlin-Andersson, and Roy Suddaby (eds), *The Sage Handbook of Organizational Institutionalism*. London: Sage, 130–148.

Zembylas, Michalinos (2003). 'Interrogating "Teacher Identity": Emotion, Resistance, and Self-Formation', *Educational Theory*, 53: 107–127.

Zemsky, Robert (2008). 'The Rain Man Cometh—Again', *Academy of Management Perspectives*, 22: 5–14.

Zietsma, Charlene and Winn, Monika (2005). *Reflections on Process and Process Theorizing: Revisiting Our Work 'Organizational Field Power Dynamics and the "War of the Woods"'*. Paper presented at the First Organization Studies Summer Workshop, Sanatorini, Greece.

Zilber, Tammar B. (2010). 'Institutional Maintenance as Narrative Acts', in Thomas B. Lawrence, Roy Suddaby, and Bernard Leca (eds), *Institutional Work: Actors and Agency in Institutional Studies of Organizations*. Cambridge/New York: Cambridge University Press, 205–235.

Zilber, Tammar B. (2010). 'Institutional Maintenance as Narrative Acts', in Thomas B. Lawrence, Roy Suddaby, and Bernard Leca (eds), *Institutional Work: Actors and Agency in Institutional Studies of Organizations*. Cambridge/New York: Cambridge University Press, 205–235.

Part III

Challenges for the Future Development of Business Schools

10

Business Schools Inside the Academy

What Are the Prospects for Interdepartmental Research Collaboration?

Ewan Ferlie, Graeme Currie, Julie Davies, and Nora Ramadan

10.1. INTRODUCTION

Established literature about the role of business schools tends towards more parochial concerns, such as their need for a more pluralist and socially reflexive mode of knowledge production (Starkey and Tiratsoo 2007; Starkey et al. 2009), or the failure of management's professionalism project expressed through the business school movement (Khurana 2007). When casting their gaze elsewhere, academic commentators examine business schools' weakening links with management practice (Bennis and O'Toole 2005). Our theme makes a novel contribution to the business school literature through exploring prospects for research collaborations with other university departments. We draw upon the case of U.K. business schools, which are typically university-based (unlike some of their European counterparts), and provide illustrations relating to collaboration with medical schools to make our analytical points. We might expect business schools and medical schools to collaborate given their similar vocational underpinnings, but at the same time, there are significant differences, such as differing paradigms of research and the extent to which the practice fields are professionalized. This means collaboration may prove challenging. In short, the case of collaboration between business schools and medical schools is likely to illuminate the challenges for business schools in 'reaching out' to other university departments.

Why is our theme of academic research collaborations beyond the business school important? Business schools may currently be experiencing a 'perfect storm' (Thomas and Cornuel 2012) of falling MBA numbers and also deep concerns about their legitimacy and what kind of knowledge it is that they produce (Ghoshal 2005: 75). UK business schools are located within publicly funded universities, sitting alongside longer-established academic departments for which the canon of academic research is taken for granted (we recognize other countries display a different institutional pattern). The question may be asked inside the university: do business schools produce knowledge with the conventional features of social science (Starkey and Tempest 2008; Thomas 2009), and how might this relate to forms of knowledge produced by other university departments?

The UK business school sector has experienced two decades of research capacity building, with new professional associations (e.g. British Academy of Management), its own peer reviewed journals (e.g. *British Journal of Management*) and major investment by the ESRC (Economic and Social Research Council) in the Advanced Institute of Management Research (AIM). Given this sustained investment, we anticipate maturing business schools would by now have developed their social science research base, and be reaching out, or 'lowering its walls', with respect to collaborating with other university departments. The latter meanwhile, given the pervasiveness of organization and management problems across all domains of life, may increasingly look to business schools to help address these. Is this too optimistic a scenario? Khurana's (2007) pessimistic conclusion, however, is that the professionalization of management project, which is inherent in the missions of business school, has failed, including its attempt to build a science base on the medical school model. This failure might imply business schools should migrate back to a dominant concern with how they relate to business practitioners, as called for by pro-practice critics (Bennis and O'Toole 2005), and sideline what were weakly developed forms of academic research.

Given their recent growth, business schools may be among the largest and most profitable departments in some universities. But how do they interact with other academic departments, especially in research? Are they co-operative or 'stand-alone'? Other academic departments may acquire negative stereotypes of business schools, seeing them as dominated by teaching, executive education and consulting. Business schools may concentrate on building and ring-fencing their financial surpluses, neglecting the fundamental research base needed for wider legitimacy within the university.

Various reformative projects have been proposed. The public interest model of the business school (Ferlie et al. 2010), for example, asserts that business schools should promote a form of 'public social science' (with conventional notions of blind peer review, declaration of financial interests or sponsorship, and eventual publication in publicly accessible journals) in their knowledge production. This stance distinguishes them from alternative knowledge producers operating in a crowded field (such as management consultants and think tanks). In pursuit of a niche position in the face of competition from other knowledge producers, business schools might take account of research policy literature. This highlights knowledge production trends as favouring more thematic and inter-disciplinary modes to tackle cross-cutting themes and promote radical innovation. If so, the capacity of business schools to develop fruitful inter-disciplinary research collaborations becomes a strategic issue for them.

We suggest that collaboration across different academic disciplines may be complex. The epistemic wall (Knorr-Cetina 1999) between different disciplines is a barrier to multi-disciplinary research, as in the sometimes fraught relationship between the natural and social sciences (Redclift 1998), each with distinctive research models and assumptions about the nature of knowledge (Campbell 2005). These epistemic differences may create inter-disciplinary conflicts (Choi and Pak 2007). Base disciplines may be seen by academics as more legitimate and influential than multi-disciplinary research, thus inter-disciplinary journals are often viewed as of lesser quality than uni-disciplinary ones (Campbell 2005). We should also consider the relative power balance between disciplines (Becher 1994; Choi and Pak 2007) and how that might affect willingness to collaborate.

We start this chapter on business schools' research engagement with other academic departments with a broad theoretical framing. We then explore some organizational literature on inter-organizational co-operation, followed by science policy literature that charts the rise of inter-disciplinary research.

After describing our methods, we present preliminary data on UK business schools' research partnerships within universities. We examine reported patterns of inter-departmental research collaboration. We take the example of reported joint research between business schools and medical schools, finding evidence of two distinctive sub-groups of stand-alone schools and active collaborators. Two case studies of collaborative schools are outlined which include an analysis of the dynamics correlated within greater research collaboration. This exploratory study concludes by elaborating a forward-looking research agenda in this important and neglected area.

10.2. A REVIEW OF TWO RELEVANT LITERATURES

10.2.1. Literature on Inter-organizational Networks and Collaboration in Public Service Settings

Research alliances between business schools and other university departments are a form of inter (or intra) organizational collaboration (at least in the UK case: the pattern may be different elsewhere) within public services organizations, rather than between private firms. We thus draw upon a literature examining networks and inter-organizational collaboration within public management studies (Klijn 2005) to orient our empirical work.

Klijn (2005) highlights two theories that might explain the development of networks within public policy settings. First, resource dependency and exchange theory (Pfeffer 1981; Aldrich 2007) argue organizations develop networks to protect key flows of resources. However, the bulk of a university department's income comes from teaching fees, and business schools typically occupy a 'cash cow' role here. Not being reliant upon other university departments, this may be a weak motivator for cross-departmental research. Rather, they are more likely to network with business firms, whose resources are more significant linked to the development of teaching income. Second, political science literature (Rhodes 1988; Marsh and Rhodes 1992) suggests that 'policy communities' (e.g. the science policy or business policy communities) develop dense, integrated, and also closed networks, cut off from each other. In university settings, dense epistemic networks tend to occur within the basic disciplines rather than between them (Knorr-Cetina 1999; Becher and Trowler 2001). Third, strong public policy networks are likely to emerge under conditions of joint production and systemic 'wicked problems' (Ferlie et al 2011), such as devising an interagency response to the cross-cutting climate change policy problem. Yet cross-over activity between university departments is often small scale or relatively simple (e.g. joint degree programmes) so this theory may be only weakly relevant.

If these three theories of network development in public management settings are not fruitful, which angles might potentially be more promising? A first question is whether a business school indeed has the strategic intent—either formally announced in a plan or emerging in collective faculty behaviours—to build research collaborations within the university as a key objective. Ferlie et al's (2010) typology of different business schools suggests that this orientation is a distinguishing characteristic of the 'public interest' model which defends traditional notions of 'public science' within the academy, but we can't assume that other university departments hold such strategic intent. Further, it may that groups of schools may be on distinct trajectories, including in their approach to research strategy, i.e. they do not all conform to the 'public interest' school (Ferlie et al. 2010). Highly institutionalist explanations of the business school field as characterized by many 'fashions' and of strong isomorphism may prove of limited value, since there may be considerable variation in the research strategies of business schools, including scope for local innovation and experiment (Starkey and Tiratsoo 2007) or even strategic choice. We return to these theoretical issues in the concluding discussion. Let us assume that empirically some business schools populate the 'public interest' box. For these schools, the question is how to realize their strategic objective of building academically-oriented research, which is likely to include building collaborations within the academy in order to maximize academic impact.

The knowledge-based view of strategy is explored here as a theoretical framing, including the resource-based view of the firm (Barney 2001; Wernerfelt 2006). Eisenhardt and Santos's overview (2006) draws mainly on private-sector-based literature which sees knowledge as a strategically significant asset for the modern 'firm', and the capacity to mobilize it as a core competence. They cite Cohen and Levinthal's (1992) concept of 'absorptive capacity', defined as an organizational ability to recognize the value of external information, assimilate it, and apply it for commercial ends. Where the academic environment is volatile and research collaborations shift, the 'dynamic capabilities' (Teece et al. 1997) concept becomes important, defined as the firm's ability to integrate, build and reconfigure internal and external competences to address high velocity environments. Knowledge-sourcing activity is an important competence addressed in the literature, often based within externally facing networks, which provide a diverse range of contacts that help to access and integrate new knowledge quickly. The process of internal knowledge transfer within a firm is also important, focusing on the nature of the relationship (and how it is shaped) between the sender and recipient of knowledge, and on knowledge brokering.

Another theme in the knowledge-based view of strategy is the role (if any) of incentives and top management pressure in stimulating internal knowledge transfer (Eisenhardt and Gahmic 2000), as well as bottom up collaborative processes (critical for powerful groups of professionals and knowledge workers). This theme is relevant because the central core in many UK universities seeks to increase its capacity to steer the university (Ferlie and Andresani 2009) and within the research domain there may be more centrally-sponsored attempts to bring academics from different departments together in novel multi-disciplinary and thematic arenas. As other parts of the university may decline during a recession, some business schools are absorbing more subjects, e.g. law.

10.2.2. Research Policy Literature: More Thematic and Inter-disciplinary Research

We now review a separate research policy literature, which suggests a long-term growth of inter-disciplinary research in academic settings, notably within science and engineering (Cummings and Keisler 2005). This shift is seen as promoting creative and radical innovation to a greater extent than is possible within one discipline. Many current scientific and social scientific agendas are broad and thematic in nature (e.g. climate change, an ageing society, new genetics technologies with their social and ethical implications) and cross-conventional disciplinary boundaries (Starkey et al. 2009).

Various 'pull' factors from the wider domain of science policy may be pulling business schools into inter-disciplinary research collaborations. National U.K. science and research policy (and funding) has moved towards broad and thematic areas. Internationally, governments seem dissatisfied with the science/society interface and seek to accelerate science-led economic growth by taking increasingly interventionist stances in funding streams (Nowotny et al. 2001). This perspective is reinforced by the 'triple helix' model (Leydesdorff and Meyer 2006), which sees government, as well as science and industry, as a major player in a co-evolving knowledge production system.

Research Councils UK currently stresses broad thematic areas such as: energy; global food security; global uncertainties; security in a changing world; living with environmental change and lifelong health and wellbeing. The U.K. Government's *Innovation and Research Strategy for Growth* (BIS 2011:16) states: 'as innovation is increasingly driven by challenges such as climate change and the ageing population, the Government will back challenge led innovation in these areas to drive interdisciplinary collaborations to develop new business models, products and processes'. For example, a major research call in autumn 2012 from the EPSRC/ESRC for proposals on the digital economy explicitly asked the established community of natural scientists who bid for the research to link up with economists and management scholars in broad multi-disciplinary teams.

A recent definition of inter-disciplinary research is provided by Rhoten and Pfirman (2007, quoted in van Rijnsoever and Hessels 2011: 464):

> 'inter-disciplinarity refers to the integration or synthesis of two or more disparate disciplines, bodies of knowledge or modes of thinking to produce a meaning, explanation or product that is more extensive and powerful than its constituent parts'.

Van Rijnsoever and Hessels' definition (2011: 464) suggests in a similar vein that inter-disciplinary research represents: 'the collaboration between scientists from different disciplines with the goal of producing new knowledge'. There are severe challenges in overcoming conceptual and methodological boundaries between different fields of research (Huutonieni et al. 2010) which may represent distinctive epistemic disciplinary-based communities (Knorr-Cetina 1999), in order to realize any vision of inter-disciplinarity.

So, is a novel mode of scientific knowledge production emerging in which traditional disciplinary boundaries erode? The general science policy literature (Hessels and van Lente 2008) reconceptualizes the production of scientific knowledge. The possible growth of inter-disciplinary science is discussed within two models in particular. First, a well-known literature explores a possible transition between a Mode 1 (based on traditional academic disciplines) and Mode 2 (dispersed and socially pluralist) knowledge production (Gibbons et al. 1994; Nowotny et al. 2001) with the greater involvement of non-academic stakeholders. Commentators write of a new mode of trans-disciplinarity which goes beyond multi-disciplinarity in the sense that the interaction of scientific disciplines is much more dynamic. Once theoretical consensus is attained, it cannot easily be reduced to disciplinary parts' (Hesselsand van Lente 2008: 741).

Nowotny et al. (2001: 106) briefly discuss multi-disciplinarity as well as trans-disciplinarity. They note there has always been multi-disciplinarity within Mode 1 knowledge production, but there appears to be a shift towards combining more historically non-adjacent disciplines, possibly because of the transfer of technologically sophisticated instrumentation from one field to another. Ziman (1994, 2000) has developed a model of 'post-academic science' in which science becomes a more collective activity, with more co-writing of articles. In addition, this model assumes 'both the practical and fundamental problems that scientists are concerned with are trans-disciplinary in nature, calling for collective effort' (Hessels and van Lente 2008: 746).

The research policy literature reflects on how to manage the complex research collaborations implied by these models. Bammer (2008) explores how to manage intellectual and other differences between partners. Cummings and Kiesler (2005) point to the high transaction costs in many multi-disciplinary research projects, especially when conducted virtually rather than face-to-face. Van Rijnsoever and Hessels (2011) explore factors associated with both kinds of inter-disciplinary research collaborations. Interestingly, they found that disciplinary collaborations, i.e. with colleagues in the same discipline but at different institutions, occur more in basic disciplines and that inter-disciplinary collaborations (across different academic disciplines) occur more in strategic disciplines, which we suggest might include business and management research.

This debate in the science policy literature has operated at a high level of generality. Some authors have creatively transferred concepts from this literature stream into the debate on the future of business schools, with the Mode 2 model proving a most influential import (see Starkey et al. 2009). The business school literature has paid less attention to the literature on Mode 1, based inter-disciplinarity, which is our focus here. Several questions emerge from the science policy literature. Within the domain of management studies, is there really a trend to broad thematic research questions which bring different disciplines together? Do concepts and instruments readily move into and out of business schools to and from other disciplines? Do radical scientific breakthroughs really occur within large multi-disciplinary teams involving management scholars?

So we have argued that Mode 1 style research co-operation between business schools and other university departments has been under studied in the current business school literature. Our initial literature review suggested theoretical perspectives drawn from the literatures on collaboration in public services settings, from the knowledge-based view of strategy, and on how science policy academic literature might help with a theoretical framing.

In this modest exploratory study, we gathered data to address the following three objectives:

- Descriptively to map the pattern of reported research collaborations between U.K. business schools and other academic departments.
- To examine an area of strategic significance in greater depth: namely research interactions between business schools and medical schools.
- To present early case study material on two promising sites for such interactions.

10.2.3. Methods and Data

We here draw on three sets of U.K. business school data largely collected through the Association of Business Schools (ABS) with its ready access to the U.K. business school community

(1) An ABS survey of UK directors of research focusing on cross-departmental research collaboration with other departments and within thematic clusters. Thirty-five institutions had responded by January 2012. See: <http://www.surveymonkey.com/s/ABS_RESEARCH>.

(2) A small-scale institutional audit of a key group of business schools to gather information on reported joint research with medical schools.

(3) Two mini case studies of business schools that reported high levels of research collaboration with their local medical schools. These early cases are based on the authors' local knowledge rather than any primary interviews.

10.2.4. Survey Findings

We received 35 responses from the web survey, giving a response rate of 32 per cent. Results are provided in Figure 10.1 and Figure 10.2. If we cluster 4- and 5-rated responses together to indicate 'high collaboration' areas, only economics approaches the 45 per cent mark and may well be partly internalized within the business schools anyway (although some deans are insistent that economics exists as a separate department outside the business school). Economics can be seen as a special case. After economics, there are reasonably-sized clusters (20–25 per cent of respondents) of high collaboration reported with engineering, medicine, law, psychology, sociology, and the arts. Given that only 30 universities in the UK have medical schools, there is high co-operation reported within that group. The low reported co-operation with geography is surprising given the importance of the sustainability thematic cluster. However, business schools may increasingly employ such

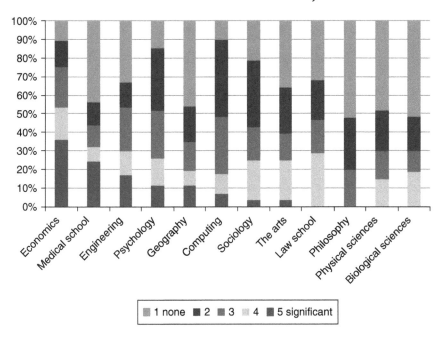

Figure 10.1. To what extent, rated on a 1–5 (highest) scale, is research collaboration taking place between the business school and other university departments?

expertise directly, for example, within a faculty group concerned with corporate social responsibility. There is less collaboration reported with law—another important professional school—than we had expected.

Generally speaking, the survey results suggest low levels of inter-disciplinary collaboration and of 'high walls' around business schools. We lack comparator data in the survey from non-business school departments in the social sciences, but U.K. business schools look cut off, as more than one respondent confirmed:

> The business school seems quite 'silo like' and isolated from other departments with the partial exception of the medical school. Business school staff rarely think in terms of applying for large ESRC grants and tend to work on quite small scale research projects. Their co-operation appears to be with other business school staff in other universities rather than other departments in the College.

The absence of a reported collaboration with philosophy may reflect either the neglect of ethical questions within business schools, the closure of departments of philosophy or the incorporation of ethics and philosophy of science within business school faculty. There appears to be further scope to collaborate on research with biological and physical sciences, with which collaboration is ranked the lowest, but around which, for example, there may be a research agenda linked to knowledge mobilization and the translation of innovation.

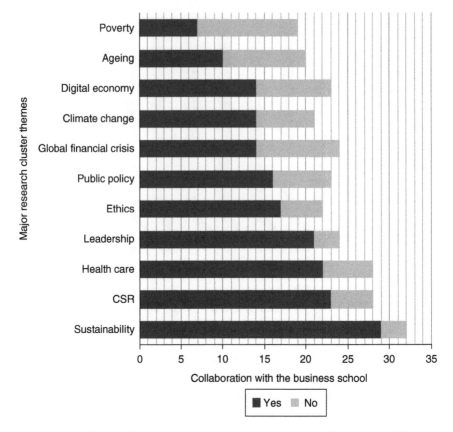

Figure 10.2. Please indicate any major research clusters established on the following themes that involve business school staff

In terms of thematic clusters, sustainability and, after that, the related field of corporate social responsibility (CSR) are the most frequently reported sites for collaboration (which should encourage stronger research collaboration with geography). They are followed by health care (medical schools), leadership and ethics (psychology), and public policy (political science). Some small-scale themes, such as ageing and poverty may gain greater attention as the public expenditure reductions bite and as an ageing population and social care become more pressing political and financial issues.

Survey respondents provided examples of supportive mechanisms being developed by the university centre to encourage cross-departmental research collaboration, such as the establishment of inter-disciplinary centres, e.g. an energy institute. Several business school directors of research referred to cross-university societal challenges that were supported with limited internal funding for collaborative projects. Several universities have appointed staff who work on cross-disciplinary opportunities. In other universities, there appears to be a more laissez-faire approach, with research clusters emerging as a bottom-up phenomenon. It still appears challenging to operationalize inter-disciplinary research in a funding system that has not yet institutionalized these demands:

> It is very difficult to get funding in a multi-disciplinary area from a funding body. There is a lack of qualified referees to review as each one is expert in their own discipline.

The narrow focus on A-rated specialist journal outputs and the lack of knowledge about journals for inter-disciplinary research appear to be major factors that act as disincentives to interdepartmental research collaboration:

> As a business school, we mainly look for top journal publications. Other departments sometimes focus on other outlets.

Respondents talked about researchers from disciplines outside the business school speaking a different language with different cultures:

> Different disciplines have evolved using their own terminology and 'ways of doing things' as well as different expectations.

The variability of research track records between units, lack of time, and poorly articulated synergies, were cited as other restraining forces. Centralized performance management systems around publication in top management journals for the national Research Excellence Framework assessment exercise appeared to have particularly strong impact, although we note such forces are emerging elsewhere as global competition between business schools intensifies:

> Instrumental pressure of publications for the Research Excellence Framework and limited research workload, coupled with high administration demands on time, leave little time for research development activity as a long-term approach.

Some respondents suggested business school faculty would benefit from informal networking opportunities with possible partners in other schools. They advocated greater awareness of inter-disciplinary funding opportunities, as well as more information on the research profiles of faculty outside the business school. They suggested new resource allocation models that encourage interdepartmental partnerships to break down a silo mentality would be helpful.

When asked how the university supports interdepartmental collaboration with business schools, respondents observed:

> The university has set up a number of university wide inter-disciplinary research themes as part of its refreshed strategic plan. Participation is encouraged but not mandatory. However, the university will use KPIs to measure the extent to which cross faculty work is taking place.

Despite such intervention, however:

> The university defines 'grand challenges' which require the creation of cross-departmental research projects. Most projects, however, originate from direct department-to-department contacts.

In the next section, we explore the results of a small-scale institutional audit on intra-university research collaboration between business and medical schools, which emerged as an important area in the survey.

10.3. MANAGEMENT AND MEDICAL SCHOOL RESEARCH INTERACTIONS: AN INSTITUTIONAL AUDIT

This major theme has been under-explored so far although there is some early case material. Kastor (2004: 85) describes low levels of interaction between the Academic Health Centre (AHC) in the University of Pennsylvania and the neighbouring (and prestigious) Wharton School (including its health economics and health management groupings), combined with the AHC's high use of management consulting, but there appears to be little material of a more systematic nature.

In teaching, there is a growing collaboration between business and medical schools, particularly in the U.S. at postgraduate level. Freudenheim (2011) notes the reasons for this: '[u]nder heavy pressure from government regulators and insurance companies, more and more physicians across the country are learning to think like entrepreneurs'. Knight (2012) also observes that 'when issues such as the rising cost of health insurance and an ageing population dominate the political agenda, many students are. . . augmenting their medical education with a joint MD/MBA. In 1993, there were five programmes in the U.S.; today there are 65, according to figures from the Association of MD/MBA Programs (AMMP)'. Such dual degrees in medicine and management are offered by top schools such as Columbia, Dartmouth, and Cornell. In Europe, Sweden's Karolinska Institutet offers joint medical and business degrees. Indeed, *The Economist* (2011) suggests that business schools that are not élite may leverage their university's medical school to provide niche medical education with management: 'To compete for students from the wider world some schools may need to specialise. . . Take the Olin Business School at Washington University in St Louis. It is popular within its region, but has found it harder to attract students from farther afield. With a renowned medical school at the university, it would seem perfectly placed to appeal to students anywhere interested in medical-sector management'. Business schools could look to medical schools for pedagogic models. Nohria (2012: 38), Dean of Harvard Business School, suggests that '[t]he clinical experience gained by fledgling doctors is an ideal example of how professional schools address the "knowing-doing gap"' which is partly being addressed in the Harvard Business School MBA by a new Field Immersion Experiences for Leadership Development programme '[t]o give MBA students a dose of real-world experience'. In Imperial College London, at undergraduate level, its Business School offers a long standing B.Sc. Medical Sciences with Management in collaboration with the Faculty of Medicine, as more recently has the Department of Management at King's College London. Students decide to come and study at the Business School in either the third or fourth year of their medical degree to equip future clinicians with an understanding of the management issues facing the health system.

10.4. RESULTS FROM CO-LOCATED BUSINESS/ MEDICAL SCHOOLS

In order to conduct an institutional audit of reported research links in the U.K., we emailed a survey to a sub-group of 11 U.K. business schools with high levels of research income (at least €1.2m in 2009/10: Source: HESA) and which also contained a medical school located within the same university. All replied and Table 10.1 summarizes these responses. Interestingly, they clustered in two strategic sub-groups: no or minimal reported research collaborations (4) and substantial reported collaboration (7). This indicates that business schools in roughly similar circumstances may be exercising some strategic choice or, at least, be on local path dependent tracks.

Table 10.1. Institutional audit of reported joint research areas between key U.K. business schools and 'their' medical schools

No or minimal reported research collaborations (4)	
Substantial reported research collaborations (7)	**Cross-site themes:** translational research; service delivery and organization; diffusion of innovations; patient safety; organizational development; leadership; implementation/improvement science. **Local themes:** re-engineering/lean; patient and public involvement; human resource management; health economics; information needs of families and patients; operations research and patient flows; mental health services, teams and culture.

Unsurprisingly, a range of research areas was reported, reflecting in part the presence of local academic champions and traditional areas of strength. A cluster of cross-site themes included: translational research (i.e. moving clinical research 'from bench to bedside'); diffusion of innovations; organizational development; patient safety and service issues; and service delivery and organization (linked to a National Institute of Health Research (NIHR) programme with substantial external and peer reviewed research funding). One site reported an NIHR funded project with two principal investigators—one each from the business and medical school. We suggest that this is evidence of novel 'hybrid knowledges' which help link business and medical schools' research activities.

10.4.1. Two Case Studies of Sites with Promising Research Interactions Between Business and Medical Schools

What might be the local contexts, structures, processes and actions that favour collaborative research relationships between business and medical schools? We now introduce two case studies of promising higher education institutions (both from our high collaboration group), before making comparative remarks.

CASE STUDY 1

This case is set in a long established, research intensive, multi-faculty university which contains Arts, Social Sciences (including Management), Natural Sciences, and a large, old and prestigious medical school. The Medical School was recently designated an Academic Health Sciences Centre (one of only five nationally). Its AHSC application mentioned potential synergy with the rest of the University, including social sciences such as Management. The strong mental health element includes well-developed research on social and community psychiatry (including user involvement) as well as trials of new drugs. It has a social science orientation (e.g. psychology), as does primary care and public health (which is open to medical sociology). These are social science 'friendly' components of the Medical School, in terms of their own interests and epistemologies. The Medical School is developing activity in the fields of Health Policy and Evaluation and Improvement Science to complement traditional biomedical research.

At the meso level, the School of Social Science is keen to foster research alliances with the Medical School, and health is a major sector for it as well. At departmental level, the self- descriptor of the 'Department of Management' (as opposed the 'Business School') indicates that it focuses on public services organizations as well as private firms. It was a strong RAE 2008 (Research Assessment Exercise) performer. Although it still operates on a medium scale, it generates a moderate surplus. There is a strong stream of research work in the Department on human resource management, including in public sector settings. It offers an M.Sc. in Public Sector Management (PSM) and has built up a PSM group of faculty that teach it. There are (small-scale) cross-departmental flows of M.Sc. students with some modules open to Medical School students. There is limited cross-departmental supervision of Ph.D. students (mainly from Management into Medicine).

Joint research with the Medical School has been developed over time by a small cluster of senior (professorial level) staff in the department with long standing personal research interests in health care management. A few senior professors in public health and psychiatry have also helped orchestrate contacts and collaboration between the Medical School and Management. This bottom-up, yet senior level, 'push' for collaboration has so far proved more influential than a formal top-down research strategy, which is so far weakly expressed. Patient safety, health policy and evaluation, and service improvement arenas in the Medical School have all proved fruitful in stimulating personal contact, dialogue, and in some cases research bids from a small number of Medical School and Management Department staff working across conventional departmental boundaries. Significant local charitable and NHS funding has been obtained which energizes such collaborations.

For these senior professors in Management, access to major AHSC sites may be helpful to their own research agendas. Such sites can be used for empirical research. These professors could also be named as co-investigators on large-scale grant applications regularly going in from the Medical School, which has a competence in spinning out large scale, multi-disciplinary bids to the National Institute of Health Research (NIHR) with its very considerable budgets (about €12bn pa). Within the Medical School, various 'pull' factors were evident. There were some senior reflective managers, either general managers or clinical managers, who found management research useful in thinking about how to manage their organizations (e.g. HRM strategy). The AHSC was in its early stages of organization development or leadership based research. Health policy and evaluation were developing as major new research areas within the AHSC, complementing traditional biomedical research. With the emergence of new and behavioural sub-disciplines or 'hybrid knowledges' (health services research; patient safety and quality research; improvement science; now implementation science), opportunities were arising to link aspects of social science (including organizational level analysis) with the clinical sciences within large scale and multi-disciplinary research bids. Future challenges include 'scaling up' the relatively limited research collaborations and discussing openly and constructively the remaining knowledge.

CASE STUDY 2

This case is set in a research intensive, multi-faculty university established in the 1960s. The University has strong research-led departments across all faculties. The Medical School, however, is a more recent development. This is a significant factor for the Medical School's stance with respect to collaboration with other departments, including the Business School. It cannot yet compete with the well-established medical schools. It seeks, therefore, to develop a 'niche' position for itself, including leadership and innovation, an area in which the Business School excels.

The Business School is a major part of the University with a well-established reputation internationally for research, teaching and corporate engagement. It has enjoyed autonomy from central control beyond that experienced by most university departments. Like many business schools, Case 2 is expected to produce a large cash surplus for strategic investment across other university departments, and to develop new collaborations which boost its income and that of other university departments. Like many business schools, it now draws many of its students from outside the UK and is being encouraged to align with University strategy for international ventures in developing, but fast growing economies. So the Business School is seeking to develop a research-focused institute in one of these fast growing economies, and has identified healthcare management research as one of three strategic themes under-serviced within the developing country. Like the Medical School, the development of collaboration for the Business School is driven by the interest and expertise of the academic faculty it is able to recruit.

However, in contrast to the Medical School, the Business School is perceived to have 'high walls' and many academic faculty remain 'inward looking' in seeking academic collaboration. For many of these academics, the pluralist nature of the Business School, particularly regarding other social science disciplines outside their own, combined with a more theoretical orientation towards knowledge development (rather than applying knowledge in practice), means they see little need to engage other departments such as the Medical School. In comparison with Case 1, the Case 2 Business School is a 'business' rather than management school, with a strong corporate culture and orientation towards the external corporate world. Reflecting this, its academic faculty and students are concentrated in the areas of marketing, strategy, accounting and finance. Public services management, and more specifically health services management, has traditionally been viewed as a relatively peripheral interest, in part because it has not generated the financial surplus expected of a business school. Public services management has traditionally been institutionalized within the Business School structure as a distinctive teaching group. With respect to a relationship with the Medical School, the Business School is favourably regarded by senior management in the Medical School as a partnership worth pursuing. However, the detail of this has not been progressed until recently. At a level below Medical School senior management, there has been some resistance to working with the Business School around the areas of leadership and innovation, which might be perceived to represent relevant expertise to be offered by any business school. Such resistance occurs on the basis that, historically, Business School research and education offerings have proved insufficiently contextualized. Instead, the Medical School has tended to look towards the Engineering School for niche management expertise in areas such as re-engineering care and 'lean'.

In summary, until recently collaboration between the Business and Medical Schools has been focused on a very limited number of funded academic research projects which have not been sustained or joined up into more institutionalized arrangements. However, there have emerged two potentially more substantive arenas for collaboration. On the 'pull' side, there is significant funding for education and research around leadership and innovation, which has caused the Medical School to look more towards the Business School. In particular, NIHR funding for translational initiatives, such as Collaborations for Leadership in Applied Healthcare Research and Care (CLAHRC), an area in which the Business School has significant expertise, has pulled the Business School and Medical School together. Meanwhile, executive education opportunities in the healthcare leadership area are many, and the Medical School has sought to collaborate with the Business School in pursuit of these, with an associated research agenda. On the 'push side', as part of overall investment in the Business School, first, academic faculty have been recruited with strong research in cognate areas for health services management, now emerging as one its research strengths. Interestingly, the public services management teaching group has been disbanded, with faculty distributed across the Business School, although the health services management faculty all 'mainstreamed' into the same teaching group, which focuses upon innovation. Included in the new recruits are academic faculty with significant engagement with applied health services research, including working with Medical School faculty in more prestigious medical schools, which even Medical School faculty beyond its senior management recognize as exhibiting the necessary contextualization of healthcare. Following meetings with the Medical School Dean and Pro-Deans, one of the 'senior' professors within this group of new recruits acts as the 'broker' between the Business School and Medical School, and is now part of the Medical School Advisory Board. In part, his motivation is that research funding in medical and other clinical sciences is larger than in social sciences, and through collaboration with the Medical Science, he and colleagues can access this funding. At the same time, second, the host university has developed high level, university wide themes, around which it expects inter-disciplinary collaboration, including healthcare. This is led by one of the senior Medical School professors, and he has invited the newly recruited senior professor in the Business School to play a significant role in the development of the healthcare theme. Meanwhile, other healthcare management experts in the Business School play key roles in an emerging institutionalized (risk sharing, investment sharing, income sharing) partnership between the Business and Medical Schools focused upon leadership, and an international initiative led by the Medical School, which encompasses organization and management in resource poor settings, specifically Africa.

The challenge for the Medical and Business Schools in this HEI (higher education institution) is to deliver research and education income, and to develop and sustain the collaboration on the ground. In the absence of this, Business School and Medical School collaboration may prove a mere dalliance, as other more fruitful collaborations are realized with other departments.

10.5. COMPARATIVE ANALYSIS AND DISCUSSION

Looking across these two cases (see Table 10.2), we make the following remarks. Our judgement was that research collaboration could be assessed as moderate to high in Case 1 and as high in Case 2. Why might this variation be the case?

At a substantive level, both sites displayed three common features which seem to promote collaboration: a Public Services or Health Services Management group of faculty (so there are faculty with an interest in working in public sector settings such as the NHS); active knowledge-brokering by a small number of senior professors (so agency as well as structure is important); and linking hybrid forms of knowledge (e.g. leadership, organizational development and change, implementation science, translational research) where both sides had a real interest in collaboration connected to income opportunities from policy sources.

In contrasting the two sites, the Business School in Case 2 was bigger, more operationally autonomous and had a bigger surplus. It was sometimes described as having 'high walls', which might well be seen as a negative factor. This negative appears to have been overcome, however, in Case 2 by three positive factors. The first was the nature of the Medical School, which in Case 2 was new, still building its profile, and seen as more flexible and willing to invest in niche areas: in essence, having 'low walls' around it. We suggest that where medical schools are more established and prestigious, they might regard the business school with some disdain as a 'trade school' with little academic credibility. In this regard, Case 1 might prove more challenging for those senior academics in the Management School that sought to progress collaboration with the Medical School. The second was a more articulated strategic framework at university level, which reinforced the activity of professorial brokers at field level, marrying a top-down push and bottom-up activity. Finally, we highlight a series of opportunities that were aligned with both the research and education mission of the Business School and Medical School that represented significant streams of income from government policy sources. We note that this final factor, whilst common across the two cases, appears particularly important for drawing a business school into collaboration, given its traditional 'high walls'.

Research collaborations between business schools and medical schools may be a positive outlier (see our data in Figures 10.1 and 10.2) when compared to research collaborations with many other university departments, including with the social sciences, which superficially might appear more promising. Why might this be the case? First, there appears to be a 'win-win' situation whereby medical schools acquire access to important organizational and management knowledge whilst management or business school researchers acquire access to major empirical sites and large research grants. Second,

Table 10.2. Business and medical school research collaborations: two case studies of promising sites (as of early 2012)

	Case Study 1	Case Study 2
Presence of a Public Services Management Group	Yes	Yes
Knowledge brokering from senior professors	Yes	Yes
Local presence of linking 'hybrid knowledges'	Yes	Yes
Status of Medical School	Old, élite; strong mental health component; AHSC	Newer, niche, more flexible; 'low walls'
Status of Business School	Smaller, smaller surplus, more centralised and integrated in mainstream university	Larger, big surplus, more operational autonomy and separate structure; 'high walls'
Strategic linking framework at university level	Weaker	Stronger
Assessed level of research co-operation	Moderate to high	High
Opportunities for collaboration with significant income attached	High	High

there are, at a deeper level, hybrid bodies of knowledge, which cross these boundaries intellectually and form an arena in which both sites can engage in dialogue. Third, there are some high status academic journals, recognized in both domains, which act as 'boundary objects': it is possible to publish jointly and in a journal recognized in both medicine and social science. However, we suggest that it is the emergence of significant sources of policy funding, for leadership education and translational research that appears particularly influential in driving inter-disciplinarity. This explains why collaboration may be realized now compared with past non-collaboration.

In future work, we would seek to theorize these substantive findings more explicitly, drawing on the heuristic of receptive and non-receptive contexts for change (Pettigrew et al. 1992), originally developed in U.K. health care settings. This model suggests that an organizational ability to progress strategic change is shaped by a configuration of various interrelated 'signs and symptoms' of receptivity (rather than one single variable), some of which seem prima facie relevant to developing research collaborations across the medical school and business school interface such as: key people leading change; change agenda and its locale; co-operative inter-organizational networks; supportive organizational culture. We return to this discussion in the conclusion.

10.6. CONCLUDING DISCUSSION

This exploratory study examined inter-disciplinary Mode 1 research occurring between university-based U.K. business schools and other local academic departments. This analytic approach has not so far been apparent in the business school literature, which has been more concerned with Mode 2 research (Starkey et al. 2009). We started to plot the reported map of U.K. business school engagement in interdepartmental and thematic research. Except for the special case of economics, the number of reported 'high collaboration' areas looks modest. We speculated that there are still 'high walls' around research in many business schools. We looked in more detail at research interactions between business schools and their local medical schools as a strategic exemplar, finding preliminary evidence of two distinct sub-groups of 'collaborative' and 'stand-alone' business schools. Our two case studies of collaborative business schools started to uncover the conditions and processes associated with collaborative research relations.

10.6.1. Developing a Future Research Agenda

Where might future research work on this important and neglected theme of business schools' academic research collaborations best be concentrated? We need, first of all, a more extensive, structured, and internationally oriented literature review of business school research collaborations to map the existing terrain. American and European research intensive universities also contain a range of academic departments, which include major business schools, so a search of the international (as well as U.K.-based) literature to uncover and synthesize existing work is an important first step. It is possible that this search might conclude that not much has been published so far.

Second, further survey-based work to extend our initial findings should be undertaken, preferably on an international basis. This work should seek to construct a typology of business schools in terms of their underpinning research strategy and orientation and identify how many emphasize inter-disciplinary academic collaborations and the correlates of that stance. For example, do schools in the U.K's Russell Group (research intensive) universities report more collaboration than teaching intensive institutions? Is there also variation within Russell Group sites?

Third, we need more intensive and focused empirical work in key collaborative areas that early work indicates are interesting. More work on business schools' research links across to the other big professional schools of medicine and law should be a priority. The research interface with health care and medical schools already appears from our exploratory study as a key area. But what about collaboration with law schools? The apparently low level of research collaboration with geography is curious and needs exploring given the reported importance of sustainability/CSR as a theme. Work on research collaboration with arts may shed light on any attempts to 'humanize' the business school. There is the intriguing question of joint research with other social sciences that are close in disciplinary terms to business schools, such as sociology, politics, and international relations but where, apart from the special case of economics, links appear to be weak. The role and extent of influence at the university centre in setting a strategic framework for research that encourages business school involvement should be further explored.

Fourth, and moving to theoretical questions, we have already suggested possible theoretical perspectives to inform future work. Attempts to construct typologies of business schools' research strategies may place limits around highly institutionalized explanations of a homogeneous field and bring in concepts of path dependence, contextual influence, strategic groups (e.g. a grouping of research intensive higher education institutions), and even strategic choice.

Our literature review suggested future work should examine the business school as a knowledge-based organization. Various models and concepts may be helpful here. The heuristic of receptive and non-receptive contexts for strategic change that was developed in U.K. health care should be explored and adapted (Pettigrew et al. 1992). The concepts of absorptive capacity and of knowledge sourcing routines may also be helpful. We suggest that the higher-level science policy literature could be applied to research dynamics within the business school sector and that it would be a novel contribution to bring two traditionally separate literatures together.

Fifth, various relatively standard social science-based methods should be employed to progress this research agenda. There appear to be few, if any, existing data sets, so primary work will be needed. Methods should include large-scale and e-mail based descriptive surveys of populations of business schools, looking at reported external research collaborations and their correlates (where it will be challenging to achieve good response rates and the number of responses needed for statistical power). In addition, case studies undertaken at various levels across the business school field will be important. There are various levels at which case study work could take place, relating to the different theoretical positions reviewed earlier:

- *At business school field level*: 'summit' institutions such as AACSB, ABS, AoM, BAM, EURAM, and EFMD represent arenas in which business school research strategies may be discussed and shaped. Do they practically engage in such conversations? How (if at all) do these institutions relate to core government policies on research and innovation, STEM subjects, and the research councils? Do they relate to learned societies in other academic disciplines? To what extent do these business school sector-wide bodies influence individual schools? Is there strong isomorphism across the field in terms of the content of, and importance placed on, research strategy at individual school level?

- *At university level*: the central steering core of the university is likely to seek to shape the research strategies of the individual department, including the business school, in a direction desired by national actors who are responsible for government policies on national competitiveness and R&D in higher education. It is possible that management reforms have strengthened the position of the university centre against traditionally autonomous departments (Paradeise et al. 2009). The creation of multi-disciplinary institutes covering broad thematic areas would be one possible approach. What are the financial, institutional levers and other incentives or penalties that the central university adopts? How much influence does such central steering have in shaping business school behaviour?

- *At business school level*: the individual business school can be seen as a knowledge-producing organization. What is its research strategy (as it is enacted in practice as well as declared in formal statements of strategy) and does it value academic collaborations with other university departments? What are the mechanisms and incentives through which any such strategy is promoted? What influence does such strategy have on the behaviours of key faculty?

- *At the individual level*: if business schools remain highly professionalized organizations, then these higher levels may have relatively little influence on individual academics, especially those with some seniority and scope for choice. Is there a 'bottom up' push for external research collaborations coming from a subset of academics? If so, what are their motivations, influence channels and characteristics? How do they relate to 'top down' research strategies and can the two reinforce each other?

- *At project level—explaining success*: it would be interesting to take a set of completed 'high impact' inter-disciplinary research projects involving business school faculty and produce a retrospective analysis of the factors and causal chain that led to such high impact.

So it will be important to assess the nature and strength of interactions between these levels within multi-level designs since the extent of 'loose coupling' (Weick 1976) may still be considerable.

These two core methods could complement each other within a mixed method approach: the survey instrument should be designed after the initial literature review and exploratory case study work to help generate propositions. Statistical patterns generated by large-scale surveys can be explored later in the field in terms of their meaningfulness to business school actors.

The case study work needs to be informed by general methodological discussion about what constitutes high quality case studies and the right balance between internal and external validity, given the weakness of descriptive single case studies (Marinetto 2012). Yin (2009) stresses the advantages of multiple sources of data (interviews, observation and documents), of purposefully selected, large scale, comparative (and we would add longitudinal) designs (e.g. Pettigrew et al. 1992 on patterns of strategic change in health care organizations), of replication across cases, and a connectedness to explicit theory and its further development.

Such case studies of business school 'knowledge work' could be ethnographically based, to including the use of research techniques such as shadowing (see Nicolini et al's 2010 cognate study of the practices of knowledge mobilization by NHS top managers). Alternatively, they could draw on the strategy-as-practice perspective (Johnson et al. 2007) to examine micropractices and artefacts of research collaboration over the cycle of an inter-disciplinary research project, for example: the construction of a joint protocol and research bid; the conduct of team meetings during a research project; how the work is divided up and then brought together; the writing of a multi-disciplinary paper; whether the collaboration endures beyond a single project.

How might this research agenda assist the future institutional development of business schools? It is our first contention that business schools still need to mature as producers of social science and research-based knowledge, both to retain legitimacy within the academy and to construct a distinctive niche within a crowded field. The development and exploitation of such an academic research capability here becomes a strategic issue for business schools. Reflecting the science policy literature, it is our second contention that a trend within knowledge production towards thematic research involves large teams drawn from various academic disciplines. If so, the ability of business schools and of individual faculty to construct productive multi-disciplinary teams with other academic disciplines represents a strategic 'core competence'. Deans and research directors, as well as vice-chancellors across the universities, should find this very interesting. These important policy issues need to be informed by relevant primary data, both quantitative and qualitative.

We hope our preliminary study and proposed research agenda will trigger more work on these important themes in the future.

REFERENCES

Aldrich, Howard (2007). *Organizations and Environments*. Stanford, CA: Stanford Business Books.

Bammer, Gabriele (2008). 'Enhancing Research Collaborations: Three Key Management Challenges', *Research Policy*, 37(5): 875–887.

Barney, Jay B. (2001). 'Is the Resource-Based "View" a Useful Perspective for Strategic Management Research? Yes', *Academy of Management Review*, 26(1): 41–56.

Becher, Tony (1994). 'The Significance of Disciplinary Differences', *Studies in Higher Education*, 19(2): 151–161.

Becher, Tony and Trowler, Paul (2001). *Academic Tribes and Territories*, 2nd edition. Buckingham: Open University Press.

Bennis, Warren and O'Toole, James (2005). 'How Business Schools Lost Their Way', *Harvard Business Review*, 83(5): 96–103.

BIS (2011). *Innovation and Research Strategy for Growth*, Department for Business, Innovation, and Skills. London: The Stationery Office.

Campbell, Lisa (2005). 'Overcoming Obstacles to Interdisciplinary Research', *Conservation Biology*, 19(2): 574–577.

Choi, Bernard C. K. and Pak, Anita W. P. (2007). 'Multidisciplinarity, Interdisciplinarity and Transdisciplinarity in Health Research, Services, Education and Policy: Promoters, Barriers and Strategies of Enhancement', *Clinical and Investigative Medicine*, 30(6): E224–E232.

Cohen, Wesley and Levinthal, Daniel (1990). 'Absorptive Capacity: A New Perspective on Learning and Innovation', *Administrative Science Quarterly*, 35(1): 128–152.

Cummings, Jonathon N. and Kiesler, Sara (2005). 'Collaborative Research Across Disciplinary and Organizational Boundaries', *Social Studies of Science*, 35(5): 703–722.

Cummings, Jonathon and Kiesler, Sara (2008). 'Who Collaborates Successfully? Prior Experience Reduces Collaboration Barriers in Distributed Inter-disciplinary Research', *Proceedings of the ACM Conference on Computer Supported Cooperative work*. 8–12 November, San Diego: California.

Eisenhardt, Kathleen and Gahmic, D. Charles (2000). 'Coevolving: At last, a Way to Make Synergies Work', *Harvard Business Review*, 78(1): 91–101.

Eisenhardt, Kathleen and Santos, Filipe (2006). '*Knowledge Based View: A New Theory of Strategy?*', in Andrew Pettigrew, Howard Thomas, and Richard Whittington (eds), *Handbook of Strategy and Management*. London: Sage, 139–164.

ESRC (2009). *ESRC Strategic Plan 2009–2014: Delivering Impact Through Social Sciences*. Swindon: ESRC.

Ferlie, Ewan and Andresani, Gianluca (2009). 'United Kingdom: From Bureau Professionalism to New Public Management?' in Catherine Paradeise, Emanuela Reale, Ivar Bleiklie, and Ewan Ferlie (eds), *University Governance: Western European Comparative Perspectives*. Dordrecht: Springer, 177–196.

Ferlie, Ewan, Fitzgerald, Louise, McGivern, Gerry, Dopson, Sue, and Bennett, Chris (2011). 'Public Policy Networks and "Wicked Problems": A Nascent Solution?', *Public Administration*, 89(2): 307–324.

Ferlie, Ewan, McGivern, Gerry, and De Moraes, Ailson (2010). 'Developing a Public Interest School of Management', *British Journal of Management*, 21: S60–S70.

Freudenheim, Milt (2011). 'Adjusting, More MDs Add MBA', *The New York Times*, 5 September.

Ghoshal, Sumantra (2005). 'Bad Management Theories are Destroying Good Management Practice', *Academy of Management Learning and Education*. 4(1): 75–81.

Gibbons, Michael, Limoges, Camille, Nowotny, Helga, Schwartzman, Simon, Scott, Peter, and Trow, Martin (1994). *The New Production of Knowledge: The Dynamics of Science and Research in Contemporary Societies*. London: Sage.

HESA Higher Education Statistics Agency. Data are available for ABS members on HESA research income: http://www.associationofbusinessschools.org/node/2000072

Hessels, Laurens K. and van Lente, Harro (2008). 'Rethinking New Knowledge Production: A Literature Review and a Research Agenda', *Research Policy*, 37(4): 740–760.

Huutonieni, Katri, Klein, Julie T., Bruun, Henrik, and Hukkinen, Janne (2010). 'Analysing Interdisciplinarity: Typology and Indicators', *Research Policy*, 39(1): 79–88.

Johnson, G., Langley, A., Melin, L., and Whittington, R. (2007). *Strategy as Practice: Research Directions and Resources*. Cambridge: Cambridge University Press.

Kastor, John (2004) *Governance of Teaching Hospitals: Turmoil at Penn and Hopkins*. Baltimore, MD: Johns Hopkins University Press.

Khurana, Rakesh (2007). *From Higher Aims to Hired Hands: The Social Transformation of American Business Schools and the Unfulfilled Promise of Management as a Profession*. Princeton, NJ: Princeton University Press.

Klijn, Erik-Hans (2005). 'Networks and Inter-organizational Management: Challenging, Steering, Evaluation and the Role of Public Actors in Public Management', in Ewan Ferlie, Laurence E. Lynn and Christopher Pollitt (eds), *The Oxford Book of Public Management*. Oxford: Oxford University Press, 257–281.

Knight, Rebecca (2012). 'A Healthy Balance', FT.com, 30 January.

Knorr-Cetina, Karin (1999). *Epistemic Cultures: How the Sciences Make Knowledge*. Cambridge, MA: Harvard University Press.

Leydesdorff, Loet and Meyer, Martin (2006). 'Triple Helix Indicators of Knowledge Based Innovation Systems: Introduction to the Special Issue', *Research Policy*, 35(10): 1441–1449.

Marinetto, Mike (2012). 'Case Studies of the Health Policy Process: a Methodological Introduction', in Mark Exworthy, Stephen Peckham, Martin Powell, and Alison Hann (eds), *Shaping Health Policy: Case Study Methods and Analysis*. Bristol: Policy Press, 21–40.

Marsh, David and Rhodes, Rod A. W. (eds) (1992). *Policy Networks in British Government*. Oxford: Clarendon Press.

Nicolini, Davide, Powell, John, and Korica, Maja (2010). *The Organisational Practices of Knowledge Mobilisation at Top Management Level in the NHS*, Protocol for NIHR HSDR Project 09/1002/36.

Nohria, Nitin (2012). 'What Business Schools Can Learn from the Medical Profession', *Harvard Business Review*, 90(1/2): 38.

Nowotny, Helga, Scott, Peter, and Gibbons, Michael (2001). *Rethinking Science: Knowledge and the Public in an Age of Uncertainty*. Cambridge: Polity Press.

Paradeise, Catherine, Reale, Emanuela, Bleiklie, Ivar, and Ferlie, Ewan (eds) (2009). *University Governance: Western European Comparative Perspectives*. Dordrecht: Springer.

Pettigrew, Andrew, Ferlie, Ewan, and McKee, Lorna (1992). *Shaping Strategic Change*. London: Sage.

Pettigrew, Andrew M. (2011). 'Scholarship with Impact', *British Journal of Management*, 22(3): 347–354.

Pfeffer, Jeffrey (1981). *Power in Organizations*. Boston, MA: Pitman.

Pfeffer, Jeffrey and Fong, Christina T. (2004). 'The Business School "Business": Some Lessons from the US Experience', *Journal of Management Studies*, 41(8): 1501–1520.

Redclift, Michael (1998). 'Dances with Wolves? Interdisciplinary Research on the Global Environment', *Global Environmental Change*, 8(3): 177–182.

Rhodes, Rod A. W. (1988). *Beyond Westminster and Whitehall: The Sub-Central Governments of Britain*. London: Unwin Hyman.

Rhoten, Diana and Pfirman, Stephanie (2007).'Women in Interdisciplinary Science: Exploring a Preference and Consequences', *Research Policy*, 36(1): 56–75.

Starkey, Ken, Hatchuel, Armand, and Tempest, Sue (2009). 'Management Research and the New Logics of Discovery and Engagement', *Journal of Management Studies*, 46(3): 547–558.

Starkey, Ken and Tempest, Sue (2008). 'A Clear Sense of Purpose? The Evolving Role of the Business School', *Journal of Management Development*, 27(4): 379–390.

Starkey, Ken and Tiratsoo, Nick (2007). *The Business School and the Bottom Line*. Cambridge: Cambridge University Press.

Teece, David, Pisano, Gary, and Shuen, Amy (1997). 'Dynamic Capabilities and Strategic Management', *Strategic Management Journal*, 18(7):509–533.

The Economist (2011). 'Trouble in the Middle. Is Time Running out for Business Schools that Aren't Quite Elite?', 15 October. 401:8755.

Thomas, Howard (2009). 'Business Schools and Management Research: A UK Perspective', *Journal of Management Development*, 28(8): 660–667.

Thomas, Howard and Cornuel, Eric (2012). 'Business Schools in Transition? Issues of Impact, Legitimacy, Capabilities and Re-invention', *Journal of Management Development*, 31(4): 329–335.

van Rijnsoever, Frank J. and Hessels, Laurens K. (2011). 'Factors Associated with Disciplinary and Interdisciplinary Research Collaboration', *Research Policy*, 40(3): 463–472.

Wernerfelt, Birger (2006). 'A Resource-Based View of the Firm', *Strategic Management Journal*, 5(2): 171–180.

Weick, Karl E. (1976). 'Educational Organizations as Loosely Coupled Systems', *Administrative Science Quarterly*, 21(1): 1–19.

Yin, Robert (2009). *Case Study Research: Design and Method*, 4th edition. London: Sage.

Ziman, John (1994). *Prometheus Bound: Science in a Dynamic Steady State*. Cambridge: Cambridge University Press.

Ziman, John (2000). *Real Science: What it Is and What it Means*. Cambridge: Cambridge University Press.

11

Strategic Choice

Taking 'Business' out of B-schools

Peter McKiernan and David Wilson

11.1. INTRODUCTION

The title of this chapter may seem paradoxical. After all, what *is* left when one takes 'business' out of business schools? Surely business is both the central premise and *raison d'être* of a business school ('b-school')? This chapter will argue that a number of pressures have forced b-schools to become synonymous largely with private, profit-making business organizations and the result has been that traditional b-schools have reached a strategic plateau where their intellectual status, rigour and practical relevance to other economic sectors (e.g. public and non-profit) and to policy and society overall are being scrutinized. We suggest that, by weakening the close ties between b-schools and for-profit organizations, b-schools would be presented with a series of strategic choices (Child 1972) that may enable them to attain greater intellectual rigour and relevance.

The massification of b-school education across the developed world over the last 20 years has been documented extensively (see, for example, Khurana 2007) with the result that many b-schools have experienced significant increases in student and staff numbers and in consequent budget increases that far outstrip many other university departments. Yet steadily, the critique of b-schools has been gaining momentum to the point where many authors have argued that they may be facing a decline in terms of relevance, student numbers and intellectual depth (Schoemaker 2008; Starkey and Tempest 2008; Starkey and Tiratsoo 2007). Others argue that the dominance of the business models that have been created by financial economics within such schools means that they are 'complicit in the current financial crisis' (Currie et al., 2010:1). Waddock sums up the b-school view, thus:

Today, we live in a world where moral compass, a sense of responsibility for the greater good and an understanding of the system as a whole are more imperative than ever for those who would assume the mantle of leadership in our largest and most powerful institutions—corporations. These attributes, of course, are equally needed in traditional and social-entrepreneurial ventures as well as in our public institutions and the non-governmental sectors. The question is: does management education as it is practised in most places today adequately prepare graduates for this world? The answer, for many, is no.

S. Waddock, Boston College, *Global Focus*, Vol 3/2, 2009, 12–15.

Inaction to such indictments from senior colleagues is to be taken seriously, as any perceived notion of ignorance reminds us of Chomsky's (1967) stinging critique of U.S. academics who, at the time of the Vietnam War, remained silent (an action which was viewed as complicit with the imperialist stance taken by the U.S.). In addition, Harney (2007) argues that the models upon which modern b-schools are created do not reflect the reality facing their current students. Originally, schools were created to professionalize management, so that both governance (and, by implication, the direct management of labour) could be improved and made more effective and efficient. In short, they taught management and how to manage (rather than how to be managed). Today's b-school students are unlikely to be managers in the ways envisaged in the 1920s, or even in the 1980s. Contemporary b-school students may manage no one. Almost certainly, they will be managed by others and, likely, they will not experience the continuity of employment (and career progression) available to their predecessors as job markets and employment are increasingly precarious (Standing 2011; Ross 2009). Some b-school students will never work in private, for-profit organizations. In many service- based economies, they are more likely to work in the public or non-profit sectors, or inter-governmental organizations (transnational public bureaucracies operating on behalf of governments). Such organizations are increasingly prevalent and varied across the world, from those fulfilling relatively temporary missions (such as feeding hungry people or helping re-settle post-war refugees) to those with long-term missions (such as the UN Security Council in its bid to prevent war).

Finally, research in business schools faces strong criticism for the production of theoretically grounded, but irrelevant research (irrelevant to either the needs of practitioners or the needs of society more widely). These criticisms are fuelled further by unfavourable comparisons of the academic nature of business schools relative to other professional schools (such as law, medicine, architecture and engineering) and to the university communities in which they reside (see, for example, Starkey and Tiratsoo, 2007; Thomas and Wilson, 2009). B-schools must endeavour to maintain their professional standing and also connect with the wide needs of society (rather than just business) in order to maintain legitimacy and credibility.

In this chapter, we develop each of these threads of argument and suggest how b-schools got to this position and how they might develop and affect change in the future. In particular, we argue that b-schools might consider a move away from teaching and researching predominantly for-profit organizations as their core subject and concentrate on a wider range of organizational types and issues of broader societal and economic concern. To reinforce, illustrate and expand our arguments, we have included data drawn from two sources: interviews with deans conducted by the authors in the U.K., Europe and Australia, and archival research using content analysis of articles by deans and deputy deans from the entire publication set of EFMD's *Global Focus* journal.

11.2. AN ANALYSIS OF CONTEXT: HOW B-SCHOOLS GOT TO WHERE THEY ARE TODAY

11.2.1.The Institutional View

In a previous paper (Wilson and McKiernan 2011), we presented a set of neo-institutional arguments (Di Maggio and Powell 1983) to situate the current context and the arguably constrained actions of b-schools. Drawing on Zucker (1987), we argued that b-schools had been subjected to decades of two broad sets of normative pressures. The first describes the pressures that emanate from rule-like patterns of action and behaviour that are imposed upon organizations by external agencies, such as state requirements and the demands of professional certification. The second describes how such pressures are embedded (Granovetter 1985) within formal organizational structures and processes. This embedding comes to characterize the whole organization as it develops norms and standard operating procedures to secure patterns of action and behaviour from its constituent individuals. As Granovetter (1985:482) argues, 'to construe actions and behaviours as independent is a grievous misunderstanding'. This neo-institutionalist view owes much to the earlier writings of Polanyi et al.. (1957), who argued that human actions and behaviours are embedded in and intricately interwoven with economic and non-economic institutions. From a b-school perspective such agencies would include the state, funding councils, ranking institutions, universities and professional associations. We noted in particular, the roles played by accreditation and regulation on the one hand, and rankings of schools and research on the other.

Accreditation by the most important bodies, the Association to Advance Collegiate Schools of Business (AACSB), European Quality Improvement System (EQUIS), and the Association of MBAs (AMBA), is meant to ensure that intending students (and wider society) can be assured that an independent agency has scrutinized a school's portfolio of activities and pronounced it to have passed its rigorous quality standards. Accreditation agencies argue that their role is to help segment the market between higher quality providers and lower quality providers in the b-school sector. Lowrie and Willmott (2009:411) describe accreditation as a 'regime'. Quoting Navarro (2008:10), Lowrie and Willmott say that the AACSB is like a 'group of foxes, guarding the MBA henhouses'. Moreover, they argue that accreditation is elitist, since it serves to diminish the value of education that takes place outside the accredited schools ('the elite'). Accreditation also serves to preserve and perpetuate 'the elite', thereby maintaining the status quo of what is considered to be a 'good' b-school. In short, they argue that accreditation stymies knowledge improvement and development in both elite schools and in non-accredited schools (which are deemed to be poor relations by default). Durand and McGuire (2005) add a dose of ethnocentrism to a similar critique of the AACSB. They argue that the AACSB is not interested in what is 'taught and not taught' outside a strictly North American model of an elite b-school. EQUIS and AMBA bring different pressures (more European for the former and more specialized around the MBA for the latter). Wilson and McKiernan (2011) argued that such accreditation has imposed isomorphic pressures on b-schools. These are 'the constraining process that forces one unit in a population to resemble other units that face the same set of environmental conditions' (DiMaggio and Powell 1983: 149).

Secondly, there are two discrete rankings for b-schools. One ranks the schools themselves (on aspects such as their MBA and their infrastructure). The other is a ranked assessment of the quality of research carried out by academic staff. Rankings of b-schools have become the subject of scrutiny by scholars as methodology, criteria and operationalization have been criticized widely and not just by the comparatively lower ranked institutions. However, as Wedlin (2007) notes, rankings have become deeply institutionalized and 'playing' the rankings game well has become a key pursuit of many b-school deans. Rankings are not simply mechanical, objective, measures. They have a strong impact on both the economic futures of schools and the morale of their staff (Kogut 2008). Rankings are scrutinized by potential students, funders and other stakeholders. Also, they are used internally by university executives as a convenient mechanism by which to judge the reputation of their own b-school and the individual performance of its staff.

Despite their failings, their ambiguity and their imprecision, such rankings have become reified. They are an accepted and expected part of the social landscape. They have become another social statistic against which a broad public can assess quality and competition within and amongst schools. But, structurally, they are altering the b-school landscape because there are large mark-ups to be earned by schools with high rankings, as Peters (2007) notes:

... a positive ranking raises a schools confidence to increase prices for future programmes. The top decile of schools, on average, charges \$79,959, indicating a rankings premium substantially above the best-fit line, while the bottom decile charges \$36,966. This is not that surprising as many of the criteria on which schools are evaluated are resource-dependent: more leads to more and exclusivity is self-fulfilling...

The snowball effect of the rankings promotes a rich get richer and poor get poorer cycle and creates a Catch 22 trap from which it is difficult to extricate oneself, win or lose...

K. Peters, Dean, Ashridge Business School, *Global Focus*, Vol 1/2, 2007, 46–49.

Once a school achieves a decent ranking, it is reluctant to take any action that might damage it. Thus, schools adopt the same conservative strategic stances and the rankings have an inherent 'stickiness' around school positions. As Eden suggests:

A number of schools, I am certain, would think about dropping their full time programmes (in favour of part academe/part practice experience) if it wasn't for the fact that, if they did, they'd fall out of the rankings.

C. Eden, International Dean, Strathclyde Business School, interview.

It is possible to explain this reification of rankings by drawing on two social theories. The first is the development of the 'knowledge society' (Thrift, 2005), where information has become increasingly transparent and visible. The second is the general trend in cultural systems toward the development of taxonomies and a range of classification systems (see, for example, Wilensky 1964; Bordieu 1984: Vaara and Fay 2011). In the U.K., each b-school receives a ranking on its research performance by a research assessment panel every five years or so. There are strong economic and social rewards for individuals in schools with excellent research and the institution itself benefits from a greater allocation of research monies. The higher the proportion of scholars publishing in highly-ranked journals (as judged by prominent 'lists', e.g. the ABS/EAJG list), the higher the perceived status of the school (Baden-Fuller et al. 2000; Borokhovich et al. 1995; Fishe 1998; Trieschmann et al. 2000). Institutions worldwide exert pressure on their faculty to publish in these 'top' journals, which has the effect of reinforcing the status (and ranking) of these journals (and the ranking of schools). The effect of this circular (institutional) process is that the ranking of journals remains relatively stable over time.

Arguably, the collective rationality which journal rankings place on schools is highly influential. The goal of achieving high-rated publications tends to dominate b-school strategy, especially as the audit deadline draws near and the academic 'transfer' market is triggered. Such dominant behavioural traits shroud the unintended consequences of the rankings. One is the confounding of image with quality of content when good scholarship is substituted by place of publication. If an article appears in a top rated (4* or A rated in the

U.S.) journal, then it might be assumed to be a high quality scholarly article. This may not be the case. The other is that b-schools come under immense pressure to organize their activities, research centres and departments to conform as closely as possible to a structure which will maximize the opportunity of staff getting 4* or A rated publications.

Besides ourselves, many other authors (for example Saunders et al. 2011; Masrani et al. 2011; Hodgkinson and Starkey 2011) have taken a convincing neo-institutional perspective to explain the current position of b-schools as remarkably similar providers worldwide of a constricted range of intellectual arguments (clustered largely around the tenets of Western capitalism). Whilst we think that these predominantly institutionalist views provide a good description of the context of b-schools, we argue here that the dynamics of this process (how b-schools got to where they are) can be illustrated more fully by utilizing the concepts and explanations of path dependency (see, for example, Sydow, Schreyogg, and Koch 2009) in tandem with those of neo-institutionalism.

One intellectual link between the two theoretical approaches lies within the slower dynamic underpinning neo-institutionalism that runs from habitualization through objectification to sedimentation. As context, all sectors (e.g. Higher Education) alter their shape over the longer term through exogenous shocks (technological, competitive, financial or policy-based, inter alia), which shake them up and trigger organizational strategic responses. If these shocks are major and incisive, they may transform a sector forever (e.g. the Dundee Jute Industry: Masrani and McKiernan 2011), giving birth to a different way of doing things. In neo-institutional theory, organizational structural designs occur through a process of *habitualization* (Tolbert and Zucker 1996). In the first, embryonic phase, when there is no defined way of doing things, responses tend to be individual as many players 'feel' for what might be a successful way of organizing for the future. Naturally, if organizations are closely knit, a replication of new structures may occur and a temporary modus operandi may emerge through experimentation, but there will be much re-invention where equilibrium may only be temporary But, if no obvious model emerges among the players, many will continue to act individually. Eventually, as competition generates sustained, good organizational performances, the associated structures are seen as representing a successful model. This causes other organizations to follow suit and begin their aculturation to the 'right' organizational recipe (Spender, 1989) for the future. This is the neo-institutional process of *objectification*.

The right way of organizing in this phase can be reinforced by external stakeholders (e.g. consultants, government bodies) who legitimize the chosen structure through active advocacy. When these structures become replete amongst many organizations *and* endure over long periods, the final process of *sedimentation* is complete. Isomorphism can drive the sector players into adopting a homogeneous form and so completing the process of institutionalization. To endure, this latter phase relies upon minimal internal challenge, few major exogenous shocks, consistently good outcomes and strong advocacy, lest de-institutionalization sets in. Of course, any major exogenous shocks or observed poor performance might lead to widespread doubting of the dominant paradigm, thus causing a new cycle to begin. Within this broader, neo- institutional process of habitualization, objectification, and sedimentation lies the more individual organizational journey of path dependence.

11.2.2. Path Dependence

Path dependence examines the processes by which self-reinforcing dynamics trap an organization into outcomes that are sub-optimal and which constrain future actions. Such constraints can be generated internally and/or externally to the organization (Pierson 2000). The basic characteristic of path dependency is that, in the early stages of a process (e.g. the formation of a b-school) few, if any, decision makers recognize that, as decisions are implemented (and accumulate) over time and 'lock in' occurs, specific courses of action become increasingly inevitable. Evolutionary economists and economic historians (such as Arthur 1989, 1994; David 1994) call such processes 'entrapping' and argue that they are a consequence of actions taken over time in an organization's history and are likely to become inefficient responses to a dynamic market. These economists were looking mostly at technological innovations (or the lack of them), but the dynamic concepts of path dependency add to our institutional understanding of how b-schools have developed.

Central to the notion of path dependence is the identification of self-reinforcing processes that are likely to accumulate in a specific path of action. These self-reinforcing dynamics lead eventually to an irreversible state of inflexibility through lock-in (David 1985). They become systemic forces in which individual actors are entrapped. Sydow, Shreyogg, and Koche (2011) provide a useful stage-based model to explain the dynamics of path dependence (see Table 11.1).[1]

Essentially, path dependence is a process during which strategic options become more and more constrained over time. Even at the pre-formation phase, there is not a hundred per cent free choice for decision makers, since there will be imprints from the past which act as constraints. But, as the process moves into the formation phase, the range of strategic options narrows significantly until the lock-in phase, where virtually all strategic actions are bound to a pre-determined path. As Sydow, Shreyogg, and Koche (2011) note, this process can be summarized in terms of decision-making, beginning with non-predictability, where there is an indeterminacy of outcome, and followed by non-ergodicity—where several outcomes are possible in transient

Table 11.1. Three Phases of Path Dependency[i]

Phase	Description of Process
Phase I—The Pre-Formation Phase	Characterized by a broad scope of action. The effect of a choice of options cannot be predicted. Once a decision is made, this choice may trigger events that unintentionally set off a self-reinforcing process. This moment of entering into the dynamics of a self-reinforcing process can be thought of as a 'critical juncture' and it indicates the end of the Pre-formation Phase.
Phase II—The Formation Phase	A new regime takes the lead: a dominant action pattern is likely to emerge, which renders the whole process increasingly irreversible. The range of options narrows, and it becomes progressively difficult to reverse the initial choice or the initial pattern of action. A path is evolving. Decision processes in Phase II are still contingent. They do not yet fully converge to a single fixed-point.
Phase III—The Lock-In Phase	Characterized by a further constriction, which eventually leads to a lock-in. The dominant decision pattern becomes fixed and gains a deterministic character; eventually, the actions are fully bound to a path. One particular choice or action pattern has become the predominant mode, and flexibility has been lost. Even new entrants to this field of action can not refrain from adopting it. When more efficient alternatives are available, individuals' and organizations' decision processes and established practices continue to reproduce this and only this particular outcome. The occurrence of a lock-in renders a system potentially inefficient and ineffective, because it loses its capability to adopt better alternatives.

Source: Adapted from Sydow; Shreyogg and Koche (2011:692)

states—but history starts to restrict the choice of alternatives. The process then enters a phase of inflexibility where decision makers are entrapped, making a shift to another option impossible. The outcome is inefficiency, since actions resulting from moving along the path lock the organization into an inferior solution.

11.2.3. Linking Neo Institutional Theories and Path-Dependence in the Context of B-schools

As Karl Marx famously observed, men make history, but not of their own choosing. The very first b-schools did not start with a strategic carte blanche. They were organizations created with a specific set of purposes in mind. Their objective was to formalize the education of future business leaders in the same way that medical schools provided for doctors. There are plenty of excellent histories of b-schools and their origins (see, for example, Williams (2010) for a history of U.K. schools whilst many U.S. schools publish their own publicly available histories). Because b-schools were created and formed with very specific purposes in mind, the pre-formation phase (see Table 11.1) was shorter than in other sectors. The heritage of formal management education lies in Europe, stemming from the first b-school in Lisbon (Portugal) in 1759, through the École Supérieure de Commerce de Paris (France) in 1819 and the German Betriebswirtschaftslehre in the late nineteenth century, to the Catholic-influenced institutions in France, Portugal, Spain and Italy at the turn of that century. Prussian administration influenced the founding of Wharton in 1881, although U.S. b-schools began earlier at Louisiana and Wisconsin in 1851 and 1852 respectively (Spender 2008). But, up until this point, there was no critical mass, and offerings were institution-specific and isolated (akin to a habitualization stage in neo-institutionalism). However, after Wharton's lead, and coupled with Harvard University offering its first masters degrees in business administration in 1908, these schools and others were well down the track to the formation phase of path dependency. As soon as it was recognized that b-schools were professional organizations (as well as expected to be profit making), they became subject to a range of influences (such as norms, expectations, accreditation and regulation) very quickly.

The model of organization (or modes of action) which then emerged revealed strikingly similar patterns in b-schools around the world. Elsewhere, we have termed this process 'global mimicry' (Wilson and McKiernan 2011). Here, we try to identify some of the patterns and themes underlying the path dependency of the process. First, it is important to recognize that b-schools have not followed a smooth, inevitable path of development. For example, in the 1950s, Harvard Business School (HBS) fees were around $800 per year and the emphasis in the classroom was on practical skills, which could apply to all levels of management. There, many acquired the skills to undertake the role of foremen, for example, in manufacturing companies. Three decades later, with the ascendancy of services over manufacturing in developed economies, the teaching of blue-collar workers appears dated and unambitious, since larger revenues were available by concentrating on more senior managerial roles and the personal development required to occupy them. Hence, the MBA began to take centre stage in this transition.

Second, by pitching the MBA as a route to potentially very senior management positions, many b-schools moved away from an emphasis on practical skills toward offering a masters degree which promised fast track upward mobility in the cadre of senior management. This shift from experiential skills to a greater emphasis on the cognitive knowledge required to be a senior manager came at a premium price (Moldoveanu and Martin 2008). By 2012, HBS's estimated costs were around $120 000 per year (estimated to be $400 000 real cost, once two years of lost wages and living expenses were taken into account). In that year, over 10 000 individuals applied for an MBA at Harvard, for fewer than 900 places. The range of options for many top global b-schools is now increasingly restricted. Schools became locked into offering premium-fee MBAs, claiming that they will significantly enhance career and earning potential. The move from practical skills to the symbolic value of the MBA represents the point at which many schools became locked in to the final stages of path dependency.

The dynamics of this journey are well described by institutional theorists (see, for example, Meyer and Rowan 1977 and Zucker 1987). They describe the influence and expectations of a wide range of stakeholders on b-schools and suggest that, once at the final stages of path dependence, there will be a strong tendency for all organizations in the sector to copy each others' strategies and structures. DiMaggio and Powell (1983) call these three types of pressure, coercive, normative and mimetic.

Coercive isomorphism is the result of formal and informal pressures exerted on b-schools by powerful agencies. Such isomorphism can arise from internal pressures (for example, from a b-school's mother university) or from external pressures (such as those exerted by the various accreditation, assessment and regulatory bodies). Full discussion of these pressures can be found in Wilson and McKiernan (2011). Here, we want to expand a little on how coercive isomorphism has been a result of the strong influence of universities and the expectations they have regarding their b-schools. This isomorphism can be observed also in schools which are independent of universities, so we might argue that such pressures are likely to originate in wider society and thus are enacted by, rather than created by, universities. The growth of b-schools and, concomitantly, the increasing emphasis on the substantive ideology of managerialism within developed societies, has been noteworthy over the last 20 years (see, for example, Grey 1994; Power 1999). Governance, managerialism (and self-management) can be argued to be ubiquitous nationally and internationally with b-schools complicit in the 'neo-colonial manifestations of these trends' (Harney, 2007: 139).

In virtually every sector of the modern economy, managerialism is dominant. In the public sector, for example, the health service in the U.K. has been managerialized to provide a more efficient and 'business-like' service (Milewa et al. 1998) as part of the new public management agenda. In the non-profit (voluntary) sector, managerialism has become a by-word for effectiveness and efficiency in NGOs (Butler and Wilson 1989; Roberts et al. 2005 and Dar and Cooke 2007). The core concern of most b-schools today is the training and development of managers at all levels. This journey has created expectations that the primary role of schools is to train and socialize managers, even though many students will never become managers (Harney 2007). Moreover, most universities expect their b-schools to be businesses in their own right, meaning more bluntly, that they are expected to make a substantial profit for their universities. B-schools are expected to operate on a high cost/high quality service model with the argument that very high fees indicate the level of investment that schools provide for their MBA cadre. The result can be very high profits for some schools and substantial benefits for their universities, which tax and often 'top slice' them. Universities then set budgets in the expectation that their b-schools will make as much or more profit in subsequent years and the coercive cycle simply repeats.

An additional coercive pressure placed upon schools by their universities is to seek and secure external sources of income, not just in the form of research grants, but in the form of philanthropic donations. These can be substantial. In the U.S., Chicago Business School received a $300 million philanthropic gift in 2008 from hedge fund manager David Booth (an alumnus). The result was not only a change of name to Chicago Booth, but also the expectation that this could be the first of many similar donations. In the U.K., Said Business School Oxford, was established in the 1990s following a generous benefaction from Mr Wafic Rida Said, which funded a new building and planned extension. Cambridge Judge Business School was founded when Sir Paul and Lady Judge provided £8 million to establish a new building for the school. Further developments and extensions have been made possible through further donations, such as those by Mr Simon Sainsbury (£5 million) and many professorships have been endowed by donations. Cass Business School in London was supported in its new building project in 2001, and the Sir John Cass Foundation continues to provide on-going support to the school. The net result is that deans of b-schools are pressured by their universities (or their boards) to seek substantial philanthropic funding in addition to other sources of revenue (such as fee income). Such a need for funding is common across schools but the American case differs from the European one, in this sense:

> American business schools used to rely on their endowments to pay higher salaries or attract students and were consequently less dependent on academic fees. In Europe, schools had to be closer to the real world with more emphasis on executive education. In both cases, there is a problem. For American schools the endowment model is good when stock prices go up but becomes a nightmare when market prices fall. For European business schools, executive education is a distinguished undertaking for many reasons but in some cases business schools only do it for financial reasons, which is not the best motivator.
>
> J. Canals, Dean, IESE, Spain, *Global Focus*, Vol. 4/1, 2010, 14–18.

Normative pressures come from a variety of sources. Accrediting agencies are one of them. The criteria by which accreditation will (or will not) be awarded are prescribed in advance of the accrediting panel's visit to the b-school. Thus, a relationship of dependency is created between the b-school and the accrediting agency. Accreditation agencies impose standards, rules and values on schools and reinforce normative expectations. This process is as important to b-schools as making a profit (Wilson and McKiernan 2011). Political power and institutional legitimacy are achieved substantially through accreditation, particularly 'triple accreditation' (EQUIS, AACSB, and AMBA), and through the various rankings of b-schools and their programmes.

In addition to accreditation, b-schools also operate in a comparatively tightly knit, inter-organizational network. Norms, developed during the education of staff, become a strong influence in the school (and the majority of academic and professional staff in b-schools have very similar educational backgrounds and achievements). In addition, inter-hiring between schools encourages isomorphism since the job specification for an academic post displays remarkable similarity across institutions internationally. People from the same educational backgrounds will tend to approach problems in much the same way and socialization reinforces these behaviours. The appointment of staff in b-schools is a process checked and influenced by powerful gatekeepers and there is a strong homogeneity to the backgrounds and qualifications of individuals who gain entry into the profession. The net effect of such conformities is to allow b-schools to interact with each other more easily and to build (normative) legitimacy in the sector.

In terms of path dependence, normative pressures can constrain choices that deviate from the dominant logic and lend support to the continued reproduction of dominant modes of operation (see Table 11.1). Normative pressures contribute substantially to lock-in.

Mimetic isomorphism occurs in all organizations, but can be seen to be a particular feature of b-schools. As Slack and Hinings (1994: 804) note:

> . . . (isomorphism) may also result from cultural expectations within the societal context in which an organization exists. Mimetic isomorphism occurs when organizations faced with uncertainty model themselves on other organizations which they perceive as successful.

B-schools are at risk of becoming increasingly similar to one another because of the content, frequency and depth of assessments by accreditation agencies and research rankings and from several other shaping forces. Furthermore, pressure to conform regionally in Europe is exacerbated by the Bologna process:

> (Sir Andrew) argues that the management education landscape in Europe has been significantly changed as a result of the Bologna agreement. The implication, he says, is that business schools (in Europe) are now able—and perhaps even required—to provide management education at every stage from pre-experience to executive education. So LBS has to compete in what is effectively a new market.
>
> G. Bickerstaffe, quoting Sir Andrew Likierman, Dean of London Business
> School, *Global Focus*, Vol 4/1, 2010, 8–1.

Besides internal pressure to conform to a norm, European schools face a peer pressure that perceives the American model of a b-school to be the ideal way of organizing:

> The current situation of management education in Europe is that of a juxtaposition of national systems largely concerned with imitating American business schools in a catch-up strategy.
>
> S. Dameron and T. Durand, *Global Focus*, Vol 3/1, 2009, 22–25.

Schools tend toward further similarity because of the tenacity and influence of institutional pressures and stakeholders. First, their significant success relative to other subjects academically and financially has made them attractive to vice-chancellors and other senior university staff. Fuelled by a popular perception of 'job secure' programmes, together with a major influx of foreign students acquiring both language and knowledge skills, many UK b-schools became rich and were often milked as 'cash cows' by university administrators.

Second, the MBA model of Executive Education has become a homogeneous offering with a standard syllabus internationally (Crainer and Dearlove 1998; Mintzberg 2004).

> The spread of knowledge has become so rapid that there is a risk of management education becoming a commodity, particularly in MBA programmes where, in the early stages, you have to offer a set of basic courses. What has become a commodity in management education is the content, the concepts—the text books, cases and so on—but what has not become a commodity yet, and hopefully never will, is the process, the way you deliver the content. The content is becoming more standardised but the process is not.
>
> Jordi Canals, Dean of IESE, Spain, *Global Focus*, Vol. 1/1 16–19, 2007.

However, despite Canals' assertion, we argue that with the massification of both undergraduate and MBA education, facilitated by the ubiquitous presence of presentation software like MS PowerPoint, even the process is becoming commoditized in tight markets. A good management teacher is able to work in most countries without having to alter content or language (English). For instance, in Singapore, where demand for business courses is strong, academic 'mercenaries' ply their lucrative trade between several institutions at the same time, equipped with the same pack of slides. More recently, there have been strong voices urging a change to the content of the MBA syllabus to include a greater coverage of ethics, leadership and entrepreneurship, creativity and innovation. However, the net result of such changes is likely to reinforce the standardization of the degree.

Third, as far as b-school researchers are concerned, there are powerful conforming pressures at work. For instance, original articles are often formed into a uniform shape or pattern, by the top journals' house style, editorial policy and reviewers' comments. Some journals, for example, have pre-prepared templates for the writing of abstracts and recommendations for the sequence of sub-headings. Nearly all journals place strict length restrictions on all articles. The end product, perhaps after two or three rounds of reviewing, is an article which arguably resembles more the views and predilections of the reviewers and the journal editor than the original piece crafted by the author. The danger is that top journals are publishing articles which may have the creative guts squeezed out of them. As Galliers observes:

> In an ideal world, a managerial problem would drive academics to look for underlying causes, and in turn solutions, the knowledge of which is then disseminated. However, this view is the exact opposite of what de facto is the case of research in academia. The vehicles of dissemination (the journals) dictate solutions—appropriate topics, methods, tools and theories—which, in turn, drive the selection of causes and problems which fit.
>
> P. Berthon and R. Galliers (Provost, Bentley College), *Global Focus*, Vol 2/1, 2008, 59–60.

Pettigrew goes further, claiming that b-school academics have become obsessed with articles and books, at the expense of impact:

> It will involve a cultural change that will shift people's focus from publishing output, writing articles and books—which to me is an intermediate good—to the final good, which is having scholarly and practical impact. At lot of the incentive systems in academia have unwittingly focused people on the intermediate good.
>
> A. Pettigrew, past Dean of Bath Management School, *Global Focus*, Vol 2/2, 2008, 8–12.

Fourth, there is explicit (and perhaps implicit) theoretical and ideological support for free market economics in nearly all schools, which, again, leads to mimetic isomorphism (see, for example, Khurana 2007; Starkey and Tempest 2008). From this perspective, isomorphism rests on the assertion that most b-schools teach capitalism and little else (Dunne et al 2008). Previously, Golembiewski (1989) had couched the argument as a problem of value-free science. He argued that value-free science is a significant danger to teaching management (and science generally) because elites will act in their own interests and discipline others by the application of knowledge, which will meet their needs (by design) and possibly the needs of others (but only by accident). It is therefore no accident to Golembiewski that free market economics became the staple and unquestioned diet of b-schools aiming their wares primarily at the global managerial class. Economic models of capitalism reflect the values of their creators and their teachers and researchers. B-schools do not 'sell (their) wares to voluntary organizations, co-operatives or trade unions, and (their) relationships with the public sector are uneasy' (Parker 2008). The result is a narrow conception of what b-schools should research and teach. As Waddock emphasizes:

> Here then is the fundamental tension facing business schools today. Most of the management theories that have been developed to date are directed at and

apply only to the developed world and we might want to acknowledge that many of those theories have not been particularly fruitful. They apply to a model of doing business that failing markets and financial institutions suggest is seriously broken and that virtually all ecologists believe is not ecologically sustainable.

> S. Waddock, Boston College, *Global Focus*, Vol 3/2, 2009. 12–15.

Along this pathway, European schools may be better prepared:

North America business schools teach business based on an economic paradigm relying on market governance with the large multinational corporation playing a key role. Entrepreneurship entered the picture only recently. In contrast, Europe has a tradition of combining large firms, SMEs, the public sector and non-profit organizations. Another path towards differentiation for European business schools could be to study all forms of organizations, including the public sector, associations or NGOs. In this sense, management is a broader world than business studies.

> S. Dameron and T. Durand, *Global Focus*, Vol 3/1, 2009, 22–25.

B-schools appear to be at the lock-in phase of the path dependence journey. Their research, teaching and foci of concern have become increasingly targeted and, so, limited to a sub-section of the economy (mainly private firms). To break out of this path dependence, b-schools need to re-think their business, broaden their horizons and reclaim the relevance that they claim to have to wider society. This represents a considerable challenge for most schools and certainly comprises a substantial area for future research which we outline in the next section.

11.3. TOWARDS A RESEARCH AGENDA

One obvious point is that research on b-schools is relatively small scale and limited in scope. To our knowledge, there has never been a comprehensive global comparative study of b-schools. Given the themes in this chapter, we would recommend a broad comparative investigation of the effects of the mass-ranking systems and the largely myopic stance taken by schools in their research and teaching towards a variety of global social and political issues. There have been strong suggestions by commentators that 'the (b-schools) that bring in the most money might be doing the least for the global economy' (Davidson 2012). There is a clear agenda here for substantial empirical evidence to support these (and associated) claims.

However, if these authors are right, then 'taking the business out of business schools' becomes a large research agenda in its own right. Western societies in particular, have placed management and business practice at the centre of contemporary life. Governments use business practices to try and make public agencies and organizations more effective and efficient, and non-profit organizations also attempt to mimic the business and management practices in the private sector to the same ends of efficiency and effectiveness. Yet, it is not only business and management practices that are at the heart of contemporary life. So, too, are climate change, environmental destruction, migration, race, war, health, and a very large gap between the world's rich and poor. Businesses operate in this context and b-schools need to address disruptive developments in the world, e.g. post-secular increases in the influence of faith on war and economies, as well as economic transitions and schisms as billions of people from China, Latin America, India, and elsewhere join the world economy.

> I am arguing that there is a moral persuasion that says that in most emerging economies everyone has to understand poverty, the markets at the bottom end of the pyramid, and the impact of politics on economics and business. In most emerging countries my impression is that politics drives economics and not the other way round. If you produce business leaders without helping them become politically and intellectually literate then you are short-changing them.
>
> N. Binedell, Director, South African Business School, *Global Focus*, Vol 1/2, 2007, 56–58.

Such a future research agenda is broadly scoped and multi-disciplinary. It is an agenda that 'critical management studies' have, so far, failed to address directly because such critiques continued to assume that managers and management were central to community life. The very focus of critical management studies (i.e., management) largely precludes the consideration of other central and substantive issues. The wider lens of multi-disciplinary research is required to examine these issues in depth and, ironically, this is a lens that b-school academics, with their varied disciplinary bases, are in pre-eminent positions to address.

> What absolutely matters is a certain balance. Business school leaders will have to dedicate themselves more to their schools' main mission – educating better people for a better world. This means reinforcing what some already do, renewing the curricula of their programmes and introducing topics that deal with responsible sustainability, social inclusion, business ethics, and individual cultural values.
>
> R. Khurana, Dean, HBR, *Global Focus*, Vol. 4/1, 2010.

Moving away from the global picture, a further research implication of our arguments focuses more locally on the nature of b-schools themselves. A key research question hinges around the differentiation-standardization axis. Should schools try and differentiate themselves by expanding their intellectual domain—at its simplest by perhaps offering a wider mix of programmes looking at a the broader economy (e.g. non- profits, public sector, illegal organizations), or consider serving populations (such as Vietnam, Poland) which do not currently have a lot of traditional b-schools? Or should they avoid such differentiation and continue down the path dependent route of standardization, doing the same things and broadly mimicking each other? We have seen that the institutional pressures are strong and various and we infer that, as a result, standardization is an easier and more common strategy than differentiation. Research here could be of direct benefit to b-school deans. For example, using well-known concepts from the field of strategic management, empirical research could identify the core competences of different schools, could identify the 'tipping points' in b-school models and paradigms, and could examine the different pressures of European, Asian, and U.S. business models, identifying strategic options (Brailsford 2011; Thomas 2012).

Stepping outside the tools and techniques of management theory itself, a further research theme, which holds promise for throwing light on the differentiation-standardization debates, is what might be termed a postcolonial approach (Young, 2001) to the globalization of b-schools and management knowledge. There is not the space here to describe fully the breadth and diversity of postcolonial theories, but the global reach and influence of b-schools is a central paradigm (or example), which permeates postcolonial theories. Post-colonialism examines the manner in which emerging societies struggle with self-determination and to what extent they incorporate or reject Western norms and conventions (such as the largely homogeneous and Western ways in which b-schools teach management).

Said (1978) described European scholars studying the Middle East and Asia. Their scholarship, he argued, was characterized by researchers ignoring the cultural and intellectual heritage of the 'Orient', imposing instead European values, norms and attitudes. Said's analysis focuses on cultural superiority (Said 1993) which allowed Europeans to control non-Europeans. However, it is only a small step to translate cultural superiority to economic superiority. Put simply, no matter what the politics or culture of a given country are, it faces a powerful process of capitalist globalization, which argues that wealth is the solution to war, poverty, racism and environmental crises. Wealth is created by business and heralded by b-schools through standardized texts of management (to teach business), and through the mantra of globalization—within which Western-based management knowledge and best practice prescriptions are dominant. Critics began to address problems of the ideological hegemony implicit in the neoliberal imperative of privatization, trade liberalization and public sector restructuring (Bello 2002; Falk 1999) and there is much further research to be done here.

Even the language of b-schools—predominantly Anglo-Saxon—has a hegemonic influence. Jankowicz (1999), for example, critiques the use of Anglo-Saxon language in creating meaning and embodying a specific culture of learning. For example, there is no direct translation in some local languages of some words used in Anglo-Saxon business discourse (such as 'marketing', 'leadership', 'manager') but also the meaning of such words poses a problem of translation and understanding, given their historical formation and origin.

> Mainly because business studies originated in North America much academic writing is produced in English. And of the academic journals recognised in such rankings as the Financial Times, 90% are American publications. Many business schools use American cases since they are in English and easily available without thinking whether they are suitable for purpose in their own country.
>
> N. Hijlkema, Vice Rector, Estonian Business School, *Global Focus*, Vol 4/1,
> 2010, 56–59.

The dominant use of the Anglo-Saxon language implies a much wider (postcolonial) issue of problematic assumptions made about the nature of management knowledge, the awareness of the contextual specificity of local management practice, and about the reproduction of values, ideology and power relations.

Case and Selvester (2000: 14) argue that such neoliberal imperatives are being constructed and reproduced through the operation of 'modern universalizing rhetorics'.

In their critique of contemporary Western education as an instrument of 'global domination' through the colonization of student knowledge, they advocate a postcolonial awareness and urge that we should 'embrace and celebrate difference rather than. . . exploit in the name of it' (Case and Selvester, 2000: 16). Research which draws upon postcolonial literatures and theoretical approaches would seem a fruitful way of constructing a research agenda which examined the globalization of b-schools and Western management education.

Finally, pedagogy itself would be another research avenue to explore, particularly since the advent of new technologies, which facilitate new models of learning, involving a wide range of digital and social media technologies. Thomas and Cornuel (2012) examine what they term 'blended learning' modules, which can not only have a global spread, but also can help the development of schools in emerging and developing nations. Notwithstanding the arguments above from postcolonial theories, the blending of the technological and the pedagogic is a potentially highly fruitful area of research as b-schools globalize their business. Fleck (2012) and Thomas and Thomas (2012) outline the many advantages of using social media platforms such as Facebook, Twitter, LinkedIn, and Google+ as well as web-based chat forums, electronic conferencing, and video. Combined with more traditional learning methods (face-to-face and text-based, for example), this constitutes what Fleck (2012) means by 'blended learning'. The linking of the technical with the pedagogic is reminiscent of the socio-technical approaches beginning in the 1960s (blending the social and the technical in the workplace) and many of the research questions, which arose in that context, can be asked of the blended learning models.

The advent of new technologies and their use in practice brings a series of changes which institutions and individuals will have to face. Some of these are already clear. For example, most b-schools are designed around a traditional university-based system of labour and cost. A lecturer, who traditionally has a wide range of freedom in how lecture material is crafted and delivered, carries out labour. Academic staff salaries are also the biggest cost for b-schools. The use of digital technologies, advances in cybernetics and robotics pose some sizeable challenges to both of these. The autonomy of the lecturer is likely to be reduced as support and design teams become involved in setting up the on-line version (which often requires compliance with rigorous external regulations). The financial base of the b-school is likely to swing toward administration and professional services being a greater cost than the employment of academic staff. Overcoming years of custom and practice presents equally significant challenges for many academic staff whose patterns of work organization will change. Intellectual property rights and plagiarism will present formidable challenges in a new technologically-driven pedagogic environment. This research arena is complex and challenging but, potentially, one of the most fruitful in the immediate future.

REFERENCES

Arthur, W. B. (1989). 'Competing Technologies, Increasing Returns, and Lock-In by Historical Events', *Economic Journal*, 99, 116–131.

Arthur, W. B. (1994). *Increasing Returns and Path Dependency in the Economy*. Ann Arbor: University of Michigan Press.

Baden-Fuller, C., Ravazzolo, F., and Schweizer T. (2000). 'Making and Measuring Reputations: The Research Ranking of European B-schools', *Long Range Planning*, 33, 621–650.

Bello, W. (2002). 'Pacific Panopticon', *New Left Review*, 16, 68-85.

Bordieu, P. (1984). *Distinction*. Cambridge M.A.: Harvard University Press.

Borokhovich, K., Bricker, R., Brunarski, K., and Simkins, B. (1995). 'Finance Research Productivity and Influence', *Journal of Finance*, 50, 1691–1717.

Butler, R. J. and Wilson, D. C. (1989). *Managing Voluntary and Non-Profit Organizations: Strategy and Structure*. London: Routledge.

Case, P. and Selvester, K. (2000). 'Close Encounters: Ideological Invasion and Complicity on an "International Management" Master's Programme', *Management Learning*, 31, 1, 11–23.

Child, J. (1972). 'Organizational Structure, Environment and Performance: The Role of Strategic Choice', *Sociology*, 6, 1, 1–22.

Chomsky, N. (1967). 'The Responsibility of Intellectuals', *New York Review of Books*, Vol 8, 3, 23 February.

Currie, G., Knights, D., and Starkey, K. (2010). 'Introduction: A Post- Crisis Critical Reflection on Business Schools', *British Journal of Management*, 21, S1-S5.

Dar, S. and Cooke B. (eds) (2007). *The New Development Management: Critiquing the Dual Modernization*. London: Zed Books.

David, P. A. (1985). 'Clio and the Economics of QWERTY', *American Economic Review*, 75, 332–337.

David, P. A. (1994). ' "Why are Institutions the 'Carriers of History?" Path Dependence and the Evolution of Conventions, Organizations and Institutions', *Structural Change and Economic Dynamics*, 5, 205–220.

Davidson, A. (2012). 'Is Michigan State Really Better Than Yale?' *The New York Times*, 7 August. <http://www.nytimes.com/2012/08/12/magazine/is-michigan-state-really-better-than-yale.html?pagewanted=all>.

Di Maggio, P. and Powell, W. (1983). 'The Iron Cage Revisited: Institutional Isomorphism and Collective Rationality in Organizational Fields', *American Sociological Review*, 48, 2, 147–160.

Dunne, S., Harvey, S., and Parker, M. (2008). 'Speaking Out: The Responsibility of Management Intellectuals: A Survey', *Organization*, 15, 2, 271–282.

Durand R. and McGuire J. (2005). 'Legitimating Agencies in the Face of Selection: The Case of AACSB', *Organization Studies*, 26, 2, 165–196.

Falk, R. A. (1999). *Predatory Globalization: A Critique*. Polity: Cambridge.

Fishe, R. (1998). 'What are the Research Standards for Full Professor of Finance?', *Journal of Finance*, 53, 1053–1079.

Fleck, J. (2012). 'Blended Learning and Learning Communities: Opportunities and Challenges', *Journal of Management Development*, 31, 4, 398–411.

Golembiewski, R. T. (1989). 'A Note on Leiter's Study: Highlighting Two Models of Burnout', *Group & Organization Studies*, 14, 5–13.

Granovetter, M. (1985). 'Economic Action and Social Structure: The Problem with Embeddedness', *American Journal of Sociology*, 91, 3, 481–510.

Grey, C. (1994). 'Career as a Project of the Self and Labour Process Discipline', *Sociology*, 28, 2, 479–497.

Harney, S. (2007) 'Socialization and the B-school', *Management Learning*, 38, 2, 139–153.

Hodgkinson, G. and Starkey K. (2011). 'Not Simply Returning to the Same Answer Over and Over Again: Reframing Relevance', *British Journal of Management*, 22, 3, 355–369.

Jancowicz, A. (1999). 'Planting a Paradigm in Central Europe. Do we Graft, or Must We Breed the Rootsock Anew?' *Management Learning*, 30, 3, 281–299.

Khurana, R. (2007). *From Higher Aims To Hired Hands: The Social Transformation of American B-schools and the Unfulfilled Promise of Management as a Profession*. Princeton: Princeton University Press.

Kogut, B. (2008). 'Rankings, Schools and Final Reflections on Ideas and Taste', *European Management Review*, 5, 4, 191–194.

Lowrie, A and H. Willmott (2009). 'Accreditation Sickness in the Consumption of Business Education: The Vacuum in AACSB Standard Setting', *Management Learning*, 40, 4, 411–420.

Masrani, S. and McKiernan, P. (2011). 'Accounting as a Legitimising Device in Voluntary Price Agreements: The Case of the Dundee Jute Industry, 1945–1960', *Critical Perspectives on Accounting*, 22, 4, 415–433.

Masrani, S., Williams, A. P. O., and McKiernan P. (2011). 'Management Education in the UK: The Roles of the British Academy of Management and the Association of B-schools', *British Journal of Management*, 22, 3, 382–400.

Meyer, J.W. and Rowan, B. (1977). 'Institutionalized Organizations: Formal Structure as Myth and Ceremony', *American Journal of Sociology*, 83, 2, 340–363.

Milewa T., Valentine J., and Calnan M. (1998). 'Managerialism and Active Citizenship in Britain's Reformed Health Service: Power and Community in an Era of Decentralisation', *Social Science & Medicine*, 47, 4, 507–517.

Moldoveanu, M. C. and Martin, R. L. (2008). *The Future of the MBA: Designing the Thinker of the Future*. Oxford: Oxford University Press.

Navarro, P. (2008). 'The MBA Core Curricula of Top-Ranked US B-schools: A Study in Failure?', *Academy of Management Learning and Education*, 7, 1, 108–123.

Parker, M. (2008). 'If Only Business Schools Wouldn't Teach Business', *The Observer*, 30 November.

Pierson, P. (2000). 'Increasing Returns, Path Dependence, and the Study of Politics', *American Political Science Review*, 94, 251–267.

Polanyi, K., Arensberg, C., and Pearson H. (eds) (1957). *Trade and Market in the Early Empires: Economics in History and Theory*. Chicago: Henry Regnery Company.

Power. M. (1997) *The Audit Society: Rituals of Verification*. Oxford: Oxford University Press.

Roberts, S. M., Jones, J. P., and Frohling, O. (2005). 'NGOs and the Globalization of Managerialism: A Research Framework', *World Development*, 33, 11, 1844–1864.

Ross, A. (ed.) (2009) *Nice Work If You Can Get it: Life and Labor in Precarious Times*. New York: New York University Press.

Said, E. (1993). *Culture and Imperialism*. New York: Random House.

Saunders, J., Wong, V., and Saunders, C. (2011). 'The Research Evaluation and Globalization of Business Research', *British Journal of Management*, 22, 3, 401–419.

Schoemaker, P. J. H. (2008). 'The Future Challenges of Business: Rethinking Management Education', *California Management Review* 50, 3, 119–139.

Slack, T., and Hinings, C. R. (1994). 'Institutional Pressures and Isomorphic Change: An Empirical Test', *Organization Studies*, 15, 6, 803–827.

Spender, J. C. (1989). *Industry Recipes: An Enquiry Into the Nature and Sources of Managerial Judgement*. Oxford: Blackwell.

Standing, G. (2011) *The Precariat: The New Dangerous Class*. London: Bloomsbury Academic.

Starkey, K. and Tiratsoo, N. (2007). *The B-school and the Bottom Line*. Cambridge: Cambridge University Press.

Starkey, K. and Tempest, S. (2008). 'A Clear Sense of Purpose? The Evolving Role of the B-school', *Journal of Management Development*, 27, 4, 379–390.

Sydow, J., Schreyogg, G., and Koch, J. (2009). 'Organizational Path Dependence: Opening the Black Box', *Academy of Management Review*, 34, 4, 689–709.

Thomas, H. and Cornuel, E. (2012). 'Business Schools in Transition? Issues of Impact, Legitimacy, Capabilities and Re-invention', *Journal of Management Development*, 31, 4, 329–335.

Thomas, H. and Wilson, A. D. (2009). 'An Analysis of the Environment and the Competitive Dynamics of Management Research', *Journal of Management Development*, 28, 8, 668–684.

Thrift, N. (2005). *Knowing Capitalism*. London: Sage.

Tolbert, P. S. and Zucker, L. G. (1996). 'The Institutionalization of Institutional Theory', in S. Clegg, C. Hardy, and W. Nord (eds), *Handbook of Organization Studies*, 175–190. London: Sage.

Trieschmann, J., Dennis, A., Northcraft, G., and Niemi, A. (2000). 'Serving Multiple Constituencies in B-schools: MBA Program Versus Research Performance', *Academy of Management Journal*, 43, 1130–1141.

Vaara, E and Fay, E. (2011). 'How Can a Bordieusian Perspective Aid Analysis of MBA Education?', *Academy of Management Learning and Education*, 10, 1, 27–40.

Wedlin, L. (2007). 'The Role of Rankings in Codifying a B-school Template: Classifications, Diffusion and Mediated Isomorphism in Organizational Fields', *European Management Review*, 4, 1, 24–39.

Wilensky, H. L. (1964). 'Mass Society and Mass Culture: Interdependence or Independence?', *American Sociological Review*, 29, 173–197.

Williams, A. P. O. (2010). *The History of UK Business and Management Education* London: Emerald.

Wilson, D. C. and McKiernan, P. (2011). 'Global Mimicry: Putting Strategic Choice Back on the B-school Agenda' *British Journal of Management* 22, 3, 457–469.

Young, R. (2001). *Postcolonialism: An Historical Introduction*. Oxford: Blackwell.

Zucker, L. G. (1987). 'Institutional Theories of Organization', *Annual Review of Sociology*, 13, 443–464.

12

Back to the Future of Management Research

Ken Starkey and Armand Hatchuel

This chapter addresses the conception and configuration of the business school and the role and nature of management research in the light of its origins and in the aftermath of the financial crisis. Our argument is that the time is ripe for a major rethink of the intellectual basis upon which the business school is grounded if it is to survive and prosper and that this has significant consequences for the future of management research.

While recognizing that there are a variety of business school models, it is the Anglo-Saxon model and particularly the American elite business school model that has emerged as triumphant. U.S. top schools dominate world rankings of both teaching and research. At its inception in Europe, it was to the U.S. that the European business school looked for inspiration. The establishment of INSEAD, for example, half a century ago was justified on the grounds that young Europeans needed to be educated with a good idea of American ideals and the free enterprise system. This view still drives much of business school debates. Recently, the dean of a leading U.S. school (Hubbard 2006) justified the role of the business school and its research base as central to entrepreneurial capitalism and the development of the new business models that are driving globalization. Critical to this, Hubbard argued, are venture capital practices, grounded in research in finance and economics, to drive new business practices. Business schools, the argument suggests, remain a key force for global business change.

Hubbard was writing before the financial crisis, but, even before the crisis, a growing number of critical voices were arguing that all was not well in the business school world, despite it being a sector which has experienced exponential global growth (Pfeffer and Fong 2003). According to Khurana's (2008) persuasive narrative, the story of the business school and management research is one of missed promise: a success in terms of demand for its products and services which hides a failure of moral purpose and a collusion with business practices that are far from optimal and sustainable. Business schools, he argues, have failed to provide the knowledge base necessary to drive the professionalization of management.

Since the financial crisis, criticisms of the business school have proliferated. The role of MBAs in top positions of leadership in companies that failed spectacularly (for example, HBOS in the U.K.) or lower down the organization as high-paid consultants and analysts in investment banks creating and (mis-)selling credit derivates has been highlighted (Tett 2009), and throws an ironic light on Hubbard's (2006) claim that the key skill taught to MBAs was the ability to assess valuations. The crisis reinforces the criticism of the impact of management research and of the business school curriculum that they are too focused on a narrow definition of analytics and have failed to provide an adequate understanding of management and leadership. While finance and a particular version of economic narrative came to dominate and define the business school agenda (Ferraro et al. 2005) and business practice (Davis 2009), business school case studies extolled the virtues of heroic leaders such as Jeff Skilling at Enron and Sir Fred Goodwin at Royal Bank of Scotland.

Debates about the nature of management research and what kind of school the business school is, or should be, continue. Should it aspire to be a professional school as suggested by Khurana (2008)? To what extent is it a serious social science school rather than a cash cow for its host university? Is the business schools' research problem that they are too limited in their social science base or too dominated by economics and finance, and a particular, narrow form of positivism? Should the business school be fundamentally redesigned to become more like a design school (Martin 2009; Starkey and Tempest 2009; Starkey et al. 2009)? We set out the issues and the parameters of our suggestions for a reframing of management research and the concept of the business school by looking at the potential contribution of three disciplines that are currently relatively peripheral to its configuration—*philosophy, law, and the arts.*

12.1. PHILOSOPHY—RETHINKING MISSION AND VALUE

Even before the financial crisis, the view from Davos at the meetings of the World Economic Forum was growing bleaker. In 2007, the year before the crisis, business leaders there were questioning the sustainability of current business models. According to Klaus Schwab, the founder of the Forum, '[l]arge parts of the population feel that business has become detached from society— that business leaders are no longer aligned with societal interest. What has come under attack now is the credibility not only of our business leaders but of business itself'. For many, the financial crisis has proved the prescience of Schwab's diagnosis. James Schiro, of Zurich Financial Services, argued that one of the main challenges faced by business leaders was the need to remove some of the uncertainty and risk that people faced and the anxiety that this gave rise to. Patrick Cescau, then CEO of Unilever, was of the opinion that '[y]ou can't have a healthy economy without a healthy community'.

Business schools have identified as one, if not their main, task the education of business leaders. Indeed it is a core claim of research-led leading schools such as Harvard and Stanford that their prime role is to educate business leaders. The Davos views of significant business leaders suggest that an important part of the business school agenda should be to confront issues of:

- aligning business and societal interests;
- working with business on the task of developing credible business leaders;
- working with business to justify the role of business, while working with business to create business practices that themselves vindicate this justification;
- developing the theory and the practice of the necessary symbiosis of healthy business, healthy economy and healthy society; and
- helping to mitigate the effects of uncertainty and risk, not least by developing better ways of avoiding and managing risk.

The problem of change is twofold. We do not wish to blame business schools for all of business's and the world's woes. Education is strongly correlated with effective management and this suggests that some of the management lessons taught in business schools might help organizations in the private and public sector become more effective. But this is an inference rather than demonstrated fact: 'We cannot infer a causal relationship from this association. . . but it is plausible that managers with an MBA or college-education are more likely to be aware of the benefits of modern management practices like lean manufacturing' (Bloom and Van Reenen 2010: 220). The financial crisis also suggests that some of these lessons might have the opposite effect. Certainly those lessons taught in certain finance classes about how to manage risks clearly contributed to the financial crisis (Delves Broughton 2008; Tett 2009; Davis 2009).

Business schools' predilection for writing fawning case studies of the latest management fad or about business leaders supposedly 'leading the revolution' (Hamel 2000) does us no credit. One need only revisit Harvard case studies of leadership at Enron and Sir Fred Goodwin of Royal Bank of Scotland to have serious reservations about the ability of business school 'research' to generate a science of business or narratives of business worthy of respect. *The Economist*'s (2009) prescription is radical: business schools 'should foster the twin virtues of scepticism and cynicism. [They] need to make more room for people who are willing to bite the hands that feed them: to prick business bubbles, expose management fads and generally rough up the most feted managers. Kings once employed jesters to bring them down to earth. It's time for business schools to do likewise'. Issues of virtue, scepticism and cynicism take us into the realm of philosophy, not one usually associated overmuch with business schools, which, in our opinion, remain unreflexive about their practices and over-certain that the knowledge they are producing is worthwhile and relevant to practice, despite evidence that the research produced by business schools has not had much impact, except in a few areas, such as finance.

'What is the good and what is value?' is one of the two most basic philosophical questions. The other is, 'What do we know and how do we know it?' Businesses are struggling for legitimacy in terms of the values they are perceived to espouse, most openly in relation to banking but it is not only financial firms which have this problem (Davis 2009). The financial crisis brings this issue to a head. 'At its core, Wall Street's failure. . . is a failure of moral leadership that no laws or regulations can ever fully address. *Goldman v. United States* is the tipping point that provides society with an opportunity to fundamentally rethink the purpose of finance' (Cohan 2010). It is a sign of the times that Goldman Sachs, the world's most successful investment bank and one that made money out of the financial crisis, while some of its clients had the opposite experience, is described by *Rolling Stone* as 'a great vampire squid' dipping its 'blood funnel' into anywhere it could extract value and extracting it. We are faced with a crisis of trust in business, a surge of antagonism towards business that reflects a failure of business leadership (Polman 2012) and, by implication, what business schools or at least their graduates, value. One of the main impediments to the election of the Republican candidate Mitt Romney (MBA, Harvard) to the U.S. Presidency in 2012 was the fact that he was employed as the chief executive of a hedge fund, Bain Capital.

The extent to which business schools have responded to the crisis is a matter of some debate and contention. Certainly some have tried. Nitin Nohria, the new dean at Harvard Business School, acknowledges that business faces a crisis of legitimacy. His plan for countering this is to develop management competence and character. He also emphasizes humility as a desirable aspect of a leader's character and has been supportive of some Harvard MBAs' attempt to promote an MBA oath similar to the Hippocratic oath of the medics. This move has met a mixed response. Some business schools have been supportive of the initiative while faculty at others, for example INSEAD, have been extremely critical. The Harvard Leadership Initiative associated with Dean Nohria, Raksh Khurana, Scott Snook and others has argued for new models of business leadership and new ways of teaching leadership (Snook et al. 2011). There are other examples, but overall change is uneven to the extent that even *The Economist* (2009) argues that business schools have shown few serious signs of reforming themselves, despite the fact that the most coveted destination for top MBA graduates was the finance industry and careers in investment banks, hedge funds, or private equity.

The knowledge challenge facing management research, the key driver of a business school that is committed to new knowledge generation, is ontological and epistemological. In terms of what is considered the core of business school knowledge, in Anglo-Saxon schools at least, economics and finance have come to dominate. Ferraro et al. (2003) argue that economics has risen to a position of epistemological and ideological dominance. This will be difficult to shift and it is unlikely that alternative perspectives will be successful in putting economics in its proper place by argument alone. Economics and finance represent a particular positivist perspective on knowledge. Grounded in a narrow ontology of the market, its philosophy of knowledge is logical empiricism and a 'logic of verification' rather than a logic of 'discovery' (Taylor 1985: 30). Economics champions a particular view of the world and its own narrative of 'worldmaking' (Goodman, 1978). Worldmaking proceeds by a process of composition which is also a process of deletion (assuming away what is considered unimportant) which can be a form of deformation. Hence, recent discussions of zombie capitalism (Harman 2009; Quiggin 2010). In the process of worldmaking, unless its proponents adopt a reflexive attitude based on inquiry rather than advocacy, the danger is that a particular representation is claimed as a 'mirror of nature' (Rorty, 1979). The 'given' in Goodman's (1978) phrase is 'acknowledged as taken', that is, interpretation is claimed as a picture of the way the world is and must be.

Agency and transaction cost theory give a very limited view of the world as best understood as a space of atomized markets, property rights and contractual relations, where individuals pursue personal advantage and collective good somehow arises as a by-product. This, in our opinion, is impossible to defend in the aftermath of the financial crisis. Research based on a narrow Anglo-Saxon economic view of markets also gave rise to some very dubious research predictions. Nobel-prize winning economist Merton Miller's (1990) injunction in his acceptance speech for this prestigious award—'Let us not waste our limited worrying capacity on second-order and largely self-correcting problems like financial leveraging. . . neither economics generally nor finance in particular. . . offer much support for [the] notion of a leverage-induced bankruptcy multiplier or a contagion effect'—now seems both optimistic and just plain wrong.

Similarly other financial economists championed a view that the new finance of risk was making markets ever more efficient and effective. Robert Merton (1997) argued that new financial vehicles (the precursor of the credit derivative) would complete markets at sustainable prices and that the flexibility they provided mean that incentive reasons for market failure were now a thing of the past. Merton's colleague, Myron Scholes, similarly argued that the new ability to finance firms using new financial instruments would change dysfunctional organizational forms, blurring the distinction between equity and debt and between a firm and its agents. The development of option technology, Scholes (1997) argued, would 'open up' new and far more effective organizational structures, citing Enron as a leading-edge example.

Even the laureate of neoliberalism and confessed admirer of the virtues of Ayn Rand's muscular individualism, former chairman of the Fed, Alan Greenspan, has admitted the errors on which his worldview were founded. Post-crisis, he confessed to having found a 'fatal flaw' in his economic ideology. Ferraro et al. (2005: 10) analyse economics's self-fulfilling theories of institutional design and management practice, arguing that there is little doubt that 'economics has won the battle for theoretical hegemony in academia and society as a whole and that such dominance becomes stronger every year'. It remains to be seen whether the financial crisis will puncture this hegemony and place economics in its appropriate place, acknowledged as one, but only one, of a nexus of disciplines that can contribute to a better knowledge of business and of society.

A crucial gap and the main weakness of economism is its lack of a theory of collective action. By this we mean a theory of all interactions and interdependancies that generate both wealth and human relations (Hatchuel 2005). Its assumption of utilitarianism ignores such basic conditions. It is difficult to justify, as the financial crisis and the business philosophy that underpinned it reveal a Darwinian rather than a communitarian logic (Fauchart and Gruber, 2011). Business is conceived as red in tooth in claw whose natural state is the survival of the fittest few. This is demonstrated in the growing gap between those at the very top of an increasingly skewed income distribution and the rest. More enlightened business leaders argue that we need a new model of business based upon a much more collaborative, inclusive form of capitalism (Paul Polman Unilever 2012). This is difficult to reconcile with what John Kay (2003) describes as the American business model based upon market fundamentalism, minimizing regulation, minimal taxation and the unrestrained pursuit of self interest. This runs counter to a view of business where legitimacy is gained not by what business does for itself but by what it does for the economy and society. The contrast is between, on the one hand, leadership that focuses upon individual and narrow sectional interests and, on the other, leadership that sees as its fundamental task the creation of a business system fit for the purpose of creating long-term and sustainable value.

Assuming that we have some concept of the common good, this suggests that we need to reflect on our philosophical assumptions, particularly from the perspective of how being an individual ('being singular') co-exists with collective action ('being plural'): 'the infinite tying, untying and retying of the social bond (Nancy 2000: xxi). Philosophy allied with empirical social science has the ability to challenge the atomistic philosophy of economics. Markets, when they work well, are actually made up of, and depend upon, networks of relationships, shared cultural norms constructed and held in common, and a moral community rather than rational egoists pursuing their own utility (McKenzie and Millo, 2003). A philosophical reflexivity on our claims to knowledge is crucial to counterbalance the myopia of intellectual arrogance. As the Chicago philosopher, Martha Nussbaum (1998: 300) warns: 'it would be catastrophic to become a nation of technically competent people who have lost their ability to think critically, to examine themselves, and to respect the humanity and diversity of others'. Philosophy provides the necessary foundation for considering issues of moral leadership in business.

Patrick Cescau, former CEO of Unilever, argues, in a contribution at Davos, that there is no dichotomy between doing business well and doing good and that 'in fact the two go hand in hand'. But Khurana (2007) argues that business schools may well have aspired to higher aims historically, yet the professional ethos that informed this aspiration has been subverted by a market and managerialist logic of a particular kind that is the antithesis of the professional ideal. Khurana traces how the growing acceptance of economics as the 'foundational discipline' of business education was a key influence in the de-legitimation of the business school's narrative of professional identity and purpose. The influential theories of Michael Jensen and others occupied centre stage and were 'catalysts in a phenomenological process' through which certain ideas, in particular the agency theory critique of management as autonomous, well-meaning and competent actors, came to be taken for granted.

A leading business school academic, one who praised the Icelandic model of banking before (with echoes of Atlantis) Iceland became 'Icelantis', defended the role of business schools against attack by arguing that the business school purpose of promoting entrepreneurialism and new business models to drive productivity was a noble one (Hubbard 2006). He also argued that business schools, like universities, should offer a 'neutral environment' for research into how to manage change in the economy and in financial markets. Of course, we support this emphasis upon neutrality but in this case it is rather undermined when Hubbard argues that the main goal of business school education is to promote venture capital practices, that private equity firms are the key drivers of necessary change, and that the ability to assess 'valuations' is the key skill transmitted to MBA students. After the financial crisis, even the *Wall Street Journal* argues that business schools need to rethink their curricula and that this need is most acute in finance and economics because a lot of things these disciplines have taken for granted are now seriously in question.

One thing that is in question is the best balance of disciplines, but it seems unsustainable that business school students should spend 95 per cent of their time learning calculations that have promoted a particular, and now discredited, view of how to maximize and share wealth (Bennis and O'Toole, 2005), and that the research that supports/vindicates/promotes this form of practice can or should retain its intellectual hegemony. As Beck (2001) argues, a simple calculation of value, based on the notion that profits rise when labour costs fall, leads to a radically different life experience in which bad news for labour markets counts as a 'victory report' for Wall Street. Michael Porter questions this simple calculus: 'How could companies think that simply shifting activities to countries with ever-lower wages was a "sustainable" solution to competitive challenges?' (Porter and Kramer 2010). The engagement with philosophy leads inexorably to questions of the good (what constitutes the good life, good business, the good organization, the good life, good value?) and questions of meaning and justice.

12.2. LAW—RESHAPING COLLECTIVE ACTION

Derek Bok, former President of Harvard University, sees business schools as having a very clear sense of purpose—to prepare future business leaders. Davis (2009) demonstrates how the purpose of business leadership changed fundamentally over the last 30 years, driven by a process in which finance replaced manufacturing at the centre of the U.S. (and one might add the U.K.) economy. Finance, driven by a fantasy of 'unimaginable' wealth creation and justified by greed becoming 'good', became 'the new American state religion... Now, all the world was a stock market, and we were all merely day traders, buying and selling various species of "capital" and hoping for the big score' (Davis 2009: vii). Driven by economic theory masquerading as fact, most notably Michael Jensen's extravagant claim that no proposition in any of the sciences is better documented than the efficient market hypothesis, the previous 'legal pragmatism' of law and economics was transformed into 'the cynical pragmatism of the shareholder value-oriented managers, as tokens of devotion to share price and ritual use of the right accountants, investment banks, directors, and alliance partners became rampant'.

In this phenomenological process, the increasing dominance of this ideology meant the 'twilight of the corporation as a social entity in the US'. Individuals were magically transformed from employees or citizens into 'investors' as everything, including talent, friends and home, became 'capital' (Davis 2009: 52–3; 99; 190). Everyman becomes trader. Delves Broughton's (2008) account of his time as a Harvard MBA testifies to the business school role in this process: 'Trading felt like the furthest possible remove from the workshop and assembly plant, and it was attracting the best minds at HBS because the rewards for doing it well were so outlandish. Yet one had to truly trust in capitalism to believe that trading like this served the goal of efficiently allocating resources in society'. There were no strong effective countervailing voices. Michael Porter's economist focus on the firm's competitive advantage as the be-all-and-end-all of strategy displaced Peter Drucker's humanistic emphasis upon the symbiotic relationship between business and society and his broad definition of the role of the business leader.

While accepting that law is no panacea for all our business woes, we recommend a renewed engagement with law as an antidote to some of the excesses of business school theory and their prescriptions for management (Segrestin and Hatchuel, 2011). It is ironic that two areas of research where the business school has proved very active—agency theory and critical management—share a deep suspicion of management motives. Agency theory, in our view, a key output from business school research, has been particularly pernicious in framing managers as a self-seeking group to be controlled by contracts and various clever technologies, including ideology, in the interests of the owners of the organization (Jensen and Meckling, 1976). We lack a view of the firm, which incentivizes collective creation rather than the conflict of interests—various aspects of law can help us fill this gap and create a more sustaining vision of corporate governance.

The challenge here is to develop a new framework of governance and law that promotes a role for management grounded in authority, responsibility, and leadership, and which encourages them to exercise their inventive capacities for the joint welfare of all stakeholders in an organization (Segrestin and Hatchuel 2011). Current frustrations with shareholder capitalism seem to be leading in the opposite direction, with the argument that it is private equity ownership of firms that will be most effective: a view promulgated in many venture capital classes (Hubbard 2006). This view has a very narrow view of management and ownership as fundamentally about direct financial control. Managerial latitude is increasingly limited and the notion of management as promoting collaborative behaviours in pursuit of a range of mutually reinforcing goals is marginalized. Reciprocity and a sense of shared property rights are minimized (Bosse et al. 2009; Asher et al. 2005; Post et al. 2002a, 2002b; Sundaramurthy and Lewis 2003).

The view of management without discretion is at odds with a philosophy of management independent and neutral in its pursuit of the best good for the organization. Blair and Stout (1999) argue that firm performance is dependent upon a range of parties (employees, shareholders, managers. . .) and that the key management task is to align the contributions of these parties in team production guided by a cooperative spirit. In the final analysis, a firm's surplus depends upon this joint effort rather than any agency relationship, which is really about the 'sharing' of rents (rent-seeking) accruing to team production rather than maximizing collective rents. The role of those at the apex of a firm's hierarchy is to provide a mediating role to balance the interests of the various parties (Lipton and Rowe 2007) and the role of the board is not to act primarily on behalf of shareholders but to act in the interests of the firm as a whole to maximize the joint welfare of the team as a whole. The focus of law in this perspective is to enable 'directors' discretion to act as mediators among all relevant corporate constituents' (Blair and Stout 1999: 806) and management's role is to enact this mediating function. This supports many of the tenets of classical management theory—Fayol, Taylor, Barnard, Parket, Follett (O'Connor 2012)—in which the essence of management is defined in terms of mediation, mobilization, and shared purpose.

There is a prevailing assumption in much business school teaching that management is an activity of free and empowered managers. However, in many (all?) economics and finance classes, this image is implicitly or actively contested. Law as currently framed does not protect the authority of management. Agency theory, a key business school artefact, suggests that managers are agents and not principals. It is not surprising that managers go over to the 'dark side' (Gelter 2009). Law provides a potential counter-balance to the excesses of agency theory. Marens and Wicks (1999) argue that managers do not risk violating the law or social norms if they choose to manage their firms in a manner that weighs the interests of other groups alongside questions of shareholder value; and that managers are not compelled to choose between the law and stakeholder ethics. According to corporation law, managers actually have considerable freedom (in law) to make decisions about a firm. They are not legally bound to reach decisions purely on the basis of concerns for the shareholder (Heracleous and Lan 2010). It is when law is refracted through agency theory that this position is obscured.

The law, if it is interpreted through a cooperative perspective on the corporation, and stakeholder theory, can serve as a counterpoint to Friedman's shareholder theory and can serve as a more compelling, inclusive and realistic account of how management can and should operate. The hope here is that a renewed narrative of management as stewardship can be developed as an antidote to an exclusive narrative of shareholder value, or the newly fashionable narrative of private equity. We need a new definition of law, based on research, which enables managers to carry out the function of stewardship and maximize collective welfare in an effective, efficient and just manner. Research should focus on aligning such a new business law with management rather than economic or finance theory.

Business as a pursuit of private value is at odds with a view of business and public value (Moore 1997). One might find out more about how to create sustainable value by talking to faculty at Kennedy School of Government at Harvard, including to Ronald Heifetz (1997) about the concept of leadership without easy answers. Business schools have tended toward easy answers and management is complicit in accepting the latest management fad if it seems to promise short-term value. The same criticism applies to particular variants of economic theory. As Stiglitz wrote in 1999, 'The *intellectual foundations* of laissez-faire economics, the view that markets by themselves will lead to efficient, let alone fair, outcomes has been stripped away. . . Today, the challenge is to get the balance right between the state and the market, between collective action at the local, national and global levels, and between government and non-governmental action'. In 2012 this challenge is even more acute.

Beside law we would also welcome more engagement with economic sociology in business schools. A sociological perspective focuses on the role of economics in performing, rather than objectively representing how markets function, and provides an interesting and necessary counterpoint to the claims of economics. It demonstrates that the existing law of the market is only one of a variety of ways of performing an economy (Callon 1998). We lack an adequate theory of effective markets and how best to organize them. This starting point, rather than the assumption that the current laws of the market as currently constituted are the equivalent of a law in physics. McKenzie and Miller's (2003) seminal analysis of the Chicago Futures Exchange (CBOE) demonstrates that effective markets are as much networks of culture and moral community as places of atomized, rational exchange. It also brings the paradox to the surface that the very markets in which economic man appears to thrive could not actually be created by man (or woman) acting in the way (rational egoism) that economics widely assumes. The invisible hand of markets is not always 'a meeting of minds and contracts negotiated between (like-minded) rational people' (Akerlof and Shiller 2009).

12.3. ART AND DESIGN—CREATING NEW WORLDS

The logic of an approach to management grounded in philosophy and law is that we expand rather than restrict the study of management and its teaching to situate it in the history of economic, social, and cultural theory and practice. In this section, we focus on management as design and the possible contribution of the arts and humanities to the business school. The financial crisis, but also, for example, the sorry tale of Long-Term Capital Management (Lowenstein 2001), demonstrate the shortcomings of an empirical approach that assumes too much by assuming away too many variables in order to arrive at what is claimed to be the most parsimonious proof of a theory. As Bennis and O'Toole (2005) argue, 'applied to business—essentially a human activity in which judgments are made with messy, incomplete, and incoherent data—statistical and methodological wizardry can blind rather than illuminate'. We live in what Ulrich Beck (2001) has described as a 'risk society' and, in some of its applications to business, finance wizardry has led to the proliferation rather than the effective management of risk. The key question that confronts us now, according to Beck, is whether the particular historical conjuncture of an Anglo-Saxon form of capitalism, and of democracy, can or should be globalized, given the risks it is creating of exhausting the physical, cultural and social foundations upon which it has depended.

The design approach adopts a radical approach to the questioning of foundations. It is premised upon a process of discovery rather than the empiricist 'logic of verification' that characterizes research in the quasi-sciences of finance and economics. Science focuses upon the question, 'Is it true?'. For design, the key question is: 'Will it work better?' (Simon 1989). The implication of this for management research and education is that the focus should be on expanding our sense of possibility, rather than the search for the one, sure answer and that the education we craft from our research should focus not on educating students to make choices among pre-designed alternatives but on training them to design new, better alternatives. Such a design philosophy situates business schools in relation to their base disciplines, e.g. social science, in a similar relationship to the one that medicine and engineering have to their various base disciplines of biology, chemistry, and physics; thus positioning management as a research-based design science (Pettigrew 2001). As Jelinek (2008) argues organizations do not conform to universal laws. They are 'suffused' with context, interpretation, expectations, hope, changing relationships, and temporality.

The key source of knowledge about the design approach lies in those companies that are leading in developing its principles—Apple, Bombardier, Intel, Saint-Gobain, for example (Hatchuel et al., 2010; Le Masson et al., 2011). Design thinking seeks to create a creative space between 'the past-data-driven world of analytical thinking and the knowing-without-reasoning world of intuitive thinking' (Martin 2009: 26). It works by generating desired unknowns and creating new previously unthinkable concepts, which become the focus for learning new ways of creating products and services (Le Masson et al. 2011). Strategic choice is conceptualized not as a choice among known alternatives in conditions of undecidability but as a process in which the capacity for decidability is enhanced through the generation of new, often previously un-thought or un-imagined options. An important aim in the design process is the 'capture of the undecidable' which the French philosopher, Alain Badiou (2008: 114), defines as follows: 'an undecidable is a statement that cannot be inscribed in any of the classes into which the norm of evaluation is supposed to be able to distribute all possible statements'. At the moment of the capture of the undecidable, the design process moves into a new state of possibility in which new norms of creation apply. The expansion of what is known is based upon a process of experimentation, knowledge acquisition, and discovery combining artistic creation (the bringing of undecidables to the surface, new conceptual models) as a new basis for choice and action) and scientific discovery based on knowledge expansion.

These new conceptual models can refer to design briefs or to new forms of organization to facilitate the process of capturing the undecidable. Hatchuel et al. (2010) illustrate this design process in Saint-Gobain Sekurit's radical innovations in automobile glazing, which led to new forms of glass technology and new forms of R&D organization, a new form of design centre. They summarize the design approach as follows: 'We conceive desired and unknown things without being able to define them; then we actively look for knowledge that helps to define these unknown things until we can give them some social and artifactual existence. . . emergent and intentional features shaping these things are interdependent and co-generated through concept-knowledge expansions'.

Huff et al. (2006) argue that management as design science is 'mindful of art and surprise'. The arts have much to teach business about creative, effective and sustainable business. For example, the architect Frank Gehry discusses his practice in terms of a range of core values, of which the economic is only one. These include 'neighborliness' and 'legacy'. The Guggenheim Museum in Bilbao, his most iconic creation, 'was done with a lot of heart and soul, working with the community, and trying to make a building that would fit in, and that worked for art' (Gehry 2004: 25). Gehry and his team have as their template 'communal spaces where people have to work together and live together' and designing 'a building that does all we want as humans from our buildings. . . it has something to do with people's pride. . . The Golden Rule? In the end, when I make a building, I think of my neighbour' (Gehry, 2004: 23, 34). The arts provide a rich source of knowledge about values-based management geared towards innovation.

Modern art has brought to culture a new approach of critical reflexivity and discovery. It stresses the necessity of tradition and reference, as well as the ability to break rules and explore new worlds. At the beginning of management history, science was a major source for critical thinking and breakthrough ventures. We know now that a false scientism in management dominated by economic orthodoxy can kill both reality and imagination. Design theory offers a new template for rediscovering sensitivity to the 'real' and the power of creation. ((Hatchuel, Starkey, and Tempest 2010). We agree with Stanford's Jim March, perhaps the world's leading management researcher, that business schools need to engage more with the arts and humanities if they are to realize their potential to create 'the performances and scripts of management education as refining the routines of reason into objects and instruments of beauty worthy of human aspiration' (Patriotta and Starkey 2008). March also argues that a key challenge for business school research is to develop 'a sense of themselves that enobles the human condition and glorifies the mind'.

12.4 THE PATH NOT TAKEN

In a recent work, Augier and March (2011) analyse what they claim was the Golden Age (the 'Camelot') of North American business schools in the period after the Second World War, 1945 to 1970. This golden age was founded upon a new commitment to fundamental scientific research. Business schools, it was argued, were to be improved by engagement with the foundational disciplines of economics and behavioural science as well as the quantitative disciplines, which would also add to their contribution to society.

Cooperation between disciplines was part of the aspiration but it was economics that became increasingly dominant. Co-production of new business school templates with engineering and information technology were proposed but these became 'unrealized' histories. Engineering schools, in particular, 'did not rise to the opportunities that were perceived by Sloan, GSIA, and others. If they had, management education might have developed in a different way, Operations research might have become more central to management education; financial economics less central. Theories of choice and of teams might have become more important; theories of markets less so. Research on the design and implementation of information technology might have become more developed; research on the theory of games and agency theory less so' (Augier and March 2011: 281).

As a result, business schools shifted from the education of the industrial manager to focus on careers in management consulting and finance. MBAs 'did not become managers of firms that produce physical products. They became experts in the management of speculation or in the management of advice' (page 282), with an unbridled 'enthusiasm for markets'. Business education became increasingly 'commodified' and 'marketized'. Interdisciplinary research and education were other casualties, 'replaced by economic intellectual imperialism as economists invaded other fields with economic tools. This resulted in substantial invasions of sociology, psychology, political science, and law by economic models, much of it stimulated by the imagination of Gary Becker' (Augier and March 2011: 307).

What are the lessons we can draw from this history? Augier and March are unequivocal: 'The key to management became the alignment of incentives for self-interested others to serve the self-interests of the managers (or his or her master [or mistress]). Business ethics became an esoteric and not conspicuously valued subject rather than part of basic socialization. When the excesses of the early twenty-first century provoked outside criticism of business school ethics and demands that business schools introduce a stronger sense of social responsibility into the curriculum, the response of the schools was, in general, minimal and often explicitly antagonistic, Significant voices, echoing the litanies of Woodstock and Chicago, maintained that the only social obligation of managers was unremitting masturbation, and social

systems worked best when individuals pursued their own self-interests without recourse to vague contrary ideas of "social good" or "public interest" '
(Augier and March 2011: 309).

In this history, there were tantalizing missed opportunities. There was
some introduction of history, philosophy of science, and even sociology, and
March himself has been a prime example of engagement with the humanities,
reflecting (March 2003) on his 'scholar's quest' and raising profound questions about the nature of scholarship and its role in the business school. He
questions, among other things, the dominance of a business school mind-set,
focused only on a 'utilitarian morality', and is critical of an instrumental attitude to learning where knowledge is valued not for its intrinsic worth but
because of its badge of certified competence. He talks, somewhat nostalgi-
cally it appears, about 'learning as a manifestation of faith in what it means
to be a human being. . . A university is only incidentally a market. It is more
essentially a temple—a temple dedicated to knowledge and a human spirit of
inquiry. It is a place where learning and scholarship are revered, not primarily
for what they contribute to personal or social well-being, but for the vision of
humanity they symbolize, sustain and pass on' (March 2003: 206).

Augier and March's vision of higher education is, indeed, of something
'higher', 'a vision not a calculation. . . a commitment, not a choice'—'[s]tudents
are not customers, they are acolytes. Teaching is not a job; it is a sacrament.
Research is not an investment; it is a testament' (Augier and March 2011: 235–
6). Managers are challenged to present themselves 'as icons and aspirations
for humanity [and] [t]he dilemmas of leadership. . . as instances of the dilemmas of life and their human resolution in management as models for achieving humanness in life'.

This challenge fits well with Nussbaum's (1997) view, which we have
already quoted, arguing that the humanities are essential to good citizenship in business. Otherwise, we face a catastrophe of being managed by technically competent people who have lost their ability to think critically and
to respect the humanity and diversity of others. These are powerful voices
arguing with Weick (2001: 574) that business schools could/should 'stand for
wisdom rather than vocation, character rather than technicalities, and mind-
fulness rather than rationality'. (We would add that the only thing that would
be more catastrophic is to become a nation of technically incompetent people
with the same asocial characteristics. We are all living witnesses to this state
of affairs.) We support the engagement with the liberal arts and its capacity
for challenging and broadening management thinking by introducing issues
of the basis of knowledge, self knowledge, wisdom and leadership (Starkey
and Tempest 2007; Starkey and Hall 2011). While there is some pessimism
about the future and the past of business schools, and while we acknowledge
the weight of some of the criticisms of business schools, we would like, in our
conclusion, to emphasize its possibilities. What this reconfiguration might

lead to is illustrated by the example of Apple. Steve Jobs' claim was that computer science is a liberal art and he himself acknowledges the impact of his liberal arts training, for example in calligraphy. For Jobs, Apple's success was based upon the alignment and integration of knowledge of technology, the humanities, liberal arts and business.

The situation of the business school cannot be divorced from the condition of the academy and of the university more broadly as a primary seat of knowledge. Frey (2010) predicts the 'withering' of academia, citing the negative impact of forces such as the rankings 'mania', the increased division of labour in research, which is driving the fragmentation of disciplines, inadequate organizational forms for research, which makes inter-disciplinarity ever more difficult, publication pressures, which lead to a growth in academic fraud, and even the dilution of the very concept of the 'university'. No doubt, all these are serious challenges and the business school has experienced them all. A dean's task is not an easy one nor does it have easy answers.

Of course, there are barriers to change in the business school, intellectual and managerial—inertia, the disciplinary tradition, staff demographics and motivations, incentive systems, leadership, and the expectations of the university and other stakeholders. Indeed, the business school still has to come to terms with its past and resolve the challenges that have been there from its beginning. The case for the establishment of Harvard Business School was justified more than a century ago by Harvard's President, Charles Norton, by arguing that if a business school were established at Harvard it 'would demonstrate a great capacity for public usefulness'. Today, one of Harvard's, and the world's most distinguished business professors, Michael Porter, argues that business schools have lost sight of the importance of shared value (Porter and Kramer 2011). Yet Abraham Flexner, one of the most important American writers on the professional school, particularly the medical school, was making a similar point in the 1930s, during the last great depression.

Flexner's (1930: 164) view of business was that it did not demonstrate the characteristics of the professions, particularly the notion of service; 'it is shrewd, energetic, and clever, rather than intellectual in character; it aims. . . at its own advantage, rather than at noble purpose within itself' and his views on Harvard Business School are directly at odds with President Norton's. '[T]he main emphasis of the School. . . is concentrated on 'getting on'—the canker of American life' (Flexner, 1930: 166). Public purpose has given way to the search by the student consumer for personal advantage. The business school still has to disprove Flexner's judgment, a task made more acute by the financial crisis. In doing this, the challenge for today's and tomorrow's business school is to align personal advantage and public purpose. Flexner (1930: 166) poses the question thus: 'Is modern business to be accepted at its own claim, or has a civilized society [and the university and the business school] some critical responsibility in respect of it?' We have suggested that to develop such critical responsibility, and to design business schools fit for the task, will require a new way of thinking the business school grounded in philosophy, law and the arts and humanities. The aftermath of the financial crisis is an opportunity for a fundamental rethinking and repositioning of the business school.

Management research and management education constitute a key arena for rethinking and reshaping the relationship between the business school and other parts of the university/academy as a place for integrating business with the faculties of science, social science, and the liberal arts and humanities. Delanty (2001) suggests that the major intellectual challenge facing the university is to reconcile the opposing domains of science and culture. The major challenge facing business schools, management research, and management education is to create new narratives of business and education that define and justify the role of management and business schools in shaping the economic, social and cultural bonds that bind us together. The justification for its central role in the future will be an enhanced capacity for promoting collective action for the greater good, not least in developing new knowledge and practices capable of building businesses and other organizations necessary for sustaining the economic system (including the ecosystem) and the social system. To meet this challenge will require a fundamental reappraisal and a systematic redesign of how business schools function, focusing upon faculty issues, student expectations, employer relations, promotion criteria, the effect of business school rankings and the relationship of business schools to business and, where they are university-based, the wider university.

12.5. TOWARDS A MANIFESTO FOR MANAGEMENT AS DESIGN—A RESPONSIBLE AND CREATIVE DISCIPLINE

One of the seminal contributions to the history of design was the Bauhaus Manifesto developed by Walter Gropius in 1919 as the basis for a new approach to the visual arts and the design of innovative buildings for the future. In this manifesto, Gropius called for 'the conscious co-operation and collaboration of all craftsman' that can only be found in the realization of a common creation (the 'building' for Gropius). He also called for the end of 'the arrogant barrier between artists and craftsmen'. The idea was that craft would revitalize spirit and inspiration and that art would find new creative paths through a better understanding of craft.

These two principles for an *aggiornamento* also make sense for management. The first principle is that responsible management is possible only when it is embedded in cooperation and collaboration, driven by a common purpose to make things happen. There is no sustainable world that can be built only on competition. Co-operation comes first as it is the condition for fair competition. The second principle is the cross fertilization between research (seen as the art of the scholar) and practice (seen as the power of the craft). This is the condition for both engagement and reflexivity in the simultaneous design of new knowledge and new worlds.

In the spirit of the Bauhaus manifesto, and of the notion of management as a design science, we conclude our chapter with key elements of what might comprise a 'Manifesto for Management' as a responsible and creative discipline aimed at creating the new goods, services, and organizations of the future. We then highlight what we consider the research implications of this agenda.

12.5.1. Purpose

1) The new management research and curriculum of the future will focus on breaking down conventional patterns of thought.

2) Its central purpose will be the study, stimulation, and design of new forms of responsible and creative collective action.

3) It will be based on establishing vital connections with the life of the community and challenging the barriers that have developed between business and society.

12.5.2. Epistemology

1) It will be based on a notion of creative unity and cooperation—of mind, body and soul, and theory and practice.

2) No one discipline, research philosophy, or definition of practice will predominate.

3) Management is essentially interdisciplinary and management research as a new type of design science will develop to reflect this.

4) A history of management facts and ideas will be developed and taught as a basic course that stimulates reflexivity, avoids fads and guru-ism, prepares commitment and innovation

12.5.3. Research and Ethics

1) The aim of management research is to integrate the arts and sciences, which provide the foundations for a complete business school

committed to the goal of sustainable management, based upon the recognition of the composite character of business as an entity.

2) Management research must re-engage with the practice of designing and building organizations in a deep way, with a commitment to producing things recognized as excellent by the range of stakeholders business serves.

3) Creative imagination depends upon the shaping of thought in the crucible of action. Collaborative research therefore assumes primacy in the hierarchy of management research approaches and philosophies.

12.5.4. Institution

A new union of research—the theoretical and the practical curriculum—with business and its stakeholders will be the primary goal. The new business school of the future will be everything in one form.

12.6. RESEARCH IMPLICATIONS

We have based our argument, in part, on our experience and research over several decades with the contested nature of management research. While a number of excellent studies of business schools, their history and current practices, have emerged in recent years, we still lack a deep knowledge of the variety of practices that business schools have adopted and general agreement about their trajectory of development, as well as the current challenges they face.

While acknowledging the variety of business schools, we tend to write about 'the business school' and are, therefore, concerned with making an argument that we assume captures the reality of a significant body of schools. This raises a number of questions that require further research. First, is it possible to write about *the* business school in a way that captures its essence as a developing institution? Second, we think Khurana's (2007) threefold categorization is a useful way of ordering business schools. The first group of business schools are the elite leading schools, located mainly in leading American research universities, but including leading non-U.S. schools such as London Business School and INSEAD. These are schools that dominate the major global rankings, such as those of the *Financial Times* and *Business Week*. In the second group of business schools are the U.S. large regional schools, AACSB-accredited, and leading non-US schools which too are increasingly AACSB accredited, but also EFMD/EQUIS and/or AMBA accredited. These schools occupy the lower ranks of business school league tables, below the elite.

The question that needs answering here is: 'To what extent are non-U.S. schools seeking to emulate the U.S. elite schools and, if so, how are they doing this? A further question concerns whether there are alternative models emerging in different national and regional contexts and what these might comprise. Research here should investigate the processes and institutional structures supporting, or not, the diffusion of the U.S. elite norm (accrediting bodies, league tables, journal rankings, for example) and what processes and alternative 'rules of the game' might lead to other trajectories of development. For example, can one talk meaningfully about the emergence of a European business school model?

The third group of business schools forms by far the largest segment of the business school market. This group includes the thousands of schools (with a very small minority of exceptions) that will never feature in the world rankings or achieve accreditation. Khurana (2007: 293) describes this third group as consisting of 'schools offering vocational programs in which academic requirements [are] modest and obtaining a degree fairly painless'! One needs further study of the role of these schools and how they can be encouraged in their development, if the name and the institutional role of the business school is to be sustained over the longer term.

We have elaborated our concerns about the current state of business schools and how they might develop. We are also aware of examples where at least some of our concerns are being addressed. The financial crisis did lead to some soul-searching among business school faculty and some deans at leading schools. But we lack a complete understanding of the range of innovations that are being developed in business schools. This can only be achieved if we have far more data, based on large-scale comparative studies of the state of the business school world. In particular, it would be interesting to secure more data on the development of inter-disciplinarity in the business school.

We are currently researching the interface of management and legal law from agency and stakeholder theory perspectives. We recognize that management research and working with business and other types of organization is not the sole prerogative of business schools. There is much important work being done in management research and education in engineering schools, for example, and in other parts of the higher education system. For example, the Kennedy School of Government at Harvard provides an interesting alternative vision of leadership education, oriented to more than corporate profit (Heifetz 1993). An important research question is how does the work being done outside the business school fit with the broad task of creating management education and management research best suited to deal with the complex global management and leadership challenges of the twenty-first century?

We also lack research into the complex relationship between research and teaching. Much of the latter is dominated by text books which do not reflect state-of the-art research. We argue for the consideration of a new curriculum in business schools. The logic of our argument is that a new curriculum would need to be grounded in new research in three broad areas:

a) *The history of management innovations in Western civilization.* Here research would adopt a design perspective showing how new management techniques are designed, adapted and changed, and the role of education in their diffusion, for example: the Roman military organization; book-keeping and the role of the monastery in medieval times; the management of the artist's workshop in the Renaissance; the interaction of research funding (from wealthy patrons) and artistic excellence; the formation and the mechanization of manufacturing in the nineteenth century; the birth of marketing and public relations. . .

b) *The development of a philosophical perspective to theorize the situation of management challenges and issues in contemporary societies.* Here research and teaching would focus on the analysis of the missions and values of management from several points of view (competence, authority, technology, general interest and benefit). Comparative research is crucial here: for example, a comparison of the role of the CEO with political statesmen; CEO's and great architects; CEOs and professional leaders, e.g. in medicine and law. Authors such as Barnard, Follett, Taylor and Fayol could be revisited as well as philosophers of power and leadership, such as Foucault of course, but also the texts of Aristotle and Plato, among others.

c) *Legal models of the enterprise and the corporation.* Here the imperative is to adopt an open perspective, rather than ideological preconceptions, on a comparison of the variety of possible organizational forms—classic corporations, cooperatives, new corporations, Anglo-Saxon, German and Scandinavian models, start-ups, and open source communities.

The overarching task here is demonstrate the strengths and weaknesses of the variety and diversity of collective action and cooperation that management researchers, students, and practitioners should take into account if we are to continue to develop the role of management as a research discipline and the role of the business school as central to the university of the twenty-first century.

NOTE

This paper is based upon the on-going study of business schools, originally funded by the U.K. ESRC, which involve interviews with deans and other members of staff in leading business schools (in the U.K., Continental Europe, and the U.S.), participant observation in various business schools, and in representative business school and management research bodies, involvement in debates about management research policy, and action research over twenty or more years with leading corporates and public sector organizations, particularly on the subjects of strategy, innovation and design (Hatchuel et al. 2010).

REFERENCES

Akerlof, G. A. and Shiller, R. J. (2009). *Animal Spirits. How Human Psychology Drives the Economy, and Why It Matters for Global Capitalism*. Princeton: Princeton University Press.

Asher, C. C., Mahoney, J. M., and Mahoney, J. T. (2005). 'Towards a Property Rights Foundation for a Stakeholder Theory of the Firm', *Journal of Management and Governance* 9: 5–32.

Augier, M. and March, J. (2011). *The Roots, Rituals, and Rhetorics of Change. North American Business Schools After the Second World War*. Stanford, CA: Stanford Business Books, Stanford University Press.

Badiou, A. (2008). *Conditions*. London: Continuum.

Beck, U. (2001). *The Brave New World of Work*. Cambridge: Polity Press.

Bennis, W. and O'Toole, J. (2005). How Business Schools Lost their Way. *Harvard Business Review*, May, 96–104.

Blair, M. M. and Stout, L. A. (1999). 'A Team Production Theory of Corporate Law', *Journal of Corporation Law* 24: 751–807.

Bloom, N. and Van Reenen, J. (2010). Why do Management Practices Differ Across Firms and Countries', *Journal of Economic Perspectives* 24: 203–224.

Bosse, D. A., Phillips, R. A., and Harrison, J. S. (2009). Stakeholders, Reciprocity, and Firm Performance', *Strategic Management Journal* 30: 447–456.

Callon, M. (ed.) (1998). *The Laws of the Market*. Oxford: Blackwell.

Cohan, W. D. (2011). *Money and Power: How Goldman Sachs Came to Rule the World*. London: Allen Lane.

Davis, G. (2009). *Managed by Markets. How Finance Re-Shaped America*. Oxford: Oxford University Press.

Delanty, G. (2001). *Challenging Knowledge: The University in the Knowledge Society*. Milton Keynes: Open University Press.

Delves Broughton, P. (2008). *What They Teach You at Harvard Business School. My Two Years Inside the Cauldron of Capitalism*. London: Viking.

The Economist (2009). 'The Pedagogy of the Privileged', 24 September 2009)

Fauchart, E. and Gruber, M. (2011). 'Darwinians, Communitarians, and Missionaries: The Role of Founder Identity in Entrepreneurship', *Academy of Management Journal* 54: 935–958.

Ferraro, F., Pfeffer, P., and Sutton, R. I. (2005). Economic Language and Assumptions Can Become Self-Fulfilling. *Academy of Management Review* 30: 8–24.

Flexner, A. (1930). *Universities. American, English, German*, reprinted in 1994. New Brunswick, New Jersey: Transaction Publishers.

Frey, B. (2010). 'Withering Academia', *Working Paper*, University of Zurich.

Gehry, F. O. (2004). 'Reflections on Designing and Architectural Practice', in R. J. Boland Jr. and F. Collopy (eds) *Managing as Designing*. Stanford, CA: Stanford University Press.

Gelter, M. (2009). 'The Dark Side of Shareholder Influence: Managerial Autonomy and Stakeholder Orientation in Comparative Corporate Governance', *Harvard International Law Journal* 50: 129–194.

Goodman, N. (1978). *Ways of Worldmaking.* Indianapolis: Hackett Publishing Company.

Hamel, G. (2000). *Leading the Revolution.* Boston, MA: Harvard Business School Press.

Harman, C. (2009). *Zombie Capitalism.* London: Bookmarks Publications.

Hatchuel, A., Starkey, K., Tempest, S., and Le Masson, P. (2010). Strategy as Innovative Design: An Emerging Perspective', *Advances in Strategic Management* (eds) 37: 3–28.

Heifetz, R. (1993). *Leadership Without Easy Answers.* Cambridge, MA: the Belknapp Press of Harvard University Press.

Hubbard, G. (2006). 'Business, Knowledge and Global Growth', *Capitalism and Society, 1,* Issue 3, 1–10. <http://www.bepress.com/cas/vol1/iss3/art1>

Huff, A. S., Tranfield, D., and Van Aken, J. E. (2006). 'Management as Design Science Mindful of Art and Surprise', *Journal of Management Inquiry* 13: 180–207.

Jensen, M. C. and Meckling, W.H. (1976). 'Theory of the Firm', *Journal of Financial Economics* 3: 305–360.

Khurana, R. (2007). *From Higher Aims to Hired Hands. The Social Transformation of American Business Schools.* Princeton: Princeton University Press.

Kay, J. (2003). *The Truth About Markets.* London: Penguin.

Lan, L. L. and Heracleous, L. (2010) Rethinking Agency Theory: The View from Law. *Academy of Management Review,* 35, 2: 294–314.

Le Masson, P., Weil, B., and Hatchuel, A. (2011) *Strategic Management of Innovation and Design.* Cambridge: Cambridge University Press.

Lipton, M. and Rowe, P. K. (2007). 'The Inconvenient Truth about Corporate Governance: Some Thoughts on Vice-chancellor Strine's Essay', *Journal of Corporation Law* 33: 63–71.

Lowenstein, R. (2001). *When Genius Failed. The Rise and Fall of Long-Term Capital Management.* London: Fourth Estate.

March, J. G. (2003). 'A Scholar's Quest', *Journal of Management Inquiry* 12, 3: 205–207.

March, J. G. and Weill, T. (2005). *On Leadership.* Malden, MA: Blackwell Publishing.

March, J. G. and Augier, M. (2007). 'The Pursuit of Relevance in Management Education', *California Management Review,* 49, 3: 129–146.

Marens, R. and Wicks, A. (1999). 'Getting Real: Stakeholder Theory, Managerial Practice and the General Irrelevance of Fiduciary Duties Owed to Shareholders', *Business Ethics Quarterly* 9: 273–293.

Martin, R. (2009). *The Design of Business.* Boston, MA: Harvard Business Press.

McKenzie, D. and Millo, Y. (2003). 'Constructing a Market. Performing Theory: The Historical Sociology of a Financial Derivates Exchange', *American Journal of Sociology* 109: 107–145.

Merton, R. C. (1997). 'Applications of Option-pricing Theory: Twenty-five Years Later', Nobel Prize lecture, 9 December. *Economic Sciences* 85–118.

Miller, M. H. (1990). 'Leverage', Nobel Prize lecture, 7 December. *Economic Sciences* 291–300.

Moore, M. (1997). *Public Value: Strategic Management in Government.* Cambridge, MA: Harvard University Press.

Nancy, J. -L. (2000) *Being Singular Plural.* Stanford: Stanford University Press.

Nusssbaum, M. (1998). *Cultivating Humanity. Classical Defence of Reform in Liberal Education*. Cambridge, MA: Harvard University Press.

O'Connor, E. S. (2012). *Creating New Knowledge in Management, Appropriating the Field's Lost Foundations*. Stanford, CA: Stanford University Press.

Patriotta, G. and Starkey, K. (2008) 'From Utilitarian Morality to Moral Imagination: Re-Imagining the Business School', *Journal of Management Inquiry* 17: 319–327.

Pettigrew, A. M. (2001). Management Research after Modernism. *British Journal of Management* 12: Special Issue, December: S61–S70.

Pfeffer, J. and Fong, C. T. (2003). The End of the Business School? Less Success than Meets the Eye. *Academy of Management Learning & Education* 1: 78–95.

Polman, P. (2102). 'Captain Planet', *Harvard Business Review*.

Porter, M. and Kramer, M. R. (2011). 'Creating Shared Value', *Harvard Business Review*, January.

Post, J. E., Preston, L. E., and Schs, S. (2002a). 'Managing the Extended Enterprise: The New Stakeholder View', *California Management Review* 45: 6–28.

Post, J. E., Preston, L. E., and Schs, S. (2002b). *Redefining the Corporation: Stakeholder Management and Organizational Wealth*. Stanford, CA: Stanford University Press.

Quiggin, J. (2010). *Zombie Economics. How Dead Ideas Still Walk Among Us*. Princeton: Princeton University Press.

Rorty, R. (1979). *Philosophy and the Mirror of Nature*. Princeton: Princeton University Press.

Scholes, M. (1997). 'Derivatives in a Dynamic Environment', Nobel Prize lecture, 9 December. *Economic Sciences* 127–154.

Segrestin, B. and Hatchuel, A. (2010). 'Beyond Agency Theory: A Post-Crisis View of Corporate Law', *British Journal of Management* 22: 484–499.

Simon, H. A. (ed.) (1989). *Models of Thought 2*. New Haven: Yale University Press.

Snook, S., Nohria, S., and Khurana, R. (eds) (2011). *Handbook of Leadership Teaching*. New York: Sage.

Starkey, K. and Hall, C. (2011). 'The Spirit of Leadership', in S. Snook, S. Nohria, and R. Khurana, (eds), *Handbook of Leadership Teaching*. New York: Sage.

Starkey, K., Hatchuel, A., Tempest, S. (2009). 'Management Research and the New Logics of Discovery and Engagement', *Journal of Management Studies* 46: 547–558.

Starkey, K. and Tempest, S. (2009). 'The Winter of our Discontent—The Design Challenge for Business Schools', *Academy of Management Learning and Education* 8: 576–586.

Stiglitz, J. (2003). *The Roaring Nineties. Seeds of Destruction*. London: Allen Lane.

Sundaramurthy, C. and Lewis, M. (2003). 'Control and Collaboration: Paradoxes of Governance', *Academy of Management Review* 28: 397–415.

Taylor, C. (1985). *Philosophy and the Human Sciences. Collected Papers*, vol 2. Cambridge: Cambridge University Press.

Tett, G. (2009). *Fool's Gold: How Unrestrained Greed Corrupted a Dream, Shattered Global Markets and Unleashed a Catastrophe*. London: Abacus.

Weick. K. E. (2001). 'Gapping the Relevance Bridge: Fashions Meet Fundamentals in Management Research', *British Journal of Management* 12: Special Issue, December: S71–S76.

13

Building a Research Agenda for the Institutional Development of Business Schools

Andrew M. Pettigrew

The purpose of this concluding chapter is to offer a forward-looking research agenda for studies of the institutional development of business schools. This is attempted in two stages. Section 13.1 of this chapter offers a brief characterization of existing research and writing on business schools. The second and main section of the chapter then focuses on three major research themes that the author believes are deserving of special attention and investment. These are: international comparative studies to examine convergence and divergence in the development of business schools; studies which map and explain performance differences between business schools in the same and in different geographical and market contexts; and finally, more micro-level studies of the processes, practices, identity, and performance of business school faculty.

13.1. CHARACTERIZING BUSINESS SCHOOL RESEARCH

The purpose of this book is to further establish the study of business schools as an important phenomenon in social science and management research. At the moment much of the existing writing on business schools falls into five categories. The first of these offers analytically important accounts of the rise and rise of business schools and of management education. In the U.S. context, key publications include Khurana's historical treaties of the social transformation of American business schools and of the professionalization of management. (Khurana 2007; Khurana and Penrice 2011). The Khurana book (2007) has been very well received for the quality of its historical scholarship and critical reflection. A more recent book by Augier and March (2011) concentrates on the development of U.S. business schools in the period of great growth from 1945 to 1970. This book chronicles patterns of development in the post-war period and raises challenges about the current analytical and value biases of business schools and management education. These challenges have also been taken up in a more direct and iconoclastic fashion by Locke and Spender (2011).

No one has yet offered a similar analytical and historical treatment of the rise of business schools in the U.K. and Europe, but a start has been made by Alan Williams in his recent book on the U.K. (2010). The Starkey and Tiratsoo book, *The Business School and the Bottom Line* (2007), offers an analysis of the development and the diffusion of the business school, drawing on a primarily U.K. database.

In the present context, it is unsurprising that there are now many viewpoint publications which reflect on the limitations of much management education (Mintzberg 2004; Pfeffer and Fong 2002) and the challenges facing business schools in a globally competitive and performance-orientated world, (e.g. Engwall and Danell 2011). Some of these viewpoint contributions offer challenges to the research base in business education and critically reflect on the character and quality of research carried out by business schools. Pettigrew (2001, 2011), Starkey et al. (2009), and Hodgkinson and Starkey (2011) are examples. These viewpoint papers represent the second of our stream of writing on business schools.

The third stream of writing is part autobiographical in character. This writing offers an analytical and prescriptive view of the leadership and management challenges of running a business school. Key recent writing here includes Lorange (2008) and Fragueiro and Thomas (2011). The latter publication by Fragueiro and Thomas is informed by personal experience, but also provides original empirical material on the strategic leadership processes in three top European business schools. As such, this is still one of the few empirical studies of business schools that explores the conduct of leadership and strategy making.

A fourth research theme in the business school literature applies variants of institutional theory (Greenwood et al. 2008) to examine the institutionalization and reputation-building processes of such schools. Indicative work here includes writing on ranking and accreditation processes and the way those processes may be producing standardizing and mimetic effects on the development of business schools (Sauder and Espelad 2009; Wedlin 2007, 2011; Lawrence et al. 2009). This tradition of work is appropriately represented in this volume.

The fifth stream of writing is a broad class of work debating the purposes and impact of business schools in the broader field of management education.

Two notable new publications in this tradition are Thomas, Lorange, and Sheth (2013) and GMAC (2013). This writing shares many of the strengths and weaknesses of the viewpoint writing mentioned above. Some of this thinking is also collected together in the recent volume by Morsing and Sauquet Rovira (2011), *Business Schools and their Contribution to Society,* and is also featured in Iniguez de Onzono (2011). In this developing tradition there is the beginning of a research-based literature on the impact of business schools. The recent study on the economic impact of business schools in the U.K. by Cooke and Galt (2010) exemplifies this work.

13.2. THREE RESEARCH THEMES FOR A FORWARD LOOKING RESEARCH AGENDA

Research into business schools is still an emergent field of inquiry. Some notable and influential studies exist and others are on their way, but this is still a relatively unpopulated and insubstantial research domain. So what are some principles that might inform the development of a forward-looking research agenda for a still developing field? One principal is theoretical and empirical embeddedness. The aim here is to encourage future research which builds on or challenges earlier theoretical development and findings. A second principle is a driver of innovation and encourages forms of questioning and methods of inquiry that have not yet reached this area of social science and yet may be well established in other fields. In social science, many notable innovations have occurred through the transfer of concepts and methods from one field to another. In the domain of business school research, there is clearly a great opportunity to transfer learning from the longer established research on the study of universities and other professionally dominated organizations such as health, law, medicine and consulting. A third shaping principle can arise from the need to link research themes to substantive problems in the research domain. In Chapter 1 of this volume, Hommel and Thomas built their view of a future research agenda for business schools largely from the major competitive challenges now facing them. Of course, a further principle to inform developments can be intellectual aspiration. This means not just framing research in terms of the limitations of a particular domain, but encouraging aspirational research in a new domain, which will influence wider social science fields. Research on business schools will only receive notable recognition when and if it not only builds that field, but begins to influence related fields of social science, organization and management inquiry.

Informed by these principles, I would like to suggest three research themes that can make a very substantial contribution to our understanding of the institutional development of business schools. Such new themes can also raise the visibility and impact of this field of research for other social science fields and for the leaders and policy makers engaged in shaping the development and impact of business schools. The three research themes are:

1) Comparative international research to map and measure similarity and variation in the development of business schools.

2) Comparative studies which map and explain performance differences between business schools in the same and in different geographical and market contexts, and

3) More micro-level studies of the processes, practices, identities and performance of business school faculty in different academic fields and in different nations of the world.

These are not research themes for the faint hearted or risk averse. Although all three themes can be expressed in terms of projects with different scales and intensity, many more will require research teams located in different countries throughout the world capable of working together using multiple research methods and drawing upon interdisciplinary theoretical research perspectives. The studies will range from the macro to the micro, but a common analytical principle will be that of embeddedness, locating the study of business school institutions in their social, political, economic and market contexts (Pettigrew 1985, 2012; Dacin, Ventresca, and Beal 1999). To different degrees, all the research themes will require not just the comparative method, but an international comparative method. (Collinson and Pettigrew 2009). A signal weakness of existing research on business schools is a lack of primary international evidence to corroborate or challenge the many observations made about convergence and divergence in the development of business schools.

An impactful research agenda on business schools will also need to complement the 'what is' pattern, generating knowledge from large sample studies, with the 'how to' knowledge, deriving from the dynamic study of phenomena over time. The most ambitious studies will seek the complementary benefits of 'what is' and 'how to' knowledge. Both forms of knowledge are a necessary condition for scholarly and policy/practice impact. The 'how to' knowledge provides the understanding of the processes and mechanisms which generate the patterns identified from large sample studies (Pettigrew 2011).

Our interest in the processes, practices and performance of business schools need not stop with analysis at the institutional level. Currently, there is a very limited literature on the identities, ideologies, working practices, needs and interests of business school faculty. The analysis of institutions should always keep in touch with parallel developments in the study of the professionals who work in them. So the more micro-level preoccupations of our third research theme are a crucial prompt to sustain the importance of the individual and the team as units of analysis.

13.2.1. Comparative International Research on Business Schools

In their recent book, *The Business School in the 21*st *Century,* Thomas, Lorange, and Sheth 2013, offer the most comprehensive account yet of the rise and rise of the business school and the challenges of delivering management education in the contemporary world. Their analysis of the evolution of business schools, and their search for identity and legitimacy, places these issues in the context of the modern university and society. They also provide the most international account yet of the variety of business school forms, identities and models throughout the world. Using a social constructionist theoretical approach, they point to the diversity of types of business school within and between nations and regions, as well as the standardizing influences in those same locations from the impact of accreditation and ranking systems. Their analysis of the possibilities of business school diversity, in amongst more conventional accounts of homogenization, is a welcome relief and keeps open the debate about the extent of convergence and divergence in business school development. However, their treatment of that debate is ultimately limited by their reliance on secondary sources to map and explain the parameters of similarity and difference. This continuing empirical deficiency, in what is an otherwise comprehensive and illuminating account, points again to the need for comparative international research to map and measure similarity and variation in the development of business schools.

The comparative method lies at the heart of social science research. Comparisons of organizations, networks or nations allow us to map and measure similarity and variation, helping us to understand the sources of difference and explain distinctiveness. Comparisons of places provide an understanding of national and regional variation and comparisons over time allow us to explain the past and the present and the emerging future (Collinson and Pettigrew 2009). All of these variants of the comparative method are now sorely needed in business school research. But what are the central mapping questions in this terrain and what kind of analytical assumptions need to be built into this kind of research?

International mapping studies require, as a minimum, some clarity about the constructs to be measured over space and time. At the moment, the typologies of business schools available in the literature are crude and undiscriminating. For example, Khurana (2007) offered a threefold typology of U.S. business schools, identifying them as elite leading schools, large regional schools, with a catch-all third category for the largest segment that offers vocational programmes with modest academic requirements. Crude typologies are unlikely to offer a discriminating classification system. The approach taken by Thomas, Lorange, and Sheft (2013) is much more sophisticated and is capable of being applied across nations and regions. Thomas et al. (2013) build up their arguments about differences between Asian, European and U.S. business schools by examining three sources of difference: institutional difference; competitive differences; and social capital differences. Using publically available resources, they are able to tabulate various aspects of the three sources of differentiation and demonstrate plausible connections with the patterns of development in business schools within the three regions.

Other approaches to assessing patterns of convergence and divergence could draw upon various critical dimensions of functionality. These include: patterns of ownership; patterns of financing; scale and structure; degrees of internationalization; product mix; faculty mix; and rates of innovation. As we shall see in the second theme in this research agenda, some of the above considerations may be crucial in explaining performance differences between business schools.

This is a reminder that comparative international research is not just about exposing patterns of similarity and difference across populations of institutions, but is also about explaining those revealed differences. Fortunately, there is now a long tradition of 'embeddedness thinking' in the social sciences, which connects the transformation of institutions to broad social, economic, political, and institutional changes. See, for example, Granovetter (1985), Dacin et al. (1999), DiMaggio (2001), and Pettigrew et al. (2003). Studies in this embeddedness tradition recognize the strength or intensity of embeddedness, the interplay between different features and levels of context, and their co-evolutionary character in explaining institutional change (Pettigrew 1985, 2012; Lewin et al. 1999). There is also a context and action debate in this literature, which any student of business school development would need to be mindful of. The progress of the development of institutions can be fruitfully examined by pointing to the enabling and constraining features of different levels of context, as well as appeals to leadership and managerial action (Pettigrew 2012).

The literatures on new organizational forms has also taken a great interest in patterns of convergence and divergence: any mapping studies of business schools can profitably draw on it. See, for example, Mayer and Whittington (1999), DiMaggio (2001), Lewin et al. (2003), and Pettigrew et al. (2003). The convergence of interest in this literature on organizational forms shows the extent to which globalizing trends for the convergence of organizational forms is being challenged by political, economic, cultural, and institutional pressures at the nation state level, which maintain local patterns of diversity. This is obviously a key question for those interested in patterns of development in business schools throughout the world.

In their 1990s' study of the development of new organizational forms in Europe, U.S., and Japan, Pettigrew et al. (2003) were able to show a common direction for organizational change across the three regions, but from different starting points and with considerable variation in pace of change over the period 1992–1997. But the common direction of change did not mask continuing real variation in forms of organizing between Europe, Japan, and the U.S.

These empirical results, which ideally would need to be repeated in subsequent studies, illustrate the challenges of conducting international mapping studies of the development of business schools. There are, of course, diverse methodological challenges in conducting these kinds of international studies. Many of these are catalogued in Collinson and Pettigrew (2008), but some scholars are now prepared to take the enhanced risks in this kind of social science research, and maintain a well-informed balance between methodological rigour and operational practicality. Aside from Pettigrew et al. (2003), the interested scholar may also turn to Bloom and Van Reenen's (2007) exemplary empirical work on measuring and explaining management practices across firms and countries, and the highly ambitious GLOBE study of culture and leadership in 62 nations (House et al. 2004, 2006), and the on-going GEM studies which explore patterns in the development of entrepreneurial activity across nation states (GEM 2005; Levie and Autio 2007).

Any developing tradition of comparative international research on business schools needs also to be sensitive to the longer established work on the internationalization of higher education. A key contributor here is Simon Marginson (King, Marginson, and Naidoo 2013; Marginson, Kaur, and Sawir 2011; Marginson, Murphy, and Peters 2009; and Peters, Marginson, and Murphy 2008). This tradition of work is important for its explicit treatment of the globalization of higher education, for locating the development of the university within debates about the influence of the knowledge economy, and for the recognition that universities are located in national university systems which are, of course, shaped by the influences of national governments and international bodies such as the European Union.

Many business schools outside North America are subject to national policy changes that can significantly impact on their national and international competitiveness. Many governments are reshaping their higher education system to increase efficiency, competitiveness and national prestige. The influence of global rankings and accreditation bodies means an increasing tendency for a single world market for universities. Both developed and developing economies are investing in education and research and development as engines of human capital development and economic growth. At the same time there are changing demands for value being placed on university systems throughout the world. The rising ethic is that universities should be funded more for what they do than for what they are by focusing funding on relevant outputs and outcomes rather than inputs.

In many societies, the ideal of a university as a stand-alone 'ivory tower' is fading. All these contextual changes at national and international levels are changing the rules of the game (North 1990, 2005), for universities and business schools, and demanding new responses from their leaders (GMAC 2013). But even a cursory examination of trends and responses suggests that the pace of change is variable in different countries, regions and disciplines. A plausible prediction is that the changing rules of the game will supplement and not supplant what we see around us in the character and functioning of business schools. But until we have a research tradition mapping and explaining the international comparative development of business schools, we can only speculate and surmise.

13.2.2. Comparative Studies which Map and Explain Performance Differences between Business Schools

Management scholars seem to have been curiously incurious about why and how certain organizations consistently out perform their comparators. Where such studies exist, they are often found wanting, sometimes because of disputes about the chosen method of performance measurement, sometimes because of the use of univariate or uni-thematic explanations of performance differences, and often because the attempts to link the determinants of performance to the performance outcome rely upon rather distant, abstracted and secondary data. But the well known challenges should not divert us from the obvious need to understand why and how certain business schools consistently out perform their comparators in the same and in different markets and geographical contexts. This is the central problem and question in business school research and the one of greatest significance from a policy and practice point of view.

In a recent article, Enders, de Boer, and Weyer (2013) take us into the heart of the problems of explaining performance differences between universities. In assessing the more general question of whether and to what extent universities are able to attain real autonomy from the state, they also address the associated question of whether autonomy matters in explaining performance differences. Their account of the condition of research in this field is not encouraging. On the one hand, they point to the 'scarce, inconclusive and methodologically problematic state of the contemporary research' (Enders et al. 2013: 5). On the other hand, they conclude from existing empirical research work that financial resources (wealth of nation, funding for higher education, budgets for universities) turn out to be correlated with university performance. They also feel confident enough to identify linkages between a university's managerial decision-making capabilities in financial and human resource matters and performance. It seems that more autonomous universities with managerial discretion, which need to compete for resources, are more research productive (Enders et al. 2013: 21).

Enders et al. (2013) note the pioneering nature of international comparative work on performance differences between universities in the U.S. and Europe (see, for example, Aghion et al. (2008, 2009)). But note the rather abstracted, distant and secondary nature of the data in such studies. Their own recommendation for the future is to open up 'the black box' of the university to greater exploration of the dynamics of university behaviour to provide a more context-sensitive treatment of the determinants of performance. This is precisely the direction of travel suggested in Shattock's (2010) recent commentary on the state of research and writing in so-called successful universities.

Shattock (2010) begins his interpretation of research into the successful university by noting the absence of empirical studies of these phenomena. He notes 'We feel instinctively we can recognise successful universities when we see them, but still there is little systematic research to identify what their characteristics might be, what criteria we use to judge them and what factors can be shown to sustain success'. (Shattock 2010: 17). Nevertheless, there are familiar factors associated with success: longevity; wealth; and prestige. Shattock mentions Gueno's (1998) study linking the age of universities to research prestige and resource accumulation in the long term. But Shattock is also wise enough to acknowledge that success cannot be down to a single factor but to a wide-ranging set of inter-related factors that are connectable to the changing purposes and performance criteria of universities over time. Given Shattock's long previous experience as a registrar in a notably successful U.K. university without age or endowment (Warwick), he is very comfortable reaching inside 'the black box' of the university to speculate about the determinants of a university's success. His list of inter-related success factors includes a strong organizational culture, a strongly competitive approach both internally and externally, an adaptability to the environment without changing fundamental identity, a willingness to take bold decisions, a conservative approach to finance in general and an open collegial approach to decision making. Shattock also points out that the best universities are as good at teaching as research and have been capable of adjusting their purposes and operational matters to the changing rules of the game in the societies where they are embedded. And, finally, Shattock is also sensitive to time and dynamics. Success is dependent upon creating and sustaining an upward momentum of positive energy and collective purpose, all intangible characteristics, which are hard to build and sustain over time.

At this time, the nearest we have to a literature on the performance of business schools is the research and writing on business school rankings, some of which is represented in this book (see Chapters 7 and 9). The recent accounts by Thomas, Lorange, and Sheth (2013) and GMAC (2013) are instructive in exposing the design fallibilities of rankings systems and discussing their reputational and other effects. Thomas et al. (2013) also offer valuable analyses of the changing profiles in these rankings systems. They demonstrate the historical ascendancy of the major U.S. schools but note the rise of a number of elite European and Asian schools in the *Financial Times* Global MBA rankings in the last 20 years, and especially in the last five years. Thomas et al. (2013) attribute the historically high rankings of the elite U.S. schools to a combination of being first, fast movers in management education, to product standardization of the MBA degree, strong and well-established brands and reputation, and, above all, significant financial strength and very large private endowments which have fuelled their strategic position in the market place (Thomas et al. 2013.43). Thomas et al. (2013) explain the recent rise of a select group of European and Asian schools partly to their skill in positioning themselves as niche players in their national and regional markets.

The interpretation of rankings data is a helpful start in explaining performance differences in business schools, but we need more contextually rich and dynamic analysis than can be supplied by secondary data. The rise and fall of Peters and Waterman's 1982 book has undermined small sample studies that look only at supposed high performers. Elsewhere (Pettigrew et al. 2001), it has been argued that this leaves the study of organizational performance with two options. Option 1 is to carry out large sample studies over time to clarify any association between the patterns of change adopted by organizations and their performance. Such a research strategy would allow the linking of 'the what' of change to organizational performance, but this would reveal very little about the process and dynamics of delivering and sustaining performance improvements. Option 2 would involve carrying out an associated set of longitudinal comparative case studies of matched pairs of organizations chosen for their respective high and low performances. Such case studies would allow researchers to ask questions about how and why the determinants of performance were linkable to different levels of performance over time.

At this stage in the development of research on business schools, one can imagine a phased set of studies starting with the analysis of matched pairs of higher and lesser performing business schools in the same country and market conditions. This way, important elements of the local higher education national policy context and market conditions could be controlled for, and attention focused on the key determinants of performance differences between the higher and lesser performers. This was the strategy adopted in the Pettigrew and Whipp (1991) study of high and low performers in four mature industry and service sectors of the U.K. economy. In this study, it was found that the higher performers differed from the lesser performers in the way they conducted environmental assessment, led change, linked strategic and operational change, managed their human resources as assets and liabilities, and managed coherence in the overall process of competition and change. Crucially, the Pettigrew and Whipp (1990) study had a 30-year time series and because of this it was possible to impose a double test on the five inter-related factors used to explain the performance differences. Thus the factors were used both to explain the differential performance of a firm in one era of business development and also to account for the loss or gain of performance relative to its comparator over time. Interestingly, the five factor model of performance determinants in the Pettigrew and Whipp (1990) study contains many elements which overlap with Shattock's (2010) set of inter-related factors explaining the relative success of universities.

One can imagine a strong research base developing on the determinants of relative business school performance by means of a series of within-nation studies of matched pairs, which might then lead to large sample studies across national boundaries. The large sample studies would then be greatly strengthened by constructs developed from the rich contextual and processual work of the smaller sample within nation studies. Of course, the large sample studies would demand associated theoretical guidance. One crucial theory of change and performance, first developed in economics by Milgrom and Roberts (1990, 1995), and by now well-established in the management literature, is that of complementarities. See Ennen and Richter (2010) for a recent review of the empirical studies using complementarities thinking. The crucial general proposition from complementarities theory is that high performing organizations are likely to be combining a number of changes at the same time and that the payoff to a full system of congruent changes is greater than the sum of its parts, some of which, if taken on their own might, even have negative effects on performance. This emphasis of the virtues of multiple congruent and coherent changes which facilitate both internal and external alignment, but which in turn demand adjustments over time as strategic and operational environments change, can deliver useful results about the factors which sustain performance differences (Pettigrew and Whittington 2003). But, as yet in the business school context, such theoretical ideas are untested by serious empirical analysis. Here lies a major opportunity for ambitious scholars of the relative performance of business schools.

13.2.3. Micro-level Studies of the Core Processes and Practices of Business Schools and their Faculty

The first two themes in this forward looking research agenda on business schools were avowedly macro in character. Both themes sought to map elements of the comparative international and performance terrain of business schools. The logic here is that in a relatively new research area there is real value in mapping important elements of the terrain before delving too deeply into the more micro analysis of the people, processes and practices within business schools themselves. The proposed mapping studies have been carefully framed to ensure strong adherence to the analytical principles of embeddedness and temporality. So the institutional development of business schools is to be studied in its political, economic, cultural, market, and international contexts, and the revealed patterns of convergence and divergence in business school development always addressed over time. The same principles apply to the analysis of performance differences between business schools within and between nations. The search for the critical performance determinants of the higher and lesser performing business schools requires an exploration of the external and internal contexts of the schools, and an analysis of the content and process of competition and change (Pettigrew 1997, 2012). In the performance studies, temporal data and questioning were present in order to appreciate not just how the determinants were developed, but how also they were sustained and adapted over time to deliver longer-term performance benefits. The same analytical logic can usefully be taken into the more micro studies of business school people, processes and practices. All processes and practices are contextually embedded and they are all best revealed through temporal analysis (Pettigrew 1997, 2012).

The potential range of micro studies of business schools is enormous. The studies could range from an appreciation of the strategic leadership processes of business schools—see, for example, the Fraguiero and Michelini chapter in this book—to the study of decision-making and change processes, the championing of educational and research innovations, the evolution of strategies and structures in business schools, and how faculty are selected, socialized and motivated to deliver performance outcomes for themselves and their institutions. All these process studies can be justified on scholarly and policy grounds since the existing empirical studies are modest and scattered.

If one was to select a single sub-theme in this micro terrain, it might be the examination of the way faculty are responding to the contextual challenges now pressing on universities and business schools throughout the world. Here there is a developing tradition of work in universities, and now more recently in business schools, that the interested scholar can draw upon. Deem, Hillyard, and Reid (2007) offer an exemplary treatment of the rise of managerialism in U.K. universities since the 1960s and discuss its effect on the management of academics, the character and identities of academic managers, and the values and identities of the professionals around them. This study is explicitly contextual and temporal. It places the study of the practices, values and career development of academic managers and academics in the context of attempts to reform the U.K. public sector and, within that, the higher education system. They note the extent to which public sector professionals in various parts of the U.K. public sector operate within 'transparency regimes. . . that monitor and control their work performance' (Deem et al. 2007: 25). In turn the rise of the new managerialism and the new public management have impacted upon, and are still impacting upon, the management structures, systems, and practices of universities, on professional academic cultures and identity, and ultimately upon the purposes, meaning and identities of universities. Their analysis profits from an examination of managerialism at the system level, the institutional level and the micro and individual level. This is one of the great strengths of the Deem et al. (2007) research and why it could be of real value to any scholar attempting to do a similar analysis in business schools.

Of course, work in this tradition is beginning in business schools. Winters earlier work on identity schisms and tensions in universities (Winter and Sarros 2002, Winter 2009, Winter and O'Donohue 2012) is now being taken forward into the study of business school academics, their identities and ideologies (Winter 2013). The value tensions in business schools are well represented in the writing on the rigour–relevance duality in business school research (Tranfield and Starkey 1998, Hodgkinson and Roussea 2009, Starkey and Tiratsoo 2007, and Pettigrew 2011). See also the chapters by McKiernan and Wilson and Starkey and Hatchuel in this volume.

Predating much of the business-school work on the responses of academics to the changing rules of the game are a variety of studies analysing the changing purposes and character of universities (Barnett 2003, Kolsakar 2008, Macfarlane 2011, and Rolfe 2013). These studies raise fundamental questions about the purposes and freedom of universities, their impact on societies and culture, their funding sources and priorities, and the core tasks and values of the scholarly life at the beginning of the twenty-first century. These kind of joint macro and micro level questions much surely be part of any research agenda on the future and fate of business schools and their professionals.

13.3. CONCLUSION

The scholarly study of business schools in their context is wide open for further development. This chapter has signalled three important sub-fields in that research domain and has in turn provided a stimulus for future research on the comparative international development of business schools, and on why and how certain business schools consistently outperform their comparators It has also encouraged micro-level studies of the the core processes and practices of business schools and their faculty. These suggestions, although embedded in our analysis of existing work, are also personal and partial. However, the suggestions have directed the reader towards questions where there are strong theoretical, empirical and methodological connections to the broad area of management and the social sciences, and where the research problematics are readily linkable to the substantive problems of business schools themselves. If research is to meet the double hurdle of scholarly and policy impact it should face both ways at the same time: into the social sciences, and into the issues facing those who are clients, funders, and leaders of business schools.

The trap for those interested in business schools as a field of study is that the field becomes an atheoretical zone of self-preoccupation. This is a danger faced by all research fields that can be contained by the substantive concerns of a sector or industry. This could easily have happened to research on another sector—for example, the study of professional service firms.

So how has the study of professional service firms avoided the intellectual isolation of a ghetto–like status? A number of factors are apparent. The first and most crucial is that some very high quality scholars were attracted to this substantive area and stuck with it. As high quality empirical studies appeared so the proponents of the field received recognition in related areas and at the same time organized themselves as a scholarly community and began to publish through special journal issues, handbooks and thematic presentations at major academic professional associations. But crucial to this developmental pathway was the desire of the proponents to build broader theoretical and empirical contributions, which not only bridged the substantive area of professional service firms to management and the social sciences, but also built new theoretical developments through the empirical studies of professional service firms. So, the study of professional service firms was not seen as an end in itself, but as a vehicle and setting to build, for example, a new corpus of work on institution theory (Greenwood et al. 2008, 2011). These are important strategic and professional lessons for all of us who are interested in the development of a vigorous and impactful set of studies of business schools in their changing contexts.

REFERENCES

Aghion, P. M., Dewatripont, C., Hoxby, M., Mas-Colell, A., and Sapir, A. (2008). *Higher Aspiration: An Agenda for Reforming European Universities*. Bruegel: Bleuprint, 5.

Aghion, P. M., Dewatripont, C., Hoxby, M., Mas-Colell, A., and Sapir, A. (2009). *The Governance and Performance of Research Universities: Evidence from Europe and the USA*. Cambridge MA: National Bureau of Economic Research.

Augier, M., and March, J. G. (2011). *The Routes, Rituals and Rhetorics of Change: North American Business Schools after the Second World War*. Stanford, CA: Stanford University Press.

Barnett, R. (2003). *Beyond all Reason: Living with Ideology in the University*. Buckingham, UK: Open University Press.

Bloom, N., and Van Reenen, J. (2007). 'Measuring and Explaining Management Practices Across Firms and Countries', *The Quarterly Journal of Economics*, Vol. CXXII, No. 4: 1351–1408.

Clark, B. R. (1998). *Creating Entrepreneurial Universities*. Oxford: IAU Press/Pergamon.

Collinson, S., and Pettigrew, A. M. (2009). 'Comparative International Business Research Methods: Pitfalls and Practicalities', in Alan Rugman (ed.), *Handbook of International Business, Second Edition*. Oxford: Oxford University Press, 765–796.

Cooke, A., and Galt, V. (2010). *The Impact of Business Schools in the UK*. London: Association of Business Schools.

Dacin, M. T., Ventresca, M. J., and Beal, B. D. (1999). 'The Embeddedness of Organizations: Dialogue and Directions', *Journal of Management*, 25, 3: 317–356.

Deem, R., Hillyard, S., and Reed, M. (2007). *Knowledge, Higher Education, and the New Managerialism*. Oxford: Oxford University Press.

DiMaggio, P. (ed.) (2001). *The Twenty First Century Firm: Changing Economic Organization in International Perspective*. Princeton, NJ: Princeton University Press.

Enders, J., DeBoer, H., and Weyer, E. (2013). 'Regulatory Autonomy and Performance: The Reform of Higher Education Revisited', *Higher Education*, 65, 1: 5–23.

Engwall, L. and Danell, R. (2011). 'Britannia and Her Business Schools', *British Journal of Management*, 22, 3: 432–442.

Ennen, E., and Richter, A. (2010). 'The Whole is More Than the Sum of the Parts—Or is it? A Review of the Empirical Literature on Complementarities on Organizations', *Journal of Management*, 36, 1: 207–233.

Fragueiro, F. and Thomas, H. (2011). *Strategic Leadership in the Business School*. Cambridge: Cambridge University Press.

GEM (2006). *Global Entrepreneurship Monitor, 2005 Executive Report*, edited by Maria Minniti, William D. Bygrave, and Erkko Autio. Babson College and London Business School.

GMAC (2013). *Disrupt or be Disrupted: A Blueprint for Change in Management Education*, edited by Brooks Holtom and Erich Dierdorff. San Francisco, CA: Jossey Bass.

Granovetter, M. S. (1985). 'Economic Action and Social Structure: The Problem of Embeddedness', *American Journal of Sociology*, 91:481–510.

Greenwood, R., Oliver, C., Sahlin, K., and Suddaby, R. (eds) (2008). *Organizational Institutionalism*. Los Angeles: Sage Publications.

Greenwood, R., Raynard, M., Codeih, F., Micekola, E., and Lounsbury, M. (2011). 'Institutional Complexity and Organizational Responses', *Academy of Management Annals*, 5: 1–55. Essex, U.K.: Routledge

Gueno, A. (1998). 'The Internationalisation of European Universities: A Return to Medieval Roots', *Minerva*, XXVI, 3: 253–270.

Hodgkinson, G. and Rousseau, D. M. (2009). 'Bridging the Rigour/Relevance Gap in Management Research, It's Already Happening', *Journal of Management Studies*, 46: 534–546.

Hodgkinson, G. and Starkey, K. (2011). 'Not Simply Returning to the Same Answer Over and Over Again: Reframing Relevance', *British Journal of Management*, 22, 3: 355–369.

House, R. J., Hanges, P. J., Javidan, M., Dorfman, P. W., and Gupta, V. (eds) (2004). *Culture, Leadership and Organization: The Globe Study of 62 Societies*. Thousand Oaks, California: Sage Publications.

House, R. J., Javidan, M., Hanges, P. J., and Dorfman, P. W. (2006). 'Understanding Cultures and Implicit Leadership Theories Across the Globe: An Introduction to Project Globe', *Journal of World Business*, 37: 3–10.

Iniguez de Onzono, S. (2011). *The Learning Curve: How Business Schools are Re-inventing Education*. London: Palgrave Macmillan.

King, R., Marginson, S., and Naidoo, R. (eds) (2013). *Handbook of Globalisation and Higher Education*. Cheltenham: Edward Elgar.

Khurana, R. (2007). *From Higher Aims to Hired Hands: The Social Transformation of American Business Schools and the Unfulfilled Promise of Management as a Profession*. Princeton NJ: Princeton University Press.

Khurana, R. and Penrice, D. (2011), 'Business Education: The American Trajectory', in M. Morsing and A. Sauquet Rovira, (eds), *Business Schools and their Contribution to Society*. London: Sage Publications, 3–15.

Kolsakar, A. (2008). 'Academic Professionalism in the Managerialist Era: A Study of English Universities', *Studies in Higher Education*, 33, 5: 513–525.

Lawrence, T. B., Suddaby, R., and Leca, B. (2009). *Institutional Work: Actor and Agency in Institutional Studies of Organizations*. Cambridge: Cambridge University Press.

Levie, J. D., and Autio, E. (2008). 'A Theoretical Grounding and Test of the GEM Model', *Small Business Economics*, 31, 3: 235–263.

Lewin, A. Y., Long, C. P., and Carroll, T. N. (1995). 'The Co-evolution of New Organizational Forms', *Organizational Science*, 10, 5: 535–550.

Locke, R. and Spender, J. C. (2011). *Confronting Managerialism: How the Business Elite and their Schools Threw our Lives out of Balance*. London: Zed Books.

Lorange, P. (2008). *Thought Leadership meets Business: How Business Schools can become Successful*. Cambridge: Cambridge University Press.

Macfarlane, B. (2011). 'Professors as Intellectual Leaders: Formation Identity and Roles', *Studies in Higher Education*, 36, 1: 57–73.

Marginson, S., Kaur, S., and Sawir, E. (eds) (2011). *Higher Education in the Asia Pacific: Strategic Responses to Globalization*. Dordrecht: Springer.

Marginson, S., Murphy, P., and Peters, M. A. (2009). *Global Creation: Space, Mobility and Synchrony in the Age of the Knowledge Economy*. New York: Peter Lang.

Mayer, M., and Whittington, R. (1999). 'Strategy, Structure and "Systemness": National Institutions and Corporate Change in France, Germany and the UK, 1950–1993'. *Organizations Studies*, 26: 933–959.

Milgrom, P. R., and Roberts, J. (1990). 'The Economics of Modern Manufacturing: Technology, Strategy and Organization', *American Economic Review*, 80: 511–528.

Milgrom, P. R., and Roberts, J. (1995). 'Complementarities and Fit: Strategy, Structure and Organizational Change in Manufacturing', *Journal of Accounting and Economics*', 19, 2/3: 179–208.

Mintzberg. H. (2004). *Managers Not MBA's: A Hard Look at the Soft Practice of Managing Management Development*. San Francisco: Berrett-Kohler Publishers.

Middlehurst, R. (1993). *Leading Academics*. Buckingham: SRHE and the Open University Press.

Morsing, M. and Sauquet Rovira, A. (eds). *Business Schools and their Contribution to Society*. London: Sage Publications.

North, D. C. (1990). *Institutions, Institutional Change and Economics*. Cambridge: Cambridge University Press.

North, D. C. (2005). *Understanding the Process of Economic Change*. Princeton, NJ: Princeton University Press.

Peters, M. A., Marginson, S., and Murphy. P. (2008). *Creativity and the Global Knowledge Economy*. New York: Peter Lang.

Pettigrew, A. M. (1985). *The Awakening Giant: Continuity and Change in ICI*. Oxford: Basil Blackwell.

Pettigrew, A. M. (1997). 'What is a Processual Analysis?', *Scandinavian Journal of Management*, 13, 4: 337–348.

Pettigrew, A. M. (2001). 'Management Research after Modernism,' *British Journal of Management*, 12: S61–S70.

Pettigrew, A. M. (2011). 'Scholarship with Impact', *British Journal of Management*, 22, 3: 347–354.

Pettigrew, A. M. (2012). 'Context and Action in the Transformation of the Firm: A Reprise', *Journal of Management Studies*, 49, 7: 1304–1328.

Pettigrew, A. M. and Whipp, R. (1991). *Managing Change for Competitive Success*. Oxford: Blackwell.

Pettigrew, A. M., Woodman, R.W., and Cameron, K.S. (2001). 'Studying Organizational Change and Development: Challenges for Future Research', *The Academy of Management Journal*, 44, 4: 697–713.

Pettigrew, A. M., Whittington, R., Melin, L., Sanchez-Runde, C., Van Den Bosch, F. A. J., Ruigrok, W., and Numagami, T. (eds) (2003). *Innovative Forms of Organizing: International Perspectives*. London: Sage Publications.

Pettigrew, A. M. and Whittington, R. (2003). 'Complementarities in Action: Organizational Change and Performance in BP and Unilever 1985–2002, in A. M. Pettigrew, R. Whittington, L. Melin, C. Sanchez-Runde, F. A. J. Van Den Bosch, W. Ruigrok, and T. Numagami, (eds), *Innovative Forms of Organizing: International Perspectives*, London: Sage Publications, 173–207.

Pfeffer, J. and Fong, C. (2002). 'The End of Business Schools? Less Success than Meets the Eye', *Academy of Management Learning and Education*, 1, 1: 78–95.

Rolfe, G. (2013) *The University in Dissent: Scholarship in the Corporate University*. London: Routledge and the Society for Research into Higher Education.

Sauder, M. and Espeland, W. N. (2009). 'The Discipline of Rankings: Tight Coupling and Organizational Change', *American Sociological Review*, 74, 1: 63–82.

Shattock, M. (2010). *Managing Successful Universities*, 2nd ed. Maidenhead: SRHE and the Open University Press.

Starkey, K. and Tiratsoo, N. (2007). *The Business School and the Bottom Line*. Cambridge: Cambridge University Press.

Starkey, K., Hatchuel, A., and Tempest, S. (2009). 'Management Research and the New Logic of Discovery and Engagement', *Journal of Management Studies*, 46: 541–558.

Thomas, H., Lorange, P., and Sheth, J. (2013). *The Business School in the Twenty First Century*. Cambridge: Cambridge University Press.

Tranfield, D. and Starkey, K. (1998). 'The Nature, Social Organization and Promotion of Management Research', *Journal of Management Studies*, 46: 547–558.

Wedlin, L. (2007). 'The Role of Rankings in Codifying a Business School Template: Classification, Diffusion and Mediated Isomorphism in Organizational Fields', *European Management Review*, 41, 1: 24–39.

Wedlin, L. (2011). 'Going Global: Rankings and Rhetorical Devices to Construct an International Field of Management Education', *Management Learning*, 42, 2: 199–218.

Williams, A. P. O. (2010). *The History of UK Business and Management Education.* Bingley: Emerald Publishing.

Winter, R. P. (2009). 'Academic Manager or Managed Academic? Academic Identity and Schisms in Higher Education', *The Journal of Higher Education Policy and Management*, 31, 2: 121–131.

Winter, R. P. (2013). 'Managing Scholarship Differently: Perspective Taking in Business Schools', paper presented to The 8th International Management Studies Conference, Manchester, 10th–12th July 2013.

Winter, R. P. and Sarros, J. C. (2002). 'The Academic Work Environments in Australian Universities: A Motivating Place to Work?', *Higher Education Research & Development*, 21, 3: 241–258.

Winter, R. P. and O'Donohue, W. (2012). 'Academic Identity Tension in the Public University: Which Values Really Matter?', *Journal of Higher Education Policy and Management*, 34, 6: 565–573.

Author Index

Subject Index